TRAVELWISE

FRENCH

Gérard Hérin

The title of the German book is *Reisewörterbuch Französisch*

English version translated
by Florence Brodkey

Phonetics by Christine Moisset

All inquiries should be addressed to:
Barron's Educational Series, Inc.
250 Wireless Boulevard
Hauppauge, NY 11788
http://www.barronseduc.com

Library of Congress Catalog Card No. 97-47438

International Standard Book No. 0-7641-7105-4 (package)
0-7641-0380-6 (book)

Library of Congress Cataloging-in-Publication Data

Hérin, Gérard
[Reisewörterbuch Französisch. English]
Travelwise French / Gérard Hérin ; translated by Florence Brodkey.
p. cm.
ISBN 0-7641-0380-6. — ISBN 0-7641-7105-4
1. French language—Conversation and phrasebooks—English.
I. Title.
PC2121.H5313 1998
448.3'421—dc21 97–47438
CIP

Printed in Hong Kong
9 8 7 6 5 4 3 2

Contents

Preface

TravelWise French is a guide to both comprehension and conversation in French. By using it you will not only acquire a series of useful words and phrases, but, more importantly, you will learn how to understand and be understood.

The most commonly heard expressions are provided for everyday situations you will encounter during your travels. These are structured as dialogues, so that you not only learn what to say, but will also understand the corresponding responses.

TravelWise French is divided into eleven topical units, which accompany you through every phase of your travel: your arrival, checking into a hotel, at the beach, and even a meeting with business associates.

With the help of phrases and word lists, as well as the additional glossary provided at the end of the book, you can readily adapt the sample sentences to your own individual, real-life situations.

The following Pronunciation Guide and the Short Grammar toward the back of the book will help familiarize you with the sounds and constructions of the French language, while pictures and useful tips provided throughout the book will help you better appreciate the special cultural features and natural scenic attractions of France.

Pronunciation

Vowels

French vowels are more complicated than those in English. But you can figure their pronunciation out easily by studying and referring to the following chart.

Note that all French vowels can be nasalized. This is shown with a capital **N**.

Note, as well, that the *h* is added to the pronunciation symbol in order to indicate a slightly lengthened vowel. In words where the vowel is not lengthened the *h* is dropped: **travail** = *(trah-vAh-yœ)* = *work*

Letters	Pronun. Symbols Used	Pronunciation	Examples
a/e	[a]	as in the exclamation *Ah!*	**acte** *deed*
	[ahn]	similar to the vowel sound in the word *gun*	**an** *year* **gouvernement** *government* **vente** *sale*
e/ê/é/i/ eu/ai	[eh]	as in the exclamation *Eh!*	**ouvert** *open* **être** *to be*
	[ay]	as in the word *day*	**échelle** *scale* **baisser** *to kiss*
	[an]	as in the article *an*	**vin** *wine*
	[ew*]	as in the word *good*	**revue** *review* **travailleur** *worker*
i/y/ie	[ee]	as in the exclamation *Eeh!*	**marchandise** *merchandise* **dynamique** *dynamic* **garantie** *warranty*

Letters	Pronun. Symbols Used	Pronunciation	Examples
o/au/aux	[o]	as in the exclamation *Oh!*	**or** *gold* **hauteur** *height*
	[oh]	as in the word *top*	**porte** *door* **homme** *man* **donne** *woman*
	[ohn]	as in *Oh no!* pronounced rapidly	**bon** *good* **montre** *he/she shows*
u/ou/eu	[oo]	as in the exclamation *Ooh!*	**vu** *seen* **bourse** *purse*
	[uuh*]	rounded lip version of [ay]	**peu** *little* **deux** *two*
	[uh]	as in the word *the*	**neuf** *nine* **soeur** *sister*

Semivowels

The following can also stand for a **y-sound** as in *yes*, and the **w-sound** as in *way.*

Letters	Pronun. Symbols Used	Pronunciation	Examples
il/ille/i	[y]	as the *y* in yes	**travail** *work* **travailleur** *worker* **bien** *well*
oi/oui	[w]	as the *w* in *way*	**voir** *to see* **oui** *yes*

Consonants

Most of the French consonants are similar to corresponding English consonants. Differences are shown in the chart below. The consonants that are not mentioned are similar to the English pronunciation.

Letters	Pronun. Symbols Used	Pronunciation	Examples
b	[b]	as in *bat*	**bien** *well*
c (hard) **c** (soft)/**ç**	[k] [s]	as in *cat* as in *sell*	**carte** *business card* **centre** *center* **français** *French*
ch	[sh]	as in *shoe*	**chemin** *street*
d	[d]	as in *day*	**dans** *in*
f/ph	[f]	as in *fair*	**faire** *to do* **photo** *photo*
g (hard) **g** (soft)/**j**	[g] [zh]	as in *gas* as in *leisure*	**grand** *big* **gestion** *management* **jour** *day*
h	silent (not pronounced)	as in *hour*	**heure** *time*
l	[l]	as in *love*	**lait** *milk*
m	[m]	as in *man*	**main** *hand*
n **gn**	[n] [ny]	as in *name* as in *canyon*	**nom** *name* **ligne** *line*
p	[p]	as in *pet*	**pain** *bread*
q	[k]	as in *quick*	**qui** *who*
r	[r]	with a guttural pronunciation	**rouge** *red*
s (voiceless)/**sc**	[s]	as in *sip*	**salle** *hall* **science** *science*
s (voiced) /**z**	[z]	as in *zip*	**prévision** *forecast* **zone** *zone*
t	[t]	as in *rent*	**taxe** *tax*
v	[v]	as in *vine*	**vin** *wine*

General Abbreviations

ACF	Automobile Club de France	French automobile association
AFP	Agence France Presse	French press agency
Av.J.-C.	avant Jésus-Christ	before Christ
Bac	Baccalauréat	secondary school graduation certificate
CEE	Communauté Economique Européenne	EEC
EDF	Electricité de France	French electricity company
etc.	et cetera	and so on
GDF	Gaz de France	French gas company
HLM	Habitation à loyer modéré	subsidized dwelling
LR	lettre recommandée	registered letter
M.	Monsieur	Sir
Mlle	Mademoiselle	Miss
Mme	Madame	Mrs.
MM.	Messieurs	Gentlemen
p.	page	page
p.ex.	par exemple	for example
P.R.	poste restante	general delivery
P.S.	post-scriptum	postscript
PTT	Télécommunications, Télématique	Telecom
PVD	Paquet avec valeur déclarée	package with declared value
SA	Société Anonyme	private company
SARL	Société à responsabilité limitée	limited company
SNCF	Société Nationale des Chemins de Fer Françaiss	French national railroad company
s.t.p.	s'il te plaît	please (you, singular)
s.v.p.	s'il vous plaît	please (you, plural)
TVA	Taxe à la valeur ajoutée	Added value tax

Abbreviations in this book

abst	abstract	abstrait
adj	adjective	adjectif
adv	adverb	adverbe
akust	audio	acoustique
art	article	article
conj	conjunction	conjonction
el	electricity	électricité
f	feminine	féminin
s.o.	someone, to someone	quelqu'un, à quelqu'un
conc	concrete	concret
m	masculine	masculin
M.	Sir	Monsieur
Mlle	Miss	Mademoiselle
Mme	Mrs. (Lady)	Madame
n/	number	numéro
pers prn	personal pronoun	pronom personnel
pl	plural	pluriel
poss prn	possessive pronoun	pronom possessif
prn	pronoun	pronom
prp	preposition	préposition
sth	something	quelque chose
qc	something	quelque chose
qn	someone	quelqu'un
rel	religion	religion
superl	superlative	superlatif
s.v.p.	please (you, pl.)	s'il vous plaît
tele	telephone, telegraph	téléphone, télégraphe

The Alphabet

A	a	a	J	j	zhee	S	s	ehs
B	b	bay	K	k	ka	T	t	tay
C	c	say	L	l	ehl	U	u	ew
D	d	day	M	m	ehm	V	v	vay
E	e	uh	N	n	ehn	W	w	doo-bluh-vay
F	f	ehf	O	o	o	X	x	eeks
G	g	zhay	P	p	pay	Y	y	ee-grehk
H	h	ash	Q	q	kew	Z	z	zehd
I	i	ee	R	r	ehr			

1 The Essentials
Les bases

Frequently Used Expressions

On le dit souvent, on l'entend souvent

Yes.	Oui. [wee]
No.	Non. [nohN]
Please.	S'il vous plaît/S'il te plaît [seel-voo-pleh/seel-voo-pleh]
Thank you!	Merci! [mehr-see]
You're welcome.	De rien. [duh-rjaN]
Pardon?	Comment? [ko-mahN]
Of course!	Naturellement! Bien entendu! [na-tew-rehl-mahN] [bjaN-nahN-tahN-dew]
Agreed/All right!	D'accord! [da-kohr]
Okay!	O.K.! [o-kay]
O.K.!	Entendu! [ahN-tahN-dew]
Excuse me.	Pardon! [par-dohN]
Just a minute, please.	Un instant, s'il vous plaît/s'il te plaît. [aN-naNs-tahN-seel-voo-pleh]
That's enough!	Ça suffit! [sa-sew-fee]
Help!	Au secours! A l'aide! [o-suh-koor] [a-lehd]
What?	Quoi? [kwa]
Which?	Lequel/Laquelle/Lesquels/Lesquelles? [luh-kehl] [la-kehl] [lay-kehl] [lay-kehl]
Who . . . to?/To whom?	A qui? [a-kee]
Who?	Qui [kee]
Where?	Où? [oo]
Where's/Where are . . .?	Où est/Où sont . . . ? [oo-eh] [oo-sohN]
Where . . . from?	D'où? [doo]
Where . . . to?	Où? [oo]

Why? Pourquoi? [poor-kwa]

Why? Pour quelle raison? [poor-kehl-reh-zohN]

What . . . for? Pour quoi faire? [poor-kwa-fehr]

What . . . for? Dans quel but? [dahN-kehl-bewt]

How? Comment? [ko-mahN]

How much? Combien? [kohm-bjaN]

How many? Combien? [kohN-bjaN]

How long? Combien de temps? [kohN-bjaN-duh-tahN]

When? Quand? A quelle heure? [kahN] [a-keh-luhr]

I'd like . . . Je voudrais . . . J'aimerais . . . [zhuh-voo-dreh] [zheh-muh-reh]

Is there . . . ?/Are there . . . ? Il y a . . . ? Est-ce qu'il y a . . .? [ee-lee-ja] [ehs-kee-lee-ja]

Numbers/Measures/Weights

Les nombres/Les mesures/Les poids

0 zéro [zay-ro]
1 un [aN]
2 deux [duuh]
3 trois [trwa]
4 quatre [katr]
5 cinq [saNk]
6 six [sees]
7 sept [seht]
8 huit [weet]
9 neuf [nuhf]
10 dix [dees]
11 onze [ohNz]
12 douze [dooz]
13 treize [trehz]
14 quatorze [ka-tohrz]
15 quinze [kaNz]
16 seize [sehz]
17 dix-sept [dee-seht]
18 dix-huit [dee-zweet]
19 dix-neuf [deez-nuhf]

20	vingt [vaN]
21	vingt et un [vaN-tay-aN]
22	vingt-deux [vaNt-duuh]
23	vingt-trois [vaNt-trwa]
24	vingt-quatre [vaNt-katr]
25	vingt-cinq [vaNt-saNk]
26	vingt-six [vaNt-sees]
27	vingt-sept [vaNt-seht]
28	vingt-huit [vaNt-weet]
29	vingt-neuf [vaNt-nuhf]
30	trente [trahNt]
31	trente et un [trahN-tay-aN]
32	trente-deux [trahNt-duuh]
40	quarante [ka-rahNt]
50	cinquante [saN-kahNt]
60	soixante [swa-sahNt]
70	soixante-dix [swa-sahNt-dees]
80	quatre-vingts [ka-truh-vaN]
90	quatre-vingt-dix [ka-truh-vaN-dees]
100	cent [sahN]
101	cent un [sahN-aN]
200	deux cents [duuh-sahN]
300	trois cents [trwa-sahN]
1,000	mille [meel]
2,000	deux mille [duuh-meel]
3,000	trois mille [trwa-meel]
10,000	dix mille [di-meel]
100,000	cent mille [sahN-meel]
1,000,000	un million [aN-mi-ljohN]
1st	premier/première [pruh-mjay/ preh-mjehr]
2nd	deuxième/second(e) [duh-zjehm] [suh-gohN]
3rd	troisième [trwa-zjehm]
4th	quatrième [ka-tree-jehm]
5th	cinquième [saN-kjehm]
6th	sixième [see-zjehm]
7th	septième [seh-tjehm]
8th	huitième [wee-tjehm]
9th	neuvième [nyh-vjehm]
10th	dixième [dee-zjehm]
1/2	un demi [aN-duh-mee]
1/3	un tiers [aN-tjehr]
1/4	un quart [aN-kar]

3/4	trois quarts [trwa-kar]
3.5%	trois virgule cinq pour cent [trwa-veer-gewl-saNk-poor-sahN]
27°C	vingt-sept degrés [vaNt-seht-duh-gray]
–5°C	moins cinq degrés [mwaN-saNk]
1998	mille neuf cent quatre-vingt dix-huit [meel-nuhf-sahN-ka-truh-vaN-dooz]
millimeter	le millimètre [luh-mee-lee-mehtr]
centimeter	le centimètre [luh-sahN-tee-mehtr]
meter	le mètre [luh-mehtr]
kilometer	le kilomètre [luh-kee-lo-mehtr]
mile	la lieue [la-ljuuh]
nautical mile	le mille marin [luh-meel-ma-raN]
square meter	le mètre carré [luh-meh-truh-ka-ray]
square kilometer	le kilomètre carré [luh-kee-lo-meh-truh-ka-ray]
acre	l'are *(m)* [lar]
hectare	l'hectare *(m)* [lehk-tar]
liter	le litre [luh-leetr]
gram	le gramme [luh-gram]
pound	la livre [luh-leevr]
kilogram	le kilogramme, le kilo [luh-kee-lo-gram] [luh-kee-lo]
a dozen	la douzaine [la-doo-zehn]

Expressions of Time

Le temps qui passe

Telling Time — L'heure

What time is it?	Quelle heure est-il? [keh-luh-reh-teel]
Can you tell me the time, please?	Vous avez l'heure, s'il vous plaît? [voo-za-vay-luhr-seel-voo-pleh]
It's (exactly/about) . . .	Il est (exactement/environ) . . . [ee-leh-tehg-zak-tuh-mahN/ahN-vee-rohN] X
three o'clock.	trois heures. [trwa-zuhr]

five past three.	trois heures cinq. [trwa-uhr-saNk]
ten past three.	trois heures dix. [trwa-zuhr-dees]
quarter past three.	trois heures et quart. [trwa-zuh-ray-kar]
half past three.	trois heures et demie. [trwa-zuh-ray-duh-mee]
quarter to four.	quatre heures moins le quart. [ka-truhr-mwaN-luh-kar]
five to four.	quatre heures moins cinq. [ka-truhr-mwaN-saNk]
noon/midnight.	midi/minuit. [mee-dee/mee-nwee]
Is this clock right?	Est-ce que cette horloge est à l'heure? [ehs-kuh-seht-ohr-lohzh-eh-ta-luhr]
It's fast/slow.	Elle avance/retarde. [ehl-a-vahNs/ruh-tard]
It's late/too early.	Il est tard/trop tôt. [eel-ay-tar/tro-to]
What time?/When?	A quelle heure?/Quand? [a-kehl-uhr] [kahN]
At one o'clock.	A une heure. [a-ewn-uhr]
At two o'clock.	A deux heures. [a-duuh-zuhr]
At about four o'clock.	Vers quatre heures. [vehr-ka-truhr]
In an hour's time.	Dans une heure. [dahN-zewn-uhr]
In two hours' time.	Dans deux heures. [dahN-duuh-zuhr]
Not before nine A.M.	Pas avant neuf heures du matin. [pa-a-vahN-nuh-vuhr-dew-ma-taN]
After eight P.M.	Après huit heures du soir. [a-pray-weet-uhr-dew-swar]
Between three and four.	Entre trois heures et quatre heures. [ahN-truh-trwa-zuhr-ay-ka-truhr]
How long?	Combien de temps? [kohN-bjaN-du-tahN]
For two hours.	Deux heures. [duuh-zuhr]
From ten to eleven.	De dix à onze. [duh-dee-zuhr-a-ohNz]
Till five o'clock.	Jusqu'à/Avant cinq heures. [zhews-ka/a-vahN-saNk-uhr]

Since when?	Depuis quelle heure? [duh-pwee-kehl-uhr]
Since eight A.M.	Depuis huit heures du matin. [duh-pwee-weet-uhr-dew-ma-taN]
For half an hour.	Depuis une demi-heure. [duh-pwee-ewn-duh-mee-uhr]
For a week.	Depuis huit jours. [duh-pwee-wee-zhuuhr]

Other Expressions of Time	**Le temps qui passe**
in the evening	le soir [luh-swar]
every half hour	toutes les demi-heures [toot-lay-duh-mee-uhr]
every other day	tous les deux jours [too-lay-zhoor]
on Sunday	dimanche [dee-mahNsh]
on the weekend	ce week-end [suh-wee-kehnd]
soon	bientôt [byaN-to]
this week	cette semaine [seht-suh-mehn]
about noon/lunchtime	vers midi [vehr-mee-dee]
yesterday	hier [ee-yehr]
today	aujourd'hui [o-zhoor-dwee]
this morning/evening	ce matin/ce soir [suh-ma-taN/suh-swar]
in two weeks	dans quinze jours [dahN-kaNz-zhoor]
within a week	en une semaine [ahN-ewn-suh-mehn]
every day	tous les jours [too-lay-zhoor]
now	maintenant [maN-tuh-nahN]
recently	l'autre jour [lo-truh-zhoor]
last Monday	lundi dernier [laN-dee-dehr-nyay]

sometimes	quelquefois [kehl-kuh-fwa]
at lunchtime	à midi [a-mee-dee]
tomorrow	demain [duh-maN]
tomorrow morning/ evening	demain matin/soir [duh-maN-ma-taN]/[swar]
in the morning	le matin [luh-ma-taN]
in the afternoon	dans l'après-midi [dahN-la-preh-mee-dee]
next year	l'année prochaine [la-nay-pro-shehn]
at night	de nuit [duh-nwee]
every hour, hourly	par heure [par-uhr]
every day, daily	par jour [par-zhoor]
during the day	pendant la journée [pahN-dahN-la-zhoor-nay]
the day after tomorrow	après-demain [a-preh-duh-maN]
about this time	à cette heure-ci [a-seht-uhr-see]
from time to time	de temps en temps [duh-tahN-zahN-tahN]
ten minutes ago	il y a dix minutes [eel-ya-dee-mee-newt]
the day before yesterday	avant-hier [a-vahN-tyehr]
during the morning	dans la matinée [dahN-la-ma-tee-nay]

Days of the Week — Les jours de la semaine

Monday	lundi [laN-dee]
Tuesday	mardi [mar-dee]
Wednesday	mercredi [mehr-kruh-dee]
Thursday	jeudi [zhuh-dee]
Friday	vendredi [vahN-druh-dee]
Saturday	samedi [sam-dee]
Sunday	dimanche [dee-mahNsh]

Months of the Year — Les mois de l'année

January	janvier [zhahN-vyay]
February	février [fay-vree-yay]
March	mars [mars]
April	avril [a-vreel]
May	mai [may]
June	juin [zhwaN]
July	juillet [zhwee-yay]
August	août [oot]
September	septembre [sehp-tahN-bruh]
October	octobre [ohk-toh-bruh]
November	novembre [no-vahN-bruh]
December	décembre [day-sahN-bruh]

Seasons — Les saisons

spring	le printemps [luh-praN-tahN]
summer	l'été *(m)* [lay-tay]
autumn/fall	l'automne *(m)* [lo-tohn]
winter	l'hiver *(m)* [lee-vehr]

Holidays — Les jours fériés

New Year's Day	le Nouvel An [luh-noo-vehl-ahN]
Epiphany	la Fête des Rois/l'Epiphanie [la-feht-day-rwa/lay-pee-fa-nee]
carnival	le carnaval [luh-kar-na-val]
Fat Tuesday	le mardi gras [luh-mar-dee-gra]
Ash Wednesday	le mercredi des cendres [luh-mehr-kruh-dee-day-sahN-druh]
Good Friday	le vendredi saint [luh-vahN-druh-dee-saN]
Easter	Pâques *(f)* [pak]
Easter Monday	le lundi de Pâques [luh-laaN-dee-duh-pak]
May 1st	la Fête du Travail [la-feht-dew-tra-va-yuh]

Summit of Mont-Blanc in the French Alps

Ascension Day	l'Ascension *(f)* [la-sahN-syohN]
Pentacost	la Pentecôte [la-pahN-tuh-kot]
Monday of Pentacost	le lundi de Pentecôte [luh-laN-dee-duh-la-pahN-tuh-kot]
Corpus Christi	la Fête-Dieu [la-feht-duh-dyuuh]
Bastille Day (July 14th)	le quatorze juillet [luh-ka-tohrz-zhwee-yay]
Assumption	l'Assomption *(f)* [la-sohNp-syohN]
All Saints Day (November 1st)	la Toussaint [la-too-saN]
Armistice Day (1st WW, November 11)	l'Armistice *(m)* [lar-mees-tees]
Christmas Eve	la veille de Noël [la-vehy-duh-no-ehl]
Christmas	Noël [no-ehl]
New Year's Eve	la Saint-Sylvestre [la-saN-seel-vehs-truh]

The Date | La date

What's the date (today)?	On est le combien aujourd'hui? [ohN-neh-luh-kohN-byaN-o-zhoor-dwee]
Today's the first of May.	Aujourd'hui, c'est le 1er mai. [o-zhoor-dwee-say-luh-pruh-myay-may]

Weather

Le temps qu'il fait

What's the weather going to be like today?	Qu'est-ce qu'il va faire comme temps, aujourd'hui? [kehs-keel-va-fehr-kohm-tahN-o-zhoor-dwee]
We'll have . . .	On va avoir . . . [ohN-va-a-vwar]
good weather.	du beau temps. [dew-bo-tahN]
bad weather.	du mauvais temps. [dew-mo-veh-tahN]
changeable weather.	un temps variable. [aN-tahN-va-ryabl]
It's going to remain fine/poor weather.	Le temps restera au beau./Le mauvais temps persistera. [luh-tahN-rehs-tuh-ra-o-bo]/ [luh-mo-vay-tahN-pehr-sees-tuh-ra]
It's going to rain/ to snow.	Il va pleuvoir/neiger. [eel-va-pluuh-vwar]/[nay-zhay]
It's cold/hot/oppressing.	Il fait froid/chaud/lourd. [eel-fay-frwa]/[sho]/[loor]
There's going to be a thunderstorm.	Un orage se prépare./Il va faire de l'orage. [aN-no-razh-suh-pray-par] [eel-va-fehr-duh-lo-razh]
It is foggy./It is windy.	Il y a du brouillard./Il fait du vent. [eel-ya-dew-broo-yar]/[eel-fay-dew-vahN]
The sun is shining.	Le soleil brille. [luh-so-lehy-breey]
The sky's clear/overcast.	Le ciel est dégagé/couvert. [luh-syehl-ay-day-ga-zhay/koo-vehr]
What's the temperature today?	Quelle température fait-il, aujourd'hui? [kehl-tahN-pay-ra-tewr-fay-teel-o-zhoor-dwi]

It's twenty degrees (Centigrade).	Il fait vingt degrés. [eel-fay-vaN-duuh-gray]
What are the roads like in . . . ?	Quel est l'état des routes dans . . . ? [kehl-ay-lay-ta-day-root-dahN]
The roads are icy.	Les routes sont verglacées. [lay-root-sohN-vehr-gla-say]
Visibility is only 20 meters/less than 50 meters.	La visibilité n'est que de vingt mètres/est de moins de cinquante mètres. [la-vee-zee-bee-lee-tay-nay-kuh-duh-vaN-mehtr]/[ay-duh-mwaN-duh-saN-kahNt-mehtr]
You need snow chains.	Il va falloir mettre des chaînes. [eel-va-fa-lwar-mehtr-day-shehn]
It's going to become warmer/colder.	Le temps va se radoucir/se rafraîchir. [luh-tahN-va-suh-ra-doo-seer/suh-ra-fray-sheer]

Word List: Weather

air	l'air *(m)* [lehr]
air pressure	la pression atmosphérique [la-pray-syohN-at-mos-fay-reek]
barometer	le baromètre [luh-ba-ro-mehtr]
calm	le calme [luh-kalm]
climate	le climat [luh-klee-ma]
cloud	le nuage [luh-new-azh]
cloudburst/downpour	la pluie torrentielle [la-plwee-to-rahN-syehl]
cloudy	nuageux [new-a-zhuuh]
cold	froid [frwa]
damp and cool	frais et humide [fray-ay-ew-meed]
dawn/dusk	l'aube/le crépuscule [lob]/[luh-kray-pews-kewl]
depression	la zone de basse pression [la-zon-duh-bas-pray-syohN]
drizzle	la bruine [la-brween]
drought	la sécheresse [la-say-shuh-rehs]
flooding, floods	l'inondation *(f)* [lee-nohN-da-syohN]
fog	le brouillard [luh-broo-yar]
frost	le gel [luh-zhehl]
gust of wind	la rafale [la-ra-fal]
hail	la grêle [la-grehl]

hailstone	les giboulées [lay-zhee-boo-lay]
hazy	brumeux [brew-muuh]
heat	la chaleur [la-sha-luhr]
heat wave	la canicule, la vague de chaleur [la-ka-nee-kewl]/[la-vag-duh-sha-luhr]
high pressure zone	la zone de haute pression [la-zon-duh-ot-pray-syohN]
high tide	la marée haute [la-ma-ray-ot]
hot	très chaud [tray-sho]
humid	lourd [loor]
ice	la glace [la-glas]
lightning	l'éclair *(m)* [lay-klehr]
low tide	la marée basse [la-ma-ray-bas]
precipitations	les précipitations *(f)* [lay-pray-see-pee-ta-syohN]
rain	la pluie [la-plwee]
rain shower	l'averse *(f)* [la-vehrs]
rainy	pluvieux [ploo-vyuuh]
sheet of ice	le verglas [luh-vehr-gla]
snow	la neige [la-nehzh]
snow powder	la (neige) poudreuse [la-nehzh-poo-druuhz]
snowstorm	la tempête de neige [la-tahN-peht-duh-nehzh]
starry	étoilé [ay-twa-lay]
sun	le soleil [luh-so-lehy]
sunny	ensoleillé [ahN-so-lay-yay]
sunrise	le lever du soleil [luh-luh-vay-dew-so-lehy]
sunset	le coucher du soleil [luh-koo-shay-dew-so-lehy]
temperature	la température [la-tahN-pay-ra-tewr]
thaw	le dégel [luh-duh-gray]
thunder	le tonnere [luh-to-nehr]
variable	variable [va-ryabl]
warm	chaud [sho]
weather forecast	les prévisions *(f)* météorologiques [lay-pray-vee-zyohN-may-tay-o-ro-lo-zheek]
weather report	le bulletin météorologique, la météo [luh-bewl-taN-may-tay-o-ro-lo-zheek]/[la-may-tay-o]
wet	humide [ew-meed]
wind	le vent [luh-vahN]
wind force	la force du vent [la-fohrs-dew-vahN]

Word List: Colors

beige	beige [behzh]
black	noir [nwar]
blue	bleu [bluuh]
brown	marron [ma-rohN]
colored	de couleur [duh-koo-luhr]
gold(en)	couleur or [koo-luhr-ohr]
gray	gris [gree]
green	vert [vehr]
lilac	lilas, mauve [lee-la],[mov]
orange	orange [o-rahNzh]
pink	rose [roz]
plain	uni [ew-nee]
purple	violet [vyo-lay]
red	rouge [roozh]
silver	couleur argent [koo-luhr-ar-zhahN]
turquoise	turquoise [tewr-kwaz]
white	blanc [blahN]
light . . .	. . . clair [klehr]
dark . . .	. . . foncé [fohN-say]
yellow	jaune [zhon]

2 Making Contact
Contacts

Saying Hello/Introductions/Getting Acquainted

Salutations/Présentations/Rencontre

Good morning!	Bonjour! [bohN-zhoor]
Good afternoon!	Bonjour! [bohN-zhoor]
Good evening!	Bonsoir! [bohN-swar]
Hello!/Hi!	Salut! [sa-lew]
What's your name? *(form.)*	Comment vous appelez-vous? [ko-mahN-voo-za-play-voo]
What's your name? *(inform.)*	Comment tu t'appelles? [ko-mahN-tew-ta-pehl]
My name is . . .	Je m'appelle X [zhuh-ma-pehl] . . .
May I introduce you?	Puis-je faire les présentations? [pweezh-fehr-lay-pray-zahN-ta-syohN]
This is . . .	C'est . . . [say]
Mrs./Ms. X.	Madame X. [ma-dam]
Miss X.	Mademoiselle X. [mad-mwa-zehl]
Mr. X.	Monsieur X. [muh-syuuh]
my husband.	mon mari. [mohN-ma-ree]
my wife.	ma femme. [ma-fam]
my son.	mon fils. [mohN-fees]
my daughter.	ma fille. [ma-feey]
my brother/my sister.	mon frère/ma sœur. [mohNfrehr] [ma-suhr]
my boyfriend/ girlfriend.	mon ami/mon amie. [mohN-na-mee] [mohN-na-mee]
my colleague.	un collègue/une collègue. [aN-koh-lehg] [ewn-koh-lehg]
How are you?	Comment allez-vous/vas-tu? [ko-mahN-ta-lay-voo]/[ko-mahN-va-tew] (Comment) ça va? [ko-mahN-sa-va]
Fine thanks. And you?	Bien, merci. Et vous-même/toi? [byaN-mehr-see][ay-voo-mehm]
Where are you from?	D'où êtes-vous?/Tu es d'où? [doo-eht-voo]/[tew-eh-doo]
I am from . . .	Je suis de . . . [zhuh-swee-duh]

Have you been here long?	Vous êtes/Tu es à X depuis longtemps? [voo-zeht]/[tew-ay-a-X-duh-pwee-lohN-tahN]
I've been here since . . .	Je suis là depuis . . . [zhu-swee-la-duh-pwee]
How long are you staying?	Vous allez/Tu vas rester combien de temps? [voo-za-lay]/[tew-va-rehs-tay-kohN-byaN-duh-tahN]
Is this your first time here?	C'est la première fois que vous venez/que tu viens ici? [say-la-pruh-myehr-fwa-kuh-voo-vuh-nay]/[kuh-tew-vyaN-ee-see]
Are you alone?	Vous êtes/Tu es seul(e)? [voo-zeht]/[tew-ay-suhl]
No, I am with my family/with friends.	Non, je suis ici avec ma famille/des amis. [nohN-zhuh-swee-a-vehk-ma-fa-meey]/[day-za-mee]
Are you staying at the Astoria Hotel/at the camping site?	Vous êtes/Tu es à l'hôtel Astoria/au camping? [voo-zeht]/[tew-ay-a-lo-tehl-as-to-rya]/[o-kahN-peeng]

Traveling Alone/Making a Date

Quand on voyage seul/Rendez-vous

Are you waiting for someone?	Vous attendez/Tu attends quelqu'un? [voo-za-tahN-day][tew-a-tahN-kehl-kaN]
Do you have any plans for tomorrow?	Vous avez/Tu as des projets pour demain? [voo-za-vay][tew-a-day-pro-zhay-poor-duh-man]
We can go together, if you wish.	On peut y aller ensemble, si vous voulez/tu veux. [ohN-puuh-ee-a-lay-ahN-sahNbl-see-voo-voo-lay]/[tew-vuuh]
Shall we go out together this evening?	On sort ensemble ce soir? [ohN-sohr-ahN-sahNbl-suh-swar]
Can I invite you for a meal?	Est-ce que je peux vous inviter/t'inviter à manger? [ehs-kuh-zhuh-puuh-voo-zaN-vee-tay]/[taN-vee-tay-a-mahN-zhay]

When shall we meet?	On se voit à quelle heure? [ohN-suh-vwa-a-kehl-uhr]
I can pick you up, if you wish.	Je peux passer vous/te prendre, si vous voulez/tu veux. [zhuh-puuh-pa-say-voo][tuh-prahN-druh-see-voo-voo-lay] [tew-vuuh]
When shall I come by?	Je viens à quelle heure? [zhuh-vyaN-a-kehl-uhr]
Let's meet at 9 o'clock . . .	On se retrouve à 9 heures . . . [ohN-suh-ruh-troov-a-nuh-vuhr]
in front of the cinema.	devant le cinéma. [duh-vahN-luh-see-nay-ma]
at the X square.	sur la placc X. [sewr-la-plas]
in the café.	au café. [o-ka-fay]
Are you married?	Vous êtes marié(e)? [voo-zeht-ma-ryay]
Have you got a boy-friend/a girlfriend?	Tu as un petit ami/une petite amie? [tew-a-aN-puh-tee-ta-mee]/[ewn-puh-teet-a-mee]
Can I take you home?	Je vous/Je te raccompagne? [zhu-voo]/[whuh-tuh-ra-kohN-pany]
I'll take you to the train station/bus stop.	Je vais vous/te conduire à la gare/à l'arrêt de bus. [zhu-vay-voo/tuh-kohN-dweer-a-la-gar]/[a-la-ray-duh-bews]
Can I see you again?	Est-ce que je peux vous/te revoir? [ehs-kuh-zhuh-puuh-voo/tuh-ruh-vwar]
I hope I'll see you again soon.	J'espère vous/te revoir bientôt. [zhehs-pehr-voo/tuh-ruh-vwar-byaN-to]
Thank you so much for a pleasant evening.	Merci beaucoup pour cette agréable soirée. [mehr-see-bo-koo-poor-seht-a-gray-abl-swa-ray]
Please leave me alone!	Laissez-moi tranquille, je vous prie! [lay-say-mwa-trahN-keel]

A Visit

Une visite

Excuse me, does Mr./Mrs./Ms. X live here?	Pardon, Mme/Mlle/M., c'est bien ici qu'habite M./Mme/Mlle X? [par-dohN-ma-dam]/[mad-mwa-zehl]/[muh-syuuh-say-byaN-ee-see-ka-beet-muh-syuuh/ma-dam/mad-mwa-zehl]
No, he's/she's moved.	Non, il/elle a déménagé. [nohN-eel/ehl-a-day-may-na-zhay]
Do you know where he's/she's living now?	Vous savez où il/elle habite maintenant?[voo-sa-vay-oo-eel/ehl-a-beet-maN-tuh-nahN]
Can I speak to Mr./Mrs./Ms. X?	Est-ce que je pourrais parler à M./Mme/Mlle X? [ehs-kuh-zhuh-poo-ray-par-lay-a-muh-syuuh/ma-dam/mad-mwa-zehl]
When will he/she be home?	Quand est-ce qu'il/elle sera à la maison? [kahN-tehs-keel/kehl/suh-ra-a-la-may-zohN]
Can I leave a message?	Est-ce que je peux laisser un message? [ehs-kuh-zhuh-puuh-lay-say-aN-may-sazh]
I'll come back later.	Je repasserai. [zhuh-ruh-pas-ray]
Come in.	Entrez./Entre. [ahN-tray]/[ahNtr]
Please, sit down.	Asseyez-vous./Assieds-toi. [a-say-yay-voo]/[a-syay-twa]
Paul asked me to convey his regards.	J'ai le bonjour à vous/te donner de la part de Paul. [zhay-luh-bohN-zhoor-a-voo/tuh-do-nay-duh-la-par-duh-pohl]
What can I get you to drink?	Qu'est-ce que je vous offre?/Qu'est-ce que tu veux boire? [kehs-kuh-zhuh-voo-zohfr]/[kehs-kuh-tew-vuuh-bwar]
Cheers!	A votre santé!/A la vôtre!/A ta santé!/A la tienne! [a-vohtr-sahNt-ay]/[a-la-vohtr]/ [a-ta-sahN-tay]/[a-la-tyehn]

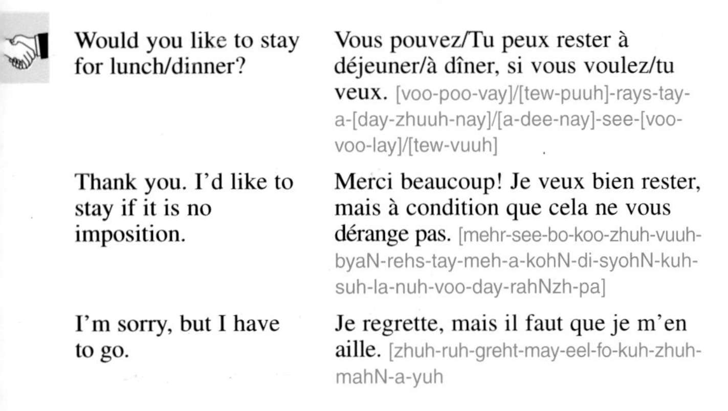

Would you like to stay for lunch/dinner?	Vous pouvez/Tu peux rester à déjeuner/à dîner, si vous voulez/tu veux. [voo-poo-vay]/[tew-puuh]-rays-tay-a-[day-zhuuh-nay]/[a-dee-nay]-see-[voo-voo-lay]/[tew-vuuh]
Thank you. I'd like to stay if it is no imposition.	Merci beaucoup! Je veux bien rester, mais à condition que cela ne vous dérange pas. [mehr-see-bo-koo-zhuh-vuuh-byaN-rehs-tay-meh-a-kohN-di-syohN-kuh-suh-la-nuh-voo-day-rahNzh-pa]
I'm sorry, but I have to go.	Je regrette, mais il faut que je m'en aille. [zhuh-ruh-greht-may-eel-fo-kuh-zhuh-mahN-a-yuh

Saying Good-bye

Départ

Good-bye/Bye-bye!	Au revoir! [o-ruh-vwar]
See you soon!	A bientôt! [a-byaN-to]
See you later!	A tout à l'heure! [a-too-ta-luhr]
See you tomorrow!	A demain! [a-duh-maN]
Good night!	Bonne nuit! [bohn-nwee]
Hi!	Salut! [sa-lew]
Have fun!	Amusez-vous/Amuse-toi bien! [a-mew-zay]/[a-mewz-twa]-[byaN]
Have a good journey!	Bon voyage! [bohN-vwa-yazh]
I'll be in touch.	Je vous donnerai de mes nouvelles. [zhuh-voo-doh-nuh-ray-duh-may-noo-vehl]
Give . . . my regards.	Bien des choses à . . . [byaN-day-shoz-a]

Asking a Favor/Expressing Thanks

Demandes et remerciements

Yes, please.	Oui, je veux bien. [wee-zhuh-vuuh-byaN]
No, thanks!	Non, merci! [nohN-mehr-see]

Could you do me a favor?	Est-ce que je peux vous demander un petit service? [ehs-kuh-zhuh-puuh-voo-duh-mahN-day-aN-puh-tee-sehr-vees]
May I?	Vous permettez? [voo-pehr-may-tay]
Can you please help me?	Vous pouvez m'aider, s.v.p.? [voo-poo-vay-may-day-seel-voo-play]
Thank you.	Merci. [mehr-see]
Thank you very much.	Merci beaucoup. [mehr-see-bo-koo]
Yes, thank you!	Merci, bien volontiers! [mehr-see-byaN-vo-lohN-tyay]
Thanks. The same to you.	Merci, vous de même/vous aussi. [mehr-see][voo-duh-mehm]/[voo-zo-see]
That's very kind of you, thank you.	C'est gentil à vous/toi, merci. [say-zhahN-tee-a-voo/twa-mehr-see]
Thank you very much for your help/trouble.	Merci beaucoup de votre aide/obligeance. [mehr-see-bo-koo-duh-vohtr-[ehd]/[o-blee-zhahNs]
Don't mention it./You're welcome.	Mais, je vous en prie./De rien. [may-zhuh-voo-zahN-pree]/[duh-ryaN]

Apologies/Regrets

Excuses/Regret

I'm sorry.	Excusez-moi/Excuse-moi. [ehks-kew-zay-mwa]/[ehks-kewz-mwa]
I must apologize.	Je vous/te dois des excuses. [zhuh-voo/tuh-dwa-day-zehks-kewz]
I'm so sorry.	Je suis navré/désolé. [zhu-swee-[na-vray]/[daay-zo-lay]
I didn't mean it.	Ce n'est pas ce que j'ai voulu dire. [suh-nay-pa-suh-khu-zhay-voo-lew-deer]
What a pity!	Dommage! [do-mazh]
I'm afraid that's impossible.	C'est malheureusement impossible. [say-ma-luuh-ruuhz-mahN-aN-po-seebl]
Maybe another time.	Une autre fois, peut-être. [ewn-o-truh-fwa-puuh-tehtr]

Congratulations/Best Wishes
Vœux/Félicitations

Congratulations!	Toutes mes félicitations! [toot-may-fay-lee-see-ta-syohN]
Happy birthday!	Bon anniversaire!/Bonne fête! [bohn-a-nee-vehr-sehr]/ [bohn-feht]
Good luck!	Bonne chance! [bohn-shahNs]
Good luck! (Break a leg!)	Merde à la puissance treize! [mehrd-a-la-pwee-sahNs-trehz]
Get well soon!	Je vous/te souhaite un prompt rétablissement! [zhuh-voo/tuh-sweht-aN-prohN-ray-ta-blees-mahN]
Happy holidays!	Passez/Passe de bonnes fêtes! [pa-say]/ [pas]-duh-bohn-feht]

Language Difficulties
Difficultés de compréhension

Pardon?	Comment? [ko-mahN]
I don't understand.	Je ne comprends pas. [zhuh-nuh-kohN-prahN-pa]
Would you repeat that, please?	Vous pouvez/Tu peux répéter, s'il vous/te plaît? [voo-poo-vay]/[tew-puuh]-[ray-pay-tay]-[seel-voo/tuh-play]
Could you please speak a little more slowly/ louder.	Vous pourriez/Tu pourrais parler un peu plus lentement/fort, s.v.p./s.t.p.? [voo-poo-ryay]/[tew-poo-ray]-[par-lay-aN-puuh-plew]-[lahN-tuh-mahN]/[fohr]-[seel-voo/tuh-play]
I understand.	Je comprends/J'ai compris. [zhuh-kohN-prahN]/[zhay-kohN-pree]
Do you speak . . .	Vous parlez/Tu parles . . . [voo-par-lay]/ [tew-parl]
German?	allemand? [al-mahN]
English?	anglais? [ahN-glay]
French?	français? [frahN-say]

I can speak a little bit.	Je parle un tout petit peu. [zhuh-parl-aN-too-puh-tee-puuh]
How do you say . . . in French?	Comment dit-on . . . en français? [ko-mahN-dee-tohN- . . . -ahN-frahN-say]
What does it mean?	Qu'est-ce que ça veut dire? [kehs-kuh-sa-vuuh-deer]
How do you pronounce this word?	Comment prononce-t-on ce mot? [ko-mahN-pro-nohNs-tohN-suh-mo]
Could you please write it down for me?	Vous pouvez/Tu peux me l'écrire, s.v.p./s.t.p.? [voo-poo-vay]/[tew-puuh]-[muh-lay-kreer]/[seel-voo/tuh-play]
Could you spell it for me, please?	Vous pouvez/Tu peux me l'épeler, s.v.p./s.t.p.? [voo-poo-vay]/[tew-puuh]-[muh-lay-play]/[seel-voo/tuh-play]

Expressing Opinions

Donner son avis

I like it/I don't like it.	ça me plaît/ça ne me plaît pas. [sa-muh-plau]/[sa-nuh-muh-play-pa]
I would prefer . . .	J'aimerais mieux/Je préférerais . . . [zheh-muh-ray-myuuh]/[zhuh-pray-fay-ruh-ray]
What I would like most would be . . .	Ce qui me plairait le plus, ce serait de . . . [suh-kee-muh-play-ray-luh-plews-suh-suh-ray-duh]
That would be great!	Ce serait chouette! [suh-sray-shweht]
With pleasure!	Avec plaisir! [a-vehk-play-zeer]
Fine!	Parfait! [par-fay]
I don't feel like it.	Je n'ai pas envie. [zhuh-nay-pa-ahN-vee]
I don't want to.	Je ne veux pas. [zhuh-nuh-vuuh-pa]
That's out of the question!	Il n'en est pas question! [eel-nahN-neh-pa-kehs-tyohN]
Certainly not!	En aucun cas! [ahN-no-kaN-ka]
I don't know yet.	Je ne sais pas encore. [zhuh-nuh-say-pa-ahN-kohr]

Maybe.	Peut-être. [puuh-tehtr]
Probably.	Probablement. [pro-ba-bluh-mahN]

Personal Information

Parler de soi

Age	L'age
How old are you?	Quel âge avez-vous/Tu as quel âge? [kehl-azh-a-vay-voo]/[tew-a-kehl-azh]
I am 39.	J'ai trente-neuf ans. [zhay-trahNt-nuh-vahN]
When is your birthday?	C'est quand votre/ton anniversaire? [say-kahN-vohtr/tohN-a-nee-vehr-sehr]
I was born on April 12, 1954.	Je suis né(e) le 12 avril 1954. [zhuh-swee-nay-luh-dooz-a-vreel-meel-nuhf-sahN-saN-kahNt-katr]

Professions/Education/ Training	Profession/Etudes/Formation
What do you do for a living?	Qu'est-ce que vous faites/tu fais comme métier? [kehs-kuh-[voo-feht]/[tew-fay]-kohm-may-tyay]
I work in a factory.	Je suis ouvrier/ouvrière. [zhuh-swee-[zoo-vree-yay]/[zoo-vree-yehr]
I work in an office.	Je suis employé(e). [zhuh-swee-zahN-plwa-yay]
I'm a civil servant.	Je suis fonctionnaire. [zhuh-swee-fohNk-syo-nehr]
I do freelance work.	J'exerce une profession libérale. [zhayg-zehrs-ewn-pro-fay-syohN-lee-bay-ral]
I'm retired.	Je suis retraité(e). [zhuh-swee-ruh-tray-tay]
I am unemployed.	Je suis au chômage. [zhuh-swee-o-sho-mazh]

I work for . . .	Je travaille chez . . . [zhuh-tra-va-yuh-shay]
I'm still at school.	Je vais encore à l'école. [zhuh-vay-ahN-kohr-a-lay-kohl]
I am in high school.	Je vais au lycée. [zhuh-vay-o-lee-say]
I am a student.	Je suis étudiant/étudiante. [zhuh-swee]-[ay-tew-dyahN]/[ay-tew-dyahNt]
Where are you studying?	Où est-ce que vous faites vos études/ tu fais tes études? [oo-ehs-kuh-voo-feht-vo-zay-tewd]/[tew-fay-tay-zay-tewd]
What are you studying?	Qu'est-ce que vous faites/tu fais comme études? [kehs-kuh-voo-feht-kohm-ay-tewd]
I am studying . . . in New York.	Je fais des études de . . . à New York. [zhuh-fay-day-zay-tewd-duh-...-a-New York]
What are your hobbies?	Quels sont vos/tes hobbies? [kehl-sohN-vo/tay-o-bee]

Word List: Professions/Education/Training

actor/actress	l'acteur/l'actrice, le comédien/la comédienne [lak-tuhr]/[lak-trees], [luh-ko may-dyaN]/[la-ko-may-dyehn]
apprentice	l'apprenti(e) [la-prahN-tee]
archaeology	l'archéologie *(f)* [lar-kay-o-lo-zhee]
architect	l'architecte *(m)* [lar-shee-tehkt]
architecture	l'architecture *(f)* [lar-shee-tehk-tewr]
art history	l'histoire *(f)* de l'art [lees-twar-duh-lar]
art school	l'école *(f)* des beaux-arts [lay-kohl-day-bo-zar]
artist	l'artiste *(m/f)* [lar-teest]
baker	le boulanger/la boulangère [luh-boo-lahN-zhay]/[la-boo-lahN-zhehr]
biologist	le/la biologiste [luh-la-bee-o-lo-zheest]
biology	la biologie [la-bee-o-lo-zhee]
blue-collar worker	l'ouvrier/l'ouvrière [loo-vree-yay]/[loo-vree-yehr]
bookkeeper	le comptable [luh-kohN-tabl]
bookseller	le/la libraire [luh/la-lee-brehr]
bricklayer	le maçon [luh-ma-sohN]

business management	la gestion des entreprises [la-zhehs-tyohN-day-zahN-truh-preez]
business school	l'école *(f)* de commerce [lay-kohl-duh-ko-mehrs]
butcher	le boucher/la bouchère [luh-boo-shay]/[la-boo-shehr]
buyer	l'acheteur/le client [lash-tuhr]/[luh-klee-yaN]
caretaker	le/la concierge [luh/la-kohN-syehrzh]
carpenter	le charpentier, le menuisier [luh-shar-pahN-tyay]/[luh-muh-nwee-zyay]
cashier	le caissier/la caissière [luh-kay-syay]/[la-kay-syehr]
certified accountant	l'expert-comptable *(m)* [lehk-spehr-kohN-tabl]
chemist	le/la chimiste [luh/la-shee-meest]
chemist/pharmacist	le pharmacien/la pharmacienne [luh-far-ma-syaN]/[la-far-ma-syehn]
chemistry	la chimie [la-shee-mee]
civil servant	le fonctionnaire [luh-fohNk-syo-nehr]
clerk	l'employé(e) [lahN-plwa-yay]
comprehensive school	le collège [luh-ko-lehzh]
computer science	l'informatique *(f)* [laN-fohr-ma-teek]
computer specialist	l'informaticien/l'informaticienne [laN-fohr-ma-tee-syaN]/[laN-fohr-ma-tee-syehn]
confectioner, pastry maker	le pâtissier/la pâtissière [luh-pa-tee-syay]/[la-pa-tee-syehr]
cook	le cuisinier/la cuisinière [luh-kwee-zee-nyay]/[la-kwee-zee-nyehr]dahN-glay]dal-mahN]
decorator	le décorateur/la décoratrice [luh-day-ko-ra-tuhr]/[la-day-ko-ra-trees]
dental technician	l'assitant(e) [la-sees-tahN]/[la-sees-tahNt]
dentist	le dentiste [luh-dahN-teest]
designer	le styliste [luh-stee-leest]
doctor	le médecin [luh-mehd-saN]
doctor's receptionist	la secrétaire médicale [la-suh-kray-tehr-may-dee-kal]
doorman	le portier/concierge [luh-pohr-tyay]/[kohN-syehrzh]
draftsman/-woman	le dessinateur/la dessinatrice industriel(le) [luh-day-see-na-tuhr]/[la-day-see-na-trees]-aN-dews-tree-yehl]

driver	le chauffeur-le conducteur/la conductrice [luh-sho-fuhr] - [luh-kohN-dewk-tuhr]/[la-kohN-dewk-trees]
driving instructor	le moniteur/la monitrice d'auto-école [luh-mo-nee-tuhr]/[la-mo-nee-trees]-do-to-ay-kohl]
economist	l'économiste *(m/f)* [lay-ko-no-meest]
editor	le rédacteur/la rédactrice [luh-ray-dak-tuhr]/[la-ray-dak-trees]
editor (movies)	le monteur [luh-mohN-tuhr]
electrician	l'électricien/l'électricienne [lay-lehk-tree-syaN]/ [lay-lehk-tree-syehn]
elementary school	l'école *(f)* élémentaire/primaire [lay-kohl-[ay-lay-mahN-tehr]/[pree-mehr]
engineer	l'ingénieur *(m)* [laN-zhay-nyuhr]
English studies	les études *(f)* d'anglais [lay-zay-tewd-
environmental officer	l'environnementaliste *(m/f)* [lahN-vee-rohn-mahN-ta-leest]
farmer	l'agriculteur *(m)* [la-gree-kewl-tuhr]
fashion model	le mannequin [luh-man-kaN]
first/second level of studies	le premier/second cycle [luh-[pruh-myay]/[suh-gohN]-seekl]
fisherman	le pêcheur [luh-pay-shuhr]
flight attendant	le steward/l'hôtesse *(f)* de l'air [luh-stew-wart]/[lo-tehs-duh-lehr]
florist	le/la fleuriste [luh/la-fluuh-reest]
forester	le garde forestier [luh-gard-fo-rehs-tyay]
French studies	les études *(f)* de français [lay-zay-tewd-duh-frahN-say]
gardener	le jardinier [luh-zhar-dee-nyay]
geography	la géographie [la-zhay-o-gra-fee]
geology	la géologie [la-zhay-o-lo-zhee]
glazier	le vitrier [luh-vee-tree-yay]
hairdresser	le coiffeur/la coiffeuse [luh-kwa-fuhr]/[la-kwa-fuuhz]
high school	le lycée [luh-lee-say]
high school student	le lycéen/la lycéenne [luh-lee-say-aN]/[la-lee-say-ehn]
history	l'histoire *(f)* [lees-twar]
housewife	la ménagère [la-may-na-zhehr]
institute	l'institut *(m)* [laNs-tee-tew]
interpreter	l'interprète *(m/f)* [laN-tehr-preht]
jeweler	le bijoutier/la bijoutière [luh-bee-zhoo-tyay]/[la-bee-zhoo-tyehr]

journalist	le/la journaliste [luh/la-zhoor-na-leest]
judge	le juge [luh-zhewzh]
laboratory technician	le laborantin/la laborantine [luh-la-bo-rahN-taN]/[la-la-bo-rahN-teen]
law	le droit [luh-drwa]
lawyer	l'avocat/e [la-vo-ka]/[la-vo-kat]
lectures	les conférences *(f)* /cours *(m)* [lay-kohN-fay-rahNs]/[koor]
librarian	le/la bibliothécaire [luh/la-bee-blee-o-tay-kehr]
locksmith	le serrurier [luh-say-rew-ryay] [ma-syaN]/[la-far-ma-syehn]
male nurse	l'infirmier *(m)* [laN-feer-myay]
management expert	le/la diplômé(e) d'une école supérieure de commerce [luh/la-dee-plo-may-dewn-ay-kohl-sew-pay-ryuhr-duh-ko-mehrs]
manager	le directeur/la directrice [luh-dee-rehk-tuhr]/[la-dee-rehk-trees]
manual worker	l'artisan *(m)* [lar-tee-zahN]
masseur/masseuse	le masseur/la masseuse [luh-ma-suhr]/[la-ma-suuhz]
mathematics	les mathématiques *(f)* [lay-ma-tay-ma-teek]
mechanic	le mécanicien [luh-may-ka-nee-syaN]
mechanical engineering	les constructions *(f)* mécaniques [lay-kohNs-trewk-syohN-may-ka-neek]
medicine	la médecine [la-mehd-seen]
meteorologist	le/la météorologiste [luh/la-may-tay-o-ro-lo-zheest]
middle school	le collège d'enseignement général (C.E.G.) [luh-ko-lehzh-dahN-seh-nyuh-mahN-zhay-nay-ral]
middle school student	le collégien/la collégienne [luh-ko-lay-zhyaN]/[la-ko-lay-zhyehn]
midwife	la sage-femme [la-sazh-fam]
motor mechanic	le mécanicien auto [luh-may-ka-nee-syaN-o-to]
music	la musique [la-mew-zeek]
musician	le musicien/la musicienne [luh-mew-zee-syaN]/[la-mew-zee-syehn]
nonmedical practitioner	le guérisseur/la guérisseuse [luh-gay-ree-suhr]/[la-gay-ree-suuhz]
notary	le notaire [luh-no-tehr]

nurse	l'infirmière *(f)* [laN-feer-myehr]
nurse for the elderly	l'infirmier/l'infirmière pour personnes âgées [laN-feer-myay]/[laN-feer-myehr] poor pehr-sohn-a-zhay]
nursery school teacher	le maître/la maîtresse [luh-mehtr]/ [la-may-trehs]
office worker	l'employé(e) de bureau [lahN-plwa-yay-duh-bew-ro]
optician	l'opticien/l'opticienne [lohp-tee-syaN]/ [lohp-tee-syehn]
painter	le peintre [luh-paN-truh]
pharmacist	le pharmacien/la pharmacienne [luh-far-ma-see]
pharmacy	la pharmacie [la-far-ma-see]
philosophy	la philosophie [la-fee-lo-zo-fee]
photographer	le/la photographe [luh/la-fo-to-graf]
physicist	le physicien/la physicienne [luh-fee-zee-syaN]/[la-fee-zee-syehn]
physics	la physique [la-fee-zeek]
physiotherapist	le/la kinésithérapeute [luh/la-kee-nay-zee-tay-ra-puht]
pilot	le pilote [luh-pee-loht]

A painter in Montmarte, Paris

plumber	le plombier [luh-plohN-byay]
policeman/-woman	l'agent *(m)* de police [la-zhahN-duh-po-lees]
political science	les sciences *(f)* politiques [lay-syahNs-po-lee-teek]
post office worker	le postier/la postière [luh-pohs-tyay]/[la-pohs-tyehr]
postman/-women	le facteur [luh-fak-tuhr]
priest	le curé *(cath.)*, [luh-kew-ray] le pasteur [luh-pas-tuhr]
professor	le professeur de faculté [luh-pro-feh-suhr-duh-fa-kewl-tay]
psychologist	le/la psychologue [luh/la-psee-ko-lohg]
psychology	la psychologie [la-psee-ko-lo-zhie]
railwayman, railway employee	l'employé *(m)* de chemin de fer [lahN-plwa-yay-duh-shuh-maN-duh-fehr]
real estate agent	l'agent *(m)* immobilier [la-zhahN-ee-mo-bee-lyay]
representative	le représentant [luh-ruh-pray-zahN-tahN]
restaurant owner	le restaurateur/la restauratrice [luh-rehs-to-ra-tuhr]/[la-rehs-to-ra-trees]
retiree	le/la retraité(e) [luh/la-ruh-tray-tay]
roofer	le couvreur [luh-koo-vruhr]
sailor	le matelot [luh-mat-lo]
salesperson	le vendeur/la vendeuse [luh-vahN-duhr]/[la-vahN-duuhz]
school	l'école *(f)* [lay-kohl]
schoolboy/-girl	l'écolier/l'écolière [lay-ko-lyay]/[lay-ko-lyehr]
scientist	le scientifique [luh-syahN-tee-feek]
secretary	le/la secrétaire [luh/la-suh-kray-tehr]
shoemaker	le cordonnier [luh-kohr-do-nyay]
skilled worker	l'ouvrier/l'ouvrière qualifié/e [loo-vree-yay]/[loo-vree-yehr]-spay-sya-lee-zay]
Slavic studies	l'étude *(f)* des langues slaves [lay-tewd-day-lahNg-slav]
social worker	le travailleur/la travailleuse social(e) [luh-tra-va-yuhr]/[la-tra-va-yuuhz]-so-syal]
sociology	la sociologie [la-so-syo-lo-zhee]
student	l'étudiant(e) [lay-tew-dyahN]/[lay-tew-dyahNt]
studies	les études *(f)* [lay-zay-tewd]
subject	la matière/discipline [la-ma-tyehr]/[dee-see-pleen] syaN-o-to]

tailor	le tailleur/la couturière [luh-ta-yuhr]/[la-koo-tew-ryehr]
tax consultant	le conseiller/la conseillère fiscal(e) [luh-kohN-seh-yay]/[la-kohN-seh-yehr]-fees-kal]
taxi driver	le chauffeur de taxi [luh-sho-fuhr-duh-tak-see]
teacher	*(high-school)* le professeur, [luh-pro-feh-suhr] *(elementary)* l'instituteur/l'institutrice [laNs-tee-tew-tuhr]/[laNs-tee-tew-trees]
technical college	l'école *(f)* supérieure d'enseignement technique [lay-kohl-sew-pay-ryuhr-dahN-say-nyuh-mahN]
technician	le technicien/la technicienne [luh-tehk-nee-syaN]/[la-tehk-nee-syehn]
theater studies	l'art *(m)* dramatique [lar-dra-ma-teek]
theology	la théologie [la-tay-o-lo-zhee]
therapist	le/la thérapeute [luh/la-tay-ra-puuht]
toolmaker	l'outilleur *(m)* [loo-tee-yuhr]
trainee	l'apprenti(e) [la-prahN-tee]
translator	le traducteur/la traductrice [luh-tra-dewk-tuhr]/[la-tra-dewk-trees]
travel guide	le guide (de voyages) [luh-geed-duh-vwa-yazh]
university	l'université *(f)* [lew-nee-vehr-see-tay]
veterinarian	le vétérinaire [luh-vay-tay-ree-nehr]
vocational school	l'école *(f)* professionnelle [lay-kohl-pro-fay-syo-nehl]
waiter/waitress	le garçon/la serveuse [luh-gar-sohN]/[la-sehr-vuuhz]
watchmaker	l'horloger *(m)* [lohr-lo-zhay]
writer	l'écrivain *(m)* [lay-kree-vyaN]

3 On the Go
En Route

Giving Directions
Comment exprimer le lieu

left	à gauche [a-gosh]
right	à droite [a-drwat]
straight ahead	tout droit [too-drwa]
in front of	devant [duh-vahN]
in back of	derrière [day-ryehr]
next to	à côté de [a-ko-tay-duh]
across from	en face de [ahN-fas-duh]
here	ici [ee-see]
there	là, là-bas [la]/[la-ba]
near	près [pray]
far	loin [lwaN]
in the direction of, toward	à, vers, en direction de [a]/[vehr]/[ahN-dee-rehk-syohN-duh]
street	la rue [la-rew]
intersection	le carrefour [luh-kar-foor]
curve	le virage [luh-vee-razh]

Car/Motorcycle/Bicycle
Voiture/Moto/Vélo

Information — Renseignements

Excuse me, how do I get to. . . please?	Pour aller à . . . s'il vous plaît? [poor-a-lay-a . . . seel-voo-play]
Can you please show me the way on the map?	Vous pouvez me montrer l'itinéraire sur la carte? [voo-poo-vay-muh-mohN-tray-lee-tee-nay-rehr-sewr-la-kart]
How far is it?	C'est à combien de kilomètres d'ici? [say-a-kohN-byaN-duh-kee-lo-mehtr-dee-see]

Excuse me, is this the road to . . .?	Pardon, Mme/Mlle/M., je suis bien sur la route de . . .? [par-dohN]-[ma-dam]/[mad-mwa-zehl]/[muh-syuuh]-[zhuh- swee-byaN-sewr-la-root-duh]
How do I get to the highway to . . .?	Pour rejoindre l'autoroute de. . . , s.v.p.? [poor-ruh-zhwaNdr-lo-to-root-duh [seel-voo-play]
Straight on until you get to . . .	Vous allez tout droit jusqu'à . . . [voo-za-lay-too-drwa-zhews-ka]
Then turn left/right at the light.	Ensuite, vous tournez à gauche/à droite au feu. [ahN-sweet-voo-toor-nay-a-gosh/a-drwat-o-fuuh]
Then take the first street to the left/right.	Ensuite, vous prenez la première rue à gauche/à droite. [ahN-sweet-voo-pruh-nay-la-pruh-myehr-rew-a-gosh/a-drwat]
Follow the sights.	Vous suivez les panneaux. [voo-swee-vay-lay-pa-no]
Is there also a scenic road to . . .?	Est-ce qu'il y a également une route peu fréquentée en direction de . . .? [ehs-keel-ya-ay-gal-mahN-ewn-root-puuh-fray-kahN-tay-ahN-dee-rehk-syohN-duh]
You're not on the right road. Drive back to. . .	Vous n'êtes pas sur la bonne route.Il faut retourner à . . . [voo-neht-pa-sewr-la-bohn-root-eel-fo-ruh-toor-nay-a]

At the Service Station / A la station-service

Where is the nearest garage/gas station, please?	Pardon, Mme/Mlle/M., où est la station-service la plus proche, s.v.p.? [par-dohN-[ma-dam]/[mad-mwa-zehl]/[muh-syuuh]-oo-ay-la-sta-syohN-sehr-vees-la-plew-prohsh]
. . . liters of . . ., please.	. . . litres, s'il vous plaît. [leetr-seel-voo-play]
regular	De l'ordinaire [duh-lohr-dee-nehr]
super	Du super [dew-sew-pehr]
diesel	Du gas-oil [dew-ga-swal]

unleaded/leaded	Du sans-plomb/. . . octanes [dew-sahN- plohN]/[ohk-tan]

The ADAC puts out a yearly map showing service stations throughout France that sell unleaded gasoline.

200 francs of super, please.	Du super, s.v.p., pour 200 francs. [dew-sew-pehr-seel-voo-lay]
Fill it up, please.	Le plein, s.v.p. [luh-plaN-seel-voo-play]
Please check the oil/the tire pressure.	Vérifiez le niveau d'huile/la pression des pneus, s.v.p. [vay-ree-fyay-[luh-nee-vo-dweel]/[la-pray-syohN-day-pnuuh]-seel-voo-play]
Could you change the oil, please?	Vous pourriez me faire une vidange, s.v.p.? [voo-poo-ryay-muh-fehr-ewn-vee-dahNzh-seel-voo-play]
I'd like to have the car washed, please.	Vous pouvez me laver la voiture, s.v.p.? [voo-poo-vay-muh-la-vay-la-vwa-tewr-seel-voo-play]
I'd like a road map of this area, please.	Je voudrais une carte routière de la région. [zhuh-voo-dray-ewn-kart-roo-tyehr-duh-la-ray-zhyohN]
Where are the toilets, please?	Où sont les W.-C., s.v.p.? [oo-sohN-lay-vay-say-seel-voo-play]

Parking — Le stationnement

Excuse me please, is there a parking lot near here?	Pardon, Mme/Mlle/M., est-ce qu'il y a un parking près d'ici, s.v.p.? [par -dohN-[ma-dam]/madmwazehl]/[muh-syuuh]-ehs-keel-ya-aN-par-king-pray-dee-see-seel-voo-play]
Can I park my car here?	Je peux garer ma voiture ici? [zhuh-puuh-ga-ray-ma-vwa-tewr-ee-see]
Could you please give me change for . . .? It is for the parking meter.	Vous pourriez me faire de la monnaie . . .? C'est pour l'horodateur. [voo-poo-ryay-muh-fehr-duh-la-mo-nay-say-poor-lo-ro-da-tuhr]

Tourmalet Pass in the Pyrenees Mountains

Is there a parking attendant?	Est-ce que le parking est gardé? [ehs-kuh-luh-par-king-ay-gar-day]
I'm afraid it is full.	Non, malheureusement, c'est complet. [nohN,ma-luuh-ruuhz-mahN-say-kohN-play]
How long can I park here?	Je peux stationner combien de temps ici? [zhuh-puuh-sta-syo-nay-kohN-byaN-duh-tahN-ee-see]
How much is it . . .	Quel est le tarif pour . . . [kehl-ay-luh-ta-reef-poor]
by the hour?	une heure? [ewn-uhr]
per day?	une journée? [ewn-zhoor-nay]
per night?	une nuit? [ewn-nwee]
Is the parking lot open all night?	Est-ce que le parking est ouvert toute la nuit? [ehs-kuh-luh-par-king-ay-oo-vehr-toot-la-nwee]

Car Trouble — Une panne

My car's broken down./ I have a flat tire.	Je suis en panne./J'ai un pneu crevé. [zuh-swee-ahN-pan]/[zhay-aN-pnuuh-kruh-vay]

Could you please call for road assistance for me?	Vous pourriez téléphoner pour moi au service de dépannage, s.v.p.? [voo-poo-ryay-tay-lay-fo-nay-poor-mwa-o-sehr-vees-duh-day-pa-nazh-seel-voo-play]
My registration number is . . .	Mon numéro minéralogique, c'est . . . [mohN-new-may-ro-new-may-ra-lo-zheek-say]
Would you please send a mechanic/a towtruck?	Est-ce que vous pouvez m'envoyer un mécanicien/une dépanneuse, s.v.p.? [ehs-kuh-voo-poo-vay-mahN-vwa-yay-aN-may-ka-nee-syaN/ewn-day-pa-nuuhz]
Could you please give me some gas?	Vous pourriez me donner un peu d'essence, s.v.p.? [voo-poo-ryaymuh-do-nay-aN-puuh-deh-sahNs-seel-voo-play]
Could you please help me change my tire?	Vous pourriez m'aider à changer la roue, s.v.p.? [voo-poo-ryay-may-day-a-shahN-zhay-la-roo]
Could you please give me a ride/tow me to the nearest garage?	Est-ce que vous pouvez me remorquer/m'emmener jusqu'au prochain garage/jusqu'à la prochaine station-service? [ehs-kuh-voo-poo-vay-muh-ruh-mohr-kay/mahN-muh-nay-zhews-ko-pro-shaN-ga-razh/zhews-ka-la-pro-shehn-sta-syohN-sehr-vees]

At the Auto Repair Shop — Au garage

Excuse me, please, is there a garage near here?	Pardon, Mme/Mlle/M., est-ce qu'il y a un garage près d'ici, s.v.p.? [par-dohN-ma-dam/mad-mwa-zehl/muh-syuuh-ehs-keel-ya-aN-ga-razh-preh-dee-see-see l-voo-play]
My car won't start.	Ma voiture ne démarre pas. [ma-vwa-tewr-nuh-day-mar-pa]
I don't know what the matter is.	Je ne sais pas quel est le problème. [xhuh-nuh-say-pa-kehl-ay-luh-pro-blehm]
Can you come with me/give me a tow, please?	Vous pouvez venir avec moi/me remorquer, s.v.p.? [voo-poo-vay-[vuh-neer-a-vehk-mwa]/[muh-ruh-mohr-kay]

There's something wrong with the engine.	J'ai des ennuis de moteur. [zhay-day-zahN-nwee-duh-mo-tuhr]
The brakes don't work.	Mes freins ne répondent pas bien. [may-fraN-nuh-ray-pohNd-pa-byaN]
. . . is/are faulty.	. . . est/sont défectueux/ défectueuse(s). [ay/sohN-day-fehk-tew-uuh(z)]
I'm losing oil.	Il y a une fuite d'huile. [eel-ya-ewn-fweet-dweel]
Could you have a look?	Vous pouvez jeter un coup d'œil, s.v.p.? [voo-poo-vay-zhuh-tay-aN-nuhy-seel-voo-play]
Change the spark plugs, please.	Changez les bougies, s.v.p. [zhahN-zhay-lay-boo-zhee-seel-voo-play]
Have you got spares for this model?	Vous avez des pièces de rechange pour ce genre de voiture? [voo-za-vay-day-pyehs-duh-ruh-shahNzh-poor-suh-zhahNr-duh-vwa-tewr]
Just carry out the essential repairs, please.	Ne faites que les réparations absolument nécessaires. [nuh-feht-kuh-lay-ray-pa-ra-syohN-ab-so-lew-mahN-nay-say-sehr]
When will the car/the motorbike be ready?	Quand est-ce que ma voiture/ma moto sera prête? [kahN-tehs-kuh-ma-vwa-tewr-suh-ra-preht]
How much will it be?	Ça va me coûter combien? [sa-va-muh-koo-tay-kohN-byaN]

A Traffic Accident — L'accident

There's been an accident.	Il y a un accident. [eel-ya-aN-nak-see-dahN]
Please call. . .	Appelez vite . . . [ap-lay-veet]
an ambulance.	une ambulance. [ewn-ahN-bew-lahNs]
the police.	la police. [la-po-lees]
the firemen.	les pompiers. [lay-pohN-pyay]
Can you look after the injured?	Vous pouvez vous occuper des blessés? [voo-poo-vay-voo-zo-kew-pay-day-blay-say]

Do you have a first aid kit?	Vous avez une trousse de secours? [voo-za-vay-ewn-troos-duh-suh-koor]
It was my/your fault.	C'est moi qui suis/vous qui êtes en tort. [say-[mwa-kee-swee]/[voo-kee-eht]-ahN-tohr]
You . . .	Vous . . . [voo]
didn't observe the right of way.	n'avez pas respecté la priorité. [na-vay-pa-rehs-pehk-tay-la-pree-o-ree-tay]
changed lanes without signaling.	avez changé de file sans clignoter. [a-vay-shahN-zhay-duh-feel-sahN-klee-nyo-tay]
were driving too fast.	rouliez trop vite. [roo-lyay-tro-veet]
were too close behind.	rouliez trop près. [roo-lyay-tro-pray]
went through a red light.	avez brûlé un feu rouge. [a-vay-brew-lay-aN-fuuh-roozh]
I was going . . . kilometers an hour.	Je roulais à . . . km/h. [zhuh-roo-lay-a] . . . [kee-lo-mehtr-uhr]
I'll give you my address and insurance number.	Je vais vous donner mon adresse et le numéro de ma police d'assurance. [zhuh-vay-voo-do-nay-mohN-na-drehs-ay-luh-new-may-ro-duh-ma-po-leesda-sew-rahNs]
Please give me your name and address/the name and address of your insurance.	Vous pouvez me donner votre nom et votre adresse/le nom et l'adresse de votre compagnie d'assurances. [ehs-kuh-voo-poo-vay-myh-do-nay-[voh-truh-nohN-ay-voh-tra-drehs]/[luh-nohN-ay-la-drehs-duh-voh-truh-kohN-pa-nee-da-se w-rahNs]
Will you act as a witness for me?	Est-ce que vous pourriez me servir de témoin? [ehs-kuh-voo-poo-ryay-muh-sehr-veer-duh-tay-mwaN]
Thank you very much for your help.	Je vous remercie beaucoup de votre aide. [zhuh-voo-ruh-mehr-see-do koo-duh-voh-trehd]

Signs and Notices

Arrêt interdit [a-ray-aN-tehr-dee]	No stopping
Attention [a-tahN-syohN]	Caution
Chaussée déformée [sho-say-day-fohr-may]	Uneven pavement
Danger [dahN-zhay]	Danger
Dérapage [day-ra-pazh]	Slippery
Descente dangereuse [day-sahNt-dahN-zhuh-ruuhz]	Steep hill
Déviation [day-vya-syohN]	Detour
Ecole [ay-kohl]	Caution—children
Entrée interdite [ahN-tray-aN-tehr-deet]	Do not enter
Fin d'interdiction de stationner [faN-daN-tehr-deek-syohN-duh-sta-syo-nay]	End of no parking zone
Gravillons [gra-vee-yohN]	Gravel
Haute tension [ot-tahN-syohN]	High voltage
Hôpital [o-pee-tal]	Hospital
Vous n'avez pas la priorité. [voo-na-vay-pa-la-pree-o-ree-tay]	You do not have the right of way.
Poids lourds [pwa-loor]	Heavy-load trucks
Priorité à droite [pree-o-ree-tay-a-drwat]	Yield to the right
Prudence [prew-dahNs]	Caution
Ralentir [ra-lahN-teer]	Reduce speed, slow down
Rappel [ra-pehl]	Reminder
Secours routier [suh-koor-roo-tyay]	Road assistance

Traffic Signs

Parking allowed only with parking disc.

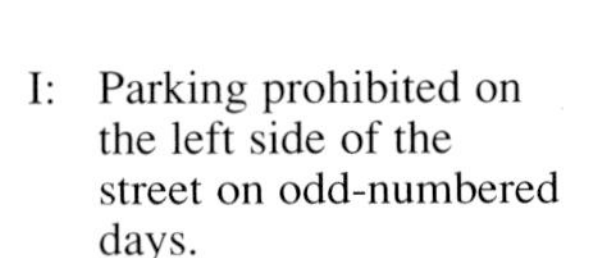

I: Parking prohibited on the left side of the street on odd-numbered days.

II: If 1–15 and 16–31, rather than I and II, appear on the sign, this means that parking is prohibited on the left side of the street from the 1st to the 15th of the month, and on the right side from the 16th to the 31st of the month.

Start of "Blue Zone." Parking allowed here only with a parking disc.

End of "Blue Zone."

Serrer à droite (à gauche) [say-ray-a-drwat/gosh]	Keep right (left)
Sortie d'autoroute [sohr-tee-do-to-root]	Highway exit
Sortie d'usine [sohr-tee-dew-zeen]	Factory exit
Sortie de véhicules [sohr-tee-duh-vay-ee-kewl]	Keep clear
Stationnement interdit [sta-syohn-mahN-aN-tehr-dee]	No parking
Chaussée défoncée [sho-say-day-fohN-say]	Uneven pavement
Virage dangereux [vee-razh-dahN-zhuh-ruuh]	Dangerous curve
Voie de dégagement [vwa-duh-day-gazh-mahN]	Service road
Zone à stationnement réglementé [zon-a-sta-syohn-mahN-ray-gluh-mahN-tay]	Short-time parking

Car/Motorcycle/Bicycle Rental — Location d'une voiture/d'une moto/d'un vélo

I'd like to rent a . . . for two days/two weeks.	Je voudrais louer . . . pour deux jours/une semaine. [zhu-voo-dray-loo-ay] [poor-[duuh-zhoor]/[ewn-suh-mehn]]
a jeep.	une voiture (tous terrains) [ewn-vwa-tewr-(too-tay-raN)]
a motorbike.	une moto [ewn-mo-to]
a scooter.	un scooter [aN-skoo-tuhr]
a moped.	une mobylette [ewn-mo-bee-leht]
a motorcycle.	un cyclomoteur [aN-see-klo-mo-tuhr]
a bicycle.	un vélo [aN-vay-lo]
How much does it cost per day/per week?	Quel est le tarif à la journée/à la semaine? [kehl-ay-luh-ta-reef-[a-la-zhoor-nay]/[a-la-suh-mehn]]
What is the charge per kilometer?	Quel est le prix au km? [kehl-ay-luh-pree-o-kee-lo-mehtr]

How much is the deposit?	Quel est le montant de la caution? [kehl-ay-luh-mohN-tahN-duh-la-ko-syohN]
I'll take the . . .	Je vais prendre la . . . /le . . . [zhuh-vay-prahN-druh-la/luh]
Would you like complementary insurance?	Vous désirez une assurance complémentaire? [voo-day-zee-ray-ewn-a-sew-rahNs-kohN-play-mahN-tehr]
Does the vehicle have comprehensive insurance?	Est-ce que le véhicule est assuré tous risques? [ehs-kuh-luh-vay-ee-kewl-ay-a-sew-ray-too-reesk]
May I see your driver's license?	Est-ce que je peux voir votre permis de conduire, s.v.p.? [ehs-kuh-zhuh-puuh-vwar-voh-truh-pehr-mee-duh-kohN-dweer-seel-voo-play]
Can I have the car right away?	Je peux prendre la voiture tout de suite? [zhuh-puuh-a-vwar-la-vwa-tewr-too-duh-sweet]
Is it possible to leave the car in . . . ?	Est-ce qu'il est possible de rendre le véhicule à . . .? [ehs-keel-ay-po-seebl-duh-rahN-druh-luh-vay-ee-kewl-a]

Word List: Car/Motorcycle/Bicycle

to accelerate	accélérer [ak-say-lay-ray]
accelerator	l'accélérateur *(m)* [lak-say-lay-ra-tuhr]
air filter	le filtre à air [luh-feeltr-a-ehr]
alarm system	le système d'alarme [luh-sees-tehm-da-larm]
alcohol level	le taux d'alcoolémie [luh-to-dal-ko-lay-mee]
all-risk insurance	l'assurance *(f)* tous risques [la-sew-rahNs-too-reesk]
antifreeze	l'antigel *(m)* [lahN-tee-zhehl]
automatic transmission	le changement de vitesse automatique [luh-shahNzh-mahN-duh-vee-tehs-o-to-ma-teek]
axle	l'axe *(m)* [laks]
ball bearing	le roulement à billes [luh-rool-mahN-a-beey]

bell	le timbre [luh-taN-bruh]
bicycle	le vélo [luh-vay-lo]
bike path	la piste cyclable [la-peest-see-klabl]
to blind, dazzle	éblouir [ay-bloo-eer]
blinker	le clignotant [luh-klee-nyo-tahN]
to brake	freiner [fray-nay]
brake	le frein [luh-fraN]
brake fluid	le liquide de frein [luh-lee-keed-duh-fraN]
brake lever	le levier de frein [luh-luh-vyay-duh-fraN]
brake lights	les stops *(m)* [lay-stohp]
brake pedal	la pédale de frein [la-pay-dal-duh-fraN]
breakdown	la panne [la-pan]
breakdown service	le service de dépannage [luh-sehr-vees-duh-day-pa-nazh]
bright lights, high beam	les feux *(m)* de route [lay-fuuh-duh-root]
broken	cassé [ka-say]
bumper	le pare-chocs [luh-par-shohk]
cable	le câble [luh-kabl]
car body	la carrosserie [la-ka-rohs-ree]
car wash	le lavage [luh-la-vazh]
carburetor	le carburateur [luh-kar-bew-ra-tuhr]
chain	la chaîne [la-shehn]
clutch	l'embrayage *(m)* [lahN-bray-yazh]
	le levier d'embrayage [luh-luh-vyay-dahN-bray-yazh]
construction site	le chantier [luh-shahN-tyay]
cooling water	l'eau *(f)* de refroidissement [lo-duh-ruh-frwa-dees-mahN]
covered parking	le parking couvert [luh-par-keeng-koo-vehr]
cylinder	le cylindre [luh-see-laNdr]
cylinder head	la culasse [la-kew-las]
defect, flaw	le défaut [luh-day-fo], le dommage [luh-do-mazh]
defective ignition	l'allumage *(m)* défectueux [la-lew-mazh-day-fehk-twuuh]
detour	la déviation [la-day-vya-syohN]
to dim one's headlights	mettre les codes [meh-truh-lay-kohd]
distributor	le delco [luh-dehl-ko]
driver's license	le permis de conduire [luh-pehr-mee-duh-kohN-dweer]
dynamo	la dynamo [la-dee-na-mo]
emergency telephone	le téléphone de secours [luh-tay-lay-fohn-duh-suh-koor]

engine	le moteur [luh-mo-tuhr]
exhaust	le tuyau d'échappement [luh-twee-yo-day-shap-mahN]
fan	le ventilateur [luh-vahN-tee-la-tuhr]
fan belt	la courroie [la-koo-rwa]
fine	l'amende *(f)* [la-mahNd]
first gear	la première [la-pruh-myehr]
flashing one's brights	l'appel *(m)* de phares [la-pehl-duh-far]
flat tire	le pneu à plat [luh-pnuuh-a pla]
four-lane road	à quatre voies [a-ka-truh-vwa]
four-wheel drive	les quatre roues motrices [lay-ka-truh-roo-mo-trees]
front axle	l'axe *(m)* avant [laks-a-ryehr]
front light	les phares *(m)* avant [lay-far-a-vahN]
front wheel	la roue avant [la-roo-a-vahN]
front-wheel drive	la traction avant [la-trak-syohN-a-vahN]
fuel injector	la pompe à injection [la-pohNp-a-aN-zhehk-syohN]
fuse	le fusible [luh-few-zeebl]
garage	l'atelier *(m)* [la-tuh-lyay]
gas	l'essence *(m)* [lay-sahNs]
gas canister	le jerrycan [luh-zhay-ree-kan]
gas pump	la pompe à essence [la-pohNp-a-ay-sahNs]
gas station	la station-service [la-sta-syohN-sehr-vees]
gas tank	le réservoir [luh-ray-zehr-vwar]
gear	la vitesse [la-vee-tehs]
gearbox	la boîte de vitesses [la-bwat-duh-vee-tehs]
gears	le changement de vitesses [luh shahNzh-mahN-duh-vee-tehs]
gearshift lever	le levier du changement de vitesses [luh-luh-vyay-duh-shahNzh-mahN-duh-vee-tehs]
to grease	graisser [gray-say]
green card	la carte verte [la-kar-tuh-vehrt]
hand brake	le frein à main [luh-fraN-a-maN]
handlebars	le guidon [luh-gee-dohN]
hazard warning light	le signal de détresse [luh-si-nyal-duh-day-trehs]
headlights	les phares [lay-far]
heating	le chauffage [luh-sho-fazh]
helmet	le casque de moto [luh-kask-duh-mo-to]
highway	l'autoroute *(f)* [lo-to-root]

to hitchhike	faire de l'auto-stop [fehr-duh-lo-to-stohp]
hitchhiker	l'auto-stoppeur/l'auto-stoppeuse [lo-to-sto-puhr/puuhz]
hood	le capot [luh-ka-po]
horn	le klaxon [luh-klak-sohn]
HP (horsepower)	CV, chevaux (vapeurs) [shuh-vo] (va-puhr)
hub	le moyeu [luh-mwa-yuuh]
ignition	l'allumage *(m)* [la-lew-mazh]
ignition key	la clé de contact [la-klay-duh-kohN-takt]
ignition short	la bougie [la-boo-zhee]
ignition switch	le contact [luh-kohN-takt]
inner tube *(tire)*	la chambre à air [la-shahN-bra-ehr]
jack	le cric [luh-kreek]
jet	le gicleur [luh-zhee-kluhr]
to knock *(engine)*	cogner [ko-nyay]
lane	la voie/file [la-vwa/feel]
lever	le levier [lluh-luh-vyay]
lever *(small)*	la manette [la-ma-neht]
license	les papiers *(m)*
license plate	la plaque d'immatriculation [la-plak-dee-ma-tree-kew-la-syohN]
luggage racks	*(bicycle)* le porte-bagages [luh-pohrt-ba-gazh] *(car)* la galerie de toît [la-gal-ree-duh-twa]
main road	la route nationale [la-root-na-syo-nal]
moped	la mobylette [la-mo-bee-leht]
motorcycle	la moto [la-mo-to]
motorized bicycle	le cyclomoteur [luh-see-klo-mo-tuhr]
mountain bike	le V.T.T. (vélo tous terrains) [luh-vay-tay-tay] (vay-lo-too-tay-raN)
mudguard	le garde-boue [luh-gar-duh-boo]
neutral (gear)	le point mort [luh-pwaN-mohr]
nut	l'écrou *(m)* [lay-kroo]
octane number	le chiffre d'octane [luh-sheefr-dohk-tan]
odometer	le compteur [luh-kohN-tuhr]
oil	l'huile *(f)* [lweel]
oil change	la vidange [la-vee-dahNzh]
oil gauge	la jauge de niveau d'huile [la-zhozh-duh-nee-vo-dweel]
parking disc	le disque de stationnement [luh-deesk-duh-sta-syohn-mahN]
parking lights	les feux *(m)* de position [lay-fuuh-duh-po-zee-syohN]

parking meter	l'horodateur *(m)* [lo-ro-da-tuhr]
parking space	la place de parking [la-plas-duh-par-keeng]
pedal	la pédale [la-pay-dal]
pedals	les pédales [lay-pay-dal]
piston	le piston [luh-pees-tohN]
pump	la pompe à air [la-pohNp-a-ehr]
racing bike	le vélo de course [luh-vay-lo-duh-koors]
radar speed check	le contrôle radar [luh-kohN-trol-ra-dar]
radiator	le radiateur [luh-ra-dya-tuhr]
rear axle	le pont arrière [luh-pohN-a-ryehr]
rear wheel	la roue arrière [la-roo-a-ryehr]
rear-wheel drive	la traction arrière [la-trak-syohN-a-ryehr]
rearview mirror	le rétroviseur [luh-ray-tro-vee-zuhr]
reflector	les réflecteurs [lay-ray-flehk-tuhr]
to release the clutch	débrayer [day-bray-yay]
rest area	l'aire *(f)* de repos [lehr-duh-ruh-po]
reverse	la marche arrière [la-marsh-a-ryehr]
reverse gear	la marche arrière [la-marsh-a-ryehr]
rim	la jante [la-zhahNt]
road map	la carte routière [la-kart-roo-tyehr]
road sign	le poteau indicateur [luh-po-to-aN-dee-ka-tuhr]
saddle	la selle [la-sehl]
saddlebag	la sacoche [la-sa-kohsh]
safety belt	la ceinture de sécurité [la-saN-tewr-duh-say-kew-ree-tay]
sandpaper	le papier de verre [luh-pa-pyay-duh-vehr]
scooter	le scooter [luh-skoo-tuhr]
screw	la vis [la-vees]
screwdriver	le tournevis [luh-toor-nuh-vees]
seal	le joint [luh-zhwaN]
service road	la voie de dégagement [la-vwa-duh-day-gazh-mahN]
shock absorber	l'amortisseur *(m)* [la-mohr-tee-suhr]
short-circuit	le court-circuit [luh-koor-seer-kwee]
snow tire	le pneu neige [luh-pnuuh-nehzh]
spare parts	les pièces *(f)* de rechange [lay-pyehs-duh-ruh-shahNzh]
spare wheel	la roue de secours [la-roo-duh-suh-koor]
spoke	le rayon [luh-ray-yohN]
stand	la quille [la-keey]
starter	le démarreur/le starter [luh-day-ma-ruhr]/[luh-star-tehr]

sunroof	le toit ouvrant [luh-twa-oo-vrahN]
suspension	la suspension [la-sews-pahN-syohN]
taillight	les feux *(m)* arrière [lay-fuuh-a-ryehr]
third party insurance	l'assurance *(f)* au tiers [la-sew-rahNs-o-tyehr]
three-speed/ten-speed bike	le vélo à trois/dix vitesses [luh-vay-lo-a-trwa/dee-vee-tehs]
tire	le pneu [luh-pnuuh]
tire repair kit	le nécessaire de réparation des pneus [luh-nay-say-sehr-duh-ray-pa-ra-syohN-day-pnuuh]
toll	le péage [luh-pay-azh]
toll road	le péage [luh-pay-azh]
tool	l'outil *(m)* [loo-tee]
to tow	remorquer [ruh-mohr-kay]
tow rope	le câble de remorquage [luh-kabl-duh-ruh-mohr-kazh]
tow truck	la dépanneuse [la-day-pa-nuuhz]
traffic jam	l'embouteillage *(m)* [lahN-boo-tay-yazh]
traffic lights	le feu *(de circulation)* [luh-fuuh]
trailer	la remorque [la-ruh-mohrk]
truck	le camion [luh-ka-myohN]
trunk	le coffre [luh-kohfr]
to turn (left/right)	tourner [toor-nay]
valve	la soupape [la-soo-pap]
warning triangle	le triangle de présignalisation [luh-tree-yahNgl-duh-pray-see-nya-lee-za-syohN]
weatherproof outfit	la combinaison imperméable [la-kohN-bee-nay-zohN-aN-pehr-may-abl]
wheel	la roue/le volant [la-roo]/[luh-vo-lahN]
windshield	le pare-brise [luh-par-breez]
windshield wiper	l'essuie-glace *(m)* [lay-swee-glas]
wing	l'aile *(f)* [lehl]
wrench	la clé anglaise [la-klay-ahN-glehz]

Airplane
Avion

At the Travel Agency/ At the Airport	A l'agence de voyages/A l'aéroport
Where is the. . . counter?	Où se trouve le guichet de la compagnie . . .? [oo-suh-troov-luh-gee-shay-duh-la-kohN-pa-nee]
When is the next flight to. . . ?	Quand part le prochain avion pour . . .? [kahN-par-luh-pro-sheh-na-vyohN-poor]
I would like to make a one-way/round-trip reservation to . . .	Je voudrais un billet d'avion pour . . ., aller simple/aller-retour. [zhuh-voo-dray-aN-bee-yay-da-vyohN-poor] . . . [a-lay-saNpl]/[a-lay-ruh-toor]
Are there still seats available?	Est-ce qu'il y a encore des places de libres? [ehs-keel-ya-ahN-kohr-day-plas-duh-leebr]
Are there also charter flights?	Est-ce qu'il y a également des vols par charters? [ehs-keel-ya-ay-gal-mahN-day-vohl-par-tshar-tehr]
How much is an economy (coach)/a first class ticket?	Combien coûte le vol en classe touristes/première classe? [kohN-byaN-koot-luh-vohl-ahN-[klas-too-reest]/[pruh-myehr-klas]]
How much luggage can I take with me?	Quelle est la franchise pour les bagages? [kehl-ay-la-frahN-sheez-poor-lay-ba-gazh]
How much does excess luggage cost per kilo?	Quel est le tarif du kilo d'excédents? [kehl-ay-luh-ta-reef-dew-kee-lo-dehk-say-dahN]
I would like to cancel this flight/to change the reservation.	Je voudrais annuler/modifier ce vol. [zhuh-voo-dray-[a-new-lay]/[mo-dee-fyay] -suh-vohl]

When do I have to be at the airport?	A quelle heure est-ce que je dois être à l'aéroport? [a-kehl-uhr-ehs-kuh-zhuh-dwa-ehtr-a-la-ay-ro-pohr]
Where is the information desk?	Où est le guichet des renseignements/la salle d'attente, s.v.p.? [oo-ay-[luh-gi-shay-day-rahN-say-nyuh-mahN]/[[la-sal-da-tahNt]-seel-voo-play]
Can I take this carry-on luggage?	Est-ce que je peux prendre cela en bagage à main? [ehs-kuh-zhuh-puuh-prahN-druh-suh-la-ahN-ba-gazh-a-maN]
Is the plane for . . . late?	Est-ce que l'avion pour . . . a du retard? [ehs-kuh-la-vyohN-poor-. . . -a-dew-ruh-tar]
How late is it going to be?	Il a combien de retard? [eel-a-kohN-byaN-duh-ruh-tar]
Has the plane from . . . already landed?	Est-ce que l'avion de . . . a atterri? [ehs-kuh-la-vyohN-duh-. . . -a-a-tay-ree]
Last call. Passengers . . . for . . . on flight number . . ., please proceed to gate . . .	Dernier rappel. Les passagers du vol numéro . . . à destination de . . . sont priés de se rendre à la porte d'embarquement numéro . . . [dehr-nyay-a-pehl][lay-pa-sa-zhay-dew-vohl-new-may-ro- . . . -a-dehs-tee-na-syohN-duh . . . -sohN- pree-yay-duh-suh- rahNdr-a-la-pohrt-dahN- bar-kuh-mahN-new-may-ro . . .]

On Board — A bord de l'appareil

Please extinguish your cigarettes. Fasten your seat belts.	Veuillez attacher vos ceintures et éteindre vos cigarettes. [vuuh-yay-a-ta-shay-vo-saN-tewr-ay-ay-taN-druh-vo-see-ga-reht]
What river/lake is this?	Quel est le nom de cette rivière/de ce lac? [kehl-ay-luh-nohN-duh-[seht-ree-vyehr]/[suh-lak]]
What is the name of this mountain?	Comment s'appelle cette montagne? [ko-mahN-sa-pehl-seht-mohN-tany]

Where are we now?	Où est-ce qu'on est? [oo-ehs-kohN-nay]
When do we land in . . .?	A quelle heure est-ce que nous allons atterrir à . . .? [a-kehl-uhr-ehs-kuh-noo-za-lohN-a-tay-reer]
We will be landing in about . . . minutes.	Nous allons atterrir dans . . . minutes environ. [noo-za-lohN-a-tay-reer-dahN-. . . -mee-newt]
What is the weather like in . . .?	Quel temps fait-il à . . .? [kehl-tahN-feh-teel-a]

Arrival — L'arrivée

See also Chapter 9–Lost and Found

I can't find my luggage/suitcase.	Je ne trouve pas mes bagages/ma valise. [zhuh-nuh-troov-pa-[may-ba-gazh]/[ma-va-leez]
My luggage is missing.	Mes bagages ont été égarés. [may-ba-gazh-ohN-ay-tay-ay-ga-ray]
My suitcase has been damaged.	Ma valise est abîmée. [ma-va-leez-ay-a-bee-may]
Where can I report it?	A qui est-ce que je dois m'adresser? [a-kee-ehs-kuh-zhuh-dwa-ma-dray-say]
Where does the air-terminal bus leave from?	Où est le départ des bus pour l'aérogare? [oo-ay-luh-day-par-day-bews-poor-la-ay-ro-gar]

Word List: Airplane

See also Word List: Train, Ship

air terminal	l'aérogare *(m)* [la-ay-ro-gar]
airline	la compagnie aérienne [la-kohN-pa-nee-a-ay-ryehn]
airline security tax	la taxe de sécurité aérienne [la-taks-duh-say-kew-ree-tay-a-ay-ryehn]
airport	l'aéroport *(m)* [la-ay-ro-pohr]
airport shuttle/bus	le bus desservant l'aéroport [luh-bews-day-sehr-vahN-la-ay-ro-pohr]
airport tax	les droits *(m)* d'aéroport [lay-drwa-da-ay-ro-pohr]

aisle	**le couloir** [luh-koo-lwar]
approach	**l'arrivée** *(f)* **l'atterissage** *(m)* [la-ree-vay]/ [la-tay-ree-sazh]
arrival	**l'arrivée** *(f)* [la-ree-vay]
to attach the seat belt	**attacher sa ceinture** [a-ta-shay-sa-saN-tewr]
boarding area	**la porte** *(f)* **d'embarquement** [la-pohrt-dahN-bar-kuh-mahN]
boarding pass	**la carte d'embarquement** [la-kart-dahN-bar-kuh-mahN]
to book	**réserver** [ray-zehr-vay]
business class	**la classe affaires** [la-klas-a-fehr]
captain	**le commandant** [luh-ko-mahN-dahN]
to cancel	**annuler** [a-new-lay]
carry-on luggage	**les bagages** *(m)* **à main** [lay-ba-gazh-a-maN]
to change	**modifier** [mo-dif-yay]
charter flight	**le charter** [luh-tshar-tehr]
to check in	**faire les formalités** *(f)* **d'embarquement** [fehr-lay-fohr-ma-lee-tay-dahN-bar-kuh-mahN]
to check out	**faire les formalités** *(f)* **de débarquement** [fehr-lay-fohr-ma-lee-tay-duh-day-bar-kuh-mahN]
connection	**la correspondance** [la-ko-rehs-pohN-dahNs]
counter	**le guichet** [luh-gee-shay]
crew	**l'équipage** *(m)* [lay-kee-pazh]
delay	**le retard** [luh-ruh-tar]
destination	**la destination** [la-dehs-tee-na-syohN]
direct flight	**le vol direct** [luh-vohl-dee-rehkt]
domestic flight	**le vol intérieur** [luh-vohl-aN-tay-ryuhr]
duty-free shop	**le duty-free** [luh-dew-tee-free]; **la boutique hors-taxes** [la-boo-teek-ohr-taks]
economy class	**la classe économique** [la-klas-ay-ko-no-meek]
emergency chute	**le toboggan d'évacuation** [luh-to-bo-gahN-day-va-kwa-syohN]
emergency exit	**la sortie de secours** [la-sohr-tee-duh-suh-oor]
emergency landing	**l'atterrissage** *(m)* **forcé** [la-tay-ree-sazh-fohr-say]
flight	**le vol** [luh-vohl]
flight timetable	**l'horaire** *(m)* **des vols** [lo-rehr-day-vohl]

helicopter	l'hélicoptère *(m)* [lay-lee-kohp-tehr]
identification tag *(on suitcase)*	l'étiquette *(f)* [lay-tee-keht]
international flight	le vol international [luh-vohl-aN-tehr-na-syo-nal]
jet	l'avion *(m)* à réaction [la-vyohN-a-ray-ak-syohN]
to land	atterrir [a-tay-reer]
landing	l'atterrissage *(m)* [la-tay-ree-sazh]
lifejacket	le gilet de sauvetage [luh-zhee-lay-duh-sov-tazh]
luggage	les bagages *(m)* [lay-ba-gazh]
luggage cart	le chariot à bagages [luh-sha-ryo-a-ba-gazh]
luggage check-in	l'enregistrement *(m)* des bagages [lahN-ruh-zhees-truh-mahN-day-ba-gazh]
luggage claim	la récupération des bagages [la-ray-kew-pay-ra-syohN-day-ba-gazh]
nonsmoking	non-fumeurs [nohN-few-muhr]
on board	à bord *(de l'appareil)* [a-bohr] (duh-la-pa-rehy]
passenger	le passager/la passagère [luh-pa-sa-zhay]/[la-pa-sa-zhehr]
pilot	le pilote [luh-pee-loht]
rear	l'arrière *(m)* [la-ryehr]
regular flight	l'avion *(m)* de ligne [la-vyohN-duh-leeny]
reservation	la réservation [la-ray-zehr-va-syohN]
route	la route aérienne [la-root-a-ay-ryehn]
runway	la piste [la-peest]
scheduled departure	le décollage prévu [luh-day-ko-lazh-pray-vew]
seat belt	la ceinture [la-saN-tewr]
security check	le contrôle de sécurité [luh-kohN-trol-duh-say-kew-ree-tay]
smoking	fumeurs [few-muhr]
steward/stewardess	le steward/l'hôtesse *(f)* de l'air [luh-stew-wart]/[lo-tehs-duh-lehr]
stopover/layover	l'escale *(f)* [lehs-kal]
take-off	le décollage [luh-day-ko-lazh]
ticket	le billet d'avion [luh-bee-yay-da-vyohN]
time of arrival	l'heure *(f)* d'arrivée [luhr-da-ree-vay]
window seat	le coin-hublot [luh-kwaN-ew-blo]

Train

Chemin de fer

At the Travel Agency/ At the Railroad Station	A l'agence de voyages/A la gare
A second/first class one-way ticket to . . ., please.	Un aller deuxième/première classe pour . . . , s.v.p. [aN-na-lay-duuh-zyehm/pruh-myehr-klas-poor-. . . -seel-voo-play]
Two round-trip tickets to . . . please.	Deux aller-retour pour . . . , s'il vous plaît. [duuh-za-lay-ruh-toor-poor-. . . -seel-voo-play]
Is there a discount for children/students/family?	Est-ce qu'il y a des réductions pour les enfants/les familles nombreuses/les étudiants? [ehs-keel-ya-day-ray-dewk-syohN-poor-lay-[zahN-fahN]/[fa-meey-nohN-bruuhz]/[zay-tew-dyahN]
I would like to reserve a seat on the . . . o'clock train to . . .	Je voudrais réserver une place dans le train de . . . heures pour . . . [zhuh-voo-dray-ray-zehr-vay-ewn-plas-daN-luh-traN-duh-. . . -uhr-poor]
A window seat?	Un coin-fenêtre? [aN-kwaN-fuh-nehtr]
I'd like to book a couchette/a sleeper on the eight o'clock train to . . .	Je voudrais réserver une couchette en wagon-lit dans le train de 20 heures pour. . . [zhuh-voo-dray-ray-zehr-vay-ewn-koo-sheht-ahN-va-gohN-lee-dahN-luh-traN-duh-vaN-tuhr-poor]
Is there a motorail service to . . .?	Est-ce qu'il y a un train autos-couchettes/autos-jour pour . . .? [ehs-keel-ya-aN-traN-o-to-koo-sheht/o-to-zhoor-poor]
How much is it for a car and four people?	Pour une voiture et quatre personnes, ça fait combien? [poor-ka-truh-pehr-sohn-sa-feh-kohN-byaN]
I'd like to check this case.	Je voudrais faire enregistrer ma valise en bagage accompagné. [zhuh-voo-dray-fehr-ahN-ruh-zhees-tray-ma-va-leez-ahN-ba-gazh-a-kohN-pa-nyay]
Where can I register my bike?	Pour les vélos, c'est quel guichet? [poor-lay-vay-lo-say-kehl-gi-shay]

Do you want to insure the luggage?	Vous voulez une assurance-bagages? [voo-voo-lay-ewn-a-sew-rahNs-ba-gazh]
Will the luggage be on the . . . o'clock train?	Est-ce que mes bagages vont partir parle train de. . . heures? [ehs-kuh-may- ba-gazh-vohN-par-teer-par-luh-traN-duh-. . . -uhr]
When will it arrive in . . .?	Quand est-ce qu'ils vont arriver à . . .? [kahN-tehs-keel-vohN-ta-ree-vay-a]
Is the train from . . . running late?	Est-ce que le train de . . . a du retard? [ehs-kuh-luh-traN-duh-. . . -a-dew-ruh-tar]
Is there a connection to . . . at . . .?	Est-ce que j'ai une correspondance pour. . . , à . . .? [ehs-kuh-zhay-ewn-ko-rehs- pohN-dahNs-poor-. . . -a]
Is there a ferry to . . .?	Est-ce que je peux prendre le ferry-boat à . . .? [ehs-kuh-zhuh-puuh-prahN-druh-luh-fay-ree-bot-a]
(Where) Do I have to change?	(Où) Est-ce que je dois changer? [oo-ehs-kuh-zhuh-dwa-shahN-zhay]
Which platform does the . . . train leave from?	Le train pour . . . part à quelle voie, s'il vous plaît? [luh-traN-poor-. . . -par-a-kehl-vwa-seel-voo-play]
The train from . . . going on to . . . is now arriving at platform 1.	Le train numéro. . . , en provenance de . . . et à destination de . . . est annoncé à la voie numéro 1. [luh-traN-new-may-ro-. . . -ahN-pro-vuh-nahNs-duh-. . . -ay-a-dehs-ti-na-syohN-duh-. . . -ay-a-nohN-say-a-la-vwa-new-may-ro-aN]
The train from . . . is running 10 minutes late.	Le train numéro . . . en provenance de . . . est annoncé avec dix minutes de retard. [luh-traN-new-may-ro-. . . -ahN-pro-vuh-nahNs-duh-. . . -ay-ta-nohN-say-a-vehk-dee-mee-newt-duh-ruh-tar]
Attention! The train in the direction of . . . is leaving. All aboard, please. Doors close automatically.	Le train à destination de . . . va partir. Attention au départ et à la fermeture automatique des portes! [luh-traN-a-dehs-tee-na-syohN-duh-. . . va-par-teer-a-tahN-syohN-o-day-par-ay-a-la-fehr-muh-tewr-o-to-ma-teek-day-pohrt]

Before boarding (for outgoing as well as for the return trip), you must validate your ticket at the orange colored validator outside the platform.

On the Train	Dans le train
Excuse me, is this seat free?	Pardon, Mme/Mlle/M., est-ce que cette place est libre, s.v.p.? [par-dohN-[ma-dam]/[mad-mwa-zehl]/[muh-syuuh]-ehs-kuh-seht-plas-eh-leebr-seel-voo-play]
Can you help me please?	Vous pouvez m'aider, s.v.p.? [voo-poo-vay-may-day-seel-voo-play]
May I open/shut the window?	Est-ce que je peux baisser/remonter la vitre, s.v.p.? [ehs-kuh-zhuh-puuh-mohN- tay-la-veetr]
Excuse me, this is a non-smoking compartment.	Je suis désolé/e, Mme/Mlle/M., mais nous sommes ici dans un comparti-ment non-fumeurs. [zhuh-swee-day-zo-lay-[ma-dam][mad-mwa-zehl]/[muh-syuuh] -may-noo-sohm-ee-see-dahN-zaN-kohN-par-tee-mahN-nohN-few-muhr]
Excuse me, that is my seat. I have got a reservation.	Je suis désolé/e, Mme/Mlle/M., mais cette place est réservée. Voilà mon ticket de réservation. [zhuh-swee-day-zo-lay-[ma-dam]/[mad-mwa-zehl]/[muh-syuuh]-may-seht-plas-ay-reh-zehr-vay-vw a-la-mohN-tee-kay]
Tickets, please.	Les billets, s'il vous plaît. [lay-bee-yay-seel-voo-play]
Does this train stop in . . .?	Est-ce que le train s'arrête à . . .? [ehs-kuh-suh-traN-sa-reht-a]
Where are we now?	Où est-ce qu'on est? [oo-ehs-kohN-neh]
How long are we stopping here?	Le train s'arrête combien de temps, s.v.p.? [luh-traN-sa-reht-kohN-byaN-duh-tahN-seel-voo-play]
Will we arrive on time?	Est-ce que nous allons arriver à l'heure? [ehs-kuh-noo-za-lohN-a-ree-vay-a-luhr]

Signs and Information

Accès aux quais [a-ksay-o-kay]	To the trains
Arrivée [a-ree-vay]	Arrival
Buffet [bew-fay]	Cafeteria
Chef de gare [shehf-duh-gar]	Stationmaster
Eau non potable [o-nohN-po-tabl]	Nonpotable water
Fumeurs [few-muhr]	Smoking
Horaire des trains [o-rehr-day-traN]	Train schedule
Lavabo [la-va-bo]	Toilet, restroom
Libre [leebr]	Vacant
Messieurs [meh-syuuh]	Gentlemen
Non-fumeurs [nohN-few-muhr]	Nonsmoking
Occupé [o-kew-pay]	Occupied
Passage souterrain [pa-sazh-soo-tay-raN]	Underground passage
Passerelle [pas-rehl]	Overpass
Quai/Voie [kay-vwa]	Platform
Renseignements [rahN-seh-nyuh-mahN]	Information
Salle d'attente [sal-da-tahNt]	Waiting room
Signal d'alarme [see-nyal-da-larm]	Emergency brake
Sortie [sohr-tee]	Exit
Toilettes [twa-leht]	Toilet, restroom
Voiture-couchettes [vwa-tewr-koo-sheht]	Sleeper car
W.-C. [vay-say]	Toilet, restroom
Wagon-lit [va-gohN-lee]	Sleeper car
Wagon-restaurant [va-gohN-rehs-to-rahN]	Restaurant car

Word List: Train

See also Word List: Plane, Ship

to arrive	arriver [a-ree-vay]
baggage check	la consigne [la-kohN-seeny]
baggage office	le guichet des bagages [luh-gee-shay-day-ba-gazh]
baggage ticket	le bulletin de consigne [luh-bewl-taN-duh-kohN-seeny]
car	le compartiment [luh-kohN-par-tee-mahN]
car number	le numéro de la voiture [luh-new-may-ro-duh-vwa-tewr]
car train (night/day)	le train auto-couchettes/autos-jour [luh-traN-o-to-koo-sheht]/[o-to-zhoor]
corridor	le couloir [luh-koo-lwar]
departure	le départ [luh-day-par]
direct train	le train direct [luh-traN-dee-rehkt]
EC (Eurocity)	l'Euro-Cités *(m)* [luuh-ro-see-tay]
emergency brake	le signal d'alarme [luh-see-nyal-da-larm]
engine	la locomotive [la-lo-ko-mo-teev]
fast train	le rapide [luh-ra-peed]
ferryboat	le ferry-boat [luh-fay-ree-bot]
to get off	descendre [day-sahNdr]
to get on	monter (dans le train) [mohN-tay-dahN-luh-traN]
group ticket	le billet de groupe [luh-bee-yay-duh-groop]
half-fare	le billet demi-tarif [luh-bee-yay-duh-mee-ta-reef]
IC (Intercity)	l'Inter-Cités *(m) (Switzerland)* [laN-tehr-see-tay]
ICE (Intercity Express)	l'Inter-Cités *(m)* express *(Switzerland)* [laN-tehr-see-tay-ehk-sprehs]
Interrail	Interrail [aN-tehr-ray]
locker	l'armoire-consigne *(f)* automatique [lar-mwar-kohN-seeny-o-to-ma-teek]
luggage	les bagages *(m)* [lay-ba-gazh]
luggage cart	le chariot à bagages [luh-sha-ryo-a-ba-gazh]
main station	la gare principale [la-gar-praN-see-pal]
nonsmoking compartment	le compartiment non-fumeurs [kohN-par-tee-mahN-nohN-few-muhr]
open car	le wagon sans compartiments [luh-va-gohN-sahN-kohN-par-tee-mahN]
platform	la voie [la-vwa]

railway station	la gare [la-gar]
reduction	la réduction [la-ray-dewk-syohN]
reservation	la réservation [ray-zehr-va-syohN]
restaurant car	le wagon-restaurant [luh-va-gohN-rehs-to-rahN]
round-trip ticket	le billet aller-retour [luh-bee-yay-a-lay-ruh-toor]
seat reservation	la réservation [la-ray-zehr-va-syohN]
sleeper car	la voiture-couchettes [la-vwa-tewr-koo-sheht]
sleeper surcharge	le supplément wagon-lit [luh-sew-play-mahN-wa-gohN-lee]
smoking compartment	le compartiment fumeurs [luh-kohN-par-tee-mahN-few-muhr]
station restaurant	le buffet de la gare [luh-bew-fay-duh-la-gar]
stop	l'arrêt *(m)* (en gare) [la-ray-ahN-gar]
subject to a supplement	avec supplément [a-vehk-sew-play-mahN]
supplement	le supplément [luh-sew-play-mahN]
T.G.V. (high speed train)	le T.G.V. (le train à grande vitesse) [luh-tay-zhay-vay]
taken	occupé [o-kew-pay]
through coach	la voiture directe [la-vwa-tewr-dee-rehkt]
ticket	le billet [luh-bee-yay]
ticket check	le contrôle des billets [luh-kohN-trol-day-bee-yay]
ticket office	le guichet des billets [luh-gee-shay-day-bee-yay]
ticket price	le prix du billet [luh-pree-dew-bee-yay]
time of departure	l'heure *(f)* de départ [luh-duh-day-par]
timetable	l'horaire *(m)* (de chemin de fer) [lo-rehr]
toilet, restroom	les toilettes *(f)* [lay-twa-leht]
train	le train [luh-trahN]
vacant	libre [leebr]
waiting room	la salle d'attente [la-sal-da-tahNt]
washroom	les lavabos *(m)* [lay-la-va-bo]
window seat	le coin-fenêtre [luh-kwaN-fuh-nehtr]

Ship
Bateau

Information — Renseignements

Information	Renseignements
Which is the best way to get to . . . by ship?	Je voudrais aller à . . . par bateau. Quel est le meilleur itinéraire? [zhuh-voo-dray-a-lay-a]. . . [par-ba-to-kehl-ay-luh-meh-yuhr-ee-tee-neh-rehr]
When does the next ship/the next ferry leave for . . .?	D'où/A quelle heure part le prochain bateau/le prochain ferry-boat pour . . .? [doo]/[a-kehl-uhr]-par-[luh-pro-shaN-ba-to]/[luh-por-shaN-fay-ree-bot]-poor]
How long does the crossing take?	La traversée dure combien de temps? [la-tra-vehr-say-dewr-kohN-byaN-duh-tahN]
What ports do we call at?	Dans quels ports fait-on escale? [dahN-kehl-pohr-feh-tohN-ehs-kal]
When do we land at . . .?	Quand est-ce qu'on arrive à . . .? [kahN-tehs-kohN-na-reev-a]
How long are we stopping at . . .?	L'escale à . . . dure combien de temps? [lehs-kal-a]. . . [dewr-kohN-byaN-duh-tahN]
I would like a ticket for . . .	Je voudrais un billet pour . . . [zhuh-voo-dray-aN-bee-yay-porr]
first class	en première classe [ahN-pruh-myehr- klas]
tourist class	en classe touristes [ahN-klas-too-reest]
a single/double cabin	une cabine pour une/deux personne(s) [ewn-ka-been-poor-ewn/duuh-pehr-sohn]
I would like a round-trip ticket at . . . o'clock.	Je voudrais un billet pour le départ de . . . heures. [zhuh-voo-dray-aN-bee-yay-poor-luh-day-par-duh]

On Board — A bord du bateau

On Board	A bord du bateau
Excuse me, I'm looking for cabin number . . .	Pardon, Mme/Mlle/M., je cherche la cabine numéro . . . [par-dohN-[ma-dam]/ [mad-mwa-zehl]/[muh-syuuh]-zhuh-shehrsh-la-ka-been-new-may-ro]

Can I have a different cabin?	Est-ce que je pourrais changer de cabine? [ehs-kuh-zhuh-poo-ray-shahN-zhay-duh-ka-been]
Where's my suitcase/ luggage?	Où est ma valise/Où sont mes bagages? [oo-ay-ma-va-leez]/[oo-sohN-may-ba-gazh]
Where's the restaurant/ lounge?	Où est la salle à manger/le salon? [oo-ay-[la-sal-a-mahN-zhay]/[luh-sa-lohN]
When are the meals served?	Les repas sont à quelle heure, s.v.p.? [lay-ruh-pa-sohN-sehr-vee-a-kehl-uhr]
Steward, would you bring me . . ., please?	Garçon/Monsieur, apportez-moi . . ., s.v.p.? [gar-sohN]/[muh-syuuh]-a-pohr-tay- mwa] . . . [seel-voo-play]
I don't feel very well.	Je ne me sens pas très bien. [zhuhn-muh-sahN-pa-tray-byaN]
Call the ship's doctor, please!	Appelez le médecin de bord, s.v.p.! [ap-lay-luh-mehd-saN-duh-bohr-seel-voo-play]
Could you give me something for sea-sickness, please?	Donnez-moi un médicament contre le mal de mer, s.v.p.? [do-nay-mwa-aN-meh-dee-ka-mahN-kohN-truh-luh-mal-duh-mehr-seel-voo-play]

Word List: Ship **See also Word List: Plane, Train**

anchor	l'ancre *(f)* [lahNkr]
booking	la réservation [la-ray-zehr-va-syohN]
bow	la proue [la-proo]
cabin	la cabine [la-ca-been]
to call at	entrer dans le port [ahN-tray-dahN-luh-pohr]
captain	le commandant [luh-ko-mahN-dahN]
car-ferry	le bac [luh-bak]
coast	la côte [la-kot]
course	le cap [luh-kap]
crew	l'équipage *(m)* [lay0kee-pazh]
crossing	la traversée [la-tra-vehr-say]
cruise	la croisière [la-krwa-zyehr]
deck	le pont [luh-pohN]
to disembark	débarquer [day-bar-kay]
to dock at	faire escale à [fehr-ehs-kal-a]
dock	l'embarcadère *(m)* [lahN-bar-ka-dehr]
to embark	embarquer [ahN-bar-kay]
excursion	l'excursion *(f)* à terre [lehk-skewr-syohN]
ferry	le bac, le ferry-boat [luh-bak]/[luh-fay-ree-bot]
harbor	le port [luh-pohr]
harbor dues, harbor fees	les droits *(m)* de port [lay-drwa-duh-pohr]
hovercraft	l'hovercraft *(m)* [lo-vuhr-kraft]
	l'aéroglisseur *(m)* [la-ay-ro-glee-suhr]
inside cabin	la cabine intérieure [la-ka-been-aN-tay-ryuhr]
knot	le nœud [luh-nuuh]
landing area, wharf	l'embarcadère *(m)* [lahN-bar-ka-dehr]
life jacket	le gilet de sauvetage [luh-zhee-lay-duh-sov-tazh]
life preserver	la bouée de sauvetage [la-bway-duh-sov-tazh]
lifeboat	le canot de sauvetage [luh-ka-no-duh-sov-tazh]
lighthouse	le phare [luh-far]
lower deck	l'entrepont *(m)* [lahN-truh-pohN]
mainland	la terre ferme, le continent [la-tehr-fehrm]/[luh-kohN-tee-nahN]
motorboat	le canot automobile [luh-ca-no-o-to-mo-beel]
on board	à bord (du bateau) [a-bohr]

outside cabin	la cabine extérieure [la-ka-been-ehk-steh-ryuhr]
quay	le quai [luh-kay]
rear deck	le bâbord [ba-bohr]
rough seas	l'état *(m)* de la mer [lay-ta-duh-la-mehr]
round trip	le circuit [luh-seer-kwee]
rowing boat	la barque à rames [la-bark-a-ram]; le canot à rames [luh-ka-no-a-ram]
rudder	la rame [la-ram]
to (set) sail	quitter le port [kee-tay-luh-pohr]
sailboat	le bateau à voiles [luh-ba-to-a-vwal]
sailor	le matelot [luh-mat-lo]
to be seasick	avoir le mal de mer [a-vwar-luh-mal-duh-mehr]
shore	le rivage [luh-ree-vazh]
starboard	tribord *(m)* [tree-bohr]
steamer, steamship	le vapeur [la-va-puhr]
stern	la poupe [la-poop]
steward	le steward [luh-stew-wart]
sun deck	le sun-deck [luh-suhn-dehk]
ticket	le billet [luh-bee-yay]
train-ferry	le ferry-boat [luh-fay-ree-bot]
upper deck	le pont supérieur [luh-pohN-sew-pay-ryuhr]
wave	la vague [la-vag]
yacht	le yacht [luh-yot]

At the Border

A la frontière

Passport Check	Contrôle des passeports
Your passport, please.	Votre passeport, s'il vous plaît. [voh-truh-pas-pohr-seel-voo-play]
Your passport has expired.	Votre passeport est périmé. [voh-truh-pas-pohr-ay-pay-ree-may]
I'm with the organized group from . . .	Je suis avec le voyage organisé de . . . [zhuh-swee-a-vehk-luh-vwa-yazh-ohr-ga-nee-zay-duh]
Can you please show me the rabies immunization certificate/health certificate for your dog/cat?	Est-ce que vous pouvez me présenter le certificat de santé/ de vaccination contre la rage pour votre chien/votre chat, s.v.p.? [ehs-kuh-voo-poo-vay-muh-pray-zahN-tay-luh-sehr-tee-fee-ka-duh-[sahN-tay]/[vak-see-na-syohN-kohN-truh-la-razh]-poor-voh-truh-shyaN/sha-seel-voo-play]
Do you have a visa?	Vous avez un visa? [voo-za-vay-aN-vee-za]
Can I get a visa here?	Est-ce que je peux obtenir le visa ici? [ehs-kuh-zhuh-puuh-ohb-tuh-neer-luh-vee-za-ee-see]

Customs	Douane
Do you have anything to declare?	Vous n'avez rien à déclarer? [voo-na-vay-ryaN-na-day-kla-ray]
No, I only have two or three presents.	Non, j'ai seulement deux ou trois cadeaux. [nohN-zhay-suhl-mahN-duuh-zoo-trwa-ka-do]
Pull over to the right/ the left, please.	Rangez-vous sur la droite/la gauche, s.v.p. [rahN-zhay-voo-sewr-la-drwat/gosh-seel-voo-play]

Open the trunk/this suitcase, please.	Ouvrez votre coffre/cette valise, s.v.p. [oo-vray-voh-truh-[kohfr]/[va-leez]-seel-voo-play]
Do I have to pay duty on this?	Il faut déclarer, ça? [eel-fo-day-kla-ray-sa]
How much duty do I have to pay?	Combien est-ce que je dois payer de droits là-dessus? [kohN-byaN-ehs-kuh-zhuh-dwa-pay-yay-duh-drwa-la-duh-sew]

Word List: At the Border

border crossing	le poste frontière [luh-pohst-frohN-tyehr]
customs check	le contrôle douanier [luh-kohN-trol-dwa-nyay]
customs office	le bureau de douane [luh-bew-ro-duh-dwan]
customs officer	le douanier [luh-dwa-nyay]
date of birth	la date de naissance [la-dat-duh-nay-sahNs]
driver's license	le permis de conduire [luh-pehr-mee-duh-kohN-dweer]
duty	la douane [la-dwan]
duty-free	exempt de droits de douane [ehg-zahN-duh-drwa-duh-dwan]
duty tax	les droits de douane [lay-drwa-duh-dwan]
entry into the country	l'entrée *(f)* [lahN-tray]
exit from the country	la sortie [la-sohr-tee]
export	l'exportation *(f)* [lehk-spohr-ta-syohN]
family name	le nom de famille [luh-nohN-duh-fa-meey]
first name	le prénom [luh-pray-nohN]
green card	la carte verte [la-kart-vehrt]
identity card	la pièce d'identité [la-pyehs-dee-dahN-tee-tay]
import	l'importation *(f)* [laN-pohr-ta-syohN]
international license plate	la plaque de nationalité [la-plak-duh-na-syo-na-lee-tay]
international vaccination certificate	le carnet international de vaccination [luh-kar-nay-aN-tehr-na-syo-nal-duh-vak-see-na-syohN]
license number plate	la plaque d'immatriculation [la-plak-dee-ma-tree-kew-la-syohN]
maiden name	le nom de jeune fille [luh-nohN-duh-zhuhn-feey]

marital status	la situation de famille [la-see-tew-a-syohN-dh-fa-meey]
married	marié [ma-ryay]
nationality	la nationalité [la-na-syo-na-lee-tay]
passport	le passeport [luh-pas-pohr]
passport check	le contrôle des passeports [luh-kohN-trol-day-pas-pohr]
place of birth	le lieu de naissance [luh-lyuuh-duh-neh-sahNs]
place of residence	le domicile [luh-do-mee-seel]
rabies	la rage [la-razh]
regulations	les prescriptions *(f)* [lay-prehs-kreep-syohN]
single	célibataire [say-lee-ba-tehr]
subject to duty	soumis aux droits de douane [soo-mee-o-drwa-duh-dwan]
valid	valable [va-labl]
visa	le visa [luh-vee-za]
widower/widow	veuf *(m)* [vuhf], veuve *(f)* [vuhv]

Local Transportation

Transports en commun

Which bus/tram/metro line goes to . . .?	Quel bus/Quel tram/Quelle ligne demétro faut-il prendre pour aller à . . .? [kehl-bews]/[kehl-tram]/[kehl-leeny-duh-meh-tro]-fo-teel-prahNdr-poor-a-lay-a]
Excuse me, where's the nearest . . .	Où se trouve . . . [oo-suh-troov]
bus stop?	l'arrêt de bus le plus proche? [la-ray-duh-bews-luh-plew-prohsh]
tram stop?	l'arrêt de tram le plus proche? [la-ray-duh-tram-luh-plew-prohsh]
metro station?	la station de métro la plus proche? [la-sta-syohN-duh-may-tro-la-plew-prohsh]
Which line goes to . . .?	C'est quelle ligne pour . . . , s.v.p.? [say-kehl-leeny-poor]. . . [seel-voo-play]
Does this bus go to . . .?	C'est bien le bus pour . . .? [say-byaN-luh-bews-poor]
What time/where does the bus leave from?	A quelle heure/D'où part le bus? [a-kehl-uhr]/[doo]-[par-luh-bews]

When's the first/last metro to . . .?	Le premier/dernier métro pour… est àquelle heure? [luh-[pruh-myay]/ [dehr-nyay]-may-tro-poor]… [ay-ta-kehl-uhr]
Which direction must I take?	Je dois aller dans quelle direction? [zhuh-dwa-a-lay-dahN-kehl-dee-rehk-syohN]
How many stops is it to . . .?	Il y a combien d'arrêts d'ici à . . .? [eel-ya-kohN-byaN-da-ray-dee-see-a]
Where do I have to get out/change?	A quel arrêt est-ce que je dois descendre/changer [a-kehl-a-ray-ehs-kuh-zhuh-dwa-[day-sahNdr]/ [shahN-zhay]

Bridge, at Langeais, over the Loire River

Can you please tell me when to get off?	Vous pourrez me faire signe quand je devrai descendre? [voo-poo-vay-muh-fehr-seeny-kahN-zhuh-duh-vray-day-sahNdr]
Where can I buy a ticket?	Où est-ce que je peux prendre mon billet? [oo-ehs-kuh-zhuh-puuh-prahNdr-mohN-bee-yay]
A ticket to…, please.	Un billet pour…, s.v.p. [aN-bee-yay-poor]
Are there one-day/ weekly/monthly tickets?	Est-ce qu'il y a également des cartes/hebdomadaires/mensuelles? [eel-ya-ay-gal-mahN-day-kart]/[ehb-do-ma-dehr]/[mahN-swehl]

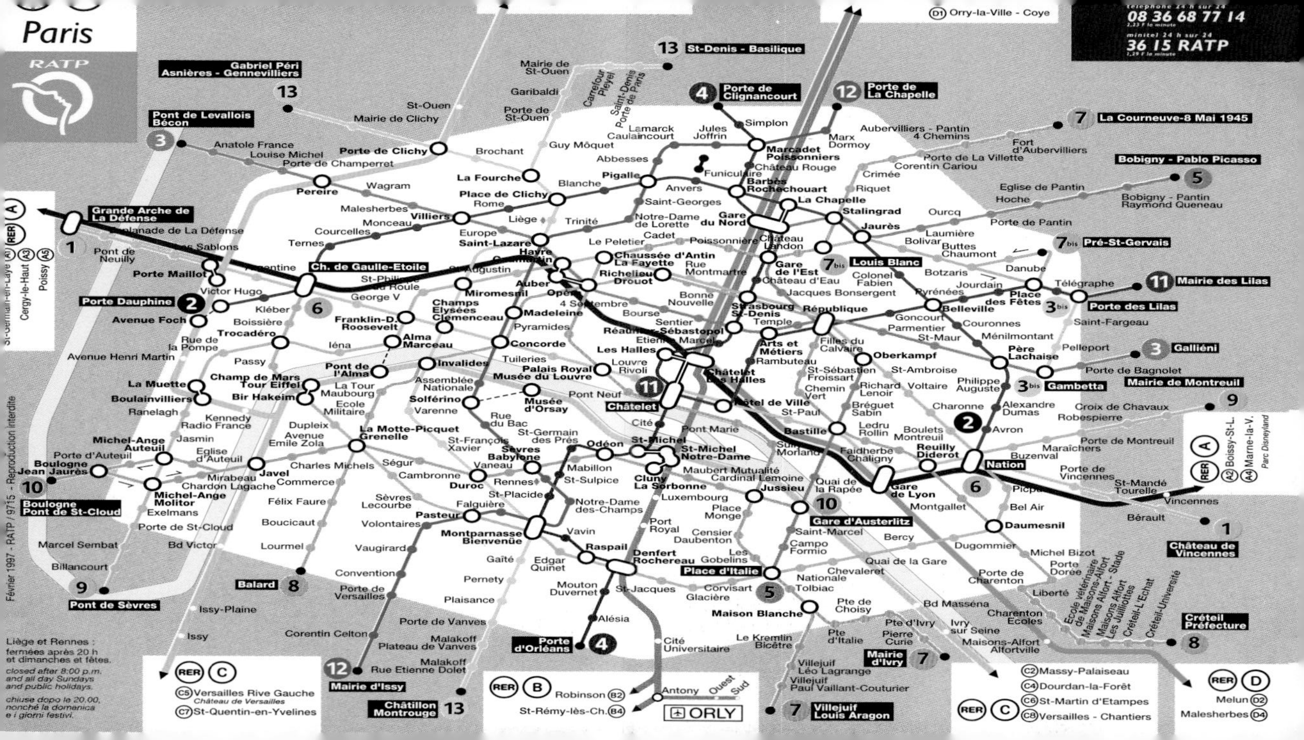

Paris
RATP
téléphone 24 h sur 24
08 36 68 77 14
2,23 F la minute
minitel 24 h sur 24
36 15 RATP
1,29 F la minute
D1 Orry-la-Ville - Coye
13 St-Denis - Basilique
Gabriel Péri
Asnières - Gennevilliers
13
Pont de Levallois
Bécon
3
4 Porte de Clignancourt
12 Porte de La Chapelle
7 La Courneuve-8 Mai 1945
Bobigny - Pablo Picasso
5
Grande Arche de La Défense
1
RER A
A1 St-Germain-en-Laye
A3 Cergy-le-Haut
A5 Poissy
7bis Pré-St-Gervais
11 Mairie des Lilas
Porte des Lilas
3 Galliéni
Mairie de Montreuil
9
RER A
A2 Boissy-St-L.
A4 Marne-la-V.
Parc Disneyland
1
Château de Vincennes
Créteil Préfecture
8
RER D
Melun D2
Malesherbes D4
RER C
C2 Massy-Palaiseau
C4 Dourdan-la-Forêt
C6 St-Martin d'Etampes
C8 Versailles - Chantiers
7 Villejuif Louis Aragon
Mairie d'Ivry
7
RER B
Robinson B2
St-Rémy-lès-Ch. B4
Antony
Ouest
Sud
ORLY
Porte d'Orléans
4
12 Mairie d'Issy
Châtillon Montrouge
13
Balard
8
RER C
C5 Versailles Rive Gauche
Château de Versailles
C7 St-Quentin-en-Yvelines
9
Pont de Sèvres
10
Boulogne Pont de St-Cloud
Porte Dauphine
2
Ch. de Gaulle-Etoile
6
Châtelet
11
Nation
Gare de Lyon
Gare d'Austerlitz
Place d'Italie
Montparnasse Bienvenüe
Louis Blanc
Gambetta
Liège et Rennes : fermées après 20 h et dimanches et fêtes.
closed after 8:00 p.m. and all day Sundays and public holidays.
chiuse dopo le 20.00, nonché la domenica e i giorni festivi.
Février 1997 - RATP / 9715 - Reproduction interdite

Taxi

Taxi

Where's the nearest taxi stand?	Pardon, Mme/Mlle/M., vous pourriez m'indiquer la station de taxis la plus proche, s.v.p.? [par-dohN-[ma-dam]/[mad-mwa-zehl]/[muh-syuuh]-voo-poo-ryay-maN-dee-kay-la-sta-syohN-duh-tak-see-la-plew-prohsh-seel-voo-play]
To the train station.	A la gare. [a-la-gar]
To the . . . Hotel.	A l'hôtel . . . [a-lo-tehl]
To . . . street.	Rue . . . [rew]
To . . . , please.	A . . ., s'il vous plaît. [a]. . .[seel-voo-play]
How much will it cost to . . .?	Il faut compter combien pour aller à . . .? [eel-fo-kohN-tay-kohN-byaN-poor-a-lay-a]
Please stop here.	Vous vous arrêtez ici, s.v.p. [voo-voo-za-ray-tay-ee-see-seel-voo-play]
Please wait. I'll be back in five minutes.	Attendez un instant. Je serai de retour dans cinq minutes. [a-tahN-day-zhuh-suh-ray-duh-ruh-toor-dahN-saN-mee-newt]
That's for you.	Voilà pour vous. [vwa-la-poor-voo]

On Foot

A pied

Excuse me, where's . . . please?	Pardon, Mme/Mlle/M., où se trouve . . . , s.v.p.? [par-dohN-[ma-dam]/[mad-mwa- zehl]/[muh-syuuh]oo-suh-troov]
Could you tell me how to get to . . . please?	Pardon, Mme/Mlle/M., pour aller à . . . , s.v.p.? [par-dohN-[ma-dam]/[mad-mwa-zhel]/[muh-syuuh]-poor-a-lay-a] [seel-voo-play]
I'm sorry, I don't know.	Je suis désolé, je ne sais pas. [zhuh-swee-day-zo-lay-zhuh-nuh-say-pa]

Which is the quickest way to . . .?	Quel est le chemin le plus court pour aller à . . .? [kehl-ay-luh-shuh-maN-luh-plew-koor-poor-a-lay-a]
How far is it to . . . (on foot)?	Le/La/Les . . . , c'est à combien d'ici, (à pied)? [luh]/[la]/[lay] . . . [say-ta-kohN-byaN-dee-see-(a-pyay)]
It's a long way./It is not far.	C'est loin/Ce n'est pas loin. [say-lwaN]/[suh-nay-pa-lwaN]
It is quite close to here.	C'est tout près d'ici. [say-too-pray-dee-see]
Go straight on. Turn left/right.	Vous allez tout droit./Vous prenez à gauche/à droite. [voo-za-lay-too-drwa]/[voo-pruh-nay-a-gosh/drwat]
The first/second street on the left/right.	La première/deuxième rue à gauche/à droite. [la-[pruh-myehr]/[duuh-zyehm]-rew-a-gosh/drwat]
Cross . . .	Vous traversez . . . [voo-tra-vehr-say]
the bridge.	le pont. [luh-pohN]
the circle/the street.	la place/la rue. [la-plas]/[la-rew]
Then ask again.	Une fois là-bas, vous redemanderez. [ewn-fwa-la-ba-voo-duh-mahN-dray]
You can't miss it.	Vous ne pouvez pas vous tromper. [voo-nuh-poo-vay-pa-voo-trohN-pay]
You can take . . .	Vous pouvez prendre. . . [voo-poo-vay-prahNdr]
the bus/the trolley.	le bus/le trolley. [luh-bews]/[luh-tro-lay]
the tram.	le tram. [luh-tram]
the metro.	le métro. [luh-may-tro]

500 m
A
B
C
1
2
3
4
5
Avenue de Villiers
Rue de Prony
Rue de Courcelles
Wagram
Demours
Pierre
Av. Niel
Rue
Av. des Ternes
B. Pereire
Pl. des Ternes
Rue du Faubourg Saint Honoré
Boulevard de Courcelles
Boul. des Batignolles
R. de Rome
Rue de Léningrad
Parc Monceau
Musée Camondo
Boulevard
Conservatoire de Musique
St Ferdinand
Salle Wagram
Salle Pleyel
Musée Jacquemart André
Boulevard
St-Augustin
Pl. St-Augustin
Rue
Haussmann
Malesherbes
Av. de la Gr. Armée
Place
Arc de Triomphe de l'Etoile
Av. Friedland
Avenue Foch
Charles de Gaulle
Avenue des Champs-Elysées
Rue La Boëtie
Salle Gaveau
St-Philippe-d.-R.
Av. V. Hugo
Lauriston
Kléber
Centre de Conférences Internationales
Rue de Ponthieu
Av. Franklin D. Roosevelt
Ste-Madeleine
Rond-Point des Champs-Elysées
Théâtre Marigny
Av. de Marigny
Avenue Gabriel
R. Royale
Rue
Théâtre du Rond Point
Avenue Marceau
Avenue George V
Avenue Montaigne
Avenue d'Iéna
Musée Guimet
Hôtel Galliéra
Place d'Iéna
Palais de Tokyo
Théâtre des Champs-Elysées
Botschaft der Bundesrepublik Deutschland
Palais
Cours la Reine
Place de la Concorde
Orangerie
Jardin
Seine
Pont de l'Alma
Pont des Invalides
Pont Alex. III
Pont de la Concorde
Avenue de New York
Palais de Chaillot
Pl. de la Résistance
Quai d'Orsay
Österreich. Botschaft
Quai Anatole France
Mus. d'Orsay
Rue de l'Université
Gare des Invalides Air Terminal
Extérieur
Branly
Pont d'Iéna
Avenue Rapp
Rue Saint Dominique
Schweizer Botschaft
Institut
Boulevard
Rue de Grenelle
Pl. des Invalides
Ste-Clotilde
l'Equipement
Quai
Champ de Mars
Avenue de la Bourdonnais
Rue Bosquet
Avenue de Suffren
Avenue de Tourville
Boulevard des Invalides
Rue de Varenne
Musée Rodin
Boute. de la Tour-Maubourg
Av. de Ségur
Breteuil
Rue de Babylone
Lowendal
St-Léon
St-François-Xavier
Unesco
Secrétariat d'Outre-Mer
Sèvres
Rue du Cherche Midi
Rue Fondary
Av. de la Motte-Picquet
Av. de Suffren
Grenelle
Boulevard Garibaldi
Place de Breteuil
Av.
Rue Cambronne
Rue de la Croix-Nivert
Avenue Émile Zola
Rue du Théâtre
Rue du Commerce
R. des Entrepreneurs
Pl. Henri Queuille
MONTPARNASSE
Place du 18 Juin 1940
Rue Lecourbe
Vaugirard
Square St Lambert
Institut Pasteur
Tour Montparnasse
Montparnasse
Avenue du Maine

PARIS
MONTMARTRE
D
E
Boul. de Clichy
Place Pigalle
Boul. de Rochechouart
Rue Blanche
Rue Pigalle
Rue N.-D. de Lorette
Av. Trudaine
Rue Condorcet
Rochechouart
Boulevard Poissonnière
St Vincent de Paul
Musée Gustave Moreau
Notre Dame de Lorette
La Fayette
St-Joseph
Place du Colonel Fabien
Rue du Faubourg St. Denis
St. Laurent
Folies Bergère
Rue de Paradis
R. d. Petites Ecuries
Rue du Faubourg
Strasbourg
Magenta
Quai de Valmy
Quai de Jemmapes
R. de la Grange
Av. Claude Vellefaux
Haussmann
Boul. Montmartre
Musée Grevin
Boul. des Italiens
Salle Favart
R. du 4. Septembre
Bourse des Valeurs
Boul. Bonne Nouvelle
Boul. St-Martin
Place de la République
Bibl. Nationale
N. D. des Victoires
Reaumur
Rue du Temple
Av. de l'Opéra
St-Roch
Rue Etienne-Marcel
St-Eustache
Bourse du Commerce
Cirque d'Hiver
Comédie Française
Turbigo
Boulevard Sébastopol
Rue Beaubourg
Rue des Archives
Musée de la Chasse
Rambuteau
Rue St. Honore
Rivoli
Forum des Halles
Centre Pompidou
Min. des Finances
Pl. du Carrousel
Palais du Louvre
St Denys
St-Germain
Théâtre du Châtelet
Tour St-Jacques
St-Merry
Boul. du Temple
Boul. Beaumarchais
Quai Malaquais
Pont des Arts
Quai de Conti
Pont Neuf
Monnaie
Théâtre de la Ville
Hôtel de Ville
Musée Carnavalet
Pl. des Vosges
Quai des Grands Augustins
ÎLE DE LA CITÉ
Hôtel Dieu
St-Gervais
St-Germain-des-Prés
St-Michel
Notre-Dame
Quai de l'Hôtel de Ville
St-Paul
R. St. Antoine
Pl. de la Bastille
ÎLE ST LOUIS
St-Severin
St-Julien-le-Pauvre
St Louis
Boul. Henri IV.
St-Sulpice
Musée de Cluny
Quai de la Tournelle
Pont de Sully
Quai Henri IV
Boul. Bourdon
Rue de la Bastille
Vaugirard
Odéon
Germain
Luxembourg
QUARTIER LATIN
Jardin du Luxembourg
Pl. Edmond Rostand
St-Etienne-du-Mont
Ecoles
Seine
Panthéon
Arènes de Lutèce
Rue Cuvier
Quai St Bernard
d'Assas
Rue Gay Lussac
Rue d'Ulm
Rue Monge
Jardin des Plantes
Pl. Valhubert
Pont d'Austerlitz
Université Paris V
Boulevard de l'Observatoire
Museum National d'Histoire Naturelle
Mosquée
Rue Buffon
Rue Claude Bernard
Montparnasse
St Médard
Rue Censier
Hôpital
Université

Word List: On the Go in Town

building	le bâtiment [luh-ba-tee-mahN]
bus	le bus [luh-bews]
church	l'église *(f)* [lay-gleez]
city bus	le bus [luh-bews]
city center	le centre-ville [luh-sahN-truh-veel]
coach	le car [luh-kar]
commuter train	le train de banlieue [luh-traN-duh-bahN-lyuuh]
conductor	le contrôleur [luh-kohN-tro-luhr]
to depart	partir [par-teer]
departure	le départ [luh-day-par]
direction	la direction [la-dee-rehk-syohN]
district	le quartier [luh-kar-tyay]
downtown	le centre-ville [luh-sahN-truh-veel]
driver	le conducteur [luh-kohN-dewk-tuhr]
end of the line	le terminus [luh-tehr-mee-news]
flat rate	le prix forfaitaire [luh-pree-fohr-feh-tehr]
to get off	descendre [day-sahNdr]
to get on	monter [mohN-tay]
house	la maison [la-meh-zohN]
house/building number	le numéro de la maison/l'immeuble [luh-new-may-ro-duh-[la-meh-zohN]/[lee-muhbl]
inspector	le contrôleur [luh-kohN-tro-luhr]
lane/alley	la ruelle [la-rew-ehl]
main street	la rue principale [la-rew-praN-see-pal]
to make an announcement on the loudspeaker	faire une annonce par haut-parleur [fehr-ewn-a-nohNs-par-o-par-luhr]
metro, subway	le métro [luh-may-tro]
one-day travel card	le billet pour une journée [luh-bee-yay-poor-la-zhoor-nay]
park	le parc, le jardin public [luh-[park]/[zhar-daN]-pew-bleek]
pedestrian zone	la zone piétonne [la-zon-pyay-tohn]
to press the button	appuyer sur le bouton [a-pwee-yay-sewr-luh-boo-tohN]
rack railway	le chemin de fer à crémaillère [luh-shuh-maN-duh-fehr-a-kray-ma-yehr]
rate per kilometer	le prix au kilomètre [luh-pree-o-kee-lo-mehtr]
receipt	le reçu [luh-ruh-sew]

side street	la rue adjacente [la-rew-ad-zha-sahNt]
sidewalk	le trottoir [luh-tro-twar]
sightseeing tour	le tour de ville (en car) [luh-toor-ahN-veel]
to stop	s'arrêter [sa-ray-tay]
stop	l'arrêt *(m)* station [la-ray]/[la-sta-syohN]
street	la rue [la-rew]
suburb	la ville de banlieue [la-veel-duh-bahN-lyuuh]
subway/metro	le métro [luh-may-tro]
to take *(ticket)*	prendre (son billet) [prahN-druh [sohN-bee-yay]
taxi driver	le chauffeur de taxi [luh-sho-fuhr-duh-tak-see]
taxi stand	la station de taxis [la-sta-syohN-duh-tak-see]
ticket machine/ticket/token vendor	la billetterie [la-bee-yeht-ree]
ticket price	le prix du billet [luh-pree-dew-bee-yay]
ticket/token	le billet [luh-bee-yay]
timetable	l'horaire *(m)* des bus/du métro/des trolleys [lo-rehr-day-bews/dew-may-tro/day-tro-lay]
tip	le pourboire [luh-poor-bwar]
train station/bus terminal	la gare des bus/cars [la-gar-day-bews/kar]
tramway/streetcar	le tram [luh-tram]
trolley	le trolley [luh-tro-lay]
to validate	composter [kohN-pos-tay]
validation machine	le composteur [luh-kohN-pos-tuhr]
weekly ticket	la carte hebdomadaire [la-kart-ehb-do-ma-dehr]
weekly/monthly ticket	la carte d'abonnement [la-kart-da-bohn-mahN]

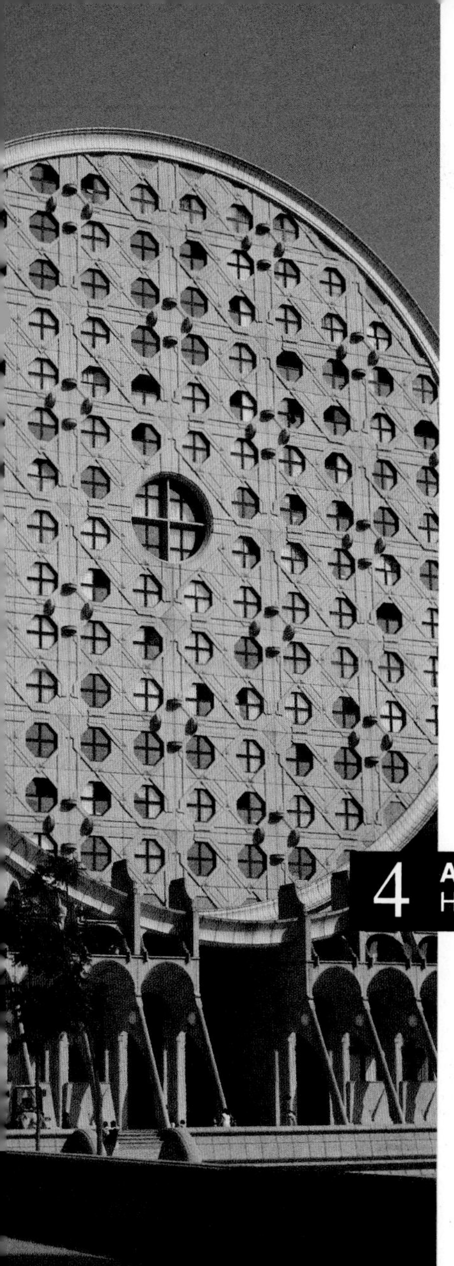

4 Accommodations
Hébergement

Information

Renseignements

Can you recommend . . ., please?	Pardon, Mme/Mlle/M., vous pourriez m'indiquer . . .? [par-dohN-[ma-dam]/[mad-mwa-zehl]/[muh-syuuh]-voo-poo-ryay-maN-dee-kay]
a good hotel	un bon hôtel [aN-bohn-o-tehl]
a cheap hotel	un hôtel pas trop cher [aN-no-tehl-pa-tro-shehr]
a guest house	une pension de famille [ewn-pahN-syohN-duh-fa-meey]
a bed and breakfast place	une chambre chez l'habitant [ewn-shahNbr-shay-la-bee-tahN]
Is it central/quiet/near the beach?	Est-ce qu'il/qu'elle est dans le centre/dans un quartier tranquille/prèsde la plage? [ehs-keel/kehl-ay-[dahN-luh-sahNtr]/[dahN-zaN-kar-tyay-trahN-keel]/[pray-duh-la-plazh]
How much will it cost a night?	Vous avez une idée du prix de la chambre? [voo-za-vay-ewn-ee-day-dew-pree-duh-la-shahNbr]
Is there a youth hostel/a camping site here?	Est-ce qu'il y a une auberge de jeunesse/un terrain de camping ici? [ehs-keel-ya-[ewn-o-behrzh-duh-zhuh-nehs]/[aN-teh-raN-duh-kahN-ping-ee-see]

Hotel/Guest House/Bed and Breakfast

Hôtel/Pension de famille/Chambre chezl'habitant

At the Reception Desk — A la réception

I've reserved a room. My name is . . .	J'ai réservé une chambre chez vous. Je m'appelle . . . [zhay-ray-zehr-vay- ewn-shahNbr-shay-voo-zhuh-ma-pehl]
Do you have any vacancies?	Est-ce que vous avez encore deschambres de libres? [ehs-kuh-voo-za-vay-ahN-kohr-day-shahN-bruh-duh-leebr]
... for one night.	... pour une nuit. [poor-ewn-nwee]
... for two days/for a week.	... pour deux jours/une semaine. [poor-[duuh-zhoor]/[ewn-suh-mehn]]

No, I'm afraid we're full.	Non, Mme/Mlle/M. Malheureusement, nous sommes complet. [nohN-[ma-dam]/[mad-mwa-zhel]/[muh-syuuh]-ma-luh-ruhz-mahN-noo-sohm-kohN-play]
Yes, what sort of room would you like?	Oui, qu'est-ce que vous désirez comme chambre? [wee-kehs-kuh-voo-day-zee-ray-kohm-shahNbr]
a single/double room	une chambre pour une/deux personne(s) [ewn-shahNbr-poor-ewn/duuh-pehr-sohn]
a double room with two beds	une chambre double, mais avec lits séparés [ewn-shahN-bruh-doobl-may-a-vehk-duuh-lee-say-pa-ray]
a quiet room	une chambre calme [ewn-shahN-bruh-kalm]
a sunny room	une chambre ensoleillée [ewn-shahN-brahN-so-leh-yay]
with a shower	avec douche [a-vehk-doosh]
with a bath	avec salle de bains [a-vehk-sal-duh-baN]
with a balcony/with a terrace	avec un balcon/une terrasse [a-vehk-[aN-bal-kohN]/[ewn-tay-ras]]
with a view of the sea	avec vue sur la mer [a-vehk-vew-sewr-la-mehr]
at the front	qui donne sur la rue [kee-dohn-sewr-la-rew]
at the back	qui donne sur la cour [kee-dohn-sewr-la-koor]
Can I see the room?	Est-ce que je peux voir la chambre? [ehs-kuh-zhuh-puuh-vwar-la-shahNbr]
I don't like this room. Show me another one, please.	Cette chambre ne me plaît pas. Vous pouvez m'en montrer une autre, s.v.p.? [seht-shahNbr-nuh-muh-play-pa-voo-poo-vay-mahN-mohN-tray-ewn-otr-seel-voo-play]
This room's very nice. I'll take it.	Cette chambre est très jolie. Je la prends. [seht-shahNbr-ay-tray-zho-lee-zhuh-la-prahN]
Can you put another bed/a cot in the room?	Est-ce que vous pouvez installer un troisième lit/un lit pour enfant? [ehs-kuh-voo-poo-vay-aNs-ta-lay-[aN-trwa-zyehm-lee]/[aN-lee]-poor-ahN-fahN]

How much is the room with . . .	Quel est le prix de la chambre, . . . [kehl-ay-luh-pree-duh-la-shahNbr]
breakfast?	petit déjeuner compris? [puh-tee-day-zhuuh-nay-kohN-pree]
breakfast and evening meal?	en demi-pension? [ahN-duh-mee-pahN-syohN]
full board?	en pension complète? [ahN-pahN-syohN-kohN-pleht]
Would you fill in the registration form, please?	Veuillez remplir cette fiche, s.v.p.? [vuuh-yay-rahN-pleer-seht-feesh-seel-voo-play]
May I see you passport/identity card?	Vous avez votre passeport/votre carte d'identité, s.v.p.? [voo-za-vay-[vohtr-pas-pohr]/[vohtr-kart-dee-dahN-tee-tay]]
Please have the luggage taken up to my room.	Vous voulez faire monter mes bagages, s.v.p.? [voo-voo-lay-fehr-mohN-tay-may-ba-gazh-seel-voo-play]
Where can I park the car?	Où est-ce que je peux garer ma voiture? [oo-ehs-kuh-zhuh-puuh-ga-ray-ma-vwa-tewr]
In our garage/parking lot.	Nous avons un garage/un parking. [noo-za-vohN-[aN-ga-razh]/[aN-par-king]]
Has the hotel got a swimming pool/a private beach?	Est-ce que l'hôtel a une piscine/une plage privée? [ehs-kuh-lo-tehl-a-[ewn-pee-seen]/[ewn-plazh-pree-vay]]

Talking to the Hotel Staff — Quand on s'adresse aux employés del'hôtel

What time is breakfast?	Le petit déjeuner, c'est à partir de quelle heure? [luh-puh-tee-day-zhuuh-nay-say-ta-par-teer-duh-kehl-uhr]
When are meal times?	Quelles sont les heures des repas? [kehl-sohN-lay-zuhr-day-ruh-pa]
Where's the restaurant?	Où est la salle à manger? [oo-ay-la-sal-a-mahN-zhay]
Where's the breakfast room?	Où est-ce qu'on peut prendre le petit déjeuner? [oo-ehs-kohN-puut-prahNdr-luh-puh-tee-day-zhuuh-nay]

Downstairs.	A l'étage au-dessous. [a-lay-tazh-o-duh-soo]
Would you like breakfast in your room?	Est-ce que vous prendrez votre petit déjeuner dans votre chambre? [ehs-kuh-voo-prahN-dray-vohtr-puh-tee-day-zhuh-nay-dahN-voh-truh-shahNbr]
I'd like breakfast in my room at . . . o'clock, please.	Faites-moi monter le petit déjeuner à . . . heures, s.v.p. [feht-mwa-mohN-tay-luh-puh-tee-day-zhuuh-nay-a] . . . [uhr-seel-voo-play]
For breakfast I'd like . . .	Au petit déjeuner, je prends . . . [o-puh-tee-day-zhuuh-nay-zhuh-prahN]
black coffee.	du café noir. [dew-ka-fay-nwar]
coffee with milk.	du café au lait. [dew-ka-fay-o-lay]
decaffeinated coffee.	du décaféiné. [dew-day-ka-fay-ee-nay]
tea with milk/lemon.	du thé au lait/au citron. [dew-tay-o-see-trohN]
herbal tea.	de la tisane. [duh-la-tee-zan]
hot chocolate.	du chocolat. [dew-sho-ko-la]
fruit juice.	un jus de fruit. [aN-zhew-duh-frwee]
a soft-boiled egg.	un œuf mollet. [aN-nuhf-mo-lay]
scrambled eggs.	des œufs brouillés. [day-zuuh-broo-yay]
eggs and bacon.	des œufs au plat avec du lard. [day-zuuh-o-pla-a-vehk-dew-lar]
bread/rolls/toasts.	du pain/des petits pains/des toasts. [dew-paN]/[[day-puh-tee-paN]/[day-tost]
a croissant.	un croissant. [aN-krwa-sahN]
butter.	du beurre. [dew-buhr]
cheese.	du fromage. [dew-fro-mazh]
sausage.	de la charcuterie. [duh-la-shar-kew-tuh-ree]
ham.	du jambon. [dew-zhahN-bohN]
honey.	du miel. [dew-myehl]
jam/marmalade.	de la confiture. [duh-la-kohN-fee-tewr]
cereal.	des céréales au lait. [day-say-ray-al-o-lay]
yogurt.	un yaourt. [aN-ya-oort]
some fruit.	des fruits. [day-frwee]
Please wake me at . . . o'clock in the morning.	Réveillez-moi à . . . heures, demain matin, s.v.p. [ray-vay-yay-mwa-a] . . . [uhr-duh-maN-ma-taN-seel-voo-play]
Could you bring me . . . please?	Est-ce que je pourrais avoir . . . [ehs-kuh-zhuh-poo-ray-a-vwar]

another towel	une serviette de toilette en plus? [ewn-sehr-vyeht-duh-twa-leht-ahN-plews]
some soap	une savonnette? [ewn-sa-vo-neht]
some hangers	des cintres? [day-saNtr]
How does... work?	Comment fonctionne . . . ? [ko-mahN-fohNk-syon]
My key, please.	Ma clé, s.v.p. [ma-klay-seel-voo-play]
Did anyone ask for me?	Est-ce que quelqu'un m'a demandé(e)? [ehs-kuh-kehl-kaN-ma-duh-mahN-day]
Are there any letters for me?	Est-ce qu'il y a du courrier pour moi? [ehs-keel-ya-dew-koo-ryay-poor-mwa]
Have you got any postcards/stamps?	Vous avez des cartes postales/des timbres? [voo-za-vay-[day-kart-pos-tal]/[day-taNbr]]
Where can I . . .	Où est-ce que je peux . . . [oo-ehs-kuh-zhuh-puuh]
mail this letter?	poster cette lettre? [pos-tay-seht-lehtr]
rent . . . ?	louer . . . ? [loo-ay]
make a phone call?	téléphoner? [tay-lay-fo-nay]
Can I leave my valuables in your safe?	Est-ce que je peux déposer mes objets de valeur dans votre coffre-fort? [ehs-kuh-zhuh-puuh-day-po-zay-may-zohb-zhay-duh-va-luhr-dahN-voh-truh-koh-fruh-fohr]
Can I leave my things here until I get back?	Est-ce que je peux laisser mes affaires ici, en attendant? [ehs-kuh-zhuh-puuh-lay-say-may-za-fehr-ee-see-ahN-na-tahN-dahN]

Complaints — Réclamations

The room hasn't been cleaned.	Ma chambre n'a pas été nettoyée. [ma-shahNbr-na-pa-ay-tay-neh-twa-yay]
The shower . . .	La douche . . . [la-doosh]
The flush . . .	La chasse d'eau . . . [la-shas-do]
The heating . . .	Le chauffage . . . [luh-sho-fazh]

The light . . . The radio . . . The television . . . does not work.	L'éclairage . . . [lay-klay-razh] La radio . . . [la-ra-dyo] Le téléviseur . . . [luh-tay-lay-vee-zuhr] ne fonctionne pas. [nuh-fohNk-syon-pa]
The tap drips.	Le robinet fuit. [luh-ro-bee-nay-fwee]
There's no (warm) water.	Il n'y a pas d'eau (chaude). [eel-nee-ya-pa-do-(shod)]
The toilet/sink is stopped up.	Les W.-C. sont bouchés/Le lavabo est bouché. [lay-vay-say-sohN-boo-shay]/[luh-la-va-bo-ay-boo-shay]
The window doesn't close/open.	Je n'arrive pas à fermer/ouvrir la fenêtre. [zhuh-na-reev-pa-a-[oo-vreer]/[fehr-may]-la-fuh-nehtr]
The key doesn't fit.	Ce n'est pas la bonne clé. [suh-nay-pa-la-bohn-klay]

Checking Out — Le départ

I'm leaving this evening/ tomorrow at . . . o'clock.	Je pars ce soir/demain à . . . heures. [zhuh-par-[suh-swar]/[duh-maN]-a-...-uhr]
By what time must I be out of the room?	Je peux occuper la chambre jusqu'àquelle heure? [zhuh-puuh-o-kew-pay-la-shahNbr-zhews-ka-kehl-uhr]
I'd like my bill, please.	Est-ce que vous pouvez préparer ma note, s.v.p.? [voo-poo-vay-pray-pa-ray-ma-noht-seel-voo-play]
Two separate bills, please.	Faites des notes séparées, s.v.p. [feht-day-noht-say-pa-ray]
Do you take American money/eurocheques?	Est-ce que vous prenez l'argent américain/les eurochèques? [ehs-kuh-voo-pruh-nay-[lar-zhahN-a-may-ree-kaN]/[lay-zuuh-ro-shehk]
Please forward any letters to me at this address.	Faites suivre mon courrier à cette adresse, s.v.p. [feht-sweevr-mohN-koo-ryay-a-seht-a-drehs-seel-voo-play]
Please have my luggage brought down.	Vous pourriez faire descendre mes bagages, s.v.p.? [voo-poo-ryay-fehr-day-sahNdr-may-ba-gazh-seel-voo-play]

Please have my luggage transferred to the station/terminal.	Est-ce que vous pourriez faire porter mes bagages à la gare/à l'aérogare, s.v.p.? [ehs-kuh-voo-poo-ryay-fehr-pohr-tay-may-ba-gazh-[a-la-gar]/[a-la-ay-ro-gar]-seel-voo-play]
Would you call a taxi for me, please?	Vous pourriez m'appeler un taxi, s.v.p.? [voo-poo-ryay-ma-play-aN-tak-see-seel-voo-play]
Thank you very much for everything! Good-bye!	Merci pour tout! Au revoir! [mehr-see-poor-too]-[o-ruh-vwar]

Word List: Hotel/Guest House/Bed and Breakfast

additional week	la semaine supplémentaire [la-smehn-sew-play-mahN-tehr]
air conditioning	la climatisation [la-klee-ma-tee-za-syohN]
armchair	le fauteuil [luh-fo-tuhy]
ashtray	le cendrier [luh-sahN-dree-yay]
baby-sitting service	la garderie [la-gar-duh-ree]
balcony	le balcon [luh-bal-kohN]
bar	le bar [luh-bar]
barbecue evening	la soirée grillades [la-swa-ray-gree-yad]
bathroom	la salle de bains [la-sal-duh-baN]
bathtub	la baignoire [la-beh-nwar]
bed	le lit [luh-lee]
bed linen	la literie [la-lee-tree]
bedside table	la table de nuit [la-ta-bluh-duh-nwee]
bidet	le bidet [luh-bee-day]
blanket	la couverture [la-koo-vehr-tewr]
bolster	le traversin [luh-tra-vehr-saN]
breakfast	le petit déjeuner [luh-put-tee-day-zhuuh-nay]
breakfast buffet	le buffet de petit déjeuner [luh-bew-fay-duh-puh-tee-day-zhuuh-nay]
breakfast room	la salle de petit déjeuner [la-sal-duh-puh-tee-day-zhuuh-nay]
cafeteria	la cafétéria [la-ka-fay-tay-rya]
category	la catégorie [la-ka-tay-go-ree]
change of linen	le changement de literie [luh-shahNzh-mahN-duh-lee-tree]
children's playground	le terrain de jeux pour les enfants [luh-

	tay-raN-duh-zhuuh-poor-lay-zahN-fahN]
to clean	nettoyer [nay-twa-yay]
closet	l'armoire *(f)* [lar-mwar]
cold water	l'eau froide [lo-frwad]
cot	le lit d'enfant [luh-lee-dahN-fahN]
dining room	la salle à manger [la-sal-a-mahN-zhay]
dinner	le dîner [luh-dee-nay]
doorman	le portier, le/la concierge [luh-pohr-tyay]/[luh/la-kohN-syehrzh]
elevator	l'ascenseur *(m)* [la-sahN-suhr]
extension cord	la rallonge [la-ra-lohNzh]
fan	le ventilateur [luh-vahN-tee-la-tuhr]
faucet	le robinet [luh-ro-bee-nay]
floor	l'étage *(m)* [lay-tazh]
full board	la pension complète [la-pahN-syohN-kohN-pleht]
glass of water	le verre à eau [luh-vehr-do]
guest house, inn	la pension de famille [la-pahN-syohN-duh-fa-meey]
half board	la demi-pension [la-duh-mee-pahN-syohN]
hanger	le cintre [luh-saNtr]
heating	le chauffage [luh-sho-fazh]
high season	la pleine saison [la-plehn-seh-zohN]
house telephone	le téléphone (de la chambre) [luh-tay-lay-fohn] (duh-la-shahNbr)
housekeeper	la femme de chambre [la-fam-duh-shahNbr]
key	la clé [la-klay]
lamp	la lampe [la-lahNp]
light switch	l'interrupteur *(m)* [laN-tay-rewp-tuhr]
lounge	le salon [luh-sa-lohN]
lunch	le déjeuner [luh-day-zhuuh-nay]
mattress	le matelas [luh-ma-tla]
minibar	le minibar [luh-mee-nee-bar]
mirror	la glace [la-glas]
motel	le motel [luh-mo-tehl]
multiple plug	la prise multiple [la-preez-mewl-teepl]
night	la nuitée [la-nwee-tay]
off season	l'arrière-saison *(f)* [la-rayehr-seh-zohN]
off season/low season	l'avant-saison *(f)* [la-vahN-seh-zohN]
pillow	l'oreiller *(m)* [lo-reh-yay]
plug	la prise [la-preez]
pool bar	le bar de la piscine [luh-bar-duh-la-pee-seen]

radio	la radio [la-ra-dyo]
reading lamp	la lampe de chevet [la-lahNp-duh-shuh-vay]
reception	la réception/le hall [la-ray-sehp-syohN]/[luh-ol]
registration	la réception [la-ray-sehp-syohN]
reservation	la réservation [la-ray-zehr-va-syohN]
room	la chambre [la-shahNbr]
room and board	le logement et la nourriture [luh-lozh-mahN-ay-la-noo-ree-tewr]
safe	le coffre-fort [luh-koh-fruh-fohr]
sheets	le drap [luh-dra]
shower	la douche [la-doosh]
shuttle bus	le car/le minibus hôtel-aéroport [luh-[kar]/[mee-nee-bews]-o-tehl-a-ay-ro-pohr]
sink	le lavabo [luh-la-va-bo]
television set	le téléviseur [luh-tay-lay-vee-zuhr]
terrace	la terrasse [la-tay-ras]
toilet	les toilettes *(f)* [lay-twa-leht]
toilet paper	le papier hygiénique [luh-pa-pyay-ee-zhyay-neek]
towel	la serviette de toilette [la-sehr-vyeht-duh-twa-leht]
TV room	la salle de télévision [la-sal-duh-tay-lay-vee-zyohN]
wading pool	la pataugeoire [la-pa-to-zhwar]
warm water	l'eau chaude [lo-shod]
wastepaper basket	la corbeille à papier [la-kohr-bey-a-pa-pyay]
water	l'eau *(f)* [lo]
window	la fenêtre [la-fuh-nehtr]
wool blanket	la couverture de laine [la-koo-vehr-tewr]

Vacation Rentals: Houses/Apartments

Maisons et appartements de vacances

Is electricity/water included in the price?	Est-ce que l'eau et l'électricité sont comprises dans le loyer? [ehs-kuh-lo-ay-lay-lehk-tree-see-tay-sohN-kohN-preez-dahN-luh-lwa-yay]
Are pets allowed?	Est-ce que les animaux domestiques sont admis? [ehs-kuh-lay-za-nee-mo-do-mehs-teek-sohN-tad-mee]

Where can we pick up the keys to the house/the apartment?	A qui faut-il s'adresser pour avoir la clé de la maison/de l'appartement? [a-kee-fo-teel-sa-dray-say-poor-a-vwar-la-klay-duh-[la-meh-zohN]/[la-par-tuh-mahN]]
Do we have to return them to the same place?	C'est là également qu'il faudra la rendre? [say-la-ay-gal-mahN-keel-fo-dra-la-rahNdr]
Where are the dustbins?	Où se trouvent les poubelles? [oo-suh-troov-lay-poo-behl]
Do we have to clean the flat before we leave?	Est-ce que nous devons faire nous-mêmes le nettoyage de fin de séjour? [ehs-kuh-noo-duh-vohN-fehr-noo-mehm-luh-nay-twa-yazh-duh-faN-duh-say-zhoor]

Word List: Vacation Rentals: Houses/Apartments

See also Word List: Hotel/Guest House/Bed and Breakfast

apartment	l'appartement *(m)* [la-par-tuh-mahN]
arrival day	le jour de l'arrivée [luh-zhoor-duh-la-ree-vay]
bedroom	la chambre à coucher [la-shahN-bra-koo-shay]
bungalow	le bungalow [luh-baN-ga-lo]
bunk bed	le lit à étages [luh-lee-a-ay-tazh]
central heating	le chauffage central [luh-sho-fazh-sahN-tral]
clean-up	le nettoyage de fin de séjour [luh-nay-twa-yazh-duh-faN-duh-say-zhoor]
coffee machine	la machine à café [la-ma-sheen-a-ka-fay]
dishwasher	le lave-vaisselle [luh-lav-veh-sehl]
eat-in nook	le coin-repas [luh-kwaN-ruh-pa]
electric cooker	la cuisinière électrique [la-kwee-zee-nyehr-ay-lehk-treek]
electricity	le courant (électrique) [luh-koo-rahN-ay-lehk-treek]
extras	les charges *(f)* [lay-sharzh]
fold-out couch	la banquette-lit [la-bahN-keht-lee]
garbage	les ordures *(f)* [lay-sohr-dewr]
gas cooker	la cuisinière à gaz [la-kwee-zee-nyehr-a-gaz]

giving of the keys	la remise des clés [la-ruh-meez-day-klay]
kitchen towel	le torchon [luh-tohr-shohN]
kitchenette	le coin-cuisine [luh-kwaN-kwee-zeen]
landlord	le propriétaire (de la maison) [luh-pro-pree-yay-tehr]
living room	la salle de séjour [la-sal-duh-say-zhoor]
lump-sum payment for electricity	la somme forfaitaire pour l'électricité [la-sohm-fohr-feh-tehr-poor-lay-lehk-tree-see-tay]
pets	les animaux *(m)* domestiques [lay-za-nee-mo-do-mehs-teek]
promotional literature	le prospectus [luh-prohs-pehk-tews]
refrigerator	le réfrigérateur/frigo [luh-ray-free-zhee-ra-tuhr]/[free-go]
rent	la location, le loyer [la-lo-ka-syohN]/[luh-lwa-yay]; *(v)* louer [loo-ay]
stove	la cuisinière [la-kwee-zee-nyehr]
studio	le studio [luh-stew-dyo]
toaster	le toasteur, le grille-pain [luh-tos-tuhr]/[greey-paN]
vacation camp, resort	le village de vacances [luh-vee-lazh-duh-va-kahNs]
vacation home/country home	la maison de vacances/de campagne [la-meh-zohN-[duh-va-kahNs]/[duh-kahN-pany]
voltage	le voltage [luh-vohl-tazh]
washing machine	la machine à laver [la-ma-sheen-a-la-vay]
water consumption	la consommation d'eau [la-kohN-so-ma-syohN-do]

Camping

Camping

Is there a campsite nearby?	Est-ce qu'il y a un terrain de camping par ici? [ehs-keel-ya-aN-teh-raN-duh-kahN-peeng-par-ee-see]
Do you have room for another camper/tent?	Est-ce que vous avez encore de la place pour une caravane/une tente? [ehs-kuh-voo-za-vay-ahN-kohr-duh-la-plas-poor-[ewn-ka-ra-van]/[ewn-tahNt]
How much does it cost per day and per person?	Quel est le tarif par jour et par personne? [kehl-ay-luh-ta-reef-par-zhoor-ay-par-pehr-sohn]

What's the charge for . . .	Quel est le tarif pour . . . [kehl-ay-luh-ta-reef-poor]
the car?	les voitures? [lay-vwa-tewr]
the camper?	les caravanes? [lay-ka-ra-van]
the mobil home?	les camping-cars? [lay-kahN-peeng-kar]
the tent?	les tentes? [lay-tahNt]
Do you rent chalets/ campers?	Est-ce que vous louez des bungalows/ des caravanes? [ehs-kuh-voo-loo-ay-day-[baN-ga-lo]/[ka-ra-van]]
Where can I park my camper/put my tent?	Où est-ce que je peux installer ma caravane/monter ma tente? [oo-ehs-kuh-zhuh-puuh-[aNs-ta-lay-ma-ka-ra-van]/[mohN-tay-ma-tahNt]]
We'll be staying for . . . days/weeks.	Nous pensons rester . . . jours/ semaines. [noo-pahN-sohN-rehs-tay] . . . [zhoor]/[suh-mehn]
Is there a grocery store here?	Est-ce qu'il y a une épicerie? [ehs-keel-ya-ewn-ay-pees-ree]
Where are...	Où sont . . . [oo-sohN]
the toilets?	les W.-C.? [lay-vay-say]
the washrooms?	les lavabos? [lay-la-va-bo]
the showers?	les douches? [lay-doosh]
Are there electric outlets here?	Est-ce qu'il y a des prises de courant dans le camp? [ehs-keel-ya-day-preez-duh-koo-rahN-dahN-luh-kahN]
Where can I exchange the gas canisters?	Où est-ce qu'on peut changer les bouteilles de gaz? [oo-ehs-kohN-puuh-shahN-zhay-lay-boo-tehy-duh-gaz]
Is the campsite guarded at night?	Est-ce que le camp est gardé, la nuit? [ehs-kuh-luh-kahN-ay-gar-day-la-nwee]
Is there a children's playground here?	Est-ce qu'il y a un terrain de jeux pour les enfants? [ehs-keel-ya-aN-teh-raN-duh-zhuuh-poor-lay-zahN-fahN]
Could you lend me . . . please?	Vous pourriez me prêter . . .? [ehs-kuh-voo-poo-ryay-muh-pray-tay]

Youth Hostels

Auberge de jeunesse

Can I rent bed linen/a sleeping bag?	Est-ce que vous pouvez me louer des draps/un sac de couchage? [ehs-kuh-voo-poo-vay-muh-loo-ay-[day-dra]/[aN-sak-duh-koo-shazh]
The front door is locked at midnight.	La porte d'entrée est fermée à partir de minuit. [la-pohrt-dahN-tray-ay-fehr-may-a-par-teer-duh-mee-nwee]

Word List: Camping/Youth Hostels

to camp	camper [kahN-pay]
camper	le camping-car [luh-kahN-peeng-kar] la caravane [la-ka-ra-van]
camping	le camping [luh-kahN-peeng]
camping guide	le guide de camping/caravaning [luh-gid-duh-kahN-peeng]/[ka-ra-va-neeng]
camping permit	la licence camping [la-lee-sahNs-duh-kahN-peeng]
campsite	le (terrain de) camping [luh-teh-raN-duh-kahN-peeng]
common room	la salle commune [la-sal-ko-mewn]
cooker	le réchaud [luh-ray-sho]
dormitory	le dortoir [luh-dohr-twar]
drinking water	l'eau *(f)* potable [lo-po-tabl]
dryer	le séchoir [luh-say-shwar]
electricity	le courant (électrique) [luh-koo-rahN-ay-lehk-treek]
electricity supply	la prise de courant [la-preez-duh-koo-rahN]
farm	la ferme [la-fehrm]
gas	le propane [luh-pro-pan]
gas canister	la bouteille de gaz [la-boo-tehy-duh-gaz]
gas cooker	le réchaud à gaz [luh-ray-sho-a-gaz]
gas refill	la cartouche de gaz [la-kar-toosh-duh-gaz]
hurricane lamp	la lampe à pétrole [la-lahNp-a-pay-trohl]
main hall	la salle commune, le foyer [la-sal-ko-mewn]/[luh-fwa-yay]
membership card	la carte de membre [la-kart-duh-mahNbr]

peg	le piquet [luh-pee-kay]
playground	le terrain de jeux pour enfants [luh-tay-raN-duh-zhuuh-poor-ahN-fahN]
plug (socket)	la prise [la-preez]
rates/charges	le tarif d'utilisation [luh-ta-reef-dew-tee-lee-za-syohN]
to rent	louer [loo-ay]
rental fees	le tarif de location [luh-ta-reef-duh-lo-ka-syohN]
reservation	la réservation [la-ray-zehr-va-syohN]
rope	la corde [la-kohrd]
sink	le lavabo (for dishwashing) [luh-la-va-bo]
sleeping bag	le sac de couchage [luh-sak-duh-koo-shazh]
student hall	la cité universitaire [la-see-tay-ew-nee-vehr-see-tehr]
tent	la tente [la-tahNt]
tent pole	le mât [luh-ma]
washroom	les lavabos *(m)* [lay-la-va-bo]
water	l'eau *(f)* [lo]
water canister	le jerrycan [luh-zhay-ree-kan]
youth group	le groupe de jeunes [luh-groop-duh-zhuuhn]
youth hostel	l'auberge *(f)* de jeunesse [lo-behrzh-duh-zhuuh-nehs]
youth hostel card	la carte des auberges de jeunesse [la-kart-day-zo-behrzh-duh-zhuuh-nehs]
youth hostel director	la direction de l'auberge de jeunesse [la-dee-rehk-syohN-duh-lo-behrzh-duh-zhuuh-nehs]
youth hostel guide	le guide des auberges de jeunesse [luh-geed-day-zo-behrzh-duh-zhuuh-nehs]

ET DE G
du Vil

5 Eating and Drinking
Gastronomie

Eating Out

Aller au restaurant

Is there . . . here?	Vous pourriez m'indiquer . . . [voo-poo-ryay-maN-dee-kay]
a good restaurant	un bon restaurant? [aN-bohN-rehs-to-rahN]
a Chinese/Italian restaurant	un restaurant chinois/italien? [aN-rehs-to-rahN-[shee-nwa]/[ee-ta-lyaN]
an inexpensive restaurant	un restaurant pas trop cher? [aN-rehs-to-rahN-pa-tro-shehr]
a fast-food restaurant	un snack/un fast food? [aN-snak/fast-food]
Where can one eat well/cheaply in the neighborhood?	Où peut-on bien manger/manger pour pas cher dans le quartier? [oo-puuh-tohN-[byaN-mahN-zhay]/[mahN-zhay-poor-pa-shehr]-dahN-luh-kar-tyay]

When looking for a place to eat or drink, one may come across the following names:
Salon de thé is a type of teahouse.

The French ***café*** is an establishment where one can get drinks and sandwiches, as well as croissants, at the counter or at a table.

The ***café-restaurant*** is a larger café, where one can have lunch or dinner.

A ***bar-tabac*** offers drinks and sandwiches like the French café, but it is also a tobacconist, where one can buy stamps.

A ***bistrot*** is a small establishment, with snacks, sandwiches, and a limited range of warm foods that are sometimes fine specialties.

A ***brasserie*** is mainly a beer establishment. Today, one thinks of it as a large ***café-restaurant***, offering various specialties.

At the Restaurant
Au restaurant

At a restaurant the gentleman lets the lady walk first.

I would like to reserve a table for four for this evening, please.	Je voudrais retenir une table pour ce soir, pour quatre personnes. [suhu-voo-dray-ruh-tuh-neer-ewn-tabl-poor-suh-swar-poor-katr-pehr-sohn]
Until what time do you serve warm meals?	Vous servez des repas chauds jusqu'à quelle heure? [voo-sehr-vay-day-ruh-pa-sho-a-kehl-uhr]
Is this table/seat free?	Est-ce que cette table/cette place est libre, s.v.p.? [ehs-kuh-seht-tabl/plas-ay-leebr-seel-voo-play]
A table for two/three, please.	Je voudrais une table pour deux/trois personnes. [zhuh-voo-dray-ewn-tabl-poor-duuh/trwa-pehr-sohn]
Where are the toilets, please?	Où sont les W.-C., s.v.p.? [oo-sohN-lay-vay-say]
This way, please.	C'est par ici. [say-par-ee-see]

Ordering

See also Breakfast, Chapter 4

Commande

Waiter, could I have . . . please.	Garçon Monsieur/Madame/Mademoiselle, . . . s.v.p. [gar-sohN] [muh-syuuh] [ma-dam]/[mad-mwa-zehl]
the menu	la carte [la-kart],
the wine list	la carte des vins [la-kart-day-vaN]
What can you recommend?	Qu'est-ce que vous me conseillez? [kehs-kuh-voo-muh-kohN-seh-yay]
Do you have vegetarian dishes/low-calorie meals?	Vous faites des plats végétariens/des repas diététiques? [voo-feht-day-pla-vay-zhay-ta-ryaN]/[day-ruh-pa-dyay-tay-teek]

Do you have children's portions?	Vous faites des demi-portions pour les enfants? [voo-feht-day-duh-mee-poh-syohN-poor-lay-zahN-fahN]
Are you ready to order?	Vous avez choisi? [voo-za-vay-shwa-zee]
What would you like for a starter/as a main course/for dessert?	Qu'est-ce que vous prendrez comme hors-d'œuvre/dessert? [kehs-kyh-voo-prahn-dray-kohm-[ohr-duhvr]/[day-sehr]
I'll have . . .	Je prendrai . . . [zhuh-prahN-dray]
As an appetizer/dessert/ main dish, I'll take . . .	Comme hors-d'œuvre/dessert/plat principal, je prendrai . . . [kohm-[ohr-duhvr]/[day-sehr]/[pla-praN-see-pal]-zhuh-prahN-dray]
I don't want a first course, thank you.	Je ne veux pas de hors-d'œuvre, merci. [zhuh-nuh-vuuh-pa-duh-ohr-duhvr-mehr-see]
I'm afraid we've run out of . . .	Nous n'avons malheureusement pas/plusde . . . [nohN-mal-uuh-ruuhz-mahN-noo-na-vohN-pa/plew-duh]
We only serve this dish as a special order.	Ce plat, nous ne le servons que sur commande. [suh-pla-noo-nuh-luh-sehr-vohN-kuh-sewr-ko-mahNd]
Could I have . . . instead of . . .?	Est-ce qu'à la place de . . . je pourrais avoir . . .? [ehs-kuh-ala-plas-duh] . . . [zhuh-poo-ray-a-vwar]
I am allergic to . . . Could you please prepare a dish without . . .?	Je n'aime pas le/la/les. . . Est-ce que vous pourriez préparer ce plat sans . . .? [zhuh- nehm-pa-/uh/la/lay...ehs-kuh-voo-poo-ryay-pray-pa-ray-suh-pla-sahN]
How would you like your steak?	Comment voulez-vous votre bifteck? [ko-mahN-voo-lay-voo-vohtr-beef-tehk]
well-done	bien cuit [byaN-kwee]
medium rare	à point [a-pwaN]
rare	saignant [seh-nyahN]
What would you like to drink?	Qu'est-ce que vous désirez comme boisson(s)? [kehs-kuh-voo-day-zee-ray-kohm-bwa-sohN]

A glass of . . ., please.	Un verre de . . ., s.v.p. [aN-vehr-duh- . . . -seel-voo-play]
Bring us a bottle/half a bottle of . . ., please.	Une bouteille/Une demi-bouteille de . . ., s.v.p. [ewn-boo-tehy]/[ewn-duh-mee-boo-tehy]-duh- . . . -seel-voo-play]
With ice, please.	Avec de la glace, s.v.p. [a-vehk-duh-la-gals-seel-voo-play]
Bon appétit!	Bon appétit! [boh-na-pay-tee]
Would you like anything else?	Vous désirez encore quelque chose? [voo-day-zee-ray-kehl-kuh-shoz]
Bring us . . ., please.	Apportez-nous . . ., s.v.p. [a-porh-tay-noo- . . . -seel-voo-play]
Could we have some more bread/water/wine, please?	Est-ce que vous pourriez nous apporter encore un peu de pain/un peu d'eau/un peu de vin, s.v.p.? [ehs-kuh-voo-poo-ryay-noo-za-pohr-tay-ahN-kohr-[aN-puuh-duh-paN]/[do]/[aN-puuh-duh-vaN]-seel-voo-play]

Complaints
Réclamations

I don't have any . . .	Je n'ai pas de . . . [zhuh-nay-pa-duh]
Have you forgotten my . . .?	Vous pensez à mon/ma/mes ..., n'est-ce pas? [voo-pahN-say-a-mohN/ma/may- . . . -nehs-pa]
I didn't order that.	Ce n'est pas ce que j'ai commandé. [suh-neh-pa-suh-kuh-zhay-ko-mahN-day]
The chicken is cold/too salty.	Le poulet est froid/trop salé. [lu-poo-lay-ay-frwa-/-tro-sa-lay]
The meat is too tough/too fat.	Cette viande est dure/trop grasse. [seht-vyahNd-ay-dewr-/-tro-gras]
The fish is not fresh.	Le poisson n'est pas frais. [luh-pwa-sohN-nay-pa-freh]
Take it back, please.	Ecoutez, vous pouvez remporter cela. [ay-koo-tay-voo-poo-vay-rahN-pohr-tay-sa]

Get the manager, please.	Allez chercher le patron, je vous prie. [a-lay-shehr-shay-luh-pa-trohN-zhuh-voo-pree]

The Check

L'addition

Could I have the bill, please?	L'addition, s.v.p.? [la-dee-syohN-seel-voo-play]
The bill, please. We are in a hurry.	L'addition, s.v.p. Nous sommes pressé(e)s. [la-dee-syohN-seel-voo-play-noo-sohm-pray-say]
I'll pay for everything together.	Je paie le tout. [zhuh-pay-luh-too]
Separate bills, please.	Vous faites des notes séparées, s.v.p. [voo-feht-day-noht-saya-pa-ray-seel-voo-play]
Is the service included?	Le service est compris? [luh-sehr-vees-ay-kohN-pree]
There seems to be a mistake in the bill.	Je crois qu'il y a une erreur dans l'addition. [zhuh-krwa-keel-ya-ewn-ay-ruhr-dahN-la-dee-syohN]
I didn't have . . . I had . . .	Je n'ai pas pris de . . . J'ai pris . . . [zhuh-nay-ap-pree-duh-. . .-zhay-pree]
Did you enjoy your meal?	C'était bon? [say-tay-bohN]
The food was excellent.	Le repas était excellent. [luh-ruh-pa-ay-tay-ehk-say-lahN]
That's for you.	Voilà pour vous. [vwa-la-poor-voo]
Keep the change.	C'est bon, vous gardez tout. [say-bohN-voo-gar-day-too]

As a Dinner Guest

Invitation à manger/Manger en compagnie

Thank you very much for the invitation.	Merci pour l'invitation. [mehr-see-poor-laN-vee-ta-syohN]
Help yourself!	Servez-vous! [sehr-vay-voo]
Cheers!	A votre santé/A la vôtre! [a-voh-truh-sahN-tay]/[a-la-votr]
Could you pass me the . . . please?	Vous pouvez me passer . . ., s.v.p.? [voo-poo-vay-muh-pa-say-...-seel-voo-play]
Would you like some more ...?	Encore un peu de . . .? [ahN-kohr-aN-puuh-duh]
No, thank you. It was plenty.	Non, merci. C'est trop. [nohN-mehr-see-say-tro]
I'm full, thank you.	Non, merci. Je n'ai plus faim. [nohN-mehr-see-zhuh-nay-plew-faN]
Do you mind if I smoke?	Je peux fumer? [zhuh-puuh-few-may]

Word List: Eating and Drinking — **See also Chapter 8, Word List: Food and Drink**

ashtray	le cendrier [luh-sahN-dree-yay]
baked	cuit(e) au four [kwee(t)-o-foor]
beer	la bière [la-byehr]
boiled	bouilli(e) [boo-yee]
bone *(fish)*	l'arête *(f)* [la-reht]
bones	l'os *(m)* [lohs]
bread	le pain [luh-paN]
breakfast	le petit déjeuner [luh-puh-tee-day-zhuuh-nay]
butter	le beurre [luh-buhr]
carafe	la carafe [la-ka-raf]
casserole	en daube [ahN-dob]
children's portion	la portion pour enfants [la-pohr-syohN-poor-ahN-fahN]
cloves	les clous *(m)* de girofle [lay-kloo-duh-zhee-rohfl]

coffeemaker	la cafetière [la-kaf-tyehr]
cold	froid(e) [frwa(d)]
to cook	faire cuire [fehr-kweer]
cook	le cuisinier/la cuisinière [luh-kwee-zee-nyay]/[la-kwee-zee-nyehr]
corkscrew	le tire-bouchon [luh-teer-boo-shohN]
cumin	le cumin [luh-kew-maN]
cup	la tasse [la-tas]
cutlery *(knife, fork, and spoon)*	les couverts *(m)* [lay-koo-vehr]
dessert	le dessert [luh-day-sehr]
diabetic	le diabétique [luh-dya-bay-teek]
dinner	le dîner [luh-dee-nay]
dish	le plat [luh-pla]
dishes	les mets *(m)* [lay-may]
draft, on tap	pression [pray-syohN]
to dress *(salad)*	assaisonner [a-say-zo-nay]
dressing *(salad)*	l'assaisonnement *(m)* [la-say-zohn-mahN]
drink	la boisson [la-bwa-sohN]
dry *(wine)*	sec [sehk]
eggcup	le coquetier [luh-kohk-tyay]
fat	gras/grasse [gra(s)]
first course	le hors-d'œuvre [luh-ohr-duhvr]
fork	la fourchette [la-foor-sheht]
french fries	les frites *(f)* [lay-freet]
fresh	frais/fraîche [freh(sh)]
fried	à la poêle [a-la-pwal]
garlic	l'ail *(m)* [la-y]
glass	le verre [luh-vehr]
grill	le gril [luh-greel]
grilled	sur le gril [sewr-luh-greel]
hard	dur(e) [dewr]
herbs	les herbes *(f)* [lay-zehrb]
homemade	(fait(e)) maison [feh(t)-meh-zohN]
hot	très chaud(e) [tray-sho(d)]
to be hungry	avoir faim [a-vwar-faN]
juicy	juteux/juteuse [zhew-tuuh(z)]
knife	le couteau [luh-koo-to]
laurel *(bay leaf)*	le laurier [luh-lo-ryay]
lean	maigre [mehgr]
lean cuisine	la cuisine diététique [la-kwee-zeen-dyay-tay-teek]
lemon	le citron [luh-see-trohN]
lunch	le déjeuner [luh-day-zhuuh-nay]

main course	le plat de résistance [luh-pla-duh-ray-zees-tahNs]
mayonnaise	la mayonnaise [la-ma-yo-nehz]
menu	la carte, le menu [la-kart]/[luh-muh-new]
menu of the day	le menu du jour [luh-muh-new-dew-zhoor]
mustard	la moutarde [la-moo-tard]
napkin	la serviette [la-sehr-vyeht]
nonalcoholic	sans alcool [sahN-zal-kohl]
noodles	les nouilles *(f)* [lay-nooy]
nutmeg	la muscade [la-mews-kad]
oil	l'huile *(f)* [lweel]
olive oil	l'huile *(f)* d'olive [lweel-do-leev]
olives	les olives *(f)* [lay-zo-leev]
onion	l'oignon *(m)* [lo-nyohN]
to order	commander [ko-mahN-day]
order	la commande [la-do-mahNd]
pan-fried dish	le plat fait à la poêle [luh-pla-feh-a-la-pwal]
paprika	le paprika [luh-pa-pree-ka]
parsley	le persil [luh-pehr-see]
pepper	le poivre [luh-pwavr]
pepper pot	la poivrière [la-pwa-vree-yehr]
plate	l'assiette *(f)* [la-syeht]
portion	la portion [la-pohr-syohN]
potatoes	les pommes *(f)* de terre [lay-pohm-duh-tehr]
prepared au gratin	gratiné(e) [gra-tee-nay]
raw	cru(e) [krew]
rice	le riz [luh-ree]
roasted	rôti(e) [ro-tee]
salad	la salade [la-sa-lad]
salad bar	le buffet de salades [luh-bew-fay-duh-sa-lad]
salt	le sel [luh-sehl]
salt container	la salière [la-sa-lyehr]
sauce	la sauce [la-sos]
saucer	la soucoupe [la-soo-koop]
to season	assaisonner [a-seh-zo-nay]
setting	le couvert [luh-koo-vehr]
slice	la tranche [la-trahNsh]
smoked	fumé(e) [few-may]
soft (egg)	(oeuf) mollet [uhf-mo-lay]
soup	la soupe [la-soop]
soup plate	l'assiette *(f)* creuse [la-syeht-kruuhz]

sour	aigre [ehgr]
specialty	la spécialité [la-spay-sya-lee-tay]
specialty of the day	le plat du jour [luh-pla-dew-zhoor]
spices	l'épice *(f)* [lay-pees]
spit-roasted	à la broche [a-la-brohsh]
spoon	la cuillère [la-kwee-yehr]
stain	la tache [la-tash]
steamed	à l'étouffée/à l'étuvée [a-lay-too-fay]/[a-lay-tew-vay]
straw	la paille [la-pa-y]
strong	fort(e) [fohr(t)]
stuffed	farci(e) [far-see]
stuffing	la farce [la-fars]
sugar	le sucre [luh-sewkr]
sweet	doux/douce [doo(s)]
sweetener	les sucrettes *(f)* [lay-sew-kreht]
tablecloth	la nappe [la-nap]
to taste	goûter [goo-tay]
taste	le goût [luh-goo]
teapot	la théière [la-tay-yehr]
teaspoon	la cuillère à thé [la-kwee-yehr-a-tay]
tender	tendre [tahNdr]
tip	le pourboire [luh-poor-bwar]
toothpick	le cure-dents [luh-kewr-dahN]
to uncork	déboucher [day-boo-shay]
to use	se servir [suh-sehr-veer]
vegetarian	végétarien/végétarienne [vay-zhay-teh-ryaN]/[vay-zhay-teh-ryehn]
vinegar	le vinaigre [luh-vee-nehgr]
waiter	le garçon [luh-gar-sohN]
waiter/waitress	le garçon/la serveuse [luh-gar-sohN]/[la-sehr-vuuhz]
water	l'eau *(f)* [lo]
water glass	le verre à eau [luh-vehr-a-o]
well done	bien cuit(e) [byaN-kwee(t)]
wine	le vin [luh-vaN]
wine glass	le verre à vin [luh-vehr-a-vaN]

Menu

Carte

Potages et Soupes	Soups
bisque d'écrevisses [beesk-day-kruh-vees]	lobster bisque
bouillabaisse [boo-ya-behs]	French Mediterranean fish soup
consommé de poulet [kohN-so-may-duh-poo-lay]	chicken soup
potage au cresson [po-tazh-o-kray-sohN]	watercress soup
soupe à l'oignon [soop-a-lo-nyohN]	onion soup
soupe de poisson [soop-duh-pwa-sohN]	fish soup
soupe à la tortue [soop-a-la-tohr-tew]	turtle soup
velouté d'asperges [vuh-loo-tay-das-pehrzh]	cream of asparagus soup

Hors-d'œuvre	Cold Hors d'oeuvres
asperges à la crème [as-pehrzh-ala-krehm]	asparagus with cream sauce
avocat vinaigrette [a-vo-ka-a-la-vee-neh-greht]	avocado with vinaigrette dressing
cœurs d'artichauts [kuhr-dar-tee-sho]	artichoke hearts
crudités variées [krew-dee-tay-va-ryay]	raw vegetables
filets de harengs [fee-lay-duh-a-rahN]	herring filets
jambon cru [zhahN-bohN-krew]	raw ham
jambon fumé [zhahN-bohN-few-may]	smoked ham
melon au porto [muh-lohN-o-pohr-to]	melon with port wine
pâté de campagne [pa-tay-duh-kahN-pany]	country paté
pâté de foie [pa-tay-duh-fwa]	liverwurst
pissenlits au lard [pee-sahN-lee-o-lar]	salad with bacon
rillettes [ree-yeht]	pork paté

salade niçoise [sa-lad-nee-swaz]	green salad, with tuna, tomatoes, olive, eggs, anchovies
salade russe [sa-lad-rews]	Russian salad
sardines à l'huile [sar-deen-a-lweel]	sardines in oil
saumon fumé [so-mohN-few-may]	smoked salmon
terrine de canard [tay-reen-duh-ka-nar]	duck paté
terrine de saumon [tay-reen-duh-so-mohN]	salmon mousse

Entrées — Entrées

bouchées à la reine [boo-shay-a-la-rehn]	pastry shells filled with mushrooms
cuisses de grenouilles [kwees-duh-gruh-nooy]	frogs' legs
escargots à la bourguignonne [ehs-kar-go-a-la-boor-gee-nyohn]	snails with garlic butter
omelette aux champignons [ohm-leht-o-shahN-pee-nyohN]	mushroom omelette
pied de porc [pyay-duh-pohr]	pork feet
quiche lorraine [keesh-lo-rehn]	quiche with egg and ham
tête de veau vinaigrette [teht-duh-vo-vee-nay-greht]	veal head with vinaigrette
tripes [treep]	tripes

Crustacés et coquillages — Shellfish and Seafood

coquilles Saint-Jacques [ko-keey-saN-zhak]	scallops
crevettes [kruh-veht]	shrimp, crabs
écrevisse [ay-kruh-vees]	crayfish
homard [o-mar]	lobster
huitres [weetr]	oysters
langouste au gratin [lahN-goost-o-gra-taN]	crayfish gratin (baked with cheese)
langoustines [lahN-goos-teen]	scampi
moules [mool]	mussels
plateau de fruits de mer [pla-to-duh-frwee-duh-mehr]	seafood platter

Poissons	Fish
Poissons de mer [pwa-sohN-duh-mehr]	Seafood
fruit de mer [frwee-duh-mehr]	shellfish
cabillaud [ka-bee-yo]	cod
calamar frit [ka-la-mar-free]	fried calamari
colin [ko-laN]	whitefish
daurade [do-rad]	sea bream
hareng [a-rahN]	herring
lotte (de mer) [loht-duh-mehr]	monkfish
maquereau [mak-ro]	mackerel
morue [mo-rew]	cod
rouget [roo-zhay]	red mullet
sole au gratin [sohl-o-gra-taN]	baked sole au gratin
turbot [tewr-bo]	turbot

Poissons d'eau douce	Freshwater Fish
anguille [ahN-geey]	eel
brochet au bleu [bro-shay-o-bluuh]	pike
carpe [karp]	carp
perche [pehrsh]	perch
petite friture [puh-teet-free-tewr]	fried fish
quenelles de brochet [kuh-nehl-duh-bro-shay]	pike dumplings
sandre [sahNdr]	zander
truite meunière [trweet-muh-nyehr]	trout rolled in flour and sautéed in butter

Viandes	Meat
agneau [a-nyo]	lamb
bœuf [buhf]	beef
mouton [moo-tohN]	mutton
porc [pohr]	pork
veau [vo]	veal
bifteck [beef-tehk]	steak
blanquette de veau [blahN-keht-duh-vo]	veal casserole
bœuf bourguignon [buhf-boor-gee-nyohN]	beef casserole with red wine
cassoulet [ka-soo-lay]	beans and lamb casserole
cochon de lait [ko-shohN-duh-leh]	suckling pig
cœur [kuhr]	heart
côte de bœuf [kot-duh-buhf]	beef chop
entrecôte [ahN-truh-kot]	type of steak
épaule [ay-pol]	shoulder chop
escalope de veau	veal cutlet
escalope panée [ehs-ka-lohp-pa-nay]	breaded veal cutlet
filet de bœuf [fee-lay-duh-buhf]	filet of beef
foie [fwa]	liver
gigot d'agneau [zhee-go-da-nyo]	leg of lamb
grillades [gree-yad]	broiled meat
jarret de veau [zha-ray-duh-vo]	veal shank
langue [lahNg]	tongue
pieds de cochon [pyay-duh-ko-shohN]	pork feet
paupiettes [po-pyeht]	thin stuffed veal
rognons [ro-nyohN]	kidneys
rôti [ro-tee]	roast
sauté de veau [so-tay-duh-vo]	sautéed veal
steak au poivre [stehk-o-pwavr]	pepper steak
steak tartare [stehk-tar-tar]	tartar steak (raw seasoned beef)

Volailles et gibier	Poultry and Game
canard à l'orange [ka-nar-a-lo-rahNzh]	duck with orange sauce
civet de lièvre [see-vay-duh-lyehvr]	wild rabbit with wine sauce
coq au vin [kohk-o-vaN]	chicken in wine sauce
cuissot de chevreuil [kwee-so-duh-shuh-vruhy]	venison (deer)
dinde aux marrons [daNd-o-ma-rohN]	turkey with chestnuts
faisan [fuh-zahN]	pheasant
lapin chasseur [la-paN-sha-suhr]	rabbit, hunter style
oie aux marrons [wa-o-ma-rohN]	goose with chestnuts
perdrix [pehr-dree]	partridge
pigeons [pee-zhohN]	pigeons
pintade [paN-tad]	guinea fowl
poule au riz [pool-o-ree]	chicken with rice
poulet rôti [poo-lay-ro-tee]	roasted chicken
sanglier [sahN-glee-yay]	wild boar

Légumes	Vegetable
choucroute [shoo-kroot]	sauerkraut
chou farci [shoo-far-see]	stuffed cabbage
chou-fleur [shoo-fluhr]	cauliflower
endives au gratin [ahN-deev-o-gra-taN]	Belgian endive with cheese
épinards [ay-pee-nar]	spinach
fenouil [fuh-nooy]	fennel
macédoine de légumes [ma-say-dwan-duh-lay-gewm]	mixed vegetables
petits pois [puh-tee-pwa]	peas

pommes de terre sautées [pohm-duh-tehr-so-tay]	fried potatoes
purée de pommes de terre [pew-ray-duh-pohm-duh-tehr]	mashed potatoes
pommes natures [pohm-na-tewr]	boiled potatoes
ratatouille niçoise [ra-ta-tooy-nee-swaz]	mixture of zucchini, eggplant, red peppers, tomato sauce and spices
tomates farcies [to-mat-far-see]	stuffed tomatoes

Pâtes et riz — Pasta and Rice

macaronis [ma-ka-ro-nee]	macaroni
nouilles [nooy]	noodles
riz au curry [ree-o-kew-ree]	rice with curry sauce

Fromages — Cheese

fromage blanc [fro-mazh-blahN]	cream cheese
fromage de chèvre [fro-mazh-duh-shehvr]	goat cheese
gruyère [grew-yehr]	Swiss cheese
petit suisse [puh-tee-swees]	soft cream cheese
roquefort [rohk-fohr]	blue cheese
yaourt [ya-oort]	yogurt

Desserts	Dessert
baba au rhum [ba-ba-o-rohm]	pastry with rum and whipped cream
beignets aux pommes [beh-nyay-o-pohm]	apple doughnuts
crème Sabayon [krehm-sa-ba-yohN]	Sabayon cream
flan [flahN]	caramel custard
gâteau [ga-to]	cake
mousse au chocolat [moos-o-sho-ko-la]	chocolate mousse
omelette norvégienne [ohm-leht-nohr-vay-zhyehn]	ice cream topped with baked meringue
pain perdu [paN-pehr-dew]	French toast
pâtisserie maison [pa-tees-ree-meh-zohN]	homemade pastries
profiteroles [pro-feet-rohl]	profiteroles
tarte aux fraises [tart-o-frehz]	strawberry tart

Fruits	Fruit
abricots [a-bree-ko]	apricots
cerises [suh-reez]	cherries
macédoine de fruits [ma-say-dwan-duh-frwee]	fruit salad
pêches [pehsh]	peaches
poires [pwar]	pears
pommes [pohm]	apples
prunes [prewn]	plums
raisin [reh-zaN]	grapes

Glaces	Ice creams
au café [o-ka-fay]	moka
au chocolat [o-sho-ko-la]	chocolate
à la fraise [a-la-frehz]	strawberry
à la pistache [a-la-pees-tash]	pistachio
à la vanille [a-la-va-neey]	vanilla
café liégeois [ka-fay-lyay-zhwa]	coffee ice cream with whipped cream
coupe maison [koop-meh-zohN]	specialty ice cream sundae
sorbet au citron [sohr-bay-o-see-trohN]	lemon sherbet

List of Beverages

Liste des Consommations

Vin rouge et vin blanc	White and Red Wine
un (verre de vin) rouge [aN-vehr-duh-vaN-roozh]	a glass of red wine
1 quart de vin blanc [kar-duh-vaN-blahN]	a quarter of a liter of white wine
1 pichet de rosé [pee-shay-duh-ro-zay]	a carafe of rosé

Appellation contrôlée	Types of Wine
Beaujolais [bo-zho-lay]	Beaujolais wine (red)
Bordeaux [bohr-do]	Bordeaux red wine (dry), sweeter white wine
Bourgogne [boor-gohny]	Burgundy wine
Champagne [shahN-pany]	Champagne
Côtes-de-Provence [kot-duh-pro-vahNs]	Côtes-de-Provence (red or rosé wines)
Côtes-du-Rhône [kot-dew-ron]	Côtes-du-Rhône (red wine)

Bière	Beer
- pression [pray-syohN]	draft beer
un demi [aN-duh-mee]	a quarter of a liter
un sérieux [aN-say-ryuuh]	a half a liter
- bouteille [boo-tehy]	a bottle of beer

Apéritifs	Aperitifs
Byrrh, Dubonnet [dew-bo-nay]	sweet wine
Pernod, [pehr-no]	drink with anis
Ricard [ree-kar]	
Suze [sewz]	aperitif with gentian

## Alcools et liqueurs	## After Dinner Drinks
Armagnac [ar-ma-nyak]	Armagnac
Calvados [kal-va-dos]	Calvados (apple liqueur)
Chartreuse [shar-truuhz]	Chartreuse (gentian liqueur)
Framboise [frahN-bwaz]	raspberry liqueur
Marc [mar]	marc
Mirabelle [mee-ra-behl]	mirabelle brandy
Rhum [rohm]	rum
Cognac [ko-nyak]	cognac

Cidre [sidr] — Apple Cider

Jus de fruits [zhew-duh-frwee] — Fruit Juice

Café et thé [ka-fay-ay-tay] — Coffee and Tea

café crème [ka-fay-krehm]	coffee with cream
café express [ka-fay-ehk-sprehs]	espresso
café au lait [ka-fay-o-lay]	coffee with milk
thé nature/au lait/au citron [tay-[na-tewr]/[o-lay]/[o-see-trohN]	tea with milk/with lemon

6 Culture and Nature
Culture et nature

At the Visitor's (Tourist) Center

Au syndicat d'initiative/A l'office detourisme

I'd like a map of the town, please.	Je voudrais un plan de . . . [zhuh-voo-dray-aN-plahN-duh]
Do you have brochures on . . .?	Vous avez des prospectus sur . . .? [zhuh-voo-dray-day-prohs-pehk-tews-sewr]
Do you have a schedule of events for this week?	Vous avez le programme des spectacles de cette semaine? [voo-za-vay-luh-pro-gram-day-spehk-takl-duh-seht-suh-mehn]
Are there sightseeing tours of the town (city)?	Est-ce qu'il y a des tours de ville en car d'organisés? [ehs-keel-ya-day-toor-ohr-ga-nee-zay-ahN-kar-dohr-ga-nee-zay]
How much does the tour cost?	Quel est le prix du billet? [kehl-ay-luh-pree-dew-bee-yay]

Places of Interest/Museums

Curiosités/Musées

What places of interest are there here?	Quelles sont les curiosités de la ville? [kehl-sohN-lay-kew-ryo-zee-tay-duh-la-veel]
We'd like to visit . . .	Nous aimerions visiter . . . [noo-zay-muh-ryohN-vee-zee-tay]
When is the museum open?	A quelle heure ouvre le musée? [a-kehl-uhr-oovr-luh-mew-zay]
When does the tour start?	La visite guidée est à quelle heure? [la-vee-zeet-ay-a -kehl-uhr]
Is there a tour in English?	Est-ce qu'il y a une visite guidée en anglais? [ehs-keel-ya-ewn-vee-zeet-gee-day-ahN-nahN-glay]
Are we allowed to take pictures here?	Est-ce qu'on peut prendre des photos? [ehs-kohN-puuh-prahNdr-day-fo-to]
What square/church is this?	Quel est le nom de cette place/cette église, s.v.p.? [kehl-ay-luh-nohN-duh-seht-[plas]/[ay-gleez]

Is this . . .?	C'est . . ., ça? [say-...-sa]
When was this building built/restored?	Quand est-ce que ce bâtiment a été construit/restauré? [kahN-tehs-kuh-suh-ba-tee-mahN-a-ay-tay-[kohNs-trwee]/[rehs-to-ray]]
From which period are these buildings?	De quelle époque date ce monument? [duh-kehl-ay-pohk-dat-suh-mo-new-mahN]
Are there others works designed by this architect in this town?	Est-ce qu'il y a en ville d'autres réalisations de cet architecte? [ehs-keel-ya-ahN-veel-do-truh-ray-a-lee-za-syohN-duh-seht-ar-shee-tehkt]
Are the excavations completed?	Est-ce que les fouilles sont terminées? [ehs-kuh-lay-fooy-sohN-tehr-mee-nay]
Where are the objects exhibited?	Où sont exposés les objets découverts? [oo-sohN-lay-zohb-zhay-day-koo-vehr]
Who has painted this work/carved this sculpture?	Qui a peint ce tableau/réalisé cette sculpture? [kee-a-[paN-suh-ta-blo]/[ray-a-lee-zay-seht-skewl-tewr]
Is there an exhibition catalog?	Est-ce qu'il y a un catalogue de cette exposition? [ehs-keel-ya-aN-ka-ta-lohg-duh-seht-ehk-spo-zee-syohN]
Do you have a poster/postcard/slide of this work?	Est-ce que vous avez ce tableau sous forme de poster/carte postale/diapo? [ehs-kuh-voo-za-vay-suh-ta-blo-soo-fohrm-duh-[pohs-tehr]/[kart-pos-tal]/[dya-po]]

Word List: Places of Interest/Museums

abbey	l'abbaye *(f)* [la-bay-ee]
altar	l'autel *(m)* [lo-tehl]
ambulatory	le déambulatoire [luh-day-ahN-bew-la-twar]
amphitheater	l'amphithéâtre *(m)* [lahN-fee-tay-a-truh]
ancient	antique [ahN-teek]
apogee	l'apogée *(m)* [la-po-zhay]
aquaduct	l'aqueduc *(m)* [lak-dewk]
arch	l'arc *(m)* [lark]
archaeology	l'archéologie *(f)* [lar-kay-o-lo-zhee]
architect	l'architecte *(m/f)* [lar-shee-tehkt]

architecture	l'architecture *(f)* [lar-shee-tehk-tewr]
arena	l'arène *(f)* [la-rehn]
art	l'art *(m)* [lar]
Art Nouveau	le style 1900 [luh-steel-meel-nuhf-sahN]
arts and crafts	les arts *(m)* décoratifs [lay-zar-day-ko-ra-teef]
baroque	le baroque [luh-ba-rohk]
bell	la cloche [la-klohsh]
bell tower	le clocher [luh-klo-shay], le carillon [luh-ka-ree-yohN]
birthplace	la ville natale [la-veel-na-tal]
bischop's place/ diocesan town	l'évêché *(m)* [lay-vay-shay]
bridge	le pont [luh-pohN]
bronze	le bronze [luh-brohNz]
Bronze Age	l'âge *(m)* de bronze [lazh-duh-brohNz]
building	le bâtiment [luh-ba-tee-mahN]
business district	la ville commerciale [la-veel-ko-mehr-syal]
bust	le buste [luh-bewst]
Byzantine	byzantin(e) [bee-zahN-taN]/[bee-zahN-teen]
candlestick	le candélabre [luh-kahN-day-lahNbr]
capital	le chapiteau [luh-sha-pee-to]
carpet	le tapis [luh-ta-pee]
carving	la sculpture sur bois [la-skewl-tewr-sewr-bwa]
castle	le château [luh-sha-to]
catacombs	les catacombes *(f)* [lay-ka-ta-kohNb]
cathedra/throne	la chaire [la-shehr]
cathedral	la cathédrale [la-ka-tay-dral]
Catholic	le catholique [luh-ka-to-leek]
cave painting	la peinture préhistorique [la-paN-tewr-pray-ees-to-reek]
ceiling	le plafond [luh-pla-fohN]
ceiling painting	la peinture sur plafonds [la-paN-tewr-sewr-pla-fohN]
Celtic	celte [sehlt]
cemetery	le cimetière [luh-seem-tyehr]
center of the city	le centre-ville [luh-sahN-truh-veel]
century	le siècle [luh-syehkl]
ceramics	la céramique [la-say-ra-meek]
changing of the guard	la relève de la garde [la-ruh-lehv-duh-la-gard]
chapel	la chapelle [la-sha-pehl]

choir	le chœur [luh-kuhr]
choir stall	la stalle [la-stal]
Christian	le chrétien [luh-kray-tyaN]
Christianity	le christianisme [luh-krees-tya-neesm]
church	*(cath)* l'église *(f)* [lay-gleez] *(ev)* le temple [luh-tahNpl]
circuit/tour	le circuit [luh-seer-kwee]
Cistercians	les cisterciens [lay-sees-tehr-syaN]
citadelle	la citadelle [la-see-ta-dehl]
city hall	la mairie [la-meh-ree], l'hôtel *(m)* de ville [lo-tehl-duh-veel]
city in ruins	la ville en ruines [la-veel-ahN-rween]
classicism	le classicisme [luh-kla-see-seesm]
cloister	le monastère [luh-mo-nas-tehr]
collage	le collage [luh-ko-lazh]
colonnade	les arcades *(f)* [lay-zar-kad]
column	la colonne [la-ko-lohn]
copperplate	la gravure sur cuivre [la-gra-vewr-sewr-kweevr]
copy	la copie [la-kopee]
Corinthian	corinthien/ne [ko-raN-tyaN]/[ko-ran-tyehn]
to cremate	incinérer [aN-see-nay-ray]
cross	la croix [la-krwa]
crucifix	le crucifix [luh-krew-see-feeks]
crypt	la crypte [la-kreept]
cubism	le cubisme [luh-kew-beezm]
cult of the dead	le culte des morts [luh-kewlt-day-mohr]
curios	les curiosités *(f)* [lay-kew-ryo-zee-tay]
customs	la coutume [la-koo-tewm]
design	le design [luh-dee-sa-y-n]
dig, excavations	les fouilles *(f)* [lay-fooy]
dome	le dôme [luh-dom], la coupole [la-koo-pohl]
doric	dorique [do-reek]
drawing	le dessin [luh-day-saN]
dynasty	la dynastie [la-dee-nas-tee]
early Gothic	le gothique primitif [luh-go-teek-pree-mee-teef]
ecclesiastic, priest	l'ecclésiastique *(m)* [lay-klay-zyas-teek]
emblem	l'emblème *(m)* [lahN-blehm]
emperor/empress	l'empereur *(m)* [lahN-puh-ruhr] /l'impératrice *(f)* [laN-pay-ra-trees]
epoch	l'époque *(f)* [lay-pohk]
etching	la gravure à l'eau-forte *(f)* [la-gra-vewr-a-lo-fohrt]

View from Notre Dame, Paris

exhibition	l'exposition *(f)* [lehk-spo-zee-syohN]
expressionism	l'expressionnisme *(m)* [lehk-spray-syo-neesm]
façade	la façade [la-fa-sad]
finds	les objets *(m)* découverts [lay-zohb-zhay-day-koo-vehr]
Flemish	flamand(e) [fla-mahN(d)]
floor plan	le plan [luh-plahN]
flying buttress	l'arc-boutant *(m)* [lark-boo-tahN]
folklore museum	le musée d'art populaire [luh-mew-zay-dar-po-pew-lehr]
font	les fonts *(m)* baptismaux [lay-fohN-ba-teez-mo]
fortress	la forteresse [la-fohr-tuh-rehs]
foundations	les fondations *(f)* [lay-fohN-da-syohN]
fountain	la fontaine [la-fohN-tehn]
fresco	la fresque [la-frehsk]
frieze	la frise [la-freez]
gable	le fronton [luh-frohN-tohN]
gallery	la galerie (de peinture) [la-gal-ree-duh-paN-tewr]
gate	la porte [la-pohrt]
glass painting	la peinture sur verre [la-paN-tewr-sewr-vehr]
gold work	l'orfèvrerie *(f)* [lohr-feh-vruh-ree]

gothic	gothique [go-teek]
Gothic	le gothique [luh-go-teek]
Gothic revival	le néo-gothique [luh-nay-o-go-teek]
graphic	l'art *(m)* graphique [lar-gra-feek]
grave/sepulcher	le tombeau [luh-tohN-bo]
greek	grec/grecque [grehk]
Greek	les Grecs *(m)* [lay-grehk]
guide	le guide [luh-geed]
guided tour	la visite guidée [la-vee-zeet-gee-day]
high Gothic	le gothique rayonnant [luh-go-teek-ray-yo-nahN]
history	l'histoire *(f)* [lees-twar]
illustration	l'illustration *(f)* [lee-lews-tra-syohN]
impressionism	l'impressionnisme *(m)* [laN-pray-syo-neesm]
influence	l'influence *(f)* [laN-flew-ahNs]
ink	l'encre *(f)* de Chine [lahN-kruh-duh-sheen]
inner courtyard	la cour intérieur [la-koor-aN-tay-ryuhr]
inscription	l'inscription *(f)* [laNs-kreep-syohN]
Ionic	ionique [ee-ro-eek]
Jew	le juif [luh-zhweef]
king/queen	le roi/la reine [luh-rwa]/[la-rehn]
library	la bibliothèque [la-bee-blee-o-tehk]
lithograph	la lithographie [la-lee-to-gra-fee]
long nave	la longue nef [la-lohNg-nehf]
mannerism	le maniérisme [luh-ma-nyay-reezm]
mannerist	de/du maniérisme [duh/dew-ma-nyay-reezm]
marble	le marbre [luh-marbr]
market	le marché [luh-mar-shay]
marketplace	les halles [lay-al]
marquetry	les marqueteries *(f)* [lay-mar-keht-ree]
mausoleum	le mausolée [luh-mo-zo-lay]
mayor/mayoress	le maire [luh-mehr]
medieval	médiéval/e [may-dyay-val]
medium	le matériau [luh-ma-tay-ryo]
Middle Ages	le Moyen Age [luh-mwa-yehn-azh]
minaret	le minaret [luh-mee-na-ray]
model	le modèle [luh-mo-dehl]
modern	moderne [mo-dehrn]
monument	le monument [luh-mo-new-mahN]
monument protection	la protection des monuments [la-pro-tehk-syohN-day-mo-new-mahN]
mosaic	la mosaïque [la-mo-za-eek]

Moslem — le musulman [luh-mew-zewl-mahN]
mosque — la mosquée [la-mos-kay]
multivision — la multivision [la-mewl-tee-vee-zyohN]
museum — le musée [luh-mew-zay]
nave — la nef centrale [la-nehf-sahN-tral]; la nef [la-nehf]
neoclassicism — le néo-classicisme [luh-nay-o-kla-see-seesm]
Norman — normand/e [nohr-mahN(d)]
the nude — le nu [luh-new]
obelisk — l'obélisque *(m)* [lo-bay-leesk]
object — l'objet *(m)* exposé [lohb-zhay-ehk-spo-zay]
oil painting — la peinture à l'huile [la-paN-tewr-a-lweel]
old city/historic district — la vieille ville [la-vyehy-veel]
opera — l'opéra *(m)* [lo-pay-ra]
order *(rel)* — les ordres *(m)* [lay-zohrdr]
organ — l'orgue *(m)* [lohrg]
original — l'original *(m)* [lo-ree-zhee-nal]
ornament — l'ornement *(m)* [lohr-nuh-mahN]
pagan — paiën/paiënne [pa-aN]/[pa-ehn]

Louvre Museum, Paris

painter — le peintre [luh-paNtr]
painting — la peinture [la-paN-tewr]
painting collection — la collection de tableaux [la-ko-lehk-syohN-duh-ta-blo]
palace — le palais [luh-pa-lay]

pantry/kitchen	l'office *(m)* [lo-fees]
parchment	le parchemin [luh-par-shuh-maN]
pastel	le pastel [luh-pas-tehl]
pavilion	le pavillon [luh-pa-vee-yohN]
photography	la photographie [la-fo-to-gra-fee]
photomontage	le montage photographique [luh-mohN-tazh-fo-to-gra-feek]
picture	le tableau [luh-ta-blo]
pilgrim	le pèlerin [luh-pehl-raN]
pilgrimage	le pèlerinage [luh-pehl-ree-nazh]
pilgrimage church	l'église *(f)* de pèlerinage [lay-gleez-duh-pehl-ree-nazh]
pillage	le pillage [luh-pee-yazh]
pillar	le pilier [luh-pee-lyay]
place of worship	le lieu de culte [luh-lyuuh-duh-kewlt]
pointed arch	l'arc *(m)* en ogive [lark-ahN-o-zheev]
pointillism	le pointillisme [luh-pwaN-tee-yeezm]
porcelain	la porcelaine [la-pohr-suh-lehn]
portal	le portail [luh-pohr-ta-y]
portrait	le portrait [luh-pohr-tray]
poster	l'affiche *(f)* [la-feesh]
pottery	la poterie [la-poht-ree]
prehistoric	préhistorique [pray-ees-to-reek]
projection	la saillie *(m)* [la-sa-yee]
Protestant	le protestant [luh-pro-tehs-tahN]
to rebuild	reconstruire [ruh-kohNs-trweer]
to reconstitute	reconstituer [ruh-kohNs-tee-tway]
relief	le relief [luh-ruh-lyehf]
religion	la religion [la-ruh-lee-zhyohN]
remains	les vestiges *(m)* [lay-vehs-teezh]
Renaissance	la Renaissance [la-ruh-neh-sahNs]
to restore	restaurer [rehs-to-ray]
restoration	la restauration [la-rehs-to-ra-syohN]
rococo	le style Louis XV [luh-steel-lwee-kaNz]
Romanesque	roman/e [ro-maN]/[ro-man]
Romanesque period	l'art *(m)* roman [lar-ro-mahN]
Romanticism	le romantisme [luh-ro-mahN-teezm]
roof	le toit [luh-twa]
rosette	la rosace [la-ro-zas]
round arch	l'arc *(m)* en plein cintre [lark-ahN-plaN-saNtr]
ruin	la ruine [la-rween]
sacristy	la sacristie [la-sa-krees-tee]
sandstone	le grès [luh-gray]

sarcophagus	le sarcophage [luh-sar-ko-fazh]
school	l'école *(f)* [lay-kohl]
sculptor	le sculpteur [luh-skewl-tuhr]
sculpture	la sculpture [la-skewl-tewr]
sightseeing tour of the town/city	le tour de ville [luh-toor-duh-la-veel]
silk screen print(ing)	la sérigraphie [la-say-ree-gra-fee]
square	la place [la-plas]
statue	la statue [la-sta-tew]
still life	la nature morte [la-na-tewr-mohrt]
Stone Age	l'âge *(m)* de pierre [lazh-duh-pyehr]
stucco	le stuc [luh-stewk]
style	le style [luh-steel]
surrealism	le surréalisme [luh-sewr-ray-a-leezm]
symbolism	le symbolisme [luh-saN-bo-leezm]
synagogue	la synagogue [la-see-na-gohg]
tapestry	la tapisserie [la-ta-pees-ree]
temple	le temple [luh-tahNpl]
terracotta	la terre cuite [la-tehr-kweet]
theater	le théâtre [luh-tay-atr]
tomb	la tombe [la-tohNb]
tombstone	la pierre tombale [la-pyehr-tohN-bal]
torso	le torse [luh-tohrs]
tour	la visite [la-vee-zeet]
tower	la tour [la-toor]
transept	le transept [luh-trahN-seht]
transept crossing	la croisée du transept [la-krwa-zay-dew-trahN-seht]
treasure chamber	la chambre du trésor [la-shaNbr-dew-tray-zohr]
triumphal arch	l'arc *(m)* de triomphe [lark-duh-tree-yohNf]
university	l'université *(f)* [lew-nee-vehr-see-tay]
vase	le vase [luh-vaz]
vault(s)	la voûte [la-voot]
Vikings	les Wikings *(m)* [lay-vee-keeng]
wall	le mur [luh-mewr]
wall painting	la peinture murale [la-paN-tewr-mew-ral]
walls	les murs *(m)* de la ville [lay-mewr-duh-la-veel]
watercolor	l'aquarelle *(f)* [la-kwa-rehl]
weaving	le tissage [luh-tee-sazh]
window	la fenêtre [la-fuh-nehtr]
wing	l'aile *(f)* [lehl]

wood carving	la sculpture sur bois [la-skewl-tewr-sewr-bwa]
woodcut	la gravure sur bois [la-gra-vewr-sewr-bwa]
work	l'œuvre *(f)* [luhvr]
early works	les œuvres *(f)* de jeunesse [lay-zuh-vruh-duh-zhuuh-nehs]
late works	les dernières œuvres *(f)* [lay-dehr-nyehr-zuhvr]
yard	la cour [la-koor]

The Musée d'Orsay, Paris

Excursions

Excursions

Can you see . . . from here?	Est-ce que, d'ici, on peut voir . . .? [ehs-kuh-dee-see-ohNuuh-vwar]
What direction is . . .?	Dans quelle direction se trouve . . .? [dahN-kehl-dee-rehk-syohN-suh-troov]
Will we pass . . .?	Est-ce que nous allons passer devantle/la . . .? [ehs-kuh-noo-za-lohN-pa-say-duh-vahN-luh/la]
Are we going to see . . ., too?	Est-ce qu'on va visiter également . . .? [ehs-kohN-va-vee-zee-tay-ay-gal-mahN]
How much free time do we have at . . . ?	On a quartier libre pendant combien de temps, à . . .? [ohN-na-kar-tyay-leebr-pahN-dahN-kohN-byaN-duh-tahN]
When are we leaving?	A quelle heure est-ce que nous repartons? [a-kehl-uhr-ehs-kuh-noo-ruh-par-tohN]
When will we be back?	A quelle heure serons-nous de retour? [a-kehl-uhr-suh-rohN-noo-duh-ruh-toor]

Word List: Excursions

amusement park	le parc de loisirs [luh-park-duh-lwa-zeer]
bird sanctuary	le parc ornithologique [luh-park-ohr-nee-to-lo-zheek]
botanical gardens	le jardin botanique [luh-zhar-daN-bo-ta-neek]
cave	la caverne [la-ka-vehrn]
cave with stalagtites and stalagmites	la grotte à stalactites et à stalagmites [la-groht-a-sta-lak-teet-ay-a-sta-lag-meet]
cliff	l'écueil *(m)* [lay-kuhy]
day trip	l'excursion *(f)* pour une journée [lehk-skewr-syohN-poor-ewn-zhoor-nay]
dike/embankment	la digue [la-deeg]
excursion	l'excursion *(f)* [lehk-skewr-syohN]
fishing port	le port de pêche [luh-pohr-duh-pehsh]
fishing village	le village de pêcheurs [luh-vee-lazh-duh-peh-shuhr]

forest/woods	la forêt [la-fo-ray]
forest fire	l'incendie *(m)* de forêt [laN-sahN-dee-duh-fo-ray]
gorge	la gorge [la-gorzh]
grotto	la grotte [la-groht]
hinterland	l'arrière-pays *(m)* [la-ryehr-pay-ee]
island tour	le tour de l'île [luh-toor-duh-leel]
landscape	le paysage [luh-pay-ee-zazh]
lava	la lave [la-lav]
market	le marché [luh-mar-shay]
moor	la lande [la-lahNd]
mountain	la montagne [la-mohN-tany]
mountain village	le village de montagne [luh-vee-lazh-duh-mohN-tany]
national park	le parc national [luh-park-na-syo-nal]
nature reserve	le parc naturel régional [luh-park-na-tew-rehl-ray-zhyo-nal]
observatory	l'observatoire *(m)* [lohb-sehr-va-twar]
open-air museum	le musée en plein air [luh-mew-zay-ahN-plehn-ehr]
panorama	le panorama [luh-pa-no-ra-ma]
pass	le col [luh-kohl]
pilgrimage site	le lieu de pèlerinage [luh-lyuuh-duh-pehl-ree-nazh]
planetarium	le planétarium [luh-pla-nay-ta-ryohm]
reef	le récif [luh-ray-seef]
sea	la mer [la-mehr]
suburb	la banlieue [la bahN-lyuuh]
surroundings	les environs *(m)* [lay-zahN-vee-rohN]
tour	le circuit [luh-seer-kwee]
valley	la vallée [la-va-lay]
vantage point	le point de vue [luh-pwaN-duh-vew]
volcano	le volcan [luh-voh-kahN]
waterfall	la chute (d'eau) [la-shewt-do]
zoo	le zoo [luh-zo-o]

Events/Entertainment
Manifestation culturelles/Distractions

Theater/Concert/Movies	Théâtre/Concert/Cinéma
What's playing at the theater tonight?	Quelle pièce est-ce qu'on joue ce soir, au théâtre? [kehl-pyehs-ehs-kohN-zhoo-suh-swar-o-tay-atr]
What's playing at the movies tomorrow night?	Qu'est-ce qu'il joue demain soir au cinéma? [kehs-keel-zhoo-duh-maN-swar-o-see-nay-ma]
Are there concerts at the cathedral?	Est-ce qu'il y a des concerts d'organisés dans la cathédrale? [ehs-keel-ya-day-kohN-sehr-dohr-ga-nee-zay-dahN-la-ka-tay-dral]
Can you recommend a good play?	Vous pouvez m'indiquer une bonne pièce de théâtre? [voo-poo-vay-maN-dee-kay-ewn-bohn-pyehs-duh-tay-atr]
When does the performance start?	A quelle heure commence la représentation? [a-kehl-uhr-ko-mahNs-la-ruh-pray-zahN-ta-syohN]
Where can I get tickets?	Où est-ce qu'on peut prendre les billets? [oo-ehs-kohN-puuh-prahNdr-lay-bee-yay]
Two tickets for this evening, please.	Deux billets pour ce soir, s.v.p. [duuh-bee-yay-poor-suh-swar]
Two seats at . . ., please.	Deux places à . . ., s.v.p. [duuh-plas-a-. . . -seel-voo-play]
Two adults and one child.	Deux adultes et un enfant. [duuh-za-dewlt-ay-aN-nahN-fahN]
A program, please.	Le programme, s.v.p. [luh-pro-gram-seel-voo-play]
When does the performance end?	A quelle heure se termine la représentation/séance? [a-kehl-uhr-suh-tehr-meen-la-[ruh-pray-zahN-ta-syohN]/[la-say-ahNs]
Where is the cloakroom?	Où est le vestiaire, s.v.p.? [oo-ay-luh-vehs-tyehr-see-voo-play]

Word List: Theater/Concert/Movies

accompaniment	l'accompagnement *(m)* [la-kohN-pa-nyuh-mahN]
act	l'acte *(m)* [lakt]
actor/actress (movie)	l'acteur/l'actrice de cinéma [lak-tuhr]/[lak-trees]-duh-see-nay-ma]
actor/actress	l'acteur/l'actrice [lak-tuhr]/[lak-trees] lecomédien/la comédienne [luh-ko-may-dyaN]/[la-ko-may-dyehn]
advance booking	la location [la-lo-ka-syohN] la réservation [la-ray-zehr-va-syohN]
ballet	le ballet [luh-ba-lay]
box	la loge [la-lozh]
box office	la caisse [la-kehs]
cabaret	le cabaret chansonniers *(m)* [luh-ka-ba-ray-shahN-so-nyay]
café-theater	le café-théâtre [luh-ka-fay-tay-atr]
chamber music concert	le concert de musique classique [luh-kohN-sehr-duh-mew-zeek-kla-seek]
choir	le chœur [luh-kuhr]
church concert	le concert en église [luh-kohN-sehr-ahN-nay-gleez]
cinema	le cinéma [luh-see-nay-ma]
circle	les galeries *(f)* [lay-gal-ree]
circus	le cirque [luh-seerk]
cloakroom	le vestiaire [luh-vehs-tyehr]
comedy	la comédie [la-ko-may-dee]
composer	le compositeur [luh-kohN-po-zee-tuhr]
concert	le concert [luh-kohN-sehr]
conductor	le chef d'orchestre [luh-sheh-duhvr]
curtain	le rideau [luh-ree-do]
dancer	le danseur/la danseuse [luh-dahN-suhr]/[la-dahN-suuhz]
drama	le drame [luh-dram]
drive-in	le cinéma en plein air [luh-see-nay-ma-ahN-plehn-ehr]
festival	le festival [luh-fehs-tee-val]
film	le film [luh-feelm]
intermission	l'entracte *(m)* [lahN-trakt]
jazz concert	le concert de jazz [luh-kohN-sehr-duh-dzhaz]
main part, lead	le rôle principal [luh-rol-praN-see-pal]
music hall show	les variétés *(f)* [lay-va-ryay-tay]

musical — l'opérette *(f)* [lo-pay-reht]; la comédie musicale [la-ko-may-dee-mew-zi-kal]
open-air theater — le théâtre en plein air [luh-tay-atr-ahN-plehn-ehr]
opera — l'opéra *(m)* [lo-pay-ra]
opera glasses — les jumelles *(f)* de théâtre [lay-zhew-mehl-duh-tay-atr]
operetta — l'opérette *(f)* [lo-pay-reht]
orchestra — l'orchestre *(m)* [lohr-kehstr]
orchestra (seats) — l'orchestre *(m)* [lohr-kehstr]
original version — la version originale [la-vehr-syohN-o-ree-zhee-nal]
part — le rôle [luh-rol]
performance — *(movie)* la séance [la-say-ahNs]; *(theater)* la représentation [la-ruh-pray-zahN-ta-syohN]

play — la pièce de théâtre [la-pyehs-duh-tay-atr]; le spectacle [luh-spehk-takl]
pop concert — le concert de musique pop [luh-kohN-sehr-duh-mew-zeek-pohp]
popular play — la pièce populaire [la-pyehs-po-pew-lehr]
premiere — la première [la-pruh-myehr]
production — la mise en scène [la-meez-ahN-sehn]
program (booklet) — le programme [luh-pro-gram]
singer — le chanteur/la chanteuse (la cantatrice) [luh-shahN-tuhr]/[la-shahN-tuuhz]/[la-kahN-ta-trees]
soloist — le/la soliste [luh/la-so-leest]
stage — la scène [la-sehn]
stage production — la mise en scène [la-meez-ahN-sehn]
subtitle/caption — le sous-titre [luh-soo-teetr]
symphony concert — le concert symphonique [luh-kohN-sehr-saN-fo-neek]
ticket — le billet [luh-bee-yay]
tragedy — la tragédie [la-tra-zhay-dee]

Moulin Rouge Nightclub

Bar/Discotheque/ Nightclub	**Bar/Discothèque/Boîte de nuit**
What can one do for entertainment here in the evening?	Quelles sont les distractions classiques ici, le soir? [kehl-sohN-lay-dees-trak-syohN-kla-seek-ee-see-luh-swar]
Is there a nice pub here?	Est-ce qu'il y a un bistrot sympa, dans le coin? [ehs-keel-ya-aN-bees-tro-saN-pa-dahN-luh-kwaN]
Where can we go dancing?	Est-ce qu'il y a une boîte/une discothèque, ici? [ehs-keel-ya-[ewn-bwat]/[ewn-dees-ko-tehk]-ee-see]
Is there a young crowd there, or is it more for older people?	Les clients sont plutôt jeunes, plutôt âgés? [lay-klee-yaN-sohN-plew-to-zhuhn-plew-to-a-zhay]
Is evening dress required?	Est-ce qu'on exige une certaine tenue vestimentaire? [ehs-kohN-nehg-zeezh-ewn-sehr-tehn-tuh-new-vehs-tee-mahN-tehr]

One drink is included in the price of admission.	Le billet d'entrée donne droit à une consommation gratuite. [luh-bee-yay-dahN-tray-dohn-drwa-a-ewn-kohN-so-ma-syohN-gra-tweet]
One beer, please.	Une bière, s.v.p. [ewn-byehr-seel-voo-play]
The same again.	La même chose, s.v.p. [la-mehm-shoz-seel-voo-play]
This round is on me.	Je paie la tournée. [zhuh-pay-la-toor-nay]
Shall we have another dance?	On danse (encore une fois)? [ohN-dahNs-ahN-kohr-ewn-fwa]
Shall we go for a walk?	On fait un petit tour avant de rentrer? [ohn-feh-aN-puh-tee-toor-a-vahN-duh-rahN-tray]

Word List: Bar/Discotheque/Nightclub

band	l'orchestre *(m)* [lohr-kehstr]
bar	le bar [luh-bar]
bouncer	le videur [luh-vee-duhr]
café	le bistrot [luh-bees-tro]
casino	le casino [luh-ka-zee-no]
to dance	danser [dahN-say]
dance music	la musique de danse [la-mew-zeek-duh-dahNs]
disc jockey	le discjockey [luh-deesk-zho-kay]
discotheque	la discothèque [la-dees-ko-tehk]
fashion show	la présentation de mode [la-pray-zahN-ta-syohN-duh-mohd]
folk dancing evening	la soirée de danse folklorique [la-swa-ray-duh-dahNs-fohl-klo-reek]
folklore	le folklore [luh-fohl-klohr]
gambling room	la salle de jeux [la-sal-duh-zhuuh]
to go out	sortir [sohr-teer]
live music	la musique en direct [la-mew-zeek-ahN-dee-rehkt]
night club	la boîte de nuit [la-bwat-duh-nwee]
show	le show [luh-sho]

7 On the Beach/Sports
A la plage/Sport

At the Swimming Pool/On the Beach

A la piscine/A la plage

Is there an . . .	Est-ce qu'il y a . . . ici? [ehs-keel-ya . . . ee-see]
outdoor pool?	une piscine en plein air [ewn-pee-seen-ahN-pleh-nehr]
indoor pool?	une piscine couverte [ewn-pee-seen-koo-vehrt]
thermal bath?	ne piscine thermale [ewn-pee-seen-tehr-mal]
An entrance ticket (with locker), please.	Un billet, s'il vous plaît (avec cabine). [aN-bee-yay-seel-voo-play-a-vehk-ka-been]
Swimmers only!	Pour les nageurs seulement! [poor-lay-na-zhuhr-suhl-mahN]
No diving!	Plongeons interdits! [plohN-zhohN-aN-tehr-dee]
No swimming!	Baignade interdite! [beh-nyad-aN-tehr-deet]
Is the beach . . . sandy? pebbled?	C'est une plage . . . [say-tewn-plazh] de sable? [duh-sabl] de galets? [duh-ga-lay]
Are there rocks?	Il y a des rochers? [eel-ya-day-ro-shay]
Are there urchins/jellyfish?	Est-ce qu'il y a des oursins/desmé-duses? [ehs-keel-ya-[day-zoor-saN]/[day-may-dewz]
How far out is it possible to swim?	On peut nager jusqu'à quelle distance du bord? [ohN-puuh-na-zhay-zhews-ka-kehl-dees-tahNs-dew-bohr]
Is the undertow strong?	Est-ce qu'il y a un courant violent? [ehs-keel-ya-aN-koo-rahN-vyo-lahN]
Is it dangerous for children?	C'est dangereux pour les enfants? [say-dahN-zhuu-ruuh-poor-lay-zahN-fahN]
When is low/high tide?	La marée basse/haute, c'est quand? [la-ma-ray-ot/bas-say-kahN]
I would like to rent . . .	Je voudrais louer . . . [zhuh-voo-dray-loo-ay]

a boat.	une barque. [ewn-bark]
a pair of water skis.	des skis nautiques. [day-skee-no-teek]
How much is it per hour/day?	Quel est le tarif à l'heure/à la journée? [kehl-ay-luh-ta-reef-[a-luhr]/[a-la-zhoor-nay]

Sports

Sport

What sporting events are there here?	Qu'est-ce qu'il y a comme manifestations sportives à . . .? [kehs-keel-ya-kohm-ma-nee-fehs-ta-syohN-spohr-teev-a]
What sports facilities are there here?	Qu'est-ce qu'on peut pratiquer comme sports, ici? [kehs-kohN-puuh-pra-tee-kay-kohm-spohr-ee-see]
Is there a golf course/tennis court/a race track here?	Est-ce qu'il y a un terrain de golf/un tennis/un hippodrome, ici? [ehs-keel-ya-[aN-tay-raN-duh-gohlf]/[aN-tay-nees]/[aN-nee-po-drom]-ee-see]
Where can one go fishing?	Où est ce qu'on peut pêcher? [oo-ehs-kohN-puuh-pay-shay]
I'd like to see the soccer match/the horse race.	Je voudrais assister au match de football/à la course de chevaux. [zhuh-voo-dray-a-sees-tay-[o-matsh-duh-foot-bol]/[a-la-koors-duh-shuh-vo]
When/Where is it?	Quand/Où est-ce qu'il/elle a lieu? [kahN/oo-ehs-keel/kehl-a-lyuuh]
How much does it cost to get in?	Combien coûte l'entrée? [kohN-byan-koot-lahN-tray]
Are there good ski slopes on the mountain?	Il y a de bonnes pistes de ski, dans les montagnes? [eel-ya-duh-bohn-pees-tuh-duh-skee-dahN-lay-mohN-tany]
At what time is the last ski lift?	La dernière remontée/descente de la télé cabine, c'est à quelle heure? [la-dehr-nyehr-[ruh-mohN-tay]/[day-sahNt]-duh-la-tay-lay-ka-been-say-a-kehl-uhr]
I'd like to go for a hike in the mountains.	Je voudrais faire une randonnée en montagne. [zhuh-voo-dray-fehr-ewn-rahN-do-nay-ahN-mohN-tany]

Can you show me an interesting route on the map?	Vous pouvez m'indiquer un itinéraire intéressant sur la carte? [voo-poo-vay-maN-dee-kay-aN-ee-tee-nay-rehr-aN-tay-ray-sahN-sewr-la-kart]
Where can I rent . . .?	Où est-ce que je peux louer . . .? [oo-ehs-kuh-zhuh-puuh-loo-ay]
I'd like to attend a . . . course.	Je voudrais prendre des cours de . . . [zhuh-voo-dray-prahN-druh-day-koor-duh]

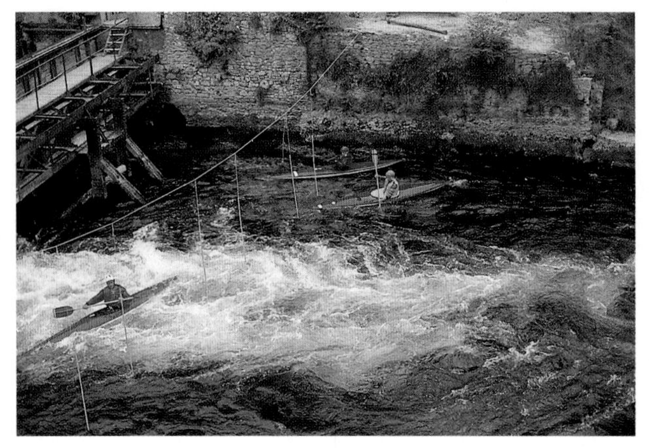

What sport do you practice?	Quel sport est-ce que vous pratiquez? [kehl-spohr-ehs-kuh-voo-pra-tee-kay]
I play . . .	Je fais du/de la . . . [zhuh-fay-[dew]/[duh-la]
I am a fan of . . .	Je suis un/e passionné/e de . . . [zhuh-swee-aN/ewn-pa-syo-nay-duh]
I like to go to . . .	J'aime bien aller . . . [zhehm-byaN-a-lay]
Can I play too?	Je peux jouer? [zhuh-puuh-zway]

Word List: Beach/Sports

aerobics	l'aérobic *(m)* [la-ay-ro-beek]
athletics	l'athlétisme *(m)* [lat-lay-teezm]
attendant	le maître-nageur [luh-meht-truh-na-zhuhr]
badminton	le volant [luh-vo-lahN]; le badminton [luh-bad-meen-tohn]
ball	la balle [la-bal]

basketball	**le basket-ball** [luh-bas-keht-bol]
bath towel	**la serviette de bain** [la-sehr-vyeht-duh-baN]
beach	**la plage** [la-plazh]
beginner	**le débutant** [luh-day-bew-tahN]
bicycle hike	**la randonnée cycliste** [la-rahN-do-nay-see-kleest]
bicycle race	**la course cycliste** [la-koors-see-kleest]
to bike	**faire du vélo** [fehr-dew-vay-lo]
biking	**le cyclisme** [luh-see-kleesm]; **le vélo** [luh-vay-lo]
bindings	**la fixation** [la-feek-sa-syohN]
boat rentals	**la location de bateaux** [la-lo-ka-syohN-duh-ba-to]
bowl game	**le jeu de boules** [luh-zhuuh-duh-bool] **la pétanque** [la-pay-tahNk]
bowling	**le bowling** [luh-boo-leeng]
bullfight	**la corrida** [la-ko-ree-da]
cable car	**le téléphérique** [luh-tay-lay-fay-reek]
canoe	**le canoé** [luh-ka-no-ay]
chair/ski lift	**le télésiège** [luh-tay-lay-syehzh]
championship	**le championnat** [luh-shaN-pyo-na]
course	**les cours** *(m)* [lay-koor]; **les leçons** *(f)* [lay-luh-sohN]
creek/inlet	**la crique** [la-kreek]
cross-country skiing	**le ski de fond**
cross-country skiing trail	**la piste de ski de fond** [la-peest-duh-skee-duh-fohN]
darts	**le jeu de fléchettes** [luh-zhuuh-duh-flay-sheht]
day pass	**le forfait-journée** [luh-fohr-fay-zhoor-nay]
defeat	**la défaite** [la-day-feht]
to dive	**faire de la plongée** [fehr-duh-la-plohN-zhay]
diving board	**le tremplin** [luh-trahN-plaN]
diving equipment	**l'équipement** *(m)* **de plongée** [lay-keep-mahN-duh-plohN-zhay]
double	**le double** [luh-doobl]
downhill skiing	**le ski alpin** [luh-skee-al-paN]
draw	**match nul** [matsh-newl]
dune	**la dune** [la-dewn]
entrance ticket	**le billet** [luh-bee-yay]
field	**le terrain de sport** [luh-tay-raN-duh-spohr]
figure skating	**le patinage artistique** [luh-pa-tee-nazh-ar-tees-teek]
to fish	**pêcher** [pay-shay]

fishing permit	le permis (de pêche) [luh-pehr-mee-duh-pehsh]
fishing rod	la canne à pêche [la-kan-a-pehsh]
fitness training	l'entretien *(m)* de la forme [lahN-truh-tyaN-duh-la-fohrm]
flippers	les palmes *(f)* [lay-palm]
football (soccer)	le football [luh-foot-bol]
football field	le terrain de football [luh-tay-raN-duh-foot-bol]
football game	le match de football [luh-matsh-duh-foot-bol]
football team	l'équipe de football [lay-keep-duh-foot-bol]
game	le match [luh-matsh]
goal	les buts *(m)* [lay-bewt]; la cage [la-kazh]
goalkeeper	le gardien de buts [luh-gar-dyaN-duh-bewt]
goggles	les lunettes *(f)* de plongée [lay-lew-neht-duh-plohN-zhay]
golf	le golf [luh-gohlf]
golf club	la crosse de golf [la-krohs-duh-gohlf]
gymnastics	la gymnastique [la-zheem-nas-teek]
halftime	la mi-temps [la-mee-tahN]
handball	le hand-ball [luh-ahNd-bal]
hang gliding	le deltaplane [luh-dehl-ta-plan]; l'aile *(f)* volante [lehl-vo-lahNt]
high-level sportsman/-woman	le sportif de bon niveau [luh-spohr-teef-duh-bohN-nee-vo]
hiking	la randonnée pédestre [la-rahN-do-nay-pay-dehstr]
hiking trail	le chemin de randonnée [luh-shuh-maN-duh-rahN-do-nay]
horse	le cheval [luh-shuh-val]
horse race	la course de chevaux [la-koors-duh-shuh-vo]
to horseback ride	faire du cheval *(m)* [fehr-dew-shuh-val] faire de l'équitation *(f)* [fehr-duh-lay-kee-ta-syohN]
horseback riding	l'équitation *(f)* [lay-kee-ta-syohN]; la promenade à cheval [la-pro-muh-nad-a-shuh-val]
ice hockey	le hockey sur glace [luh-o-kay-sew-glas]
ice rink	la patinoire [la-pa-tee-nwar]
ice skating	le patinage [luh-pa-tee-nazh]
inflatable mattress	le matelas pneumatique [luh-mat-la-pnuuh-ma-teek]

intermediate slope lift station	l'arrêt *(m)* intermédiaire du téléski [la-ray-aN-tehr-may-dyehr-dew-tay-lay-skee]
jazz dancing	la jazz-dance [la-dzhaz-dahNs]
to jog	faire du jogging [fehr-dew-dzho-geen]
jogging	le jogging [luh-dzho-geen]
judo	le judo [luh-zhew-do]
karate	le karaté [luh-ka-ra-tay]
lawn	la pelouse [la-puh-looz]
lift station	le point de départ du téléski [luh-pwaN-duh-day-par]
to lose	perdre [pehrdr]
lounge chair	la chaise-longue [la-shehz-lohNg]
match	la compétition [la-kohN-pay-tee-syohN]
miniature golf	le minigolf [luh-mee-nee-gohlf]
motor racing	le motocyclisme [luh-mo-to-see-kleesm] la moto [la-mo-to]
motorboat	le canot automobile [luh-ka-no-o-to-ma-teek]
mountaineering	l'alpinisme *(m)* [lal-pee-neezm]
net	le filet [luh-fee-lay]
nonswimmer	le non-nageur [luh-nohN-na-zhuhr]
nudist beach	la plage de nudistes [la-plazh-duh-new-deest]
paddleboat	le canoé [luh-ka-no-ay] le kayak [luh-ka-yak]
parachuting	le parachutisme [luh-pa-ra-shew-teezm]
paraglider	l'amateur *(m)* de parapente [la-ma-tuhr-duh-pa-ra-pahNt]
paragliding	le parapente [la-pa-ra-pahNt]
pebble	le galet [luh-ga-lay]
pedal boat	le pédalo [luh-pay-da-lo]
polo	le polo [luh-po-lo]
private beach	la plage privée [la-plazh-pree-vay]
race	la course [la-koors]
racket	la raquette [la-ra-keht]
rafting	le rafting [luh-raf-teeng]
regatta	les régates *(f)* [lay-ray-gat]
to ride on a sled	aller en traîneau; faire de la luge [a-lay-ahN-tray-no]/[fehr-duh-la-lewzh]
to row	(faire de) l'aviron *(m)* [fehr-duh-la-vee-rohN]
rowboat	la barque [la-bark]
rubber ring	la bouée [la-boo-ay]
rugby	le rugby [luh-rewd-bee]

to sail	le vol à voile [luh-vol-a-vwal]
sailboat	le bateau à voiles [luh-ba-to-a-vwal]
sailing	faire de la voile [fehr-duh-la-vwal]
sand	le sable [luh-sabl]
sauna	le sauna [luh-so-na]
score/result	le résultat [luh-ray-zewl-ta]
sea fishing	la pêche sportive [la-pehsh-spohr-teev]
seawater swimming pool	la piscine avec eau de mer [la-pee-seen-a-vehk-o-duh-mehr]
shower	la douche [la-doosh]
singles	le simple [luh-saNpl]
skateboard	le skateboard [luh-skeht-bohrd] laplanche à roulettes [la-plahNsh-a-roo-leht]
skates	les patins *(m)* à glace [lay-pa-taN-a-glas]
ski	le ski [luh-skee]
to ski	skier; faire du ski [skee-yay]/[fehr-dew-skee]
ski classes	les cours *(m)*/leçons *(f)* de ski [lay-koor]/[lay-luh-sohn]-duh-skee]
ski goggles	les lunettes *(f)* de ski [lay-lew-neht-duh-skee]
ski instructor	le moniteur de ski [luh-mo-nee-tuhr-duh-skee]
ski lift station	le point d'arrivée du téléski [luh-pwaN-da-ree-vay-dew-tay-lehs-kee]
ski poles	les bâtons *(m)* [lay-ba-tohN]
ski tow	le téléski [luh-tay-lay-skee]; le remonte-pente [luh-ruh-mohNt-pahNt]
skittles	le jeu de quilles [luh-zhuuh-duh-keey]
sled	le traîneau [luh-tray-no]; la luge [la-lewzh]
snorkel	le tuba [luh-tew-ba]
solarium	le solarium [luh-so-la-ryohm]
sportsman/-woman	le sportif/la sportive [luh-spohr-teef]/[la-spohr-teev]
squash	le squash [luh-skwash]
start	le départ [luh-day-par]
sun umbrella	le parasol [luh-pa-ra-sohl]
to surf	faire de la planche à voile [fehr-duh-la-plahNsh-a-vwal]
surfboard	la planche à voile [la-plahNsh-a-vwal]
surfing	le surf [luh-suhrf]
to swim	nager [na-zhay]
swimmer	le nageur [luh-na-zhuhr]

swimming pool	la piscine [la-pee-seen]
table tennis	le tennis de table [luh-tay-nees-duh-tabl]
	le ping-pong [luh-peeng-pohNg]
team	l'équipe *(f)* [lay-keep]
tennis	le tennis [luh-tay-nees]
tennis racket	la raquette de tennis [la-ra-keht-duh-tay-nees]
ticket office	la caisse [la-kehs]
umpire/referee	l'arbitre *(m)* [lar-beetr]
victory/win	la victoire [la-veek-twar]
volleyball	le volley-ball [luh-vo-lay-bol]
water polo	le water-polo [luh-wa-tehr-po-lo]
week pass	le forfait-semaine [luh-fohr-fay-suh-mehn]
to win	gagner [ga-nyay]
windbreak	le pare-vent [luh-par-vahN]
wrestling	la lutte [la-lewt]

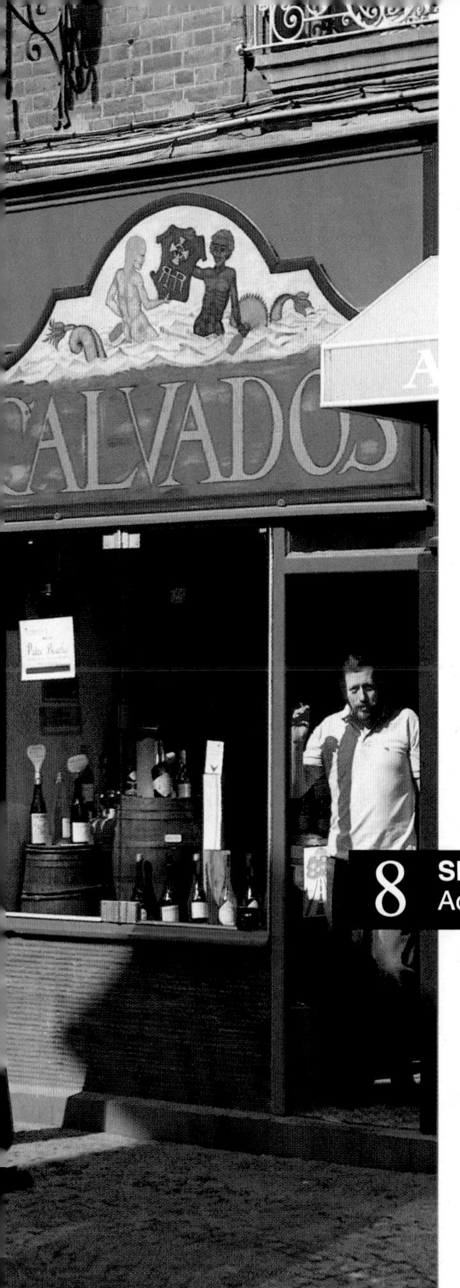

8 Shopping/Stores
Achats/Magasins

Questions/Prices
Questions/Prix

opening hours	horaires d'ouverture [o-rehr-doo-vehr-tewr]
open/closed/closed for vacation	ouvert/fermé/vacances jusqu'au… [oo-vehr]/[fehr-may]/[va-kahNs]-zhews-ko]
Where can I find . . .?	Où est-ce qu'on peut acheter . . .? [oo-ehs-kohN-puuh-a-shuh-tay]
Can you recommend a . . . shop?	Vous pourriez m'indiquer un magasin de . . .? [voo-poo-ryay-maN-dee-kay-aN-ma-ga-zaN-duh]
Are you being helped?	On vous sert? [ohN-voo-sehr]
Thank you, I'm just looking around.	Je regarde. [zhuh-ruh-gard]
I'd like . . .	J'aimerais . . . [zhay-muh-ray]
Have you got . . .?	Vous avez . . .? [voo-za-vay]
Could I have a look at . . ., please.	Donnez-moi/Montrez-moi . . ., s.v.p. [do-nay-mwa]/[mohN-tray-mwa]-seel-voo-play]
A pair of . . ., please.	Une paire de . . . s.v.p. [ewn-pehr-duh] . . . [seel-voo-play]
A piece of . . ., please.	Un/Une . . . s.v.p. [aN/ewn] . . . [seel-voo-play]
Could you show me another . . .?	Vous pourriez m'en montrer un autre/une autre, s.v.p.? [voo-poo-ryay-mahN-mohN-tray-aN/ew-notr-seel-voo-play]
Do you have anything cheaper?	Vous n'avez pas quelque chose de moins cher? [voo-na-vay-pa-kehl-kuh-shoz-duh-mwaN-shehr]
I like this. I'll take it.	Ça me plaît. Je le/la/les prends. [sa-muh- play-zhuh-luh/la/lay-prahN]
How much is it?	Combien ça coûte? [kohN-byaN-sa-koot]
Do you take . . .	Vous prenez . . . [voo-pruh-nay] des
American dollars?	dollars américains? [day-do-lar-a-may-ree-kaN]
Eurochecks?	les eurochèques? [lay-zuuh-ro-shehk]
credit cards?	les cartes de crédit? [lay-kart-duh-kray-dee]

traveler's checks?	les chèques de voyage? [lay-shehk-duh-vwa-yazh]
Could you please wrap it for me?	Vous pourriez me l'emballer? [voo-poo-ryay-muh-lahN-ba-lay]

Word List: Stores

antique shop	la boutique d'antiquaire [la-boo-teek-dahN-tee-kehr]
art dealer	le marchand d'objets d'art [luh-mar-shahN-dohb-zhay]
bakery	la boulangerie [la-boo-lahNzh-ree]
beauty parlor	l'institut *(m)* de beauté [laNs-tee-tew-duh-bo-tay]
bookstore	la librairie [la-lee-bray-ree]
boutique	la boutique [la-boo-teek]
butcher's	la boucherie [la-boosh-ree]
candy store	la confiserie [la-kohN-feez-ree]
cheese store	la fromagerie [la-fro-ma-zhuh-ree]
dairy products store	la crémerie [la-krehm-ree]
delicatessen	l'épicerie *(f)* fine [lay-pees-ree-feen]
department store	le grand magasin [luh-grahN-ma-ga-zaN]
dietetic food store	le magasin de produits diététiques [luh-ma-ga-zaN-duh-pro-dwee-dyay-tay-teek]
drugstore	la pharmacie [la-far-ma-see]
dry cleaner	la teinturerie [la-taN-tewr-ree]
electrical goods	l'électricien *(m)* [lay-lehk-tree-syaN]
fish store	la poissonnerie [la-pwa-sohn-ree]
flea market	le marché aux puces [luh-mar-shay-o-pews]
florist	le/la fleuriste [luh/la-fluh-reest]
fruit store	la fruiterie [la-frwee-tuh-ree]
furniture store	le magasin de meubles [luh-ma-ga-zaN-duh-muhbl]
furrier	le fourreur [luh-foo-ruhr]
grocery store	l'épicerie *(f)* [lay-ees-ree]
hairdresser	le salon de coiffure [luh-sa-lohN-duh-kwa-fewr]
hardware store	la quincaillerie [la-kaN-ka-yuh-ree]
health food store	le magasin de produits diététiques [luh-ma-ga-zaN-duh-pro-dwee-dyay-tay-teek]
jeweler's	la bijouterie [la-bee-zhoo-tuh-ree]

launderette	la laverie [la-lav-ree]
laundry	le pressing [luh-pray-seeng]; la blanchisserie [la-blahN-shee-suh-ree]
leathergoods store	la maroquinerie [la-ma-ro-keen-ree]
market	le marché [luh-mar-shay]
music store	le magasin de musique [luh-ma-ga-zaN-duh-mew-zeek]
newsstand	le marchand de journaux [luh-mar-shaN-duh-zhoor-no]
old book shop	la boutique de livres d'occasion [la-boo-teek-duh-lee-vruh-do-ka-syohN]
optician	l'opticien *(m)* [lohp-tee-syaN]
pastry shop	la pâtisserie [la-pa-tee-suh-ree]
perfumery	la parfumerie [la-par-fewm-ree]
pharmacy (supermarket-type)	la droguerie [la-drohg-ree]
photographic materials	le photographe [luh-fo-to-graf]
record store	le disquaire [luh-dees-kehr]
second-hand shop	la boutique de fripes [la-boo-teek-duh-freep]
self-service	le libre-service [luh-lee-bruh-sehr-vees]
shoe store	le magasin de chaussures [luh-ma-ga-zaN-duh-sho-sewr]
shoemaker's/shoe repair	le cordonnier [luh-kohr-do-nyay]
souvenir store	la boutique de souvenirs [la-boo-teek-duh-soov-neer]
sporting goods store	le magasin d'articles de sport [luh-ma-ga-zaN-dar-teekl-duh-spohr]
stationer's	la papeterie [la-pa-peht-ree]
supermarket	le supermarché [luh-sew-pehr-mar-shay]
tailor	le tailleur/la couturière [luh-ta-yuhr]/[la-koo-tew-ryehr]
tobacconist's	le bureau de tabac [luh-bew-ro-duh-ta-ba]
toy store	le magasin de jouets [luh-ma-ga-zaN-duh-zway]
travel agency	l'agence *(f)* de voyages [la-zhahNs-duh-vwa-yazh]
vegetable store	le marchand de primeurs [luh-mar-shaN-duh-pree-muhr]
watchmaker's	l'horloger *(m)* [lohr-lo-zhay]
wine and spirits store	le commerce de vins et spiritueux [luh-ko-mehrs-duh-vaN-ay-spee-ree-twuuh]
wine merchant's	le marchand de vins [luh-mar-shahN-duh-vaN]

Groceries

Denrées alimentaires

What can I get you?	Vous désirez? [voo-day-zee-ray]
I'd like . . . please.	Donnez-moi . . ., s.v.p. [do-nay-mwa...seel-voo-play]
a kilo of . . .	un kilo de . . . [aN-kee-lo-duh]
ten slices of . . .	dix tranches de . . . [dee-trahNsh-duh]

a piece of . . .	un morceau de . . . [aN-mohr-so-duh]
a package of . . .	un paquet de . . . [aN-pa-kay-duh]
a glass of . . .	un verre de . . . [aN-vehr-duh]
a can of . . .	une boîte de . . . [ewn-bwat-duh]
a bottle of . . .	une bouteille de . . . [ewn-boo-tehy-duh]
a bag of . . .	un sac en plastique de . . .[aN-sak-ahN-plas-teek-duh]
Can I give you a little more?	Est-ce que je peux vous en donner un peu plus? [ehs-kuh-zhuuh-puuh-voo-zahN-do-nay-aN-puuh-plews]
Can I get you anything else?	Et avec ça? [ay-a-vehk-sa]
Could I try some of this please?	Est-ce que je peux goûter? [ehs-kuh-zhuh-puuh-goo-tay]
No, thank you. That's all.	Non, merci. C'est tout. [nohN-mehr-see-say-too]

Word List: Groceries

almonds	les amandes *(f)* [lay-za-mahNd]
apples	les pommes *(f)* [lay-pohm]
apricots	les abricots *(m)* [lay-za-bree-ko]
artichokes	les artichauts *(m)* [lay-zar-tee-sho]
asparagus	l'asperge *(f)* [las-pehrzh]
avocado	l'avocat *(m)* [la-vo-ka]
bananas	les bananes *(f)* [lay-ba-nan]
basil	le basilic [luh-ba-zee-leek]
beans	les haricots *(m)* [lay-a-ree-ko]
beef	le bœuf [luh-buhf]
beer	la bière [la-byehr]
Belgian endive	l'endive *(f)* [lahN-deev]
blackberries	les mûres *(f)* [lay-mewr]
bread	le pain [luh-paN]
butter	le beurre [luh-buhr]
buttermilk	le petit-lait [luh-puh-tee-lay]
cabbage	le chou [luh-shoo]
cake	le gâteau [luh-ga-to]
calamari	la seiche [la-sehsh]
Camembert cheese	le camembert [luh-ka-mahN-behr]
canned goods	les conserves *(f)* [lay-kohN-sehrv]
carrots	les carottes *(f)* [lay-ka-roht]
cauliflower	le chou-fleur [luh-shoo-fluhr]
celery	le céleri [luh-sehl-ree]
champagne	le champagne [luh-shahN-pany]
cheese	le fromage [luh-fro-mazh]
cherries	les cerises *(f)* [lay-suh-reez]
chestnuts	les marrons *(m)* [lay-ma-rohN]
chicken	le poulet [luh-poo-lay]
chickpeas	les pois chiches *(m)* [lay-pwa-sheesh]
chocolate	le chocolat [luh-sho-ko-la]
chocolate bar	la barre de chocolat [la-bar-duh-sho-ko-la]
chop	la côtelett [la-kot-leht]
chopped meat	la viande hâchée [la-vyahNd-a-shay]
coconut	la noix de coco [la-nwa-duh-ko-ko]
coffee	le café [luh-ka-fay]
cold cuts	la charcuterie [la-shar-kewt-ree]; les tranches *(f)* de charcuterie/de viande froide [lay-trahNsh-duh-shar-kewt-ree]/[vyahNd-frwad]
cooked ham	le jambon cuit/blanc/de Paris [luh-zhahN-bohN-[kwee]/[blahN]/[duh-pa-ree]]

cookies	les biscuits *(m)* [lay-bees-kwee]
corn	le maïs [luh-ma-ees]
crab	les crabes *(m)* [lay-krab]
cream	la crème [la-krehm]
cucumber	le concombre [luh-kohN-kohNbr]
dates	les dattes *(f)* [lay-dat]
eel	l'anguille *(f)* [lahN-geey]
eggplant	les aubergines *(f)* [lay-zo-behr-zheen]
eggs	les œufs *(m)* [lay-zuuh]
fennel	le fenouil [luh-fuh-nooy]
figs	les figues *(f)* [lay-feeg]
fish	le poisson [luh-pwa-sohN]
fishballs	les boulettes *(f)* de poisson [lay-boo-leht-duh-pwa-sohN]
flour	la farine [la-fa-reen]
foie gras	le foie gras [luh-fwa-gra]
fresh	frais/fraîche [fray]/[frehsh]
fruit	les fruits *(m)* [lay-frwee]
garlic	l'ail *(m)* [la-y]
goat cheese	le fromage de chèvre [luh-fro-mazh-duh-shehvr]

goulash | le goulasch [luh-goo-lash]
grapefruit | le pamplemousse [luh-pahN-pluh-moos]
grapes | les raisins [lay-reh-zaN]
green beans | les haricots *(m)* verts [lay-a-ree-ko-vehr]
ham | le jambon [luh-zhahN-bohN]
herring | les harengs *(m)* [lay-a-rahN]
honey | le miel [luh-myehl]
ice | la glace [la-glas]
jam | la confiture [la-kohN-fee-tewr]
lamb | l'agneau *(m)* [la-nyo]
leeks | le poireau [luh-pwa-ro]
lemonade | la limonade [la-lee-mo-nad]
lemons | les citrons *(m)* [lay-see-trohN]
lentils | les lentilles *(f)* [lay-lahN-teey]
lettuce | la laitue [la-leh-tew]
licorice | le réglisse [luh-ray-gleez]
liverwurst | le pâté de foie [luh-pa-tay-duh-fwa]
mackerel | le maquereau [luh-mak-ro]
mandarin orange | les mandarines *(f)* [la-mahN-da-reen]
margarine | la margarine [la-mar-ga-reen]
mayonnaise | la mayonnaise [la-ma-yo-nehz]
meat | la viande [la-vyahNd]

melon | le melon [luh-muh-lohN]
milk | le lait [luh-lay]
muësli | le musli [luh-mew-slee]
mulberries | les mûres *(f)* [lay-mewr]
mussels | les moules *(f)* [lay-mool]
mustard | la moutarde [la-moo-tard]
mutton | le mouton [luh-moo-tohN]
nonalcoholic beer | la bière sans alcool [la-byehr-sahN-zal-kohl]
noodles | les nouilles *(f)* [lay-nooy]
oatmeal | les flocons *(m)* d'avoine [lay-flo-kohN-da-vwan]
oil | l'huile *(f)* [lweel]
olives | les olives *(f)* [lay-zo-leev]
onions | les oignons *(m)* [lay-zo-nyohN]
orange juice | le jus d'orange [luh-zhew-do-rahNzh]
orangeade | l'orangeade *(f)* [lo-rahN-zhad]
oranges | les oranges *(f)* [lay-zo-rahNzh]
oysters | les huîtres *(f)* [lay-zweetr]
paprika | le paprika [luh-pa-pree-ka]; le piment [luh-pee-mahN]
parsley | le persil [luh-pehr-see]
pastries | les pâtisseries *(f)* [lay-pa-tees-ree]

peaches	les pêches *(f)* [lay-pehsh]
pears	les poires *(f)* [lay-pwar]
peas	les petits pois *(m)* [lay-puh-tee-pwa]
pepper	le poivre [luh-pwavr]
perch	la perche [la-pehrsh]
pineapple	l'ananas *(m)* [la-na-nas]
plums	les prunes *(f)* [lay-prewn]
pork	le porc [luh-pohr]
potatoes	les pommes *(f)* de terre [lay-pohm-duh-tehr]
pumpernickel bread	le pain noir [luh-paN-nwar]
rabbit	le lapin [luh-la-paN]
raisins	les raisins *(m)* secs [lay-ray-zaN-sehk]
raw ham	le jambon cru [luh-zhahN-bohN-krew]
red pepper	le poivron [luh-pwa-vrohN]
red wine	le vin rouge [luh-vaN-roozh]
rice	le riz [luh-ree]
rolls	les petits pains [lay-puh-tee-paN]
saffron	le safran [luh-sa-frahN]
salad	la salade [la-sa-lad]
salami	le salami [luh-sa-la-mee]
salt	le sel [luh-sehl]
sandwich bread	les sandwichs *(m)* [lay-sahN-dweetsh]
sausage	la saucisse [la-so-sees]
sausages	les saucisses *(f)* [lay-so-sees]
scallops	les coquilles *(f)* [lay-ko-keey]; les palourdes *(f)* [lay-pa-loord]
sea bream	la daurade [la-dorad]
semolina	la semoule [la-suh-mool]
shrimp	les crevettes *(f)* [lay-kruh-veht]
skim milk	le lait écrémé [luh-lay-ay-kray-may]
smoked meat	la viande fumée [la-vyahNd-few-may]
soft cheese	le fromage à pâte molle [luh-fro-mazh-a-pat-mohl]
sole	la sole [la-sohl]
soup	la soupe [la-soop]
sour cream	la crème aigre [la-krehm-ehgr]
spaghetti	les spaghettis *(m)* [lay-spa-gay-tee]
spice cake	le pain d'épice [luh-paN-day-pees]
spinach	les épinards *(m)* [lay-zay-pee-nar]
spring water	l'eau *(f)* minérale [lo-mee-nay-ral]
squash	la courge [la-koorzh]
strawberries	les fraises *(f)* [lay-frehz]
sugar	le sucre [luh-sewkr]

sweets	les friandises *(f)* [lay-free-yahN-deez]
swordfish	l'espadon *(m)* [lehs-pa-dohN]
tea	le thé [luh-tay]
teabag	le sachet de thé [luh-sa-shay-duh-tay]
thyme	le thym [luh-taN]
toast	le toast [luh-tost]
tomatoes	les tomates *(f)* [lay-to-mat]
treated	traité(e) (à l'insecticide) [tray-tay-a-laN-sehk-tee-seed]
tuna	le thon [luh-tohN]
veal	le veau [luh-vo]
vegetables	les légumes *(m)* [lay-lay-gewm]
vinegar	le vinaigre [luh-vee-nehgr]
waffle	les gaufres *(f)* [lay-gofr]
walnuts	les noix *(f)* [lay-nwa]
watermelon	la pastèque [la-pas-tehk]
whipped cream	la crème chantilly [la-krehm-shahN-tee-yee]
white beans	les haricots *(m)* blancs [lay-a-ree-ko-blahN]
white bread	le pain blanc [luh-paN-blahN]
white cheese	le fromage blanc [luh-fro-mazh-blahN]
white wine	le vin blanc [luh-vaN-blahN]
whole wheat bread	le pain complet [luh-paN-kohN-play]
wine	le vin [luh-vaN]
yogurt	le yaourt [luh-ya-oort]

Drugstore Items

Articles de droguerie

Word List: Drugstore Items

adhesive tape	le sparadrap [luh-spa-ra-dra]
after-shave lotion	la lotion après-rasage [la-lo-syohN-a-pray-ra-zazh]
baby bottle	le biberon [luh-bee-brohN]
body lotion	le lait de beauté [luh-lay-duh-bo-tay]
body/talcum powder	le talc [luh-talk]
brush	la brosse [la-brohs]
cleansing milk	le lait démaquillant [luh-lay-day-ma-kee-yahN]
clothes brush	la brosse à habits [la-brohs-a-a-bee]
comb	le peigne [luh-pehny]

condom	le préservatif [luh-pray-zehr-va-teef]
cotton swab	le cotton-tige [luh-ko-tohN-teezh]
cotton wool	le coton hydrophile [luh-ko-tohN-ee-dro-feel]
cream	la crème [la-krehm]
cream for dry/normal/ oily skin	la crème pour peau sèche/normale/ grasse [la-krehm-poor-po-sehsh]/[nohr-mal]/[gras]
curlers	les bigoudis *(m)* [lay-bee-goo-dee]
deodorant	le déodorant [luh-day-o-do-rahN]
diapers	les couches *(f)* [lay-koosh]; les couches-culottes *(f)* [lay-koosh-kew-loht]
dish towel	le torchon [luh-tohr-shohN]
dishwashing brush	la brosse pour la vaisselle [la-brohs-poor-la-vay-sehl]
dishwashing liquid	le produit pour laver la vaisselle [luh-pro-dwee-poor-la-vay-la-vay-sehl]
eye shadow	le fard à paupières [luh-far-a-po-pyehr]
eyebrow pencil	le crayon à sourcils [luh-kray-yohN-a-soor-see]
eyeliner	l'eye-liner *(m)* [la-y-ly-nuhr]
face powder	la poudre pour le visage [la-poo-druh-poor-luh-vee-zazh]
hair band	l'élastique *(m)* [lay-las-teek]
hair gel	le gel pour les cheveux [luh-zhehl-poor-lay-shuh-vuuh]
hair remover	la crème épilatoire [la-krehm-day-pee-la-twar]
hair spray	le fixateur [luh-feek-sa-tuhr]
hairbrush	la brosse à cheveux [la-brohs-a-shuh-vuuh]
hairpins	les épingles *(f)* à cheveux [lay-zay-paNgla-shuh-vuuh]
hand cream	la crème pour les mains [la-krehm-poor-lay-maN]
laundry	la lessive [la-lay-seev]
lipstick	le rouge à lèvres [luh-roozh-a-lehvr]
mascara	le rimmel [luh-ree-mehl]; le mascara [luh-mas-ka-ra]
mirror	la glace [la-glas]
moisturizing cream	la crème hydratante [la-krehm-ee-dra-tahNt]
mouthwash	l'eau *(f)* dentifrice [lo-dahN-tee-frees]
nail scissors	les ciseaux *(m)* à ongles [lay-see-zo-a-ohNgl]

nailbrush	la brosse à ongles [la-brohs-a-ohNgl]
nailfile	la lime à ongles [la-leem-a-ohNgl]
nailpolish	le vernis à ongles [luh-vehr-nee-a-ohNgl]
nailpolish remover	le dissolvant [luh-dee-sohl-vahN]
pacifier	la tétine [la-tay-teen]
perfume	le parfum [luh-par-faN]
powder	la poudre [la-poodr]
protection factor (suncream)	l'indice *(m)* de protection [laN-dees-duh-pro-tehk-syohN]
razor	le rasoir mécanique [luh-ra-zwar-may-ka-neek] *(el)* le rasoir électrique [luh-ra-zwar-ay-lehk-treek]
razor blade	la lame de rasoir [la-lam-duh-ra-zwar]
rouge	le rouge à joues [luh-roozh-a-zhoo]
safety pins	les épingles *(f)* à nourrice [lay-zay-paN-gla-noo-rees]
sanitary napkins	les serviettes *(f)* hygiéniques [lay-sehr-vyeht-ee-zhyay-neek]
shampoo	le shampooing [luh-shahN-pwaN]
shampoo for oily/normal/ dry hair	le shampooing pour cheveuxgras/nor-maux/secs [luh-shahNpwaN-poor-shuh-vuuh-[gra]/[nohr-mo]/[sehk]]
shampoo to prevent/fight dandruff	le shampooing antipelliculaire [luh-shahN-pwaN-ahN-tee-pay-lee-kew-lehr]
shaving brush	le blaireau [luh-bleh-ro]
shaving soap	le savon à barbe [luh-sa-vohN-a-barb]
soap	le savon [luh-sa-vohN]
sponge	l'éponge *(f)* [lay-pohNzh]
stain remover	le détachant [luh-day-ta-shahN]
styling mousse	la mousse structurante (pour les cheveux) [la-moos-strewk-tew-rahNt-poor-lay-shuh-vuuh]
suntan lotion	la crème solaire [la-krehm-so-lehr]
suntan oil	l'huile *(f)* solaire [lweel-so-lehr]
tampons	les tampons *(m)* [lay-tahN-pohN]
tissues	les mouchoirs *(m)* en papier [lay-moo-shwar-ahN-pa-pyay]
toilet paper	le papier hygiénique [luh-pa-pyay-ee-zhyay-neek]
toilet water	l'eau *(f)* de Cologne [lo-duh-ko-lohny]
toothbrush	la brosse à dents [la-brohs-a-dahN]
toothpaste	le dentifrice [luh-dahN-tee-frees]
travel kit	la trousse de toilette [la-troos-duh-twa-leht]
tweezers	la pince à épiler [la-paNs-a-ay-pee-lay]
washcloth	le gant de toilette [luh-gahN-duh-twa-leht]

Tobacco Products

Au bureau de tabac

A packet/carton of filter-tipped/plain... cigarettes, please.	Un paquet/Une cartouche de... filtre/ sans filtre, s.v.p. [aN-pa-kay]/[ewn-kar-toosh]-duh...[feeltr]/[sahN-feeltr]-seel-voo-play]
Do you have American cigarettes?	Vous avez des cigarettes américaines? [voo-za-vay-day-see-ga-reht-[a-may-ree-kehn]/[mahN-tohl]
Ten cigars/cigarillos, please.	Dix cigares/cigarillos, s.v.p. [dee-[see-gar]/[see-ga-ree-yos]-seel-voo-play]
A package/can of cigarette/pipe tobacco, please.	Un paquet/Une boîte de tabac pour cigarettes/pipes. [aN-pa-kay]/[ewn-bwat]-duh-ta-ba-poor-[see-ga-reht]/[peep]]
A box of matches/ A lighter, please.	Une boîte d'allumettes/Un briquet, s.v.p. [ewn-bwat-da-lew-meht]/[aN-bree-kay]-seel-voo-play]

Clothing/Leather Goods/Dry Cleaning

Vêtements/Cuirs/Nettoyage

See also Chapter 1—Colors

Can you show me. . .?	Est-ce que vous pouvez me montrer . . .? [ehs-kuh-voo-poo-vay-muh-mohN-tray]
Do you have a particular color in mind?	Quel coloris désirez-vous? [kehl-ko-lo-ree-day-zee-ray-voo]
I'd like something in brown.	Je voudrais du marron. [zhuh-voo-dray-dew-ma-rohN]
I'd like something to match this.	Je voudrais quelque chose qui aille avec ça. [zhuh-voo-dray-kehl-kuh-shoz-kee-a-y-a-vehk-sa]
Can I try it on?	Je peux l'essayer? [zhuh-puuh-lay-say-yay]
What size do you take?	Quelle taille faites-vous? [kehl-tay-feht-voo]
It's too . . .	Il est trop . . . pour moi. [eel-ay-tro . . . poor-mwa]

tight/big. short/long. small/big.	étroit/large [ay-trwa]/[larzh] court/long [koor]/[lohN] petit/grand [puh-tee]/[grahN]
It's a good fit. I'll take it.	Il me va. Je le prends. [eel-muh-va-zhuh-luh-prahN]
It's not quite what I wanted.	Ce n'est pas tout à fait ce que je voulais. [suh-nay-pa-too-ta-fay-suh-kuh-zhuh-voo-lay]
I'd like a pair of . . . shoes.	Je voudrais une paire de . . . [zhuh-voo-dray-ewn-pehr-duh]
I have a size . . .	Je chausse du . . . [zhuh-shos-dew]
They are too tight.	Elles me serrent. [ehl-muh-sehr]
They are too narrow/ wide.	Elles sont trop petites/grandes. [ehl-sohN-tro-[puh-teet]/[grahNd]]
Give me also a tube of shoe cream/a pair of shoelaces, please.	Donnez-moi aussi une boîte de cirage/des lacets. [do-nay-mwa-o-see-[ewn-bwat-duh-see-razh]/[day-la-say]]
I'd like to have new soles put on these shoes.	Je voudrais faire ressemeler ces chaussures. [zhuh-voo-dray-fehr-ruh-suh-muh-lay-say-sho-sewr]
Could you put on new heels, please?	Est-ce que vous pouvez changer les talons, s.v.p.? [ehs-kuh-voo-poo-vay-shahN-zhay-lay-ta-lohN-seel-voo-play]
I'd like to have these things cleaned/washed.	Je voudrais faire nettoyer/laver ces affaires. [zhuh-voo-dray-fehr-[nay-twa-yay]/[la-vay]-may-za-fehr]
When will they be ready?	Quand est-ce qu'elles seront prêtes? [kahN-tehs-kehl-suh-rohN-preht]

Word List: Clothing/Leather Goods/Dry Cleaning

backpack	le sac à dos, le sac de montagne [luh-sak-a-do, luh-sak-duh-mohN-tany]
bag	la sacoche, le sac [la-sa-kohsh, luh-sak]
bathing cap	le bonnet de bain [luh-bo-nay-duh-baN]
bathing suit (one piece)	le maillot une pièce [luh-ma-yo-ewn-pyehs]
bathing trunks	le maillot de bain [luh-ma-yo-duh-baN]

bathrobe	le peignoir de bain [luh-peh-nywar-duh-baN]
beach shoes	les chaussures *(f)* de plage [lay-sho-sewr-duh-plazh]
belt	la ceinture [la-saN-tewr]
bikini	le bikini [luh-bee-kee-nee]
blazer	le blazer [luh-bleh-zuhr]
blouse	le chemisier [luh-shuh-mee-zyay]
boots	les bottes *(f)* [lay-boht]
bow tie	le nœud papillon [luh-nuuh-pa-pee-yohN]
bra	le soutien-gorge [luh-soo-tyaN-gorzh]
button	le bouton [luh-boo-tohN]
cap	la casquette [la-kas-keht]
carry-on bag	le sac de voyage [luh-sak-duh-vwa-yazh]
checked	à carreaux [a-ka-ro]
clogs	les sabots [lay-sa-bo]
coat	le manteau [luh-mahN-to]; lepardessus [luh-par-duh-sew]
collar	le col [luh-kohl]
color	la couleur [la-koo-luhr]
cotton	le coton [luh-ko-tohN]
dress	la robe [la-rohb]
to dry clean	nettoyer (à sec) [nay-twa-yay-a-sehk]
evening dress	la robe du soir [la-rohb-dew-swar]
fur coat	le manteau en fourrure [luh-mahN-to-ahN-foo-rewr]
fur jacket	la veste en fourrure [la-vehst-ahN-foo-rewr]
gloves	les gants *(m)* [lay-gahN]
handbag	le sac à main [luh-sak-a-maN]
handkerchief	le mouchoir [luh-moo-shwar]
hat	le chapeau [luh-sha-po]
hose	les bas *(m)* [lay-ba]
to iron	repasser [ruh-pa-say]
jacket	la veste [la-vehst]
jeans	le jean [luh-dzheen]
jogging pants	le pantalon de jogging [luh-pahN-ta-lohN-duh-dzho-geeng]
leather coat	le manteau en cuir [luh-mahN-to-ahN-kweer]
leather jacket	la veste en cuir [la-vehst-ahN-kweer]
leather trousers	le pantalon en cuir [luh-pahN-ta-lohN-ahN-kweer]
linen	le lin [luh-laN]; la toile [la-twal]

lining — la doublure [la-doo-blewr]
machine washable — qu'on peut laver à la machine [kohN-puuh-la-vay-a-la-ma-sheen]
miniskirt — la mini-jupe [la-mee-nee-zhewp]
nightgown — la chemise de nuit [la-shuh-meez-duh-nwee]
overall — la salopette [la-sa-lo-peht]
pajamas — le pyjama [luh-pee-zha-ma]
pantyhose, tights — les collants *(m)* [lay-ko-lahN]
parka — l'anorak *(m)* [la-no-rak]
permanent press — qui ne se repasse pas [kee-nuh-suh-ruh-pas-pa]
petticoat — le slip [luh-sleep]; le jupon [luh-zhew-pohN]
pullover — le pull-over [luh-pewl-o-vehr]
raincoat — l'imperméable *(m)* [laN-pehr-may-abl]
robe — la robe de chambre [la-rohb-duh-shahNbr]
rubber boots — les bottes *(f)* en caoutchouc [lay-boht-ahN-ka-o-tshoo]
sandals — les sandales *(f)* [lay-sahN-dal]
scarf — le foulard [luh-foo-lar]
shawl — le châle, l'écharpe *(f)* [luh-shal]/]lay-sharp]

shirt — la chemise [la-shu-meez]
shoe — la chaussure [la-sho-sewr]
shoe brush — la brosse à chaussures [la-brohs-a-sho-sewr]
shoe cream — le cirage [luh-see-razh]
shoe size — la pointure [la-pwaN-tewr]
shorts — le short [luh-shohrt]
silk — la soie [la-swa]
ski boots — les chaussures *(f)* de ski [lay-sho-sewr-duh-skee]
ski pants — le pantalon de ski [luh-pahN-ta-lohN-duh-skee]
skirt — la jupe [la-zhewp]
sleeve — la manche [la-mahNsh]
slip — le slip [luh-sleep]
slippers — les pantoufles *(f)* [lay-pahN-toofl]
snap — le bouton-pression [luh-boo-tohN-pray-syohN]
socks — les chaussettes *(f)* (montantes) [lay-sho-seht-mohN-tahNt]
sole — la semelle [la-suh-mehl]
stockings, hose — les bas *(m)* de soie [lay-ba-duh-swa]

striped	rayé(e) [ray-yay]
suede coat	le manteau en daim [luh-mahN-to-ahN-daN]
suede jacket	le blouson en daim [luh-bloo-zohN-ahN-daN]; la veste en daim [la-vehst-ahN-daN]
suit (for men)	le costume [luh-kos-tewm]
suit (for women)	le tailleur [luh-ta-yuhr]
suitcase	la valise [la-va-leez]
sundress	la robe d'été [la-rohb-day-tay]
sun hat	le chapeau de paille [luh-sha-po-duh-pa-y]
synthetic fiber	la fibre synthétique [la-feebr-saN-tay-teek]
T-shirt	le tee-shirt [luh-tee-shuhrt]
tennis shoes	les tennis *(f)* [lay-tay-nees]; les baskets *(m)* [lay-bas-keht]
terrycloth	le tissu-éponge [luh-tee-sew-ay-pohNzh]
tie	la cravate [la-kra-vat]
tracksuit	le survêtement de jogging [luh-sewr-veht-mahN-duh-dzho-geeng]
trousers	le pantalon [luh-pahN-ta-lohN]
umbrella	le parapluie [luh-pa-ra-plwee]
underwear	les sous-vêtements *(m)* [lay-soo-veht-mahN]
underwear/singlet	le maillot de corps [luh-ma-yo-duh-kohr]
vest	la veste [la-vehst]; le gilet [luh-zhee-lay]
water shoes	les chaussures *(f)* en plastique pour la baignade [lay-sho-sewr-ahN-plas-teek-poor-la-bay-nyad]
wool	la laine [la-lehn]
wool jacket	la veste en laine [la-vehst-ahN-lehn]
zipper	la fermeture éclair [la-fehr-muh-tewr-ay-klehr]

Books and Stationery

A la librairie/A la papeterie

I'd like . . .	Je voudrais . . . [zhuh-voo-dray]
an American newspaper.	un journal américain. [aN-zhoor-nal-a-may-ree-kaN]
a magazine.	un magazine. [aN-ma-ga-zeen]
a travel guide.	un guide touristique. [aN-geed-too-rees-teek]

Word List: Books and Stationery

adhesive tape	le scotch [luh-skohtsh]
ballpoint pen	le stylo à bille [luh-stee-lo-a-beey]
city map	le plan (de la ville) [luh-plahN-duh-la-veel]
colored pencil	le crayon de couleur [luh-kray-yohN-duh-koo-luhr]
coloring book	le livre à colorier [luh-leevr-a-ko-loh-ryay]
detective story	le roman policier [luh-ro-mahN-po-lee-syay]
envelope	l'enveloppe *(f)* [lahN-vuh-loh]
felt pen	le feutre [luh-fuutr]
fountain pen	le stylo à plume [luh-stee-lo-a-plewm]
glue	la colle [la-kohl]
magazine	le magazine [luh-ma-ga-zeen]
newspaper	le journal [luh-zhoor-nal]
notebook	le carnet [luh-kar-nay]
notepad	le bloc-notes [luh-blohk-noht]
novel	le roman [luh-ro-mahN]
pad of paper	le bloc de papier à dessin [luh-blohk-duh-pa-pyay-a-day-saN]
paper	le papier [lu-pa-pyay]
paper clips	les trombones *(m)* [lay-trohN-bohn]
pencil	le crayon [luh-kray-yohN]
pencil sharpener	le taille-crayon [luh-ta-y-kray-yohN]
picture postcard	la carte postale illustrée [la-kart-pos-tal-ee-lews-tray]
playing cards	le jeu de cartes [luh-zhuuh-duh-kart]
pocketbook	le livre de poche [luh-leevr-duh-pohsh]
road map	la carte (géographique) [la-kart-zhay-o-gra-feek]; la carte routière [la-kart-roo-tyehr]
rubber eraser	la gomme [la-gohm]
stamp	timbre [luh-taNbr]
thumbtacks	les punaises *(f)* [lay-pew-nehz]
travel guide	le guide touristique [luh-geed-too-rees-teek]
wrapping paper	le papier cadeaux [luh-pa-pyay-ka-do]
writing paper	le papier à lettres [luh-pa-pyay-a-lehtr]

Household Items

Articles ménagers

Word List: Household Items

aluminum foil	le papier d'aluminium [luh-pa-pyay-da-lew-mee-nyohm]
bottle opener	l'ouvre-bouteilles *(m)* [loo-vruh-boo-tehy]
broom	le balai [luh-ba-lay]
brush	la balayette [la-ba-lay-yeht]
bucket	le seau [luh-so]
camp chair	la chaise de camping [la-shehz-duh-kahN-peeng]
camp table	la table de camping [la-tabl-duh-kahN-peeng]
can opener	l'ouvre-boîtes *(m)* [loo-vruh-bwat]
candles	les bougies *(f)* [lay-boo-zhee]
cellophane	l'emballage *(m)* pour conservation de saliments [lahN-ba-lazh-poor-kohN-sehr-va-syohN-day-za-lee-mahN]
charcoal	le charbon de bois [luh-shar-bohN-duh-bwa]
clothesline	l'étendoir *(m)* [lay-tahN-dwar]
clothespins	les pinces *(f)* à linge [la-paNs-a-laNzh]
cooler	la glacière [la-gla-syehr]
corkscrew	le tire-bouchon [luh-teer-boo-shohN]
cutlery	les couverts *(m)* [lay-koo-vehr]
dustpan	la pelle [la-pehl]
fire starter/lighter	la pastille d'allumage pour le gril [la-pas-teey-da-lew-mazh-poor-luh-greel]
glass	le verre [luh-vehr]
grill	le gril [luh-greel]
liquid warmer	le chauffe-liquide [luh-shof-lee-keed]
methylated spirits/ methyl alcohol	l'alcool *(m)* à brûler [lal-kohl-a-brew-lay]
paper napkin	les serviettes *(f)* en papier [lay-sehr-vyeht-ahN-pa-pyay]
paraffin	le pétrole [luh-pay-trohl]
plastic bag	le sac en plastique [luh-sak-ahN-plas-teek]
pocket knife	le couteau de poche [luh-koo-to-duh-pohsh]

saucepan	la marmite [la-mar-meet]
sun umbrella	le parasol [luh-pa-ra-sohl]
thermos flask	la bouteille Thermos [la-boo-tehy-tehr-mos]
trashbag	le sac à ordures [luh-sak-a-ohr-dewr]
windshield	le pare-vent [luh-par-vahN]

Electrical Goods and Photographic Supplies

Chez l'électricien et le photographe

I'd like . . .	Je voudrais . . . [zhuh-voo-dray]
film for this camera.	une pellicule pour cet appareil. [ewn-pay-lee-kewl-poor-seht-a-pa-rehy]
color film for prints/ slides.	une pellicule couleur (pour diapos). [ewn-pay-lee-kewl-koo-luhr-poor-dya-po]
film with 36/20/12 exposures.	une pellicule pour 36/20/12 photos. [ewn-pay-lee-kewl-poor-36/20/12-fo-to]
Could you put the film in the camera for me, please?	Vous pourriez mettre la pellicule dans l'appareil, s.v.p.? [voo-poo-ryay-mehtr-la-pay-lee-kewl-dahN-la-pa-rehy-seel-voo-play]
Would you develop this film for me, please?	Vous pourriez me développer cette pellicule, s.v.p.? [voo-poo-ryay-muh-day-vlo-pay-seht-pay-lee-kewl]
I'd like one print of each of these negatives, please.	Faites-moi une épreuve pour chacun de ces négatifs, s.v.p. [feht-mwa-ewn-ay-pruhv-poor-sha-kaN-duh-say-nay-ga-teef-seel-voo-play]
What size?	Quel format désirez-vous? [kehl-fohr-ma-day-zee-ray-voo]
Seven by ten./Nine by nine.	Du sept dix./Du neuf neuf. [dew-seht-dees]/[dew-nuhf-nuhf]
Would you like glossy or mat?	Vous désirez du brillant ou du grain de soie? [voo-day-zee-ray-dew-bree-yahN-oo-dew-graN-duh-swa]
When can I pick up the photos?	Quand est-ce que je peux venir chercher les photos [kahN-tehsk-kuh-zhuh-puuh-vuh-neer-shehr-shay-lay-fo-to]

The viewfinder/shutter doesn't work.	Le viseur/Le déclencheur ne fonctionne plus. [luh-vee-zuhr]/[luh-day-klahN-shuhr]-nuh-fohNk-syohn-plew]
This is broken. Can you please fix it?	C'est cassé. Vous pouvez réparer ça, s.v.p.? [say-ka-say-voo-poo-vay-ray-pa-ray-sa-seel-voo-play]

Word List: Electrical Goods and Photographic Supplies

adapter	l'adaptateur *(m)* [la-dap-ta-tuhr]
aperture	le diaphragme [luh-dya-fragm]
battery	la pile [la-peel]
black-and-white film	le film en noir et blanc [luh-feelm-nwar-ay-blahN]
camcorder	le caméscope [luh-ka-mehs-kohp]
camera	la caméra [la-ka-may-ra]
cassette	la cassette [la-ka-seht]
CD/CD-ROM	le CD/le (disque) compact [luh-say-day]/[luh-deesk-kohN-pakt]
extension cord/lead	la rallonge [la-ra-lohNzh]
film speed	la sensibilité [la-sahN-see-bee-lee-tay]
film spool	le transport de bande/de pellicule [luh-trahNs-pohr-duh-[bahNd]/[pay-lee-kewl]]
flash	le flash [luh-flash]
flash cube	le flash [luh-flash]
hair dryer	le sèche-cheveux [luh-sehsh-shuh-vuuh]
headphones	les écouteurs *(m)* [lay-zay-koo-tuhr]
lens	la lentille [la-lahN-teey] l'objectif *(m)* [lohb-zhehk-teef]
light bulb	l'ampoule *(f)* [lahN-pool]
light meter	le photomètre [luh-fo-to-mehtr]
passport picture	la photo d'identité [la-fo-to-dee-dahN-tee-tay]
plug	la prise (mâle) [la-preez-mal]
pocket calculator	la calculette [la-kal-kew-leht]
pocket flashlight	la lampe de poche [la-lahNp-duh-pohsh]
record	le disque [luh-deesk]
self-timer	le déclencheur automatique [luh-day-klahN-shuhr-o-to-ma-teek]
shutter	l'obturateur *(m)* [lohb-tew-ra-tuhr]
shutter release	le déclencheur [luh-day-klahN-shuhr]
speaker	le haut-parleur le baffle [luh-o-par-luhr]/[luh-bafr]

super-8 film	le film super-8 [luh-feelm-sew-pehr-weet]
telephoto lens	le téléobjectif [luh-tay-lay-ohb-zhehk-teef]
tripod	le pied [luh-pyay]
video camera	la caméra vidéo [la-ka-may-ra-vee-day-o]
videocassette	la vidéocassette [la-vee-day-o-ka-seht]; le film vidéo [luh-feelm-vee-day-o]
videocassette recorder	le magnétoscope [luh-ma-nyay-to-skohp]; le lecteur de cassettes [luh-lehk-tuhr-duh-ka-seht]
videotape	le film vidéo [luh-feelm-vee-day-o]
viewfinder	le viseur [luh-vee-zuhr]
walkman	le walkman, le baladeur [luh-wok-man]/[luh-ba-la-duhr]

At the Optician

Chez l'opticien

Could you repair these glasses/this frame for me please?	Je voudrais faire réparer ces lunettes/la monture? [zhuh-voo-dray-fehr-ray-pa-ray-[say-lew-neht]/[la-mohN-tewr]]
One of the lenses of my glasses is broken.	Un de mes verres est cassé. [aN-duh-may-vehr-ay-ka-say]
I'm nearsighted/farsighted.	Je suis myope/hypermétrope. [zhuh-swee-[myohp]/[ee-pehr-may-trohp]
What's your acuity/eye prescription?	Quelle est votre acuité visuelle? [kehl-ay-vohtr-a-kwee-tay-vee-zwehl]
in the right eye . . ., in the left eye . . .	œil droit . . ., [uhy-drwa] . . . œil gauche . . . [uhy-gosh] . . .
When can I pick up the glasses?	Quand est-ce que je peux venir les chercher? [kahN-tehs-kuh-zhuh-puuh-vuh-neer-lay-shehr-shay]
I need . . .	Il me faudrait . . . [eel-muh-fo-dray]
some storing solution	du liquide de conservation [dew-lee-keed-duh-kohN-sehr-va-sohN]
some cleansing solution	du liquide de nettoyage [dew-lee-keed-duh-nay-twa-yazh]
for hard/soft contact lenses.	pour lentilles dures/molles. [poor-lahN-teey-dewr/mohl]

I'm looking for . . .	Je voudrais . . . [zhuh-voo-dray]
some sunglasses.	des lunettes de soleil. [day-lew-neht-duh-so-lehy]
some binoculars.	des jumelles. [day-zhew-mehl]

At the Watchmaker/Jeweler

Chez l'horloger/Chez le bijoutier

My watch doesn't work. Could you have a look at it?	Ma montre ne marche plus. Vous pourriez la regarder, s.v.p.? [ma-mohNtr-nuh-marsh-plew-voo-poo-ryay-la-ruh-gar-day-seel-voo-play]
I would like a nice souvenir/present.	Je voudrais un joli souvenir/cadeau. [zhuh-voo-dray-aN-zho-lee-[soov-neer]/[ka-do]
How much do you want to spend?	Quel prix voulez-vous y mettre? [kehl-pree-voo-lay-voo-ee-mehtr]
I'd like something that is not too expensive.	Je voudrais quelque chose de pas trop cher. [zhuh-voo-dray-kehl-kuh-shoz-duh-pa-tro-shehr]

Word List: Watchmaker/Jeweler

bracelet	le bracelet [luh-bras-lay]
brooch	la broche [la-brohsh]
coral	le corail [luh-ko-ra-y]
costume jewelry	les bijoux *(m)* fantaisie [lay-bee-zhoo-fahN-tay-zee]
crystal	le cristal [luh-krees-tal]
earrings	les boucles *(f)* d'oreilles [lay-boo-kluh-do-rehy]
gold	l'or *(m)* [lohr]
jewelry	les bijoux *(m)* [lay-bee-zhoo]
necklace	le collier [luh-ko-lyay]
pearl	la perle [la-pehrl]
pendant	le pendentif [luh-pahN-dahN-teef]
ring	la bague [la-bag]
silver	l'argent *(m)* [lar-zhahN]
turquoise	la turquoise [la-tewr-kwaz]
watchband	la montre-bracelet [la-mohNtr-bras-lay]

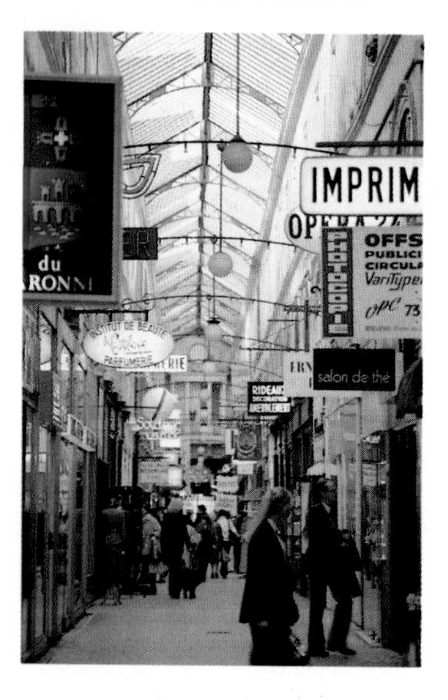

At the Hairdresser/Barber

Chez le coiffeur

Can I make an appointment for tomorrow?	Est-ce que je peux prendre rendez-vous pour demain? [ehs-kuh-zhuh-puuh-prahNdr-rahN-day-voo-poor-duh-maN]
How would you like your hair done?	Quelle coiffure/coupe de cheveux désirez-vous? [kehl-[kwa-fewr]/[koop-duh-shuuh-vuuh]-day-zee-ray-voo]
Shampoo and blow-dry/set, please.	Shampooing et brushing, s.v.p. [shahN-pwaN-ay-bro-sheeng-seel-voo-play]
Wash and cut/Dry cut, please.	Une coupe avec/sans shampooing, s.v.p.[ewn-koop-[a-vehk]/[sahN]-shahN-pwaN-seel-voo-play]
I'd like…	Je voudrais... [zhuh-voo-dray]
a perm.	une permanente. [ewn-pehr-ma-nahNt]
to have my hair dyed/tinted.	une coloration/un rinçage. [ewn-ko-lo-ra-syohN]/[aN-raN-sazh]

to have my hair highlighted.	me faire teindre des mèches. [muh-fehr-tahNdr-day-mehsh]
Leave it long, please.	Laissez-les longs, s.v.p. [lay-say-lay-lohN-seel-voo-play]
Just trim the ends.	Les pointes seulement. [lay-pwaNt-suhl-mahN]
Not too short/Very short/ A bit shorter, please.	Pas trop courts/Très courts/Un peu plus courts, s.v.p. [pa-tro-koor]/[tray-koor]/ [aN-puuh-plew-koor]-seel-voo-play]
A bit (more) off the back/front/top/A bit shorter, please.	Enlevez-en un peu derrière/devant/ dessus/sur les côtes. [ahN-luh-vay-an-puh-[day-ryehr]/[duh-vahN]/[duh-sew]/ [sewr-lay-ko-tay]
Cut above/below the ears, please.	Dégagez les oreilles./Laissez les oreilles couvertes. [day-ga-zhay-lay-zo-rehy]/[lay-say-lay-zo-rehy]
The part on the left/ right, please.	La raie à gauche/à droite, s.v.p. [la-ray-a-gosh/drwat-seel-voo-play]
A razor cut, please.	Une coupe au rasoir, s.v.p. [ewn-koop-o-ra-zwar-seel-voo-play]
Would you tease it a bit, please?	Crêpez un peu, s.v.p. [kray-pay-aN-puuh-seel-voo-play]
No/Not too much hair spray, please.	Pas de/Un peu de laque seulement. [pa-duh]/[ppuuh-duh]-lak-suhl-mahN]
I'd like a shave, please.	Un rasage, s.v.p. [aN-ra-zazh-seel-voo-play]
Would you trim my beard, please.	Vous me taillez la moustache/la barbe, s.v.p. [voo-muh-ta-yay-[la-moos-tash]/[la-barb]-seel-voo-play]
Can you give me a manicure?	Vous pouvez me faire les mains, s.v.p. [voo-poo-vay-muh-fehr-lay-maN-seel-voo-play]
Thank you. That's fine.	Merci beaucoup. ça va très bien. [mehr-see-bo-koo-sa-va-tray-byaN]

Word List: Hairdresser/Barber

bangs	la coupe à la Jeanne d'Arc [la-koop-a-la-zhan-dark]
beard	la barbe [la-barb]
blond	blond(e) [blohN(d)]
to blow-dry	faire un brushing [fehr-aN-bro-sheeng]
to comb	peigner [pay-nyay]
curlers	les bigoudis *(m)* [lay-bee-goo-dee]
curls	les boucles *(f)* [lay-bookl]
dandruff	les pellicules *(f)* [lay-pay-lee-kewl]
dry hair	les cheveux secs [lay-shuh-vuuh-sehk]
to dye	faire une coloration [fehr-ewn-ko-lo-ra-syohN]
eyebrows	les sourcils *(m)* [lay-soor-see]
hair	les cheveux [lay-shuh-vuuh]
hair loss	la chute des cheveux [la-shewt-day-shuh-vuuh]
hair set	la mise en plis [la-meez-ahNplee]
hair spray	la laque [la-lak]
haircut	la coupe [la-koop]
hairpiece	le postiche [luh-pohs-teesh]
hairstyle	la coiffure [la-kwa-fewr] la coupe de cheveux [la-koop-duh-shuh-vuuh]
layered cut	la coupe en dégradé [la-koop-ahN-day-gra-day]
moustache	la moustache [la-moos-tash]
oily hair	les cheveux gras [lay-shuh-vuuh-gra]
parting	la raie [la-ray]
perm	la permanente [la-pehr-ma-nahNt]
to set	faire une mise en plis [fehr-ewn-meez-ahN-plee]
shampoo	le shampooing [luh-shahN-pwaN]
to have a shave	se faire raser [suh-fehr-ra-zay]
sideburns	les pattes *(f)* [lay-pat]
to style	coiffer [kwa-fay]
to tint	faire un rinçage [fehr-aN-raN-sazh]
to trim	rafraîchir [ra-fray-sheer]
wig	la perruque [la-pay-rewk]

9 Services
Services

Money Matters

Questions d'argent

Excuse me, where is the nearest bank/money exchange office?	Pardon, Mme/Mlle/M., je cherche une banque/un bureau de change. [par-dohN-[ma-dam]/[mad-mwa-zehl]/[muh-syuuh]-zhuh-shehrsh-ewn-bahNk-duh-shahNzh]
What time does the bank open/close?	La banque ouvre/ferme à quelle heure? [la-bahNk-oovr/fehrm-a-kehl-uhr]
I'd like to change . . . U.S. dollars for French francs.	Je voudrais changer . . . U.S. dollars en francs français. [zhuh-voo-dray-shahN-zhay . . . U.S.-do-lars-ahN-frahN-[frahN-say.]
What is the current exchange rate?	Le dollar est à combien aujourd'hui? [luh-do-lar-ay-ta-kohN-byaN-o-zhoor-dwee]
How many francs do I get for $100?	Pour cent dollars, on a combien de francs, s.v.p.? [poor-sahN-do-lar-ohN-na-kohN-byaN-duh-frahN-seel-voo-play]
I'd like to cash this traveler's check, Euro-check/money order.	Je voudrais encaisser ce chèque de voyage/cet eurochèque/ce mandat. [zhuh-voo-dray-ahN-kay-say-[suh-shehk-duh-vwa-yazh]/[seht-uuh-ro-shehk]/[suh-mahN-da]
What is the maximum I can cash on one check?	Quelle est la somme maximale que je peux retirer? [kehl-ay-la-sohm-mak-see-mal-kuh-zhuh-puuh-ruh-tee-ray]
Can I see your credit card, please?	Votre carte (de chèque), s.v.p.? [voh-truh-kart (duh-shehk)-seel-voo-play]
May I see your passport/identity card, please?	Vous avez votre passeport/une pièce d'identité, s.v.p.? [voo-za-vay-[voh-truh-pas-pohr]/[ewn-pyehs-dee-dahN-tee-tay]-seel-voo-play]
Sign here, please.	Vous signez ici, s.v.p. [voo-see-nyay-ee-see-seel-voo-play].

100
CENT FRANCS
X.120
BANQUE DE FRANCE
285136
500
E.221
CINQ CENTS FRANCS
10330
50
Cinquante Francs
358130
200
BANQVE DE FRANCE
781265
M.044
DEVX CENTS FRANCS
BANQUE de FRANCE
20
671213
VINGT FRANCS
F.022

I'd like to withdraw… U.S. dollars/francs from my account/savings account.	Je voudrais retirer . . . U.S. dollars/ francs de mon compte/livret de caisse d'épargne. [zhuh-voo-dray-ruh-tee-ray... U.S.-do-lars/frahN-duh-mohN-[kohNt]/[lee-vray-duh-kehs-day-parny]
Has any money been transferred for me?	Est-ce qu'on a viré de l'argent à mon compte? [ehs-kohN-na-lee-vray-duh-lar-zhahN-a-mohN-kohNt]
Go to the cashier, please.	Vous allez à la caisse, s.v.p. [voo-za-lay-a-la-kehs]
Bills, please.	Seulement des billets, s.v.p. [suhl-mahN-day-bee-yay-seel-voo-play]
Some small change too, please.	Un peu de petite monnaie également. [aN-uuh-duh-puh-teet-mo-nay-ay-gal-mahN]
I'd like four 200-franc bills and the rest in small change, please.	Vous me donnez quatre billets de deux cents et le reste en petite monnaie, s.v.p. [voo-muh-do-nay-katr-bee-yay-duh-duuh-sahN-ay-luh-rehst-ahN-puh-teet-mo-nay-seel-voo-play]
I've lost my traveler's checks. What do I have to do?	J'ai perdu mes chèques de voyage. Qu'est-ce qu'il faut que je fasse? [zhay-pehr-dew-may-shehk-duh-vwa-yazh-kehs-keel-fo-kuh-zhuh-fas]

Word List: Money Matters

account	le compte [luh-kohNt]
amount	le montant [luh-mohN-tahN]; la somme [la-sohm]
bank	la banque [la-bahNk]
bank account	le compte en banque [luh-kohNt-ahN-bahNk]
bank card	la carte (de chèque) [la-kart-duh-shehk]
bank charges	les frais *(m)* bancaires [lay-fray-bahN-kehr]
bank code number	le code établissement [luh-kohd-ay-ta-blees-mahN]
banknote	le billet [luh-bee-yay]
cash	les espèces *(f)* [lay-zehs-pehs]

to cash a check	encaisser un chèque [ahN-kay-say-aN-shehk]
change	le change [luh-shahNzh]
to change	changer [shahN-zhay]
check	le chèque [luh-shehk]
check book	le carnet de chèques [luh-kar-nay-duh-shehk]
coin	la pièce de monnaie [la-pyehs-duh-mo-nay]
commission	la commission [la-ko-mee-syohN]
credit card	la carte de crédit [la-kart-duh-kray-dee]
currency	les devises *(f)* [lay-duh-veez]
to deposit	verser [vehr-say]
Eurocheck	l'eurochèque *(m)* [luuh-ro-shehk]
exchange office	le bureau de change [luh-bew-ro-duh-shahNzh]
exchange rate	le cours de change [luh-koor-duh-shahNzh]
form	le formulaire [luh-fohr-mew-lehr]
in cash	en espèces [ahN-ehs-pehs]
money	l'argent *(m)* [lar-zhahN]
money order	le mandat [luh-mahN-da]
to pay	payer [pay-yay]
payment	le paiement [luh-pay-mahN]
PIN number	le numéro de code [luh-new-may-ro-duh-kohd]
receipt	le reçu [luh-ruh-sew]
savings account	le compte d'épargne [luh-kohNt-day-parny]; le livret de caisse d'épargne [luh-lee-vray-duh-kehs-day-parny]
savings bank	la caisse d'épargne [la-kehs-day-parny]
savings book	le livret de caisse d'épargne [luh-lee-vray-duh-kehs-day-parny]
to sign	signer [see-nyay]
signature	la signature [la-see-nya-tewr]
small change	la monnaie [la-mo-nay]
Swiss franc	le franc suisse [luh-frahN-swees]
transfer	le virement [luh-veer-mahN]
transfer form	le mandat-carte [luh-mahN-da-kart]
transfer order	le mandat de paiement [luh-mahN-da-duh-peh-mahN]
traveler's check	le chèque de voyage [luh-shehk-duh-vwa-yazh]
window (in a bank)	le guichet [luh-gee-shay]

wire transfer	le mandat télégraphique [luh-mahN-da-tay-lay-gra-feek]
to withdraw	retirer [ruh-tee-ray]
to write a check	tirer un chèque [tee-ray-aN-shehk]

At the Post Office

A la poste

Where is the nearest post office/mailbox/ postbox?	Où se trouve le bureau de poste le plus proche/la boîte aux lettres la plus proche? [oo-suh-troov-[luh-bew-ro-duh-pohst-luh-plew-prohsh]/[la-bwat-o-lehtr-la-plew-prosh]
How much does a letter/postcard cost . . .	Quel est le tarif d'affranchissement des lettres/cartes postales . . . [kehl-ay-luh-ta-reef-da-frahN-shees-mahN-day-[lehtr]/[kart-pos-tal]]
to the United States?	pour les Etats-Unis [lay-zay-ta-zew-nee]
to Canada?	pour le Canada? [poor-luh-ka-na-da]
Three . . . Francs stamps, please.	Trois timbres à . . . francs, s.v.p. [trwa-taN-bra...frahN-seel-voo-play]

One can get stamps not only at the post office, but also at the tobacco shop.

I'd like to send this letter . . .
Je voudrais envoyer cette lettre . . . [zhuh-voo-dray-ahN-vwa-yay-seht-lehtr]

registered.
en recommandé. [ahN-ruh-ko-mahN-day]

by airmail.
par avion. [par-a-vyohN]

express.
en exprès. [ahN-ehk-sprehs]

How long does a letter to the United States take?
Quels sont les délais postaux pour les Etats Unis? [kehl-sohN-lay-day-lay-pohs-to-poor-lay-zay-ta-zew-nee]

Do you also have stamps for collectors?
Vous avez des timbres de collection? [voo-za-vay-day-taNbr-duh-ko-lehk-syohN]

This set/One each of those, please.
Donnez-moi cette série-là/un timbre de chaque série, s.v.p. [do-nay-mwa-seht-say-ree-la]/[aN-taNbr-duh-sahk-say-ree]-seel-voo-play]

Held Mail — Poste restante

Are there any letters for me? My name's . . .
Est-ce qu'il y a du courrier pour moi? Mon nom est . . . [ehs-keel-ya-dew-koo-ryay-poor-mwa-mohN-nohN-ay]

No, there is nothing for you.
Non, il n'y a rien. [nohN-eel-nee-ya-ryaN]

Yes, there is something for you. Could I see your passport, please?
Oui, il y a deux lettres. Vous avez une pièce d'identité? [wee-eel-ya-duuh-lehtr-voo-za-vay-ewn-pyehs-dee-dahN-tee-tay]

Telegrams/Faxes — Télégrammes/Téléfax

I'd like to send a telegram, please.
Je voudrais envoyer un télégramme. [zhuh-voo-dray-ahN-vwa-yay-aN-tay-lay-gram]

Can you please help me to fill in the form?
Vous pouvez m'aider à remplir le formulaire, s.v.p.? [voo-poo-vay-may-day-a-rahN-pleer-luh-fohr-mew-lehr-seel-voo-play]

How much is one word?	Quel est le tarif par mot? [kehl-ay-luh-ta-reef—par-mo]
Up to 10 words it costs . . ., each additional word is . . .	Jusqu'à dix mots, c'est . . ., et c'est . . . par mot en plus. [zhews-ka-dee-mo-say . . . ay-say . . . par-mo-ahN-plews]
Will the telegram be delivered today to . . .?	Est-ce que mon télégramme va arriver aujourd'hui à . . .? [ehs-kuh-mohN- tay-lay-gram-va-a-ree-vay-o-zhoor-dwee-a]
Can I send a fax from here to . . .?	Est-ce que je peux envoyer un fax à . . ., d'ici? [ehs-kuh-zhuh-puuh-ahN-vwa-yay-aN-faks-a . . . dee-see]

Word List: Post Office

See Word List: Money Matters

address	l'adresse *(f)* [la-drehs]
addressee	le destinataire [luh-dehs-tee-na-tehr]
airmail, by	par avion [par-a-vyohN]
cash on delivery (COD)	contre remboursement [kohN-truh-rahN-boor-suh-mahN]
collection	la levée [la-luh-vay]
customs declaration	la déclaration en douane [la-day-kla-ra-syohN-ahN-dwan]
declaration of value	la déclaration de valeur [la-day-kla-ra-syohN-duh-va-luhr]
destination	la destination [la-dehs-tee-na-syohN]
dispatch form	le bulletin d'expédition [luh-bewl-taN-dehk-spay-dee-syohN]
envelope	l'enveloppe *(f)* [lahN-vlohp]
express letter	la lettre exprès [la-lehtr-ehk-sprehs]
fax	le fax [luh-faks]
fee	la taxe [la-taks] le tarif [luh-ta-reef]
to fill in	remplir [rahN-pleer]
form	la formule [la-fohr-mewl]
to forward	faire suivre [fehr-sweevr]
held mail	poste restante [pohst-rehs-tahNt]
letter	la lettre [la-lehtr]
to mail	poster *(lettre)* [pos-tay]; envoyer *(télégramme)* [ahN-vwa-yay]
mailbox	la boîte aux lettres [la-bwat-o-lehtr]
mailman	le facteur [luh-fak-tuhr]

main post office	la poste centrale [la-pohst-sahN-tral]
opening hours	les heures *(f)* d'ouverture des guichets [lay-zuhr-doo-vehr-tewr-day-gee-shay]
package	le paquet [luh-pa-kay]; le colis [luh-ko-lee]
post office	le bureau de poste [luh-bew-ro-duh-pohst]
postage	le port [luh-pohr]
postcard	la carte postale [la-kart-pos-tal]
printed matter	l'imprimé *(m)* [laN-pree-may]
receipt	le récépissé [luh-ray-say-pee-say]
registered letter	la lettre recommandée [la-lehtr-ruh-ko-mahN-day]
to send	envoyer [ahN-vwa-yay]; expédier [ehk-spay-dyay]
sender	l'expéditeur *(m)* [lehk-spay-dee-tuhr]
special issue stamp	le timbre de collection [luh-taN-bruh-duh-ko-lehk-syohN]
to stamp	affranchir [a-frahN-sheer]
stamp	le timbre [luh-taNbr]
stamp machine	le distributeur automatique de timbres [luh-dees-tree-bew-tuhr-o-to-ma-teek-duh-taNbr]
telegram	le télégramme [luh-tay-lay-gram]
telex	le télex [luh-tay-lehks]
weight	le poids [luh-pwa]
window	le guichet [luh-gee-shay]
zip code	le code postal [luh-kohd-pos-tal]

Telephoning

Téléphone

Could I use your telephone?	Est-ce que je peux téléphoner? [ehs-kuh-zhuuh-puuh-tay-lay-fo-nay]
Excuse me, I am looking for the nearest phone booth?	Pardon, Mme/Mlle/M., je cherche une cabine téléphonique. [par-dohN-[ma-dam]/[mad-mwa-zehl]/[muh-syuuh]-zhuh-shehrsh-ewn-ka-been-tay-lay-fo-neek]
Can I have a phone card, please?	Je voudrais une télécarte? [zhuh-voo-dray-ewn-tay-lay-kart]
Can you give me some change? I need to make a phone call.	Vous pouvez me faire de la monnaie, s.v.p.? C'est pour téléphoner. [voo-poo-vay-muh-fehr-duh-la-mo-nay-seel-voo-play-say-poor-tay-lay-fo-nay]

1 Introduisez dans la fente ci-dessus un jeton de téléphone.
2 Décrochez le combiné.
3 Attendez la tonalité, puis formez le numéro d'appel de votre correspondant.
4 Quand vous entendrez celui-ci, enfoncez le bouton.
5 En cas de non réponse, de fausse manœuvre ou d'occupation, raccrochez le combiné et le jeton vous sera rendu.

Attention

A partir de cet appareil il n'est pas possible d'obtenir de communications interurbaines ou régionales.

1. Put the token in the slot.
2. Lift the receiver.
3. Listen for the dial tone, then dial the number.
4. When you hear the voice, push the button.
5. If there is no answer, a wrong number, or a busy signal, hang up. The token will be refunded.

Attention

Only local calls can be dialed, from this telephone.

One can find a phone number on the screen of the Minitel in every post office.

Do you have a phone directory for . . . ?	Vous avez l'annuaire de . . .? [voo-za-vay-la-nwehr-duh]
What's the national code for . . .?	Quel est l'indicatif de . . .? [kehl-ay-laN-dee-ka-teef-duh]
Information, can you please give me the number for . . .	Allô, les renseignements? Donnez-moi le numéro de . . . [a-lo-lay-rahN-seh-nyuh-mahN-do-nay-mwa-luh-new-may-ro-duh]
I'd like to make a call to . . .	Je voudrais téléphoner à . . ., s.v.p. [zhuh-voo-dray-tay-lay-fo-nay-a . . . seel-voo-play]
I'd like to make a collect call to . . .	Je voudrais un numéro en P.C.V. [zhuh-voo-dray-aN-new-may-ro-ahN-pay-say-vay]
Can you put me through to . . . please?	Passez-moi . . ., s.v.p.? [pa-say-mwa-seel-voo-play]
Booth number . . .	Cabine numéro . . . [ka-been-new-may-ro]
The line is busy.	La ligne est occupée. [la-leeny-ay-o-kew-pay]
There's no answer.	Ça ne répond pas. [sa-nuh-ray-pohN-pa]
Hold the line, please.	Ne quittez pas. [nuh-kee-tay-pa]
This is . . . speaking.	Mme/Mlle/M. . . à l'appareil. [ma-dam]/mad-mwa-zehl]/[muh-syuuh]...a-la-pa-rehy]
Hello, who is speaking?	Allô? Qui est à l'appareil? [a-lo-kee-ay-ta-la-pa-rehy]
Can I speak to Mr./Mrs./Ms. . ., please?	Est-ce que je pourrais parler à Mme/Mlle/M. . . s.v.p.? [ehs-kuh-zhuh-poo-ray-par-lay-a-[ma-dam]/[mad-mwa-zehl]/[muh-syuuh]...seel-voo-play]
I'll put you through.	Je vous le/la passe. [zhuh-voo-luh/la pas]
I'm sorry, he's/she's not here/at home.	Je suis désolé/e, il/elle n'est pas là. [zhuh-swee-day-zo-lay-eel/ehl-nay-pa-la]
When will he/she be back?	Quand est-ce qu'il/elle sera de retour? [kahN-tehs-keel/kehl-suh-ra-duh-ruh-toor]
Can he/she call back?	Il/Elle peut vous rappeler, si vous voulez? [eel/ehl-puuh-voo-rap-lay-see-voo-voo-lay]

Yes, my number is . . .	D'accord. Mon numéro, c'est le . . . [da-kohr-mohN-new-may-ro-say-luh]
Would you like to leave a message?	Vous voulez laisser un message? [voo-voo-lay-lay-say-aN-may-sazh]
Would you tell him/her that I called?	Dites-lui que j'ai téléphoné? [deet-lwee-kuh-zhay-tay-lay-fo-nay]
Could you give him/her a message?	Vous pourriez lui faire une commission? [voo-poo-ryay-lwee-fehr-ewn-ko-mee-syohN]
I will call back later.	Je rappellerai. [zhuh-ra-pehl-ray]
The number you have reached is not in service.	Il n'y a pas d'abonné au numéro que vous avez demandé. [eel-nee-ya-pa-da-bo-nay-o-new-may-ro-kuh-voo-za-vay-duh-mahN-day]

Word List: Telephoning

to answer the phone	décrocher [day-kro-shay]
answering machine	le répondeur automatique [luh-ray-pohN-duhr-o-to-ma-teek]
busy	occupé [o-kew-pay]
to call	appeler [ap-lay]; téléphoner à [tay-lay-fo-nay-a]
charge	la taxe [la-taks]; le tarif [luh-ta-reef]
collect call	l'appel *(m)* en P.C.V. [la-pehl-ahN-pay-say-vay]
to dial a number	composer le numéro [kohN-po-zay-luh-new-may-ro]
to dial direct	composer directement [kohN-po-zay-dee-rehk-tuh-mahN]
information/directory	les renseignements *(m)* [lay-rahN-seh-nyuh-mahN]
international call	un appel pour l'étranger [aN-na-pehl-poor-lay-trahN-zhay]
local call	la communication en ville [la-ko-mew-nee-ka-syohN-ahn-veel]
long-distance call	la communication interurbaine [la-ko-mew-nee-ka-syohN-aN-tehr-ewr-behn]
national code	l'indicatif *(m)* [laN-dee-ka-teef]
phone booth	la cabine téléphonique [la-ka-been-tay-lay-fo-neek]

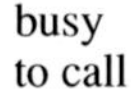

phone call	le coup de téléphone [luh-koo-duh-tay-lay-fohn]; la communication [la-ko-mew-nee-ka-syohN]; l'entretien *(m)* téléphonique [lahN-truh-tyaN-tay-lay-fo-neek]
phone card	la télécarte [la-tay-lay-kart]
phone number	le numéro de téléphone [luh-new-may-ro]
receiver	le combiné [luh-kohN-bee-nay]
repair service	le service des dérangements [lay-sehr-vees-day-day-rahNzh-mahN]
switchboard	le standard [luh-stahN-dar]
telephone	le téléphone [luh-tay-lay-fohn]
telephone book	l'annuaire *(m)* [la-nwehr]
telephone exchange	l'inter(urbain) [laN-tehr-ewr-baN]

At the Police Station

Au poste de police/Au commissariat

See also Unit 3, Car/Motorcycle/Bicycle

The police station can be reached by calling the emergency number 17 and the fire department by calling 18.

Where's the nearest police station, please?	Où est le commissariat de police le plus proche, s.v.p.? [oo-ay-luh-ko-mee-sa-rya-duh-po-lees-luh-plew-prohsh-seel-voo-play]
I'd like to report a theft/a loss/an accident.	Je voudrais faire une déclaration de vol/de perte/d'accident. [zhuh-voo-dray-fehr-ewn-day-kla-ra-syohN-duh-[vohl]/[pehrt]/[ak-see-dahN]
My . . . has been stolen.	On m'a volé . . . [ohN-ma-vo-lay]
handbag/purse	mon sac à main. [mohN-sak-a-maN]
wallet	mon portefeuille. [mohN-pohr-tuh-fuhy]
camera	mon appareil-photo. [mohN-na-pa-rehy-fo-to]
car/bike	ma voiture/mon vélo. [ma-vwa-tewr]/[mohN-vay-lo]
My car has been broken into.	On a fracturé la porte de ma voiture. [ohN-na-frak-tew-ray-la-pohrt-duh-ma-vwa-tewr]
. . . has been stolen from my car.	On a volé . . . dans ma voiture. [ohN-na-vo-lay...dahN-ma-vwa-tewr]

I've lost . . .	J'ai perdu . . . [zhay-pehr-dew]
My son/my daughter has been missing since . . .	Mon fils/Ma fille a disparu . . . [mohN-es]/[ma-feey]-a-dees-pa-rew]
This man keeps bothering me.	Cet homme ne cesse de m'importuner. [seht-ohm-nuh-sehs-duh-maN-pohr-tew-nay]
Could you help me, please?	Vous pouvez m'aider, s.v.p.? [voo-poo-vay-may-day-seel-voo-play]
When exactly did this happen?	Ça s'est passé quand exactement? [sa-say—pa-say-kahN-ehg-zak-tuh-mahN]
We'll look into the matter.	On va s'en occuper. [ohN-va-sahN-no-kew-pay]
I've got nothing to do with it.	Je ne suis pour rien dans cette histoire. [zhuh-nee-swee-poor-ryaN-dahN-seht-ees-twar]
Your name and address, please.	Votre nom et votre adresse, s.v.p. [voh-truh-nohN-ay-voh-tra-drehs-seel-voo-play]
Get in touch with the American/Canadian consulate.	Adressez-vous au consulat des Etats-Unis, du Canada, s.v.p. [a-dray-say-voo-o-kohN-sew-la-[day-zay-ta-zew-nee]/[dew-ka-na-da]-seel-voo-play]

Word List: Police

to arrest	arrêter [a-ray-tay]
to beat up	rouer de coups [roo-ay-duh-koo]
to break into/open	fracturer [frak-tew-ray]
to confiscate	confisquer [kohN-fees-kay]
car keys	les clés *(f)* de voiture [lay-klay-duh-vwa-tewr]
car radio	l'autoradio *(m)* [lo-to-ra-dyo]
car registration	la carte grise [la-kar-tuh-greez]
court	le tribunal [luh-tree-bew-nal]
crime	le crime [luh-kreem]
documents, papers	les papiers *(m)* [lay-pa-pyay]
drugs	la drogue [la-drohg]
fraud	la fraude [la-frod]
guilt	la culpabilité [la-kewl-pa-bee-lee-tay]
to harass	importuner [aN-pohr-tew-nay]
identity card	la pièce d'identité [la-pyehs-dee-dahN-tee-tay]

judge	le juge [luh-zhewzh]
key	la clé [la-kay]
lawyer	l'avocat *(m)* [la-vo-ka]
to lose	perdre [pehrdr]
mugging	l'agression *(f)* [la-gray-syohN]; le hold-up [luh-old-uhp]
passport	le passeport [luh-pas-pohr]
pickpocket	le voleur à la tire [luh-vo-luhr-a-la-teer]; le pickpocket [luh-peek-po-keht]
police	la police [la-po-lees]
police car	la voiture de police [la-vwa-tewr-duh-po-lees]
policeman/policewoman	l'agent *(m)* de police [la-zhahN-duh-po-lees]
preventive detention	la détention préventive [la-day-tahN-syohN-pray-vahN-teev]
prison	la prison [la-pree-zohN]
purse	le porte-monnaie [luh-pohrt-mo-nay]
rape	le viol [luh-vyohl]
to report	faire une déclaration [fehr-ewn-day-kla-ra-syohN]
theft	le vol [luh-vohl]
thief	le voleur [luh-vo-luhr]

Lost and Found

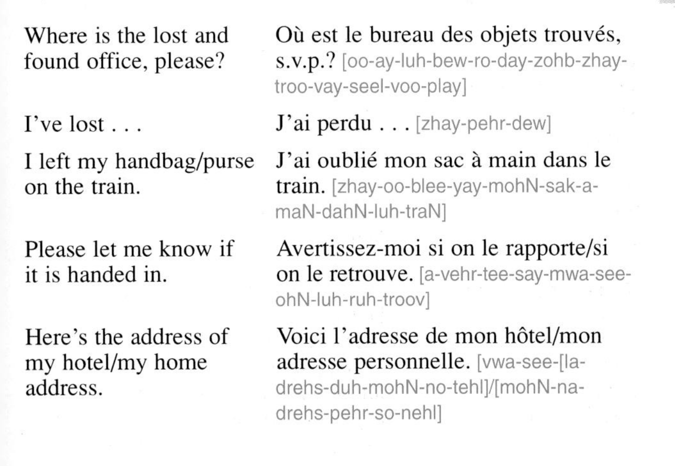

Bureau des objets trouvés

Where is the lost and found office, please?	Où est le bureau des objets trouvés, s.v.p.? [oo-ay-luh-bew-ro-day-zohb-zhay-troo-vay-seel-voo-play]
I've lost . . .	J'ai perdu . . . [zhay-pehr-dew]
I left my handbag/purse on the train.	J'ai oublié mon sac à main dans le train. [zhay-oo-blee-yay-mohN-sak-a-maN-dahN-luh-traN]
Please let me know if it is handed in.	Avertissez-moi si on le rapporte/si on le retrouve. [a-vehr-tee-say-mwa-see-ohN-luh-ruh-troov]
Here's the address of my hotel/my home address.	Voici l'adresse de mon hôtel/mon adresse personnelle. [vwa-see-[la-drehs-duh-mohN-no-tehl]/[mohN-na-drehs-pehr-so-nehl]

POSTES
HEURES DES LEVÉES
JOURS OUVRABLES
SAMEDI
11H45
BUREAU LE PLUS PROCHE
DECIZE
NE PAS JETER DE JOURNAUX
DANS CETTE BOITE

10 Health
La santé

At the Pharmacy

A la pharmacie

Where's the nearest pharmacy (with all-night service)?	Vous pourriez m'indiquer une pharmacie (de garde), s.v.p.? [voo-poo-ryay-maN-dee-kay-ewn-far-ma-see-duh-gard-seel-voo-play]
Can you give me something for . . .?	Donnez-moi quelque chose contre . . ., s.v.p.? [do-nay-mwa-kehl-kuh-shoz-kohN-truh] . . . [seel-voo-play]
You need a prescription for this.	Ce médicament n'est délivré que sur ordonnance. [suh-may-dee-ka-mahN-nay-day-lee-vray-kuh-sewr-ohr-do-nahNs]
I will wait, if you wish.	Je peux attendre, si vous voulez. [zhuh-puuh-a-tahNdr-see-voo-voo-lay]
When can I pick it up?	Quand est-ce que je peux venir le chercher? [kahN-tehs-kuh-zhuh-puuh-vuh-neer-luh-shehr-shay]

Word List: Pharmacy See also Word List: Doctor/Dentist/Hospital

after meals	après les repas [a-pray-lay-ruh-pa]
antibiotics	l'antibiotique *(m)* [lahN-tee-byo-teek]
antidote	l'antidote *(m)* [lahN-tee-doht]
aspirin	l'aspirine *(f)* [las-pee-reen]
bandage	le tricostéril [luh-tree-ko-stay-reel]; le sparadrap [luh-spa-ra-dra]
before meals	avant les repas [a-vahN-lay-ruh-pa]
birth control pills	la pillule (anticonceptionnelle) [la-pee-lewl-ahN-tee-kohN-sehp-syo-nehl]
camomile tea	la camomille [la-ka-mo-meey]
cardiac stimulant	le médicament pour la circulation [luh-may-dee-ka-mahN-poor-la-seer-kew-la-syohN]
condom	le préservatif [luh-pray-zehr-va-teef]
cotton wool	le coton hydrophile [luh-ko-tohN-ee-dro-feel]
cough syrup	le sirop contre la toux [luh-see-ro-kohN-truh-la-too]
disinfectant	l'antiseptique *(m)* [lahN-tee-sehp-teek]

drops	les gouttes *(f)* [lay-goot]
drops for a stomachache	les gouttes *(f)* pour les maux d'estomac [lay-goot-poor-lay-mo-dehs-to-ma]
eardrops	le collyre liquide [luh-ko-leer-lee-keed]
elastic bandage	le bandage élastique [luh-bahN-dazh-ay-las-teek]
eyedrops	les gouttes *(f)* pour les oreilles [lay-goot-poor-lay-zo-rehy]
gauze bandage	la gaze [la-gaz]
glucose	le glucose [luh-glew-koz]
headache pills	les cachets *(m)* contre les maux de tête [lay-ka-shay-kohN-truh-lay-mo-duh-teht]
insect repellent	l'insecticide *(m)* [laN-sehk-tee-seed]
insulin	l'insuline *(f)* [laN-sew-leen]
iodine	la teinture d'iode [la-taN-tewr-dyohd]
laxative	le laxatif [luh-lak-sa-teef]
let it disolve in your mouth	laisser fondre dans la bouche [lay-say-fohN-druh-dahN-la-boosh]
lozenges	les pastilles *(f)* contre le mal de gorge [lay-pas-teey-kohN-truh-luh-mal-duh-gorzh]
medicine	le médicament [luh-may-dee-ka-mahN]
mouthwash	le gargarisme [luh-gar-ga-reezm]
ointment	la pommade [la-po-mad]
ointment for burns	la pommade contre les brûlures [la-po-mad-kohN-truh-lay-brew-lewr]
on an empty stomach	jeûn [a-zhaN]
painkillers	les cachets *(m)* contre la douleur [lay-ka-shay-kohN-truh-la-doo-luhr]
powder	la poudre [la-poodr]
prescription	l'ordonnance *(f)* [lohr-do-nahNs]
remedy	le remède [luh-ruh-mehd]
sedative, tranquilizer	le tranquillisant [luh-trahN-kee-lee-zahN] le calmant [luh-kal-mahN]
sleeping pills	les somnifères *(m)* [lay-sohm-nee-fehr]
sunburn	le coup de soleil [luh-koo-duh-so-lehy]
suppository	les suppositoires *(m)* [lay-sew-po-zee-twar]
tablet	le comprimé [luh-kohN-pree-may]; le cachet [luh-ka-shay]
to take	prendre [prahNdr]
thermometer	le thermomètre [luh-tehr-mo-mehtr]

At the Doctor

Chez le médecin

Can you recommend a good . . .?	Vous pourriez m'indiquer un bon . . . s.v.p.? [voo-poo-ryay-maN-dee-kay-aN-bohN . . . seel-voo-play]
doctor	médecin [mehd-saN]
eye specialist	ophtalmo [ohf-tal-mo]
gynecologist	gynécologue [zhee-nay-ko-lohg]
ear, nose and throat specialist	oto-rhino(-laryngologiste) [o-to-ree-no]
dermatologist	dermatologue [dehr-ma-to-lohg]
healer	guérisseur [gay-ree-suhr]
specialist for internal medicine	spécialiste des maladies internes [spay-sya-leest-day-ma-la-dee-aN-tehrn]
pediatrician	pédiatre [pay-dyatr]
neurologist	neurologue [nuuh-ro-lohg]
GP (general practitioner)	généraliste [zhay-nay-ra-leest]
urologist	urologue [ew-ro-lohg]
dentist	dentiste [dahN-teest]
Where is his/her practice/office?	Où se trouve son cabinet, s.v.p.? [oo-suh-troov-sohN-ka-bee-nay-seel-voo-play]
What are his/her office hours?	Quelles sont ses heures de consultation? [kehl-sohN-say-zuhr-duh-kohN-sewl-ta-syohN]
What's the trouble?	Qu'est-ce qui ne va pas? [kehs-kee-nuh-va-pa]
I don't feel well.	Je ne me sens pas très bien. [zhuh-nuh-muh-sahN-pa-byaN]
I have a temperature.	J'ai de la fièvre. [zhay-duh-la-fyehvr]
I can't sleep.	Je ne dors pas la nuit. [zhuh-nuh-dohr-pa-la-nwee]
I often feel sick/nauseated.	J'ai souvent des nausées/vertiges. [zhay-soo-vahN-[day-no-zay]/[day-vehr-teezh]
I fainted.	J'ai eu une syncope. [zhay-ew-ewn-saN-kohp]

I have a bad cold.	Je suis très enrhumé. [zhuh-swee-tray-zahN-rew-may]
I have a headache/a sore throat.	J'ai mal à la tête/à la gorge. [zhay-mal-a-la-teht/gohrzh]
I have a cough.	Je tousse beaucoup. [zhuh-toos-bo-koo]
I have been stung/bitten.	J'ai été piqué/mordu. [zhay-ay-tay-[pee-kay]/[mohr-dew]
I have an upset stomach.	J'ai une indigestion. [zhay-ewn-aN-dee-zhehs-tyohN]
I have diarrhea./I am constipated.	J'ai la diarrhée./Je suis constipé. [zhay-la-dya-ray]/[zhuh-swee-kohNs-tee-pay]
The food doesn't agree with me./I can't stand the heat.	Je digère mal./Je ne supporte pas la chaleur. [zhu-dee-gehr-mal]/[zhuh-nuh-sew-pohrt-pa-la-sha-luhr]
I've hurt myself.	Je me suis blessé. [zhuh-muh-swee-blay-say]
I fell down.	Je suis tombé. [zhuh-swee-tohN-bay]
I think I've broken/sprained . . .	Je crois que je me suis cassé/foulé . . . [zhuh-krwa-kuh-zhuh-muh-swee-[ka-say]/[foo-lay]
Where does it hurt?	Où est-ce que vous avez mal? [oo-ehs-kuh-voo-za-vay-mal]
I've got a pain here.	J'ai mal ici. [zhay-mal-ee-see]
Does that hurt?	C'est ici que vous avez mal? [say-tee-see-kuh-voo-za-vay-mal]
I have high/low blood pressure.	Je fais de l'hypertension/del'hypo-tension. [zhuh-fay-[duh-lee-pehr-tahN-syohN]/[duh-lee-po-tahN-syohN]
I'm a diabetic.	Je suis diabétique. [zhuh-swee-dya-bay-teek]
I'm pregnant.	J'attends un enfant/Je suis enceinte. [zha-tahN-aN-nahN-fahN]/[zhuh-swee-zahN-saNt]
I had recently . . .	J'ai eu récemment . . . [zhay-ew-ray-sa-mahN]

Get undressed, please./ Lift your sleeve.	Déshabillez-vous/Retroussez votre manche, s.v.p. [day-za-bee-yay-voo]/ [ruh-troo-say-voh-truh-mahNsh]-seel-voo-play]
Take a deep breath. Hold your breath, please.	Inspirez profondément. Retenez votre respiration. [aNs-pee-ray-pro-fohN-day-mahN-ruh-tuh-nay-voh-truh-rehs-pee-ra-syohN]
Open your mouth.	Ouvrez la bouche. [oo-vray-la-boosh]
Put your tongue out.	Tirez la langue. [tee-ray-la-lahNg]
Cough, please.	Toussez, s.v.p. [too-say-seel-voo-play]
How long have you been feeling like this?	Depuis combien de temps vous sentez-vous ainsi? [duh-pwee-kohN-byaN-duh-tahN-voo-sahN-tay-voo-aN-see]
How is your appetite?	Vous avez de l'appétit? [voo-za-vay-duh-la-pay-tee]
I've lost my appetite.	Je n'ai pas d'appétit. [zhuh-nay-pa-da-pay-tee]
Do you have a vaccination certificate?	Vous avez un certificat de vaccination? [voo-za-vay-aN-sehr-tee-fee-ka-duh-vak-see-na-syohN]
I've been vaccinated against...	Je suis vacciné(e) contre... [zhuh-swee-vak-see-nay-kohNtr]
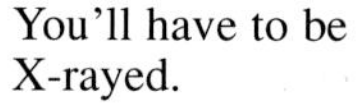 You'll have to be X-rayed.	Il faut que vous vous fassiez faire une radio. [eel-fo-kuh-voo-voo-fa-syay-fehr-ewn-ra-dyo]
I need to do a blood/ urine test.	C'est pour une analyse de sang/ d'urine. [say-poor-ewn-a-na-leez-[duh-sahN]/[dew-reen]]
I'll have to send you to a specialist.	Il va falloir consulter un spécialiste. [eel-va-fa-lwar-kohN-sewl-tay-aN-spay-sya-leest]
You'll have to have an operation.	Il va falloir vous faire opérer. [eel-va-fa-lwar-voo-fehr-o-pay-ray]
You need a few days in bed.	Vous allez garder le lit pendant deux ou trois jours. [voo-za-lay-gar-day-luh-lee-pahN-dahN-duuh-zoo-trwa-zhoor]

It's nothing serious.	Il n'y a rien de grave. [eel-nee-ya-ryaN-duh-grav]
Can you give me/ prescribe something for … ?	Vous pouvez me donner/me prescire quelque chose contre..., s.v.p.? [voo-poo-vay-[muh-do-nay]/[muh-prehs-kreer]-kehl-kuh-shoz-kohNtr-...-seel-voo-play]
I usually take …	Normalement, je prends... [nohr-mal-mahN-zhuh-prahN]
Take one tablet/pill before you go to bed.	Vous prendrez un comprimé chaque soir, avant de vous coucher. [voo-prahN-dray-an-kohN-pree-may-shak-swar-a-vahN-duh-voo-koo-shay]
Here's my international medical insurance card.	Voici ma feuille de maladie internationale. [vwa-see-ma-fuhy-duh-ma-la-dee-aN-tehr-na-syo-nal]
Can you give me a doctor's certificate, please?	Vous pouvez me faire un certificat médical, s.v.p.? [voo-poo-vay-muh-fehr-aN-sehr-tee-fee-ka-may-dee-kal-seel-voo-play]

At the Dentist

Chez le dentiste

I have a (terrible) toothache.	J'ai (très) mal aux dents. [zhay-(tray)-mal-o-dahN]
This tooth (at the top/ bottom/front/back) hurts.	C'est cette dent-là (en haut/en bas/ devant/derrière) qui me fait mal. [say-seht-dahN-la-(ahN-o/ahN-ba/duh-vahN/day-ryehr)-kee-muh-fay-mal]
I've lost a filling.	J'ai perdu un plombage. [zhay-pehr-dew-aN-plohN-bazh]
I've broken a tooth.	Je me suis cassé une dent. [zhuh-muh-swee-ka-say-ewn-dahN]
I'll have to fill it.	Je vais vous faire un plombage. [zhuh-vay-voo-fehr-aN-plohN-bazh]
I'll do only a temporary job.	Je ne vous ferai qu'un traitement provisoire. [zhuh-nuh-voo-fuh-ray-kaN-treht-mahN-pro-vee-zwar]

It will have to come out.	Il faut que je l'arrache. [eel-fo-kuh-zhuh-la-rash]
This tooth needs a crown.	Il faut que je mette une couronne à cette dent. [eel-fo-kuh-zhuh-meht-ewn-koo-rohn-a-seht-dahN]
I'd like an injection, please. /I don't want an injection.	Faites-moi une piqûre/Ne me faites pas de piqûre, s.v.p. [feht-mwa-ewn-pee-kewr]/[nuh-muh-feht-pa-duh-pee-kewr]-seel-voo-play]
Rinse well, please.	Rincez-vous bien la bouche. [rahN-say-voo-byaN-la-boosh]
Can you repair these dentures, please?	Vous pouvez réparer cette prothèse? [voo-poo-vay-ray-pa-ray-seht-pro-tehz]
Come again in two days so that I can have a look at it.	Repassez après-demain, s.v.p., pour que je voie ce que ça donne. [ruh-pa-say-a-pray-duh-maN-seel-voo-play-poor-kuh-zhuh-vwa-suh-kuh-sa-dohn]
See your dentist as soon as you get home.	Dès votre retour chez vous, vous irez voir votre dentiste. [day-voh-truh-ruh-toor-shay-voo-voo-zee-ray-vwar-voh-truh-dahN-teest]

At the Hospital

A l'hôpital

How long will I have to stay here?	Combien de temps est-ce que je vais devoir rester ici? [kohN-byan-duh-tahN-zhuh-vay-duh-vwar-rehs-tay-ee-see]
I can't sleep. Could you give me a painkiller/a sleeping pill, please?	Je n'arrive pas à m'endormir. Donnez-moi un cachet contre la douleur/un somnifère, s.v.p.? [zhuh-na-reev-pa-a-dohr-meer-do-nay-mwa-[aN-ka-shay-kohN-truh-la-doo-luhr]/[aN-sohm-nee-fehr]-seel-voo-play]
When can I get up?/leave the room?	Quand est-ce que je pourrai me lever/sortir de la chambre? [kahN-tehs-kuh-zhuh-poo-ray-[muh-luh-vay]/[sohr-teer-duh-la-shahNbr]

Please give me a certificate stating how long I was in the hospital, together with the diagnosis.	Faites-moi un certificat indiquant la durée de mon séjour à l'hôpital ainsi que le diagnostic, s.v.p. [feht-mwa-aN-sehr-tee-fee-ka-aN-dee-kahN-la-dew-ray-duh-mohN-say-zhoor-a-lo-pee-tal-aN-see-kuh-luh-dyag-nohs-teek-seel-voo-pla]

Word List: Doctor/Dentist/Hospital

abscess	l'abcès *(m)* [lab-say]
AIDS	le sida [luh-see-da]
allergy; to be allergic to . . .	l'allergie *(f)* [la-lehr-zhee]; être allergique à . . . [eh-tra-lehr-zhee-ka]
anesthetic	l'anesthésie *(f)* [la-nehs-tay-zee]
angina	l'angine *(f)* [lahN-zheen]
ankle	la cheville [la-shuh-veey]
appendicitis	l'appendicite *(f)* [la-paN-dees]
appendix	l'appendice *(m)* [la-paN-dees]
arm	le bras [luh-bra]
asthma	l'asthme *(m)* [lasm]
attack	l'attaque *(f)* [la-tak]; la crise [la-kreez]
back	le dos [luh-do]
backache	la douleur *(f)* dorsale [la-doo-luhr-dohr-sal]
bladder	la vessie [la-vay-see]
to bleed	saigner [say-nyay]
bleeding	le saignement [luh-say-nyuh-mahN]
blood	le sang [luh-sahN]
blood group	le groupe sanguin [luh-groop-sahN-gaN]
blood poisoning	la septicémie [la-sehp-tee-say-mee]
blood pressure (high/low)	la tension (l'hypertension*(f)*/l'hypotension) *(f)* [la-tahN-syohN]/[lee-pehr-tahN-syohN]/[lee-po-tahN-syohN]
blood test	l'analyse *(f)* de sang [la-na-leez-duh-sahN]
blood transfusion	la transfusion (sanguine) [la-trahNs-few-zyohN-sahN-geen]
bone	l'os *(m)* [lohs]
brain	le cerveau [luh-sehr-vo]
to breathe	respirer [rehs-pee-ray]
broken	cassé(e) [ka-say]
bronchial tubes	les bronches *(f)* [lay-brohNsh]
bronchitis	la bronchite [la-brohN-sheet]
burn	la brûlure [la-brew-lewr]
bypass (surgery)	le by-pass [luh-ba-y-pas]

cancer	le cancer [luh-kahN-sehr]
cardiac infarction	l'infarctus *(m)* [laN-fark-tews]
to catch a cold	prendre froid [prahN-druh-frwa]
certificate	l'attestation *(f)* [la-tehs-ta-syohN]; le certificat [luh-sehr-tee-fee-ka]
chest	la poitrine [la-pwa-treen]
chickenpox	la varicelle [la-va-ree-sehl]
cholera	le choléra [luh-ko-lay-ra]
circulatory disorder	les troubles *(m)* de la circulation [lay-troo-bluh-duh-la-seer-kew-la-syohN]
to have a cold	enrhumé [ahN-rew-may]
cold	le rhume (de cerveau) [luh-rewm]
colic	la colique [la-ko-leek]
collarbone	la clavicule [la-kla-vee-kewl]
concussion	la commotion cérébrale [la-ko-mo-syohN-say-ray-bral]
constipation	la constipation [la-kohNs-tee-pa-syohN]
contagious	contagieux/contagieuse [kohN-ta-zhyuuh(z)]
contusion	la contusion [la-kohN-tew-zyohN]
cough	la toux [la-too]
cramp	la crampe [la-krahNp]
crown	la couronne [la-koo-rohn]
cut	la coupure [la-koo-pewr]
department	le service [luh-sehr-vees]
diabetes	le diabète [luh-dya-beht]
diagnosis	le diagnostic [luh-dyag-nohs-teek]
diarrhea	la diarrhée [la-dya-ray]
diet	le régime [luh-ray-zheem]
digestion	la digestion [la-dee-zhehs-tyohN]
digestive trouble	les troubles *(m)* digestifs [lay-troobl-dee-zhehs-teef]
digestive tube	le tube digestif [luh-tewb-dee-zhehs-teef]
diphtheria	la diphtérie [la-deef-tay-ree]
to disinfect	désinfecter [day-zaN-fehk-tay]
dizzy spell/vertigo	le vertige [luh-vehr-teezh]
doctor's office	le cabinet [luh-ka-bee-nay]
doctor's visit	la consultation [la-kohN-sewl-ta-syohN]
to dress	panser [pahN-say]
dressing	le pansement [luh-pahNs-mahN]
ear	l'oreille *(f)* [lo-rehy]
elbow	le coude [luh-kood]
examination	l'examen *(m)* [lehg-za-maN]
eyes	les yeux *(m)* [lay-zyuuh]

face	**le visage** [luh-vee-zazh]
fainted	**évanoui(e)** [ay-va-noo-ee]
fainting	**l'évanouissement** *(m)* [lay-va-nwees-mahN] la syncope [la-saN-kohp]
fever	**la fièvre** [la-fyehvr]; **la température** [la-tahN-pay-ra-tewr]
filling *(tooth)*	**le plombage** [luh-plohN-bazh]
finger	**le doigt** [luh-dwa]
flu	**la grippe** [la-greep]
food poisoning	**l'intoxication** *(f)* **alimentaire** [laN-to-ksee-ka-syohN-a-lee-mahN-tehr]
foot	**le pied** [luh-pyay]
fracture	**la fracture** [la-frak-tewr]
gallbladder	**la vésicule biliaire** [la-vay-zee-kewl-bee-lyehr]
gas	**les vents** *(m)* [lay-vahN]
German measles	**la rubéole** [la-rew-bay-ohl]
gland	**la glande** [la-glahNd]
growth	**la grosseur** [la-gro-suhr]; **la tumeur** [la-tew-muhr]
gums	**les gencives** *(f)* [lay-zhahN-seev]
hand	**la main** [la-maN]
hay fever	**le rhume des foins** *(m)* [lay-rewm-day-fwaN]
head	**la tête** [la-teht]
headache	**le mal de tête** [luh-mal-duh-teht]
hearing	**l'ouïe** *(f)* [lwee]
heart	**le cœur** [luh-kuhr]
heart attack	**la crise cardiaque** [la-kreez-kar-dyak]
heart failure	**la déficience cardiaque** [la-day-fee-syahNs-kar-dyak]
heart specialist	**le cardiologue** [luh-kar-dyo-lohg]
heart trouble	**les troubles** *(m)* **cardiaques** [lay-troobl-kar-dyak]
heartburn	**les aigreurs** *(f)* **d'estomac** [lay-zay-gruhr-dehs-to-ma]
hemorrhage	**l'hémorragie** *(f)* [lay-mo-ra-zhee]
hemorrhoids	**les hémorroïdes** *(f)* [lay-zay-mo-ro-eed]
hernia	**la hernie** [la-ehr-nee]
hip	**la hanche** [la-ahNsh]
to be hoarse	**être enroué** [ehtr-ahN-roo-ay]
hospital	**l'hôpital** *(m)* [lo-pee-tal]
to hurt	**faire mal** [fehr-mal]
incisor	**l'incisive** *(f)* [laN-see-zeev]

infection	l'infection *(f)* [laN-fehk-syohN]
inflammation	l'inflammation *(f)* [laN-fla-ma-syohN]
infusion	la perfusion [la-pehr-few-zyohN]
insomnia	les insomnies *(f)* [lay-zaN-sohm-nee]
intestine	l'instestin *(m)* [laN-tehs-taN]
jaundice	la jaunisse [la-zho-nees]
jaw	la mâchoire [la-ma-shwar]
joint	l'articulation *(f)* [lar-tee-kew-la-syohN]
kidney	le rein [luh-raN]
kidney stone	le calcul rénal [luh-kal-kewl-ray-nal]
knee	le genou [luh-zhuh-noo]
leg	la jambe [la-zhahNb]
limbs	les membres *(m)* [lay-mahNbr]
lip	la lèvre [la-lehvr]
liver	le foie [luh-fwa]
loss of appetite	le manque d'appétit [luh-mahNk-da-pay-tee]
lower abdomen	le bas-ventre [luh-ba-vahNtr]
lumbago	le tour de reins le lumbago [luh-toor-duh-raN]/[luh-laN-ba-go]
lung	le poumon [luh-poo-mohN]
malaria	la malaria [la-ma-la-rya]
measles	la rougeole [la-roo-zhohl]
medical insurance	la caisse d'assurance-maladie [la-kehs-da-sew-rahNs-ma-la-dee]
medical insurance form	la feuille de maladie/de soins [lay-fuhy—duh-ma-la-dee]/[duh-swaN]]
menstruation	les règles *(f)* [lay-rehgl]
migraine	la migraine [la-mee-grehn]
miscarriage	la fausse-couche [la-fos-koosh]
molar	la molaire [la-mo-lehr]
mouth	la bouche [la-boosh]
mumps	les oreillons *(m)* [lay-zo-reh-yohN]
muscle	le muscle [luh-mews-kluh]
nausea	la nausée [la-no-zay]
neck	le cou [luh-koo] la gorge [la-gohrzh]
nephritis	la néphrite [la-nay-freet]
nerve	les nerfs *(m)* [lay-nehr]
nervous	nerveux [nehr-vuuh]
nose	le nez [luh-nay]
nosebleed	les saignements *(m)* de nez [lay-seh-nyuuh-mahN-duh-nay]
nurse	l'infirmière *(m)*/*(f)* [laN-feer-myehr]

operation/surgery	l'opération *(f)* [lo-pay-ra-syohN]
otitis (inflammation of the middle ear)	l'otite *(f)* [lo-teet]
pacemaker	le stimulateur cardiaque [luh-stee-mew-la-tuhr-kar-dyak]
pains	les douleurs *(f)* [lay-doo-luhr]
paralysis	la paralysie [la-pa-ra-lee-zee]
pneumonia	la pneumonie [la-pnuuh-mo-nee]
poisoning	l'empoisonnement *(m)* [lahN-pwa-zohn-mahN]
polio	la polio(myélite) [la-po-lyo-may-leet]
pregnancy	la grossesse [la-gro-sehs]
to prescribe	prescrire [prehs-kreer]
prosthesis	la prothèse [la-pro-tehz]
pulled ligament/muscle	le claquage (musculaire) [luh-kla-kazh-mews-kew-lehr]
to pull *(tooth)*	arracher [a-ra-shay]
pulse	le pouls [luh-poo]
pus	le pus [luh-pew]
rash, pimples	l'éruption *(f)* [lay-rewp-syohN]; les boutons [lay-boo-tohN] *(m)*
respiratory problems	les troubles *(m)* respiratoires [lay-troobl-rehs-pee-ra-twar]
rheumatism	le rhumatisme [luh-rew-ma-teezm]
rib	la côte [la-kot]
rib cage	la cage thoracique [la-kazh-to-ra-seek]
scar	la cicatrice [la-see-ka-trees]
scarlet fever	la scarlatine [la-skar-la-teen]
sciatica	la sciatique [la-sya-teek]
sexual organs	les organes génitaux [lay-zohr-gan-zhay-nee-to]
shinbone	le tibia [luh-tee-bya]
shiver	le frisson [luh-free-sohN]
shot	la piqûre [la-pee-kewr]
shoulder	l'épaule *(f)* [lay-pol]
sick	malade [ma-lad]
sickness	la maladie [la-ma-la-dee]
sinusitis	la sinusite [la-see-new-zeet]
skin	la peau [la-po]
skin disease	la maladie de la peau [la-ma-la-dee-duh-la-po]
skull	le crâne [luh-kran]
smallpox	la variole [la-va-ryohl]
sore throat	le mal de gorge [luh-mal-duh-gohrzh]

specialist	le spécialiste [luh-spay-sya-leest]
spine	la colonne vertébrale [la-ko-lohn-vehr-tay-bral]
splint	l'éclisse *(f)* [lay-klees]; la gouttière [la-goo-tyehr]
sprained	foulé(e) [foo-lay]
sting	la piqûre [la-pee-kewr]
to stitch	recoudre [ruh-koodr]
stitch (in the side)	le point de côté [luh-pwaN-duh-ko-tay]
stomach	l'estomac *(m)* [lehs-to-ma]; le ventre [luh-vahNtr]
stomachache	le mal *(m)* d'estomac [luh-mal-dehs-to-ma]
stools/bowel movement	les selles *(f)* [lay-sehl]
stroke	l'embolie *(f)* [lahN-bo-lee]
sunstroke	l'insolation *(f)* [laN-so-la-syohN]
to suppurate	suppurer [sew-pew-ray]
surgeon	le chirurgien [luh-shee-rewr-zhyaN]
to sweat	transpirer [trahNs-pee-ray]
sweat	la sueur [la-swuhr]
swelling	l'enflure *(f)* [lahN-flewr]
swollen	enflé(e) [ahN-flay]
tetanus	le tétanos [luh-tay-ta-nos]
to throw up	vomir [vo-meer]
toe	l'orteil *(m)* [lohr-tehy]
tongue	la langue [la-lahNg]
tonsilitis	l'inflammation *(f)* des amygdales [laN-fla-ma-syohN-day-za-mee-dal]
tonsils	les amygdales *(f)* [lay-za-mee-dal]
tooth	la dent [la-dahN]
toothache	le mal de dents [luh-mal-duh-dahN]
torn ligament	la rupture de tendon [la-rewp-tewr-duh-tahN-dohN]
tympanum/eardrum	le tympan [luh-taN-paN]
typhoid	la typhoïde [la-tee-fo-eed]
ulcer	l'ulcère *(m)* [lewl-sehr]
ultrasound	l'échographie *(f)* [lay-ko-gra-fee]
ultraviolet light treatment	le traitement à rayons ultraviolets [luh-treht-mahN-a-ray-yohN-ewl-tra-vyo-lay]
urine	l'urine *(f)* [lew-reen]
to vaccinate	vacciner [vak-see-nay]
vaccination	la vaccination [la-vak-see-na-syohN]
vaccination card	le carnet de vaccinations [luh-kar-nay-duh-vak-see-na-syohN]

vein/artery	la veine [la-vehn] l'artère *(f)* [lar-tehr]
venereal disease	la maladie vénérienne [la-ma-la-dee-vay-nay-ryehn]
virus	le virus [luh-vee-rews]
visiting hours	les heures *(f)* de visites [lay-zuhr-duh-vee-zeet]
waiting room	le salon d'attente [luh-sa-lohN-da-tahNt]
whooping cough	la coqueluche [la-ko-klewsh]
without consciousness	sans connaissance [sahN-ko-neh-sahNs]
to wound	blesser [blay-say]
wound	la blessure [la-bleh-sewr]; la plaie [la-play]
to X-ray	faire une radio(graphie) [fehr-ewn-ra-dyo]
X-ray	la radio(graphie) [la-ra-dyo-gra-fee]
yellow fever	la fièvre jaune [la-fyeh-vruh-zhon]

At a Health Resort

En cure

Is treatment in this establishment covered by the insurance?	Est-ce que cet établissement thermal est conventionné? [ehs-kuh-seht-ay-ta-blees-mahN-tehr-mal-ay-kohN-vahN-syo-nay]
What is your doctor's diagnosis?	Quel est le diagnostic de votre médecin? [kehl-ay-luh-dyag-nohs-teek-duh-voh-truh-mehd-saN]
How many more treatments do I have?	J'ai encore combien de séances de soins de prévues? [zhay-ahN-kohr-kohN-byaN-duh-say-ahNs-duh-swaN-duh-pray-vew]
I would like a few additional sessions of . . .	Je voudrais quelques séances supplémentaires de . . . [zhuh-voo-dray-kehl-kuh-say-ahNs-sew-play-mahN-tehr-duh]
Could I change the time/date of the appointment?	Est-ce que je pourrais changer l'heure/la date du rendez-vous? [ehs-kuh-zhuh-poo-ray-shahN-zhay-[luhr]/[la-dat]-dew-rahN-day-voo]

Word List: Health Resort

1,000-calorie diet	le régime sur une base de 1000 calories [luh-ray-zheem-sew-ewn-baz-duh-sahN-ka-lo-ree]
administrative personnel	le personnel administratif de l'établissement [luh-pehr-so-nehl-ad-mee-nees-tra-teef-duh-lay-ta-blees-mahN]
air therapy	l'aérothérapie *(f)* [la-ay-ro-tay-ra-pee]
bath	le bain [luh-baN]
breathing exercices	les exercices *(m)* respiratoires [lay-zehg-zehr-sees-rehs-pee-ra-twar]
convalescent home	la maison de repos [la-meh-zohN-duh-ruh-po]; le préventorium [luh-pray-vahN-to-ryohm]
diet	le régime [luh-ray-zheem]
foot bath	le bain de pieds [luh-baN-duh-pyay]
to give a massage	masser [ma-say]
health cure	la cure [la-kewr]
health cure establishment	l'établissement *(m)* thermal [lay-ta-blees-mahN-tehr-mal]
hot air	l'air *(m)* chaud [lehr-sho]
inhalation	l'inhalation *(f)* [lee-na-la-syohN]
invigorating climate	le climat vivifiant [luh-klee-ma-vee-vee-fyahN]
massage	le massage [luh-ma-sazh]
massage of the connective tissues	le massage du tissu conjonctif [luh-dew-tee-sew-kohN-zhohNk-teef]
massages	les massages *(m)* au jet [lay-ma-sazh-o-zhay]
masseur/masseuse	le masseur [luh-ma-suhr]/la masseuse [la-ma-suuhz]
mineral water health cure	la cure d'eau minérale [la-kewr-do-mee-nay-ral]
mineral water source	la source d'eau minérale [la-soors-do-mee-nay-ral]
mud bath	le bain de boue [luh-baN-duh-boo]
physiotherapy	la physiothérapie [la-fee-zyo-tay-ra-pee]
pump room	la buvette [la-bew-veht]
radiation	les rayons *(m)* [lay-ray-yohN]
reeducation/rehabilitation	la rééducation [la-ray-ay-dew-ka-syohN] la postcure [la-pohst-kewr]
remedy	le remède [luh-ruh-mehd]; le médicament [luh-may-dee-ka-mahN]

rest cure	la cure de repos [la-kewr-duh-ruh-po]
saltwater bath	le bain d'eau salée [luh-baN-do-sa-lay]
steam bath	le bain de vapeur [luh-baN-duh-va-puhr]
taxes	la taxe de séjour [la-taks-duh-say-zhoor]
thermal bath	le bain thermal [luh-baN-tehr-mal]
thermal bath pool	la piscine thermale [la-pee-seen-tehr-mal]
thermal source	la source thermale [la-soors-tehr-mal]
treatment	la séance de soins [lay-say-ahNs-duh-swaN]; le traitement (médical) [luh-treht-mahN-may-dee-kal]
underwater massage	le massage dans l'eau [luh-ma-sazh-dahN-lo]
yoga	le yoga [luh-yo-ga]

11 Business Trip
Voyage d'affaires

On the Way to a Business Meeting

Le long chemin qui mène au partenaire en affaires

Where is the main entrance?	Où se trouve l'entrée principale? [oo-suh-troov-lahN-tray-praN-see-pal]
Can you tell me how to get to . . ., please?	Je cherche M./Mme/Mlle . . . [zhuh-shehrsh-[muh-syuuh]/[ma-dam]/ [mad-mwa-zehl]
My name is . . . I am from . . .	Je suis . . ., de l'entreprise . . . [zhuh-swee . . . duh-lahN-truh-preez]
Can I speak to . . . please?	Est-ce que je peux parler à . . .? [ehs-kuh-zhuh-puuh-par-lay-a]
Could you tell . . . I am here please?	Veuillez annoncer mon arrivée à . . .? [vuuh-yay-a-nohN-say-mohN-na-ree-vay-a]
I have an appointment with . . .	J'ai rendez-vous avec . . . [zhay-rahN-day-voo-a-vehk]
. . . is expecting you.	. . . vous attend. [voo-za-tahN]
He/She is still in a meeting.	Il/Elle est en conférence. [eel/ehl-ay-tahN-kohN-fay-rahNs]
I'll take you to . . .	Je vais vous conduire auprès de . . . [zhuh-vay-voo-kohN-dweer-o-pray-duh]
I am sorry I am late.	Veuillez excuser mon retard. [vuuh-yay-ehk-skew-zay-mohN-ruh-tar]
Please sit down.	Asseyez-vous. [a-say-yay-voo]
Would you like something to drink?	Je vous offre quelque chose à boire? [zhuh-voo-zohfr-kehl-kuh-shoz-a-bwar]
Did you have a good trip?	Vous avez fait bon voyage? [voo-za-vay-feh-bohN-vwa-yazh]
How much time do we have?	Nous avons combien de temps devant nous? [noo-za-vohN-kohN-byaN-duh-tahN-duh-vahN-noo]
When does your flight leave?	A quelle heure part votre avion? [a-kehl-uhr-par-vohtr-a-vyohN]
I need an interpreter.	Il me faut un interprète. [eel-muh-fo-aN-naN-tehr-preht]

Word List: Business Meeting

appointment	le rendez-vous [luh-rahN-day-voo]
building	le bâtiment [luh-ba-tee-mahN]
company	la firme [la-feerm]; l'entreprise *(f)* [lahN-truh-preez]
conference room	la salle de conférence [la-sal-duh-kohN-fay-rahNs]
deadline	la date limite [la-dat-lee-meet]
delay	les délais *(m)* [lay-day-lay]
department	le service, le département [luh-sehr-vees]/[luh-day-par-tuh-mahN]
doorman	le portier [luh-pohr-tyay]; le concierge [luh-kohN-syehrzh]
entrance	l'entrée *(f)* [lahN-tray]
floor	l'étage *(m)* [lay-tazh]
interpreter	l'interprète *(m/f)* [laN-tehr-preht]
meeting	la conférence [la-kohN-fay-rahNs]; la réunion [la-ray-ew-nyohN]
office	le bureau [luh-bew-ro]
reception	la réception [la-ray-sehp-syohN]; l'accueil *(m)* [la-kuhy]
secretary	le/la secrétaire [luh/la-suh-kray-tehr]
secretary's office	le secrétariat [luh-suh-kray-ta-rya]

Negotiations/Conferences/Trade Fairs

Négociations/Conférence/Foire-exposition

I am looking for the . . . stand.	Je cherche le stand de l'entreprise . . . [zhuh-shehrsh-luh-stahNd-duh-lahN-truh-preez]
Go to the hall . . ., stand number . . .	Vous allez dans la halle/la salle . . ., stand numéro . . . [voo-za-lay-dahN-la-al/sal . . . stahNd-new-may-ro]
We manufacture . . .	Nous produisons/fabriquons . . . [noo-pro-dwee-zohN]/[noo-fa-bree-kohN]
We deal in . . .	Nous commercialisons . . . [noo-ko-mehr-sya-lee-zohN]
Do you have information on . . .?	Est-ce que vous avez de la documentation sur . . .? [ehs-kuh-voo-za-vay-duh-la-do-kew-mahN-ta-syohN-sewr]

We can send you detailed information on . . .	Nous pouvons vous envoyer de la documentation détaillée sur ... [noo-poo-vohN-voo-zahN-vwa-yay-duh-la-do-kew-mahN-ta-syohN-day-ta-yay-sew]
Who should I contact about…?	Quelle est la personne compétente pour ...? [kehl-ay-la-pehr-sohn-kohN-pay-tahNt-poor]
Could you let us have a quote?	Est-ce que vous pourriez nous faire parvenir une offre? [esh-kuh-voo-poo-ryay-noo-fehr-par-vuh-neer-ewn-ohfr]
We should arrange a meeting.	Il serait bon que nous convenions d'une rencontre. [eel-suh-ray-bohN-kuh-noo-kohN-vuh-nyohN-dewn-rahN-kohNtr]
Here is my business card.	Tenez, voici ma carte de visite. [tuh-nay-vwa-see-ma-kart-duh-vee-zeet]

Word List: Negotiations/Conferences/Trade Fairs

advertising	la publicité [la-pew-blee-see-tay]
advertising campaign	la campagne publicitaire [la-kahN-pany-pew-blee-see-tehr]
advertising material	la documentation [la-do-kew-mahN-ta-syohN]
agenda	l'ordre *(m)* du jour [lohr-druh-dew-zhoor]
branch/subsidiary	la succursale [la-sew-kewr-sal]; la filiale [la-fee-lyal]
brochure	le prospectus [luh-prohs-pehk-tews]
business card	la carte de visite [la-kart-duh-vee-zeet]
business connections	les relations *(f)* d'affaires [lay-ruh-la-syohN-da-fehr]
business partner	le partenaire en affaires [luh-par-tuh-nehr-ahN-na-fehr]
catalog	le catalogue [luh-ka-ta-lohg]
commercial traveller	le représentant de commerce [luh-ruh-pray-zahN-tahN-duh-ko-mehrs]
concessionary	le concessionnaire [luh-kohN-say-syo-nehr]
condition	la condition [la-kohN-dee-syohN]
conference	la conférence [la-kohN-fay-rahNs]; la réunion [la-ray-ew-nyohN]

confirmation of order	la confirmation de l'ordre/de la commande [la-kohN-feer-ma-syohN-[duh-lohrdr]/[duh-la-ko-mahNd]]
contact person	la personne compétente [la-pehr-sohn-kohN-pay-tahNt]
contract	le contrat [luh-kohN-tra]
cooperation	la coopération [la-ko-o-pay-ra-syohN]
cost	le coût [luh-koo]
customer	le client/la cliente [luh/la-klee-yahN(t)]
delivery	la livraison [la-lee-vray-zohN]
delivery time	les délais *(m)* de livraison [lay-day-lay-duh-lee-vray-zohN]
discount	l'escompte *(m)* [lehs-kohNt]; la remise [la-ruh-meez]
distribution	la vente [la-vahNt]
distribution network	le réseau des points de vente [luh-ray-zo-day-pwaN-duh-vahNt]
estimate	le devis [luh-duh-vee]
exhibitor	l'exposant *(m)* [lehk-spo-zahN]
export	l'exportation *(f)* [lehk-spohr-ta-syohN]
exporter	l'exportateur *(m)* [lehk-spohr-ta-tuhr]
financing	le financement [luh-fee-nahNs-mahN]
floor plan	le plan de la halle/de la salle [luh-plahN-duh-la-al/sal]
freight	le fret [luh-freht]; la cargaison [la-kar-gay-zohN]
group *(company)*	le groupe [luh-grooo]; le cartel [luh-kar-tehl]
guarantee	la garantie [la-ga-rahN-tee]
hall	la halle [la-al]; la salle [la-sal]
import	l'importation *(f)* [laN-pohr-ta-syohN]
importer	l'importateur *(m)* [laN-pohr-ta-tuhr]
information material	la documentation [la-do-kew-mahN-ta-syohN]
information stand	le stand d'information [luh-stahNd-daN-fohr-ma-syohN]
insurance	l'assurance *(f)* [la-sew-rahNs]
invoice	la facture [la-fak-tewr]
joint venture	le joint-venture [luh-zhwohNt-vaN-tyewr]
leasing	le leasing [luh-lee-seeng]
licence contract	le contrat de licence [luh-kohN-tra-duh-lee-sahNs]
list of exhibitors	la liste des exposants [la-leest-day-zehk-spo-zahN]

manufacturer	le producteur [luh-pro-dewk-tuhr]; le fabricant [luh-fa-bree-kahN]
marketing	le marketing [luh-mar-kay-teeng]
meeting	la rencontre [la-rahN-kohNtr]
meeting/conference	la conférence [la-kohN-fay-rahNs]
merchandise	la marchandise [la-mar-shahN-deez]
minutes (of a meeting)	le procès-verbal [luh-pro-say-vehr-bal] le compte-rendu (de réunion) [luh-kohNt-rahN-dew-duh-ray-ew-nyohN]
offer	l'offre *(f)* [lohfr]
order	l'ordre *(m)* [lohrdr]; la commande [la-ko-mahNd]
packing/packaging	l'emballage *(m)* [lahN-ba-lazh]
price	le prix [luh-pree]
price list	le prix-courant [luh-pree-koo-rahN]; les tarifs *(m)* [lay-ta-reef]
pro forma invoice	la facture pro forma [la-fak-tewr-pro-fohr-ma]
production	la production [la-pro-dewk-syohN]
public relations	les relations *(f)* publiques [lay-ruh-la-syohN-pew-bleek]
retailer	le détaillant [luh-day-ta-yahN]
sales promotion	la promotion des ventes [la-pro-mo-syohN-day-vahNt]
sales representative	le représentant *(m)* [luh-ruh-pray-zahN-tahN] l'agent *(m)* [la-zhahN]
sales tax	l'impôt *(m)* sur le chiffre d'affaires [laN-po-sewr-luh-sheefr-da-fehr]
sample	l'échantillon *(m)* [lay-shahN-tee-yohN]
seller	le vendeur [luh-vahN-duhr]
selling/buying contract	le contrat d'achat/de vente [luh-kohN-tra-[da-sha]/[duh-vahNt]
sole agent/agency	l'agent *(m)* général [la-zhaN-zhay-nay-ral]
stand	le stand (d'exposition) [luh-stahNd-dehks-pohr-ta-syohN]
stocklist	le catalogue [luh-ka-ta-lohg]
supplier	le fournisseur [luh-foor-nee-suhr]
terms of the contract	les conditions *(f)* du contrat [lay-kohN-dee-syohN-dew-kohN-tra]
terms of payment	les conditions *(f)* de paiement [lay-kohN-dee-syohN-duh-peh-mahN]
terms of supply	les conditions *(f)* de livraison [lay-kohN-dee-syohN-duh-lee-vray-zohN]
to be interested	être intéressé par [eh-traN-tay-ray-say-par]

trade fair	la foire-exposition [la-fwar-ehk-spo-zee-syohN]; la foire [la-fwar]; l'exposition [lehk-spo-zee-syohN]
trade fair hostess	l'hôtesse *(f)* d'accueil [lo-tehs-da-kuhy]
trade fair manager	la direction de la foire [la-dee-rehk-syohN-duh-la-fwar]
training	la formation [la-fohr-ma-syohN]; l'initiation *(f)* [lee-nee-sya-syohN]
transportation	le transport [luh-trahNs-pohr]
value added tax (VAT)	la taxe à la valeur ajoutée (T.V.A.) [la-tay-vay-a]
wholesaler	le grossiste [luh-gro-seest]

Business Equipment

Equipement

Could you make me some copies of this document, please?	Est-ce que vous pourriez me faire des copies de ce document? [ehs-kuh-voo-poo-ryay-muh-fehr-day-ko-pee-duh-suh-do-kew-mahN]
I need an overhead projector for my talk.	Pour ma conférence, j'aurai besoin d'un rétro-projecteur. [poor-ma-kohN-fay-rahNs-zho-ray-buh-zwaN-daN-ray-tro-pro-zhehk-tuhr]
Could you get me . . . please?	Est-ce que vous pourriez me procurer . . .? [ehs-kuh-voo-poo-ryay-muh-pro-kew-ray]

Word List: Business Equipment

catalog	le catalogue [luh-ka-ta-lohg]
color copier	la photocopieuse couleurs [la-fo-to-ko-pyuuhz]
copy	la copie [la-ko-pee]
disk	la disquette [la-dees-keht]
display material	les produits *(m)* exposés [lay-pro-dwee-ehk-spo-zay]
extension cord	la rallonge [la-ra-lohNzh]
fax	le fax [luh-faks]
marker	le feutre [luh-fuuhtr]

marker for transparencies	le marqueur pour transparents [luh-mar-kuhr-poor-trahNs-pa-rahN]
microphone	le micro [luh-mee-kro]
modem	le modem [luh-mo-dehm]
overhead projector	le rétro-projecteur [luh-ray-tro-pro-zhehk-tuhr]
PC	le PC/l'ordinateur *(m)* personnel, l'ordinateur *(m)* individuel [luh-pay-say]/[lohr-dee-na-tuhr-pehr-so-nehl]/[lohr-dee-na-tuhr-aN-dee-vee-dwehl]
pencil	le crayon [luh-kray-yohN]; le stylo [luh-stee-lo]
photocopier	la photocopieuse [la-fo-to-ko-pyuuhz]
printer	l'imprimante *(f)* [laN-pree-mahNt]
telephone	le téléphone [luh-tay-lay-fohn]
telex	le télex [luh-tay-lehks]
videocassette recorder	le magnétoscope [luh-ma-nyay-tohs-kohp]
word processing system	le système de traitement de textes [luh-sees-tehm-duh-treht-mahN-duh-tehkst]
writing pad	le bloc-notes [luh-blohk-noht]

A Short Grammar

Articles

Forms

	Definite Article	Indefinite article
Singular Masculine Feminine	**le** train the train **la** ville the city	**un** train a train **une** ville a city
Plural for both genders	**les** trains the trains villes the cities	**des** trains trains villes cities

In front of nouns starting with a vowel or an h, the article changes

a) *le* and *la* into *l'*: l'avion the airplane, l'heure the hour
b) *un* with liaison: un avion
c) *les* and *des* with liaison: les heures
des avions

Prepositions + Article

The prepositions *à* and *de* contract with the following article *le* and *les* in one word:

à + le > au   de + le > du
à + les > aux   de + les > des

Je vais **au** cinéma. I go to the movie theatre	La valise **du** touriste est lourde. The tourist's suitcase is heavy.
J'écris **aux** copains. I write to the pals.	Je viens **des** Etats-Unis. I come from the United States.

!

Partitive Article

The partitive article is composed of *de* + definite article. It describes a part of a whole.

Definite Measure/ Quantity	Je mange **du** pain.	I eat some bread.
	Je bois **de l'**eau.	I drink some water.
	Je prends **de la** confiture.	I take some jam.

Use of de

When the noun is preceded by an adverb or a word of quantity or measure, use *de*.

Definite Measure/ Quantity	**un litre de** vin	a liter of wine
	une tasse de café	a cup of coffee
	un kilo d'oranges	a kilo of oranges
	un million de francs	one million francs
As well as	**beaucoup de** fruits	a lot of fruit
	un peu de fromage	a little cheese
	trop de limonade	too much lemonade

Nouns

Plural

Generally, the plural of a noun is formed by adding an *-s* to the singular form, but it is not sounded.

le train	the train	la route	the road
les trains	the trains	les routes	the roads

! Nouns that, in the singular, end in *-x, -z, -s*, do not change in the plural.

le prix	the price	le nez	the nose	le cas	the case
les prix	the prices	les nez	the noses	les cas	the cases

Subject/Direct Object/Indirect Object/Possession

The subject and direct object have the same form. The indirect object complement uses *à*; possession uses *de*

Subject (Who? What?)	**Le** café italien est fort. The Italian coffee is strong. **Le** musée Rodin est fermé. The Rodin Museum is closed.
Direct Object (What?)	Le garçon apporte **le** café. The waiter is bringing the coffee. Je cherche **le** musée Rodin. I am looking for the Rodin Museum.
Indirect Object (To whom?)	J'écris une lettre **à** mon père. I am writing a letter to my father. J'écris une lettre **à** ma sœur. I am writing a letter to my sister.
Possession (Whose?)	Où est le sac **de** Françoise? Where is Françoise's handbag? Où est la voiture **du** voisin? Where is the neighbor's car?

Adjectives

Agreement Noun/Adjective

The adjective always agrees in gender and number with the noun it qualifies. The feminine form of the adjective is normally formed by adding *-e* to the masculine singular. If the masculine form already ends in *-e*, the feminine singular remains the same. The plural is normally formed by adding *-s* to the masculine or feminine singular.

	Singular	Plural
Masculine	**Le** livre est passionnant. The book is thrilling.	**Les** livres sont passion-**nants**. The books are thrilling.
Feminine	**La** revue est intéressant**e**. The magazine is interesting.	**Les** revues sont intéres-san**tes**. The magazines are interesting.

Position of Adjectives

An adjective is usually placed **after** a noun.

un film **passionnant** a thrilling movie un voyage **fatigant** a tiring trip une voiture **rouge** a red car

A few adjectives are placed **before** the noun.

un **bon** restaurant a good restaurant un **petit** café a small café une **grande** maison a big house

Comparatives and Superlatives of Adjectives

grand → **plus grand que** → **le plus grand**
big — bigger than — the biggest

- The comparative is formed by adding *plus* or *moins*.

plus grand	Paris est **plus** grand **que** Lyon. Paris is larger than Lyons.
moins grand	Toutes les autres villes sont **moins** grandes. All the other towns are less large/not as large.

aussi grand	La Pologne est **aussi** grande **que** la Norvège. Poland is as large as Norway.

- To form the superlative, place the appropriate definite article in front of the comparative.

le plus grand	New York est **la plus** grande ville **du** monde. New York is the largest city in the world.

!

- Note the irregular forms of the comparative and superlative of *bon*:

bon → **meilleur** → **le meilleur**
good — better — the best

Adverbs

Forms

There are irregular adverbs, for instance:

beaucoup	**bien**	**mal**	**vite**
a lot	well	badly	fast

and regular adverbs that are formed by adding *-ment* to the feminine form of the adjective.

lent/e	Il marche lente**ment**.	He walks slowly.

For the adjectives that end in *-e*, that only have one form, add *-ment* to this form.

simple	Elle s'exprime simple**ment**.	She expresses herself simply.

Regular Comparative

The adverb behaves like the adjective:

vite quickly	→	**plus vite** more quickly	→	**le plus vite** the most quickly

Irregular Comparative

bien well	→	**mieux** better	→	**le mieux** the best
beaucoup much	→	**plus** more	→	**le plus** the most
peu little	→	**moins** less	→	**le moins** the least

A conduit **mieux que** B. A drives better than B.	C'est C qui conduit **le mieux** des trois. C drives the best of the three.
Elle mange **plus que** son mari. She eats more than her husband.	C'est leur fils qui mange **le plus.** Their son eats the most.
Tu gagnes **moins qu'**elle. You earn less than she does.	C'est moi qui gagne **le moins.** I earn the least of all.

!

Verbs

Present

a) **avoir, être**

avoir to have			être to be		
j'	ai	I have	je	suis	I am
tu	as	you have	tu	es	you are
il/elle	a	he/she has	il/elle	est	he/she is
nous	avons	we have	nous	sommes	we are
vous	avez	you have	vous	êtes	you are
ils/elles	ont	they have	ils/elles	sônt	they are

The *nous* form can be expressed with two forms in French, *on* and *nous*. *On* is a spoken form: *nous* is a written form. After *on* the verb is in the third person singular.

On va au cinéma.
Nous allons au cinéma. We are going to the movies.

b) **regular verbs**

The French verbs are arranged in three regular conjugation types according to the ending of their infinitive.

-er		-ir				-re	
parler to speak		finir to finish		partir to leave		vendre to sell	
je	parle	je	finis	je	pars	je	vends
tu	parles	tu	finis	tu	pars	tu	vends
il	parle	il	finit	il	part	il	vend
elle	parle	elle	finit	elle	part	elle	vend
nous	parlons	nous	finissons	nous	partons	nous	vendons
vous	parlez	vous	finissez	vous	partez	vous	vendez
ils	parlent	ils	finissent	ils	partent	ils	vendent
elles	parlent	elles	finissent	elles	partent	elles	vendent

- The group of verbs ending in *-er* is the largest.
- Most of the verbs in *ir* are conjugated like *finir.*
- Only a few verbs follow the model of *partir.*

dormir to sleep servir to use
sentir to smell sortir to go out

Present Perfect (Passé composé)

The present perfect is formed with the present indicative of the auxiliary (helping) verb *avoir* (to have) and *être* (to be) + the past participle of the verb you want to use.

The past participle is formed by dropping the last letter from the infinitive:

parl**er**	fin**ir**	part**ir**	vend**re**
parl**é** spoken	fin**i** finished	part**i** gone	vend**u** sold

Irregular forms are, for example:

avoir	être	recevoir	faire	prendre
eu had	été been	reçu received	fait done	pris taken

The *passé composé* of most verbs is formed by using *avoir*. For the verbs that form their present perfect with *être*, the past participle agrees in gender and number with the subject of the verb.

Present perfect with *avoir*			Present perfect with *être*		
j'	**ai**	été	je	**suis**	} parti/partie
tu	**as**		tu	**es**	
il	**a**	eu	il	**est**	parti
elle	**a**		elle	**est**	partie
nous	**avons**	fini	nous	**sommes**	} partis/parties
vous	**avez**		vous	**êtes**	
ils	**ont**	reçu	ils	**sont**	partis
elles	**ont**	parlé	elles	**sont**	parties

!

● Note:
All reflexive verbs are conjugated with *être*.

Il s'**est** lavé. He washed himself.

Future and Conditional

Future		Conditional		Future	Conditional
je	parler**ai** I shall speak	je	parler**ais** I would speak	je partir**ai** I shall leave	je partir**ais** I would leave
tu	parler**as**	tu	parler**ais**		
il	parler**a**	il	parler**ait**		
elle	parler**a**	elle	parler**ait**	je prendr**ai**	je prendr**ais**
nous	parler**ons**	nous	parler**ions**	I will take	I would take
vous	parler**ez**	vous	parler**iez**		
ils	parler**ont**	ils	parler**aient**		
elles	parler**ont**	elles	parler**aient**		

- To form a future, one often uses the irregular verb *aller* in the present tense followed by the infinitive of the verb.

je	vais	partir	I will go
tu	vas	parler	you will speak
il	va	boire	he will drink
nous	allons	voyager	we will travel
vous	allez	sortir	you will go out
ils	vont	payer	they will pay

- To express a request or a hopeful question, one can use the conditional.

Je **voudrais** louer une voiture.	I would like to rent a car.
Est-ce que je **pourrais** avoir le plan de la ville?	Could I have a map of the city?

!

Imperative

The imperative of the group of verbs in *-er* ends in the you-form in *-e*, for all the other verbs, it ends in *-s*.

To order someone	parler	venir
in the *tu*-form: in the *vous*-form:	parle speak! parl**ez** spreak!	viens come! ven**ez** come!

Common irregular verbs

aller to go — allé gone

Present:	je vais I go, tu vas, il va, nous allons, vous allez, ils vont
Present perfect:	je suis allé I have gone, tu es allé etc.
Future:	j'irai I shall go, tu iras, il ira, nous irons, vous irez, ils iront
Conditional:	j'irais I would go, tu irais, il irait, nous irions, vous iriez, ils iraient

avoir to have — eu had

Present:	j'ai I have, tu as, il a etc.
Present perfect:	j'ai eu I have had, etc.
Future:	j'aurai I shall have, tu auras, etc.
Conditional:	j'aurais I would have, tu aurais, etc.

boire to drink — bu drunk

Present:	je bois I drink, tu bois, il boit, nous buvons, vous buvez, ils boivent
Present perfect:	J'ai bu I have drunk, tu as bu, il a bu, etc.
Future:	je boirai I shall drink, tu boiras, etc.
Conditional:	je boirais I would drink, tu boirais, etc.

connaître to know — connu known

Present:	je connais I know, tu connais, il connaît, nous connaissons, vous connaissez, ils connaissent
Present perfect:	j'ai connu I have known, etc.
Future:	je connaîtrai I shall know, tu connaîtras, etc.
Conditional:	je connaîtrais I would know, tu connaîtrais, etc.

croire to believe — cru believed

Present:	je crois I believe, tu crois, il croit, nous croyons, vous croyez, ils croient
Present perfect:	j'ai cru I have believed, etc.
Future:	je croirai I shall believe, tu croiras, etc.
Conditional:	je croirais I would believe, tu croirais, etc.

devoir must — dû had

Present:	je dois I must, tu dois, il doit, nous devons, vous devez, ils doivent
Present perfect:	j'ai dû I have had to, etc.
Future:	je devrai I shall have to, tu devras, etc.
Conditional:	je devrais I should have to, tu devrais, etc.

dire to say — dit said

Present:	je dis I say, tu dis, il dit, nous disons, vous dites, ils disent
Present perfect:	j'ai dit I have said, etc.
Future:	je dirai I shall say, tu diras, etc.
Conditional:	je dirais I would say, tu dirais, etc.

être to be — été been

Present:	je suis I am, tu es, il est, nous sommes, vous êtes, ils sont
Present perfect:	j'ai été I have been, etc.
Future:	je serai I shall be, tu seras, etc.
Conditional:	je serais I would be, tu serais, etc.

faire to do — fait done

Present:	je fais I do, tu fais, il fait, nous faisons, vous faites, ils font
Present perfect:	j'ai fait I have done, etc.
Future:	je ferai I shall do, tu feras, etc.
Conditional:	je ferais I would do, tu ferais, etc.

mettre to put, to set — mis put, set

Present:	je mets I put, I set, tu mets, il met, nous mettons, vous mettez, ils mettent
Present perfect:	j'ai mis I have put, set, etc.
Future:	je mettrai I shall put, set, tu mettras, etc.
Conditional:	je mettrais I would put, set, tu mettrais, etc.

pouvoir to be able to, can — pu been able to

Present:	je peux I can, tu peux, il peut, nous pouvons, vous pouvez, ils peuvent
Present perfect:	j'ai pu I have been able to, etc.
Future:	je pourrai I shall be able to, tu pourras, etc.
Conditional:	je pourrais I could, tu pourrais, etc.

prendre to take — pris taken

Present:	je prends I take, tu prends, il prend, nous prenons, vous prenez, ils prennent
Present perfect:	j'ai pris I have taken, etc.
Future:	je prendrai I shall take, tu prendras, etc.
Conditional:	je prendrais I would take, tu prendrais, etc.

savoir to know — su known

Present:	je sais I know, I can, tu sais, il sait, nous savons, vous savez, ils savent
Present perfect:	j'ai su I have known, etc.
Future:	je saurai I shall know, tu sauras, etc.
Conditional:	je saurais I would have known, tu saurais, etc.

!

venir to come — venu come

Present:	je viens I come, tu viens, il vient, nous venons, vous venez, ils viennent
Present perfect:	je suis venu I have come, etc.
Future:	je viendrai I shall come, tu viendras, etc.
Conditional:	je viendrais I would come, tu viendrais, etc.

voir to see — vu seen

Present:	je vois I see, tu vois, il voit, nous voyons, vous voyez, ils voient
Present perfect:	j'ai vu I have seen, etc.
Future:	je verrai I shall see, tu verras, etc.
Conditional:	je verrais I would see, tu verrais, etc.

vouloir to want — voulu wanted

Present:	je veux I want, tu veux, il veut, nous voulons, vous voulez, ils veulent
Present perfect:	j'ai voulu . . . I have wanted . . ., etc.
Future:	je voudrai . . . I shall want . . ., tu voudras, etc.
Conditional:	je voudrais I would want, tu voudrais, etc.

Verb + Object

1. **Transitive verbs** (that take a direct object)

aider			to help
applaudir			to applaud
écouter	quelqu'un	someone	to listen (to)
remercier			to thank
rencontrer			to meet

2. **Intransitive verbs** (that take an indirect object)

demander			to ask
parler	à quelqu'un	someone	to speak (to)
téléphoner			to phone

3. Verbs with direct and indirect object

J'ai donné un jus d'orange à l'enfant.	
Direct object	Indirect
Indirect	Direct object
I gave the child an orange juice.	

When a verb takes a direct object and a complement introduced by a preposition, the direct object comes before the other complement.

donner quelque chose à quelqu'un	to give something to someone
demander quelque chose à quelqu'un	to ask something of someone

4. Verbs with *de*

avoir besoin **de** quelque chose	to need something
s'occuper **de** quelque chose	to take care of something
profiter **de** quelque chose	to take advantage of something
remercier quelqu'un **de** quelque chose	to thank someone for something

Order of Elements in a Sentence

The regular order of elements in the sentence is:

Subject →	Verb →	Object
Paul Paul	prend takes	le train. the train.
Paul Paul	a pris took	le train. the train.

There are several interrogative constructions:

- Ton frère est venu? Has your brother come?
  (The order is the regular order, but the tone rises.)
- Est-ce que ton frère est venu? Has your brother come?
  (Put est-ce que in front of the subject.)
- Où est ta voiture? Where is your car?
  (The subject comes after the verb. After an interrogative word, the tone of the sentence rises.)

The Negation

Non no

Encore une bière? — **Non,** merci.	Another beer? — No, thank you.

Ne . . . pas does not

Il **ne** vient **pas.**	He does not come.
Il **n'**est **pas** venu.	He has not come.

Ne . . . pas de no

Je **n'**ai **pas** d'argent.	I have no money.

Ne . . . personne/rien/jamais/plus no one, nothing, never, not anymore

Il **ne** connaît **personne.**	He knows no one.
Il **ne** veut **rien.**	He wants nothing.
Il **ne** fume **jamais.**	He never smokes.
Il **ne** fume **plus.**	He does not smoke anymore.

The Pronouns

Personal Pronouns

1. Subject, Direct/Indirect Object Pronouns

	Subject (who?)		Indirect Object (to whom?)		Direct Object (whom?)	
Sing. 1st Pers.	je	I	moi	to me	me	me
2nd Pers.	tu	you	toi	to you	te	you
3rd Pers.	il/elle	he/she/it	lui	to him/to her	le/la	him/her/it
			se	oneself	se	himself/herself
Plur. 1st Pers.	nous	we	nous	to us	nous	us
2nd Pers.	vous	you	vous	to you	vous	you
3rd Pers.	ils/elles	they	eux	to them	les	them
			se	themselves	se	themselves

Instead of the 1st person plural *nous* one uses *on* in the spoken language.

On va au café? Are we going to the coffee shop?

The direct and indirect object are placed before the verb. If a verb has both a direct and indirect pronoun complement the order is:

① Indirect Object		② Direct Object		③ Indirect Object
me te se nous vous	before	le la les	before	lui leur

① ②
Je **te la** donne. I give it to you.

① ②
Je **la leur** donne. I give it to them.

!

2. Disjunctive pronouns

	Singular		Plural	
1st Person	moi	me/I	nous	us/we
2nd Person	toi	you	vous	you
3rd Person	lui/elle	him/he, her/she	eux/elles	them/they

Stressed pronouns
Moi, j'ai déjà mangé. I have already eaten.
After a preposition
Nous partirons sans eux. We will leave without them.
With an imperative
Donne-le-moi. Give it to me.
(*but:* Ne me le donne pas. Don't give it to me.)

3. "y" and "en"

y = there *en* = of
are used as personal pronouns.

Vous allez à Paris/en France ?	Vous mangez du poisson ?
–Oui, j'**y** vais demain.	–Oui, j'**en** mange quelquefois.
Are you travelling to Paris/to France?	Are you eating fish?
–Yes, (I am travelling there) tomorrow.	–Yes, (I eat it) sometimes.

4. Reflexive pronouns and reflexive verbs

The reflexive pronouns are placed before the verb. All reflexive

Present			Present perfect			
Je	**me**	souviens.	Je	**me**	**suis**	souvenu(e).
I remember.			I have remembered.			
Tu	**te**	souviens.	Tu	**t'**	**es**	souvenu(e).
Il	**se**	souvient.	Il	**s'**	**est**	souvenu.
Elle	**se**	souvient.	Elle	**s'**	**est**	souvenue.
Nous	**nous**	souvenons.	Nous	**nous**	**sommes**	souvenu(e)s.
Vous	**vous**	souvenez.	Vous	**vous**	**êtes**	souvenu(e)s.
Ils	**se**	souviennent.	Ils	**se**	**sont**	souvenus.
Elles	**se**	souviennent.	Elles	**se**	**sont**	souvenues.

Possessive pronouns

verbs are conjugated with *être* (to be).

Number Number	Singular masculine feminine		Plural both genders
Singular	**mon** / **ton** / **son** } sac **ma** / **ta** / **sa** } veste	my your his/her	**mes** / **tes** / **ses** } enfants
Plural	**notre** / **votre** / **leur** } sac, veste	our your their	**nos** / **vos** / **leurs** } enfants

- *Son/Sa* are used whether the owner is masculine or feminine. *Leur* is used when there are several owners.

  sa clé his/her key
  leur clé their key

Demonstrative pronouns

Before masculine nouns that begin with a vowel or an h, *ce*

Singular		Plural
Masculine	**ce** livre this book	**ces** enfants these children
Feminine	**cette** voiture this car	

becomes *cet:*

cet avion this airplane

Relative Pronouns

Subject (who? what?)	qui	le restaurant **qui** est fermé the restaurant that is closed
Object (whom? what?)	que	le crayon **que** j'ai perdu the pencil that I lost

Interrogative Words

Who?	**Qui** est venu?	Who has come?
Whom? To whom?	**Qui** as-tu vu?	Whom did you see?
To what?	**A qui** écris-tu?	Whom do you write to?
Of whom?	**De qui** parles-tu?	Of whom are you talking?
What?	**Qu'est-ce que** tu fais? **Que** fais-tu?	What are you doing?
Which?	**Quel** est ton livre? **Quelle** est sa voiture?	Which is your book? Which is your car?
How much?	**Combien de** kilomètres?	How many kilometers?
How many?	Ça coûte **combien?**	How much does it cost?
Where?	**Où** se trouve . . .?	Where does one find …?
Where?	**Où** vas-tu?	Where are you going?
Where from?	**D'où** venez-vous?	Where are you coming from?
When?	**Quand** pars-tu?	When are you leaving?
At what time?	**A quelle heure** arrive-t-elle?	At what time does she arrive?
How long?	**Combien de temps** a-t-il mis?	How long did it take?
How?	**Comment** vas-tu?	How are you?
Why?	**Pourquoi** est-il parti?	Why has he left?

English-French Dictionary

A

abbreviation l'abréviation *(f)* [a-bray-vya-syohN]
able, to be . . . être capable de [eh-truh-ka-pabl]; pouvoir [poo-vwar]; *(to do)* savoir [sa-vwar]
about à peu près [a-puuh-pray]; environ [ahN-vee-rohN]
above . . . all avant tout [a-vahN-too]
abroad à l'étranger [a-lay-trahN-zhay]
absent absent(e) [ab-sahN(t)]
absolutely not absolument pas
abuse l'abus *(m)*
abuse *(v)* abuser de [a-bew-zay-duh]
accelerate *(v)* accélérer [ak-say-lay-ray]
accept *(v)* accepter [ak-sehp-tay]
acceptance l'acceptation *(f)* [lak-sehp-ta-syohN]
accident l'accident *(m)* [lak-see-dahN]
accident, to have an avoir un accident [a-vwar-ahN-nak-see-dahN]
acclimated, to get s'acclimater [sa-klee-ma-tay]
accommodations l'hébergement *(m)* [lay-behr-zhuh-mahN]
accompany *(v)* accompagner [a-kohN-pa-nyay]
accuracy l'exactitude *(f)* [leg-zak-tee-tewd]
acquaintance la connaissance, la rencontre [la-rahN-kohNtr]
action l'acte *(m)*, l'action *(f)* [lak-syohN]
activity l'activité *(f)* [lak-tee-vee-tay]
actual(ly) *(adj)* véritable [vay-ree-tabl]; *(adv)* en fait [ahN-feht], à vrai dire [a-vray-deer]
add *(v)* ajouter [a-zhoo-tay]
add up *(v)* faire le total de [fehr-luh-to-tal-duh]
additional supplémentaire, en plus [ahN-plews]
address l'adresse *(f)* *f* [la-drehs]
address *(v)* adresser [a-dray-say]
administration l'administration *(f)* [lad-mee-nees-tra-syohN]
admire *(v)* admirer [ad-mee-ray]
adult l'adulte *(m/f)* [la-dewlt]
advance, in par avance [par-a-vahNs]
advantage l'avantage *(m)* [la-vahN-tazh]
advantageous avantageux, -euse [a-vahN-ta-zhuuh(z)]
advertisement la publicité [la-pew-blee-see-tay]; *(newspaper, magazine)* l'annonce *(f)* [la-nohNs]
advice le conseil; **to ask for** demander conseil à qn [duh-mahN-day-kohN-sehy-a-kehl-kaN]
advise *(v)* conseiller [kohN-seh-yay]
after après [a-pray]
afternoon l'après-midi *(m)* [la-pray-mee-dee]
afterwards après [a-pray]
again de nouveau; **once again** encore une fois [ahN-kohr-ewn-fwa]
against contre [kohNtr]
against, to be être contre [eh-truh-kohNtr]
age l'âge *(m)* [lazh]
agency l'agence *(f)* [la-zhahNs]
agent l'intermédiaire *(m)* [laN-tehr-may-dyehr]
agree *(v)* consentir à [kohN-sahN-teer-a] convenir de [kohN-vuh-neer-duh] être d'accord [eh-truh-da-kohr] se mettre d'accord [suh-meh-truh-da-kohr]
agree upon *(v)* convenir de [kohN-vuh-neer-duh]
agreeable agréable [a-gray-abl]
aim le but; *(trip)* la destination [la-dehs-tee-na-syohN]
air l'air *(m)* [lehr]
air *(v)* aérer [a-ay-ray]
alarm clock le réveil [luh-ray-vehy]
alcohol, denatured l'alcool *(m)* à brûler [lal-kohl-a-brew-lay]
algae les algues *(f pl)* [lay-zalg]
alive vivant(e) [vee-vahN(t)]
all tous, toutes [toos]/[toot]
all, not at pas du tout [pa-dew-too]
allowed, to be pouvoir [poo-vwar]
almost presque [prehsk]
alone seul [suhl]
along le long de [luh-lohN-duh]
already déjà [day-zha]
also aussi [o-see]
although bien que [byaN-kuh]
always toujours [too-zhoor]
ambulance l'ambulance *(f)* [lahN-bew-lahNs]

among entre [ahNtr]; **among others** entre autres [ahN-trotr]
amount la somme [la-sohm], le montant [luh-mohN-tahN]
ample copieux, -euse *(adj)* [ko-pyuuh(z)]; abondamment *(adv)* [a-bohN-da-mahN]
amuse *(v)* amuser [a-mew-zay]; **amuse oneself** se distraire [suh-dees-trehr]
and et [ay]
angry en colère [ahN-ko-lehr]
angry, to be angry about s'irriter de [see-ree-tay]
animal l'animal *(m)* [la-nee-mal]
announce *(v)* annoncer [a-nohN-say]
announcement l'information *(f)* [laN-fohr-ma-syohN]
annoying fâcheux, -euse [fa-shuuh(z)]
annual par an *(adv)* [par-ahN]
another un autre [aN-notr]; **another time** une autre fois [ewn-otr-fwa]
answer la réponse [la-ray-pohNs]
answer *(v)* répondre [ray-pohNdr]
anxious soucieux,-euse [soo-syuuh(z)]
anyone n'importe qui [naN-pohr-tuh-kee]; le premier venu [luh-pruh-myay-vuh-new]
apartment l'appartement *(m)* [la-par-tuh-mahN]
apparently apparemment [a-pa-ra-mahN]
appear *(v)* apparaître [a-pa-rehtr]
appetite l'appétit *(m)* [a-pay-tee]
applause les applaudissements *(m pl)* [lay-za-plo-dees-mahN]
appointment le rendez-vous [luh-rahN-day-voo]
approach *(v)* s'approcher [sa-pro-shay]
area la région [la-ray-zhyohN]
around autour de [o-toor-duh]; *(time)* à [a]; *(place)* vers [vehr]
arrive *(v)* arriver [a-ree-vay]
article l'article *(m)* [lar-teekl]
as for me pour ma part [poor-ma-par]
as if comme si [kohm-see]
ask *(v)* interroger [aN-tay-ro-zhay]
ask for *(v)* demander [duh-mahN-day]; réclamer [ray-kla-may]
ask someone for something demander qc à qn [duh-mahN-day-kehlk-shoz-a-kehl-kaN]
asleep, to fall s'endormir [sahN-dohr-meer]
association l'association *(f)* [la-so-sya-syohN]
assumption la supposition [la-sew-po-zee-syohN]
assure *(v)* assurer [a-sew-ray]

at à [a]; **the post office** à la poste [a-la-pohst]
at breakfast/lunch/dinner à table [a-tabl]
Atlantic l'Atlantique *(m)* [lat-lahN-teek]
attack *(v)* agresser [a-gray-say]
attempt l'essai *(m)* [lay-say]
attendant le gardien [luh-gar-dyaN]
attention attention [a-tahN-syohN]; **pay attention** *(v)* faire attention [fehr-a-tahN-syohN]
attentive attentif, -ive [a-tahN-teef]/[a-tahN-teev]
audience le public [luh-pew-bleek]
aunt la tante [la-tahNt]
authorities l'administration *(f)* [lad-mee-nees-tra-syohN]
automatic automatique [o-to-ma-teek]
available en vente [ahN-vahNt]
average moyen(ne) *(adj)* [mwa-yaN]/[mwa-yehn]; **on the average** en moyenne *(adv)* [ahN-mwa-yehn]
avoid *(v)* éviter [ay-vee-tay]
awake réveillé(e) [ray-vay-yay]
aware of, to be remarquer [ruh-mar-kay]
away parti(e) [par-tee]

B

baby le bébé [luh-bay-bay]
bachelor le célibataire [luh-say-lee-ba-tehr]
back de retour [duh-ruh-toor]
back, at the à l'arrière [a-la-ryehr]
backpack le sac à dos [luh-sak-a-do]; le sac de montagne [luh-sak-duh-mohN-tany]
backwards en arrière [ahN-na-ryehr]
bad grave; **worse** pire; **at worst** le pire [luh-peer]
bad mauvais(e) [mo-veh(z)]; **I feel bad** j'ai mal au cœur [zhay-mal-o-kuhr]
bad(ly) mauvais(e) *(adj)* [mo-veh(z)]; mal *(adv)* [mal]
bag *(small)* le sachet [luh-sa-shay]
ball le ballon [luh-ba-lohN]; la balle [la-bal]; *(party)* le bal [luh-bal]
ban l'interdiction *(f)* [laN-tehr-deek-syohN]
bandage le pansement [luh-pahNs-mahN]
bank *(river)* la rive [la-reev]; *(sea)* le bord [luh-bohr]; le rivage [luh-ree-vazh]
bank la banque [la-bahNk]
basket le panier [luh-pa-nyay]
bath le bain [luh-baN]; **to take a bath** prendre un bain [prahN-draN-baN]; *(swimming pool)* se baigner [suh-bay-nyay]

battery *(auto)* la batterie [la-bat-ree]; les accus *(m pl)* [lay-za-kew]; *(flashlight)* la pile [la-peel]
bay la crique [la-kreek]
be *(v)* être [ehtr]; se trouver [suh-troo-vay]; être [ehtr]
beach la plage [la-plazh]
beam le rayon [luh-reh-yohN]; *(water)* le jet d'eau [luh-zhay-do]
bear *(v)* supporter [sew-pohr-tay]
beautiful beau [bo]; bel(le) [behl]
beauty la beauté [la-bo-tay]
because parce que [pars-kuh]
because of à cause de [a-koz-duh]
become *(v)* devenir [duh-vuh-neer]
bed le lit [luh-lee]; **to go to bed** aller se coucher [a-lay-suh-koo-shay]
bee l'abeille [la-behy]
before *(space)* devant [duh-vahN]; *(time)* avant [a-vahN]; avant que [a-vahN-kuh]
begin *(v)* commencer [ko-mahN-say]; débuter [day-bew-tay]
beginning le commencement [luh-ko-mahNs-mahN]; le début [luh-dew]
behavior la conduite [la- kohN-dweet]
behind derrière [deh-ryehr]
Belgian le/la Belge [luh/la-behlzh]
Belgium la Belgique [la-behl-zheek]
believe *(v)* croire [krwar]
bell la sonnette [la-so-neht]
belong *(v)* to appartenir [a-par-tuh-neer]
below en bas [ahn-ba]
bench le banc [luh-bahN]
bend le virage [luh-vee-razh]
besides d'autre part [do-truh-par]; en outre [ahN-nootr]
best le/la meilleur(e) [luh/la-meh-yuhr]
bet le pari [luh-pa-ree]; *(v)* parier [pa-ryay]
better mieux [myuuh]; meilleur(e) [meh-yuhr]
between entre [ahNtr]; *(among several)* parmi [par-mee]
beyond de l'autre côté (de) [duh-lotr-ko-tay-duh]; au-delà de [o-duh-la-duh]
big grand(e) [grahN(d)]; important(e) [aN-pohr-tahN(t)]
bill la facture [laa-fak-tewr]; *(in a restaurant, café)* l'addition *(f);* [la-dee-syohN]; *(in a hotel)* la note [la-noht]
binoculars les jumelles *(f pl)* [lay-zhew-mehl]
bird l'oiseau *(m)* [lwa-zo]
birth la naissance [la-neh-sahNs]
bit, a un peu [aN-puuh]
bite *(v)* mordre [mohrdr]
bitter amer, -ère [a-mehr]
blanket la couverture [la-koo-vehr-tewr]
blind aveugle [a-vuhgl]
blossom *(v)* fleurir [fluuh-reer]
blow le coup [luh-koo]
board, to go on monter à bord [mohN-tay-a-bohr]
boat la barque [la-bark] le bateau [luh-ba-to]
body le corps [luh-kohr]
bolt le verrou [luh-vay-roo]
book le livre [luh-leevr]
book *(v)* *(seat)* retenir [ruh-tuh-neer]; réserver [ray-zehr-vay]
border la frontière [luh-frohN-tyehr]
boring ennuyeux, -euse [ahN-nwee-yuuh(z)]
born né(e) [nay]
boss le patron [luh-pa-trohN]
both tous/toutes les deux [too/toot-lay-duuh]
bother *(v)* importuner [aN-pohr-tew-nay]
bottle la bouteille [la-boo-tehy]
box la boîte [la-bwat]
box office la caisse [la-kehs]
boy le garçon [luh-gar-sohN]
branch la succursale [la-sew-kewr-sal]
break *(v)* casser [ka-say]
break off *(v)* interrompre [aN-teh-rohNpr]
breakfast, to have *(v)* prendre son petit déjeuner [prahNdr-sohN-puh-tee-day-zhuuh-nay]; déjeuner [day-zhuuh-nay]
breath le souffle [luh-soofl]
briefcase le porte-documents [luh-pohrt-do-kew-mahN]
bright clair(e) [klehr]
bring *(v)* apporter [a-pohr-tay]; *(with)* emporter [ahN-pohr-tay]
bring back *(v)* rapporter [ra-pohr-tay]
broad large [larzh]
broken cassé(e) [ka-say]; en panne [ahN-pan]
brother le frère [luh-frehr]
brother-in-law le beau-frère [luh-bo-frehr]
brown marron [ma-rohN]; *(tanned)* bronzé(e) [brohN-zay]; *(hair)* brun [braN]
brush la brosse [la-brohs]
brush *(v)* brosser [bro-say]
build *(v)* construire [kohN-dweer]
building le bâtiment [luh-ba-tee-mahN]
bunch of flowers le bouquet [luh-boo-kay]
burn *(v)* brûler [brew-lay]
burst *(v)* éclater [ay-kla-tay]; crever [kruh-vay]
bush le buisson [luh-bwee-sohN]
business l'affaire *(f)* [la-fehr]
business hours les horaires *(m pl)* d'ouverture [lay-so-rehr-doo-vehr-tewr]

busy occupé(e) [o-kew-pay]
but mais [meh]
button le bouton [luh-boo-tohN]
buyer l'acheteur *(m)* [lash-tuhr]; le client [luh-klee-yaN]
by means of grâce à [gras-a]; *(passive)* par [par]
by de [duh]; *(passive)* par [par]
by day/night de jour [duh-zhoor]/de nuit [duh-nwee]
bye-bye Salut! [sa-lew]

C

cabin la cabine [la-ka-been]
café le salon de thé [luh-sa-lohN-duh-tay]
calculate *(v)* calculer [kal-kew-lay]
call *(v)* appeler [ap-lay]
call for *(v)* aller chercher [a-lay-shehr-shay]
called, to be s'appeler [sa-play]
calm calme [kalm]
calm down *(v)* se calmer [suh-kal-may]
camera *(photo)* l'appareil *(m)* [la-pa-rehy]; l'appareil-photo *(m)* [la-pa-rehy-fo-to]
can *(food)* la boîte de conserve [la-bwat-duh-kohN-sehrv]
canal le canal [luh-ka-nal]
cancel *(v)* *(room)* décommander [day-ko-mahN-day]; *(train or flight ticket)* annuler [a-new-lay]
candle la bougie [la-boo-zhee]
capable (of) capable [ka-pabl]
capital la capitale [la-ka-pee-tal]
car la voiture [la-vwa-tewr]; **drive a car** conduire
card la carte [la-kart]; **entrance card** le billet [luh-bee-yay]; **postcard** la carte postale [la-kart-pohs-tal]; **card game** le jeu de cartes [luh-zhuuh-duh-kart]
care le soin [luh-swar]
care, take care of *(v)* surveiller [sewr-veh-yay]
careful prudent(e) *(adj)* [prew-dahN(t)]; soigneusement *(adv)* [swa-nyuuhz-mahN]
careless imprudent(e) [aN-prew-dahN(t)]; négligent(e); [nay-glee-zhahN(t)]
carry *(v)* porter [pohr-tay]
carry out *(v)* *(work)* accomplir [a-kohN-pleer]
case, in any à toutes fins utiles [a-toot-faN-zew-teel]

case, in case of au cas où [o-ka-zoo]
castle le château [luh-sha-to]
cat le chat [luh-sha]
catch *(v)* attraper [a-tra-pay]
cause la cause [la-koz]
cause *(v)* causer [ko-zay]
caution la caution [la-ko-syohN]; la précaution [la-pray-ko-syohN]; attention! [a-tahN-syohN]
ceiling le plafond [luh-pla-fohN]
celebration la fête [la-feht]
center le centre [luh-sahNtr]
central central(e) [sahN-tral]
certain(ly) certain(e) *(adj)* [sehr-taN]/[sehr-tehn]; sûrement *(adv)* [sewr-mahN]
certainly certainement *(adv)* [sehr-tehn-mahN]
certainly! absolument *(adv)* [ab-so-lew-mahN]
certify *(v)* attester [a-tehs-tay]
chain la chaîne [la-shehn]; *(necklace)* le collier [luh-ko-lyay]
chair la chaise [la-shehz]
chance, by par hasard [par-a-zar]
change le changement [luh-shaNzh-mahN]; le change [luh-shahNzh]; l'appoint *(m)* [la-pwaN]; *(v)* *(money)* changer [shahN-zhay]; échanger [ay-shahN-zhay]; modifier [mo-dee-fyay]
change, to give *(money)* rendre [rahNdr]
English Channel la Manche [la-mahNsh]
chapel la chapelle [la-sha-pehl]
charming ravissant(e) [ra-vee-sahN(t)]
chauffeur le chauffeur [luh-sho-fuhr]
cheap bon marché [bohN-mar-shay]
cheat *(v)* tromper [trohN-pay]
check *(v)* *(baggage)* faire enregistrer [fehr-ahN-ruh-zhees-tray]; *(v)* vérifier [vay-ree-fyay]
cheerful gai(e) [gay]
chest la caisse [la-kehs]
child l'enfant *(m/f)* [lahN-fahN]
choice le choix [luh-shwa] *(f)*
choir le chœur [luh-kuhr]
choose *(v)* choisir [shwa-zeer]; *(politics)* voter [vo-tay]
cigar le cigare [luh-see-gar]
cigarette la cigarette [la-see-ga-reht]
cigarillo le cigarillo [luh-see-ga-ree-yo]
circumstances les circonstances *(f pl)* [lay-seer-kohNs-tahNs]
city la ville [la-veel]; **city map** le plan de la ville [luh-plahN-duh-la-veel]
class la classe [la-klas]
clean propre [prohpr]
clean *(v)* nettoyer [nay-twa-yay]; faire le ménage [fehr-luh-may-nazh]
cleaner la teinturerie [la-taN-tewr-ree]
clear clair(e) [klehr]

clever intelligent(e) [aN-tay-lee-zhahN(t)] rusé(e) [rew-zay]
cliff le rocher [luh-ro-shay]
climate le climat [luh-klee-ma]
climb *(v)* monter [mohN-tay]
close *(v)* fermer [fehr-may]
closed fermé(e) [fehr-may]
cloth le drap [luh-dra]; *(rug)* le chiffon [luh-shee-fohN]; *(head)* le foulard [luh-foo-lar]
clothing les vêtements *(m pl)* [lay-veht-mahN]
cloudy couvert [koo-vehr]
coal le charbon [luh-shar-bohN]
coast la côte [la-kot]
coffee le café [luh-ka-fay]
coin la monnaie [la-mo-nay]; la pièce de monnaie [la-pyehs-duh-mo-nay]
coincidence le hasard [luh-a-zar]
cold froid(e) [frwa(d)]
cold, to be avoir froid [a-vwar-frwa]
colleague le collègue [luh-ko-lehg]; le confrère [luh-kohN-frehr]
collect *(v)* collectionner [ko-lehk-syo-nay]; recueillir [ruh-kuuh-yeer]
collection la collection [la-ko-lehk-syohN]
collision le choc [luh-shohk]; la collision [la-ko-lee-zyohN]
color la couleur [la-koo-luhr]
colored coloré(e) [ko-lo-ray]
colorful multicoloré varié(e) [va-ryay]
come *(v)* venir [vuh-neer]
come back *(v)* revenir [ruhv-neer]
come from *(v)* être originaire (de) [eh-tro-ree-zhee-nehr-duh]
come in *(v)* entrer [ahN-tray]
come to *(v)* s'élever à [say-luh-vay-a]
come in! entrez! [ahN-tray]
comfort le confort [luh-kohN-fohr]
comfortable confortable [kohN-fohr-tabl]
common commun(e) *(adj)* [ko-maN]/[ko-mewn]; ensemble [ahN-sahNbl] *(adv)*; usuel(le) [ew-zwehl]
company l'entreprise *(f)* [lahN-truh-preez]
compare *(v)* comparer [kohN-pa-ray]
comparison la comparaison [la-kohN-pa-reh-zohN]
compass la boussole [la-boo-sohl]
compel *(v)* forcer [fohr-say]
compensation la compensation [la-kohN-pahN-sa-syohN]
competition le concours [luh-kohN-koor]
complain *(v)* faire une réclamation [fehr-ewn-ray-kla-ma-syohN]
complain of/about *(v)* se plaindre de [suh-plaN-druh-duh]
complaint la plainte [la-plaNt]; la réclamation [la-ray-kla-ma-syohN]
complete complet, -ète [kohN-lay]/[kohN-pleht]
complete *(v)* achever [a-shuh-vay]
compulsion la contrainte [la-kohN-traNt]
conceal *(v)* cacher [ka-shay]; tenir secret [tuh-neer-suh-kray]
concerning concernant [kohN-sehr-nahN]
condition l'état *(m)* [lay-ta]; la condition [la-kohN-dee-syohN]
condolence(s) les condoléances *(f pl)* [lay-kohN-do-lay-ahNs]
condom le préservatif [luh-pray-zehr-va-teef]
confidence la confiance [la-kohN-fyahNs]
confident confiant(e) [kohN-fyahN(t)]
confirm *(v)* confirmer [kohN-feer-may]
congratulate *(v)* féliciter [fay-lee-see-tay]
congratulations les félicitations *(f pl)* [lay-fay-lee-see-ta-syohN]
connect *(v)* relier [ruh-lyay]; *(telephone)* passer (qn) [pa-say-kehl-kaN]
connection la relation [la-ruh-la-syohN]; *(telephone)* la communication [la-ko-mew-nee-ka-syohN]
conscientious consciencieux, -euse [kohN-syahN-syuuh(z)]
conscious conscient(e) [kohN-syaN(t)]
consent le consentement [luh-kohN-sahNt-mahN]
consent to *(v)* consentir [kohN-sahN-teer]
considerable considérable [kohN-see-day-rabl]
consideration les égards *(m pl)* [lay-zay-gar]
constitution la constitution [la-kohNs-tee-tew-syohN]
consulate le consulat [luh-kohN-sew-la]
consult *(v)* consulter [kohN-sewl-tay]
consume *(v)* consommer [kohN-so-may]
consumption la consommation [la-kohN- so-ma-syohN]
contact le contact [luh-kohN-takt]
contain *(v)* contenir [kohN-tuh-neer]
container le récipient [luh-ray-see-pyahN]
content le contenu [luh-kohN-tuh-new]
continue *(v)* continuer [kohN-tee-nway]
contraceptive le contraceptif [luh-kohN- tra-sehp-teef]
contract le contrat [luh-kohN-tra]
contrary le contraire [luh-kohN-trehr]; **to the contrary** au contraire [o-kohN-trehr]
control *(v)* contrôler [kohN-tro-lay]
conversation la conversation [la-kohN-vehr-sa-syohN]

conversion le change [luh-shahNzh]; la conversion [la-kohN-vehr-syohN]
convince *(v)* convaincre [kohN-vaNkr]
cook faire la cuisine [fehr-la-kwee-zeen]
cooked *(medium)* à point [a-pwaN]
cool frais [fray]; fraîche [frehsh]
copy la copie [la-ko-pee]
corner l'angle *(m)* [lahNgl]; le coin [luh-kwaN]
correct correct(e) [do-rehkt]
cost le coût [luh-koo]; les frais *(m pl)* [lay-freh]
cost *(v)* coûter [koo-tay]
correspondence la correspondance [la-ko-rehs-pohN-dahNs]
costume le costume régional/folklorique [luh-kos-tewm-ray-zhyo-nal]/[fohl-klo-reek]
cottage la cabane [la-ka-ban]; *(mountain)* le chalet [luh-sha-lay]
cough *(v)* tousser [too-say]
count *(v)* compter [kohN-tay]
counter le guichet [luh-gee-shay]
countryman le compatriote [luh-kohN-pa-tree-oht]
coupon *(check)* le talon [luh-ta-lohN]
course le cours [luh-koor]
court le tribunal [luh-tree-bew-nal]
courtyard la cour [la-koor]
cousin le cousin, la cousine [luh-koo-zaN]/[la-koo-zeen]
cover *(v)* couvrir [koo-vreer]
cow la vache [la-vash]
crazy fou, folle [foo]/[fohl]
creative créatif, -ive [kray-a-teef]/[kray-a-teev]
credit le crédit [luh-kray-dee]
criticize *(v)* critiquer [kree-tee-kay]
cross *(v)* traverser [tra-vehr-say]
crossing la traversée [la-tra-vehr-say]; le passage [luh-pa-sazh]
crossroad le carrefour [luh-kar-foor]
cry *(v)* pleurer [pluh-ray]
culture la culture [la-kewl-tewr]; la civilisation [la-see-vee-lee-za-syohN]
cup le gobelet [luh-gohb-lay]
curious curieux, -euse [kew-ryuuh(z)]
current le courant [luh-koo-rahN]
curtain le rideau [luh-ree-do]
custom la douane [la-dwan]
customs, to clear dédouaner [day-dwa-nay]
customer le/la client(e) [luh/la-klee-yahN(t)]
cut *(v)* couper [koo-pay]

D

damage *(v)* endommager [ahN-do-ma-zhay]
damage le dégât [luh-day-ga]; le dommage [luh-do-mazh]; **damage compensation** le dédommagement [luh-day-do-mazh-mahN]
dance la danse [la-dahNs]
danger le danger [luh-dahN-zhay]
dangerous dangereux, -euse [dahN-zhuuh-ruuh(z)]
dare *(v)* oser [o-zay]
dark obscur(e) [ohb-skewr]; sombre [sohNbr]
darling chéri [luh-shay-ree]; chérie [la-shay-ree]
date la date [la-dat]
daughter la fille [la-feey]
day le jour [luh-zhoor]
day, every tous les jours [loo-lay-zhoor]
day, the other l'autre jour [lo-truh-zhoor]
dead mort(e) [mohr(t)]
deadline la date limite [la-dat-lee-meet]; les délais *(m pl)* [lay-day-lay]
death la mort [la-mohr]
decide *(v)* décider (de) [day-see-day-duh]
decision la décision [la-day-see-zyohN]
decline *(v)* refuser [ruh-few-zay]
deep profond(e) [pro-fohN(d)]
defend *(v)* défendre [day-fahNdr]
definite(ly) définitif, -ive *(adj)* [day-fee-nee-teef]/[day-fee-nee-teev]; définitivement *(adv)* [day-fee-nee-teev-mahN]
degree le degré [luh-duh-gray]
delay l'ajournement *(m)* [la-zhoor-nuh-mahN]
delay *(v)* différer [dee-fay-ray]
delete *(v)* supprimer [sew-pree-may]
delighted ravi(e) [ra-vee]
deliver *(v)* livrer [lee-vray] remettre [ruh-mehtr]
demand la revendication [la-ruh-vahN-dee-ka-syohN]
demand *(v)* exiger [ehg-zee-zhay]
dense *(fog)* épais [ay-pay]
deny *(v)* nier [nee-yay]
departure le départ [luh-day-par]
deposit le gage [luh-gazh]; *(bottle)* la consigne [la-kohN-seeny]
deposit *(v)* déposer [day-po-zay]
describe *(v)* décrire [day-kreer]
description la désignation [la-day-zee-nya-syohN]
desire l'envie *(f)* [lahN-vee]

desperate désespéré(e) [day-zehs-pay-ray]
destroy *(v)* détruire [day-trweer]
detail le détail [luh-day-ta-yuh]
detailed en détail [ahN-day-ta-yuh] détaillé(e) [day-ta-yay]
determined, to be être décidé(e) [eh-truh-day-see-day]
detour le détour [luh-day-toor]
develop *(v)* développer [day-vlo-pay]
development le développement [luh-day-vlohp-mahN]
diagnostic le diagnostic [luh-dyag-nohs-teek]
dial *(v)* composer (un numéro)[kohN-po-zay-aN-new-may-ro]
die *(v)* mourir [moo-reer]
difference la différence [la-dee-fay-rahNs]
different différent(e) [dee-fay-rahN(t)]
different(ly) autrement *(adv)* [o-truh-mahN]
difficult difficile [dee-fee-seel]
difficulty la difficulté [la-dee-fee-kewl-tay]
direct(ly) direct(e) [dee-rehkt]; directement *(adv)* [dee-rehk-tuh-mahN]
direction la direction [la-dee-rehk-syohN]
director le directeur [luh-dee-rehk-tuhr]; *(high school)* le proviseur [luh-pro-vee-zuhr]
directory la liste [la-leest]
dirt la saleté [la-sal-tay]
dirty sale [sal]
disadvantage l'inconvénient *(m)* [laN-kohN-vay-nyahN]
disappear disparaître [dees-pa-rehtr]
disappointed déçu(e) [day-sew]
discount la remise [la-ruh-meez]
discover découvrir [day-koo-vreer]
dish *(food)* le plat [luh-pla]
disorder le désordre [luh-day-zohrdr]
dispatch *(v)* expédier [ehk-spay-dyay]
dissatisfied mécontent, [may-kohN-tahN]
distance l'éloignement *(m)* [laay-lwa-nyuh-mahN]; l'intervalle *(m)* [laN-tehr-val]; la distance [la-dees-tahNs]
distant éloigné(e) [ay-lwa-nyay]
distinct clair(e) [klehr]
distinguish *(v)* distinguer [dees-taN-gay]; **distinguish oneself from** *(v)* se distinguer de [suh-dees-taN-gay-duh]
distinguished distingué(e) [dees-taN-gay]
distribute répartir [ray-par-teer]
distribution la répartition [la-ray-par-tee-syohN]
distrust *(v)* se méfier de [suh-may-fyay-duh]
disturb *(v)* déranger [day-rahN-zhay]
disturbance le dérangement [luh-day-rahNzh-mahN]; l'interruption *(f)* [laN-tay-rewp-syohN]
divide *(v)* diviser [dee-vee-zay]
do *(v)* faire [fehr]
doctor le docteur [luh-dohk-tuhr]
document le document [luh-do-kew-mahN]
dog le chien [luh-shyaN]
doll la poupée [la-poo-pay]
donkey l'âne *(m)* [lan]
door la porte [la-pohrt]; *(house)* la porte d'entrée [la-pohrt-dahN-tray]
door, front la porte de la maison/de l'immeuble [la-pohrt-duh-la-meh-zohN]/[lee-muhbl]
double double [doobl]
doubt le doute [luh-doot]; **without a doubt** sans aucun doute [sahN-zo-kaN-doot]; *(v)* douter de [doo-tay-duh]
doubtful douteux, -euse [doo-tuuh(z)]; incertain(e) [aN-sehr-taN]/[aN-sehr-tehn]
down vers le bas [vehr-luh-ba]; en bas [ahN-ba]
downhill en descendant [ahN-day-sahN-dahN]
draft le courant d'air [luh-koo-rahN-dehr]; le plan [luh-plahN]; le projet [luh-pro-zhay]; l'esquisse *(f)* [lehs-kees]
draw *(v)* dessiner [day-see-nay]
dreadful affreux, -euse [a-fruuh(z)]
dream le rêve [luh-rehv]
dress *(v)* s'habiller [sa-bee-yay]
drink *(v)* boire [bwar]
drinkable potable [po-tabl]
drip *(v)* tomber goutte à goutte [tohN-bay-goot-a-goot]
driver le chauffeur [luh-sho-fuhr]
drop la goutte [la-goot]
drunk soûl(e) [sool]; ivre [eevr]; *(lightly)* éméché(e) [ay-may-shay]; **to get drunk** se soûler [suh-soo-lay]
dry sec [sehk], sèche [sehsh]
dry *(v)* sécher [say-shay]
durable résistant(e) [ray-zees-tahN(t)]
duration la durée [la-dew-ray]
during pendant *(prp)* [pahN-dahN]; pendant que *(conj)* [pahN-dahN-kuh]
dust la poussière [la-poo-syehr]
duty le devoir [luh-duh-vwar]

E

earlier plus tôt [plew-to]; autrefois [o-truh-fwa]
early tôt [to]
earn *(v)* gagner [ga-nyay]; *(be worth)* mériter [may-ree-tay]
earnings le gain [luh-gaN]
earth la terre [la-tehr]
earthenware la poterie [la-poht-ree]
East l'Est *(m)* [lehst]
easy facile [fa-seel]
eat *(v)* manger [mahN-zhay]
edge le bord [luh-bohr]
edible comestible [ko-mehs-teebl]
education l'éducation *(f)* [lay-dew-ka-syohN]; l'instruction *(f)* [laNs-trewk-syohN]
effect l'effet *(m)* [lay-fay]
effective efficace [ay-fee-kas]
effort l'effort *(m)* [lay-fohr]
egg l'œuf [luhf] *(m)*; **eggs** les œufs *(m pl)* [lay-zuuh]
either, . . . or ou [oo] . . . ou [oo]; ou bien [oo-byaN] . . . ou bien [oo-byaN]
electric électrique *(adj)* [ay-lehk-treed]; à l'électricité *(adv)* [a-lay-lehk-tree-see-tay]
elevator l'ascenseur *(m)* [la-sahN-suhr]
elsewhere ailleurs [a-yuhr]
emancipated émancipé(e) [ay-mahN-see-pay]
embassy l'ambassade *(f)* [lahN-ba-sad]
emergency, in case of en cas d'urgence [ahN-ka-dewr-zhahNs]
employ *(v) (formula)* appliquer [a-plee-kay]; *(v)* employer [ahN-plwa-yay]
empty vide [veed]
enclosure *(letter)* la/les pièce(s) jointe(s) [la/lay-pyehs-zhwaNt]
end la fin [la-faN]; **in the end** finalement [fee-nal-mahN]; *(v)* se terminer [suh-tehr-mee-nay]
engaged, to get engaged se fiancer avec [suh-fee-yahN-say-a-vehk]
English anglais(e) [ahN-gleh(z)]
enjoy *(v)* jouir de [zweer-duh]; savourer [sa-voo-ray]
enjoyment le plaisir [luh-pleh-zeer]
enormous puissant(e) [pwee-sahN(t)]
enough assez [a-say]; suffisamment [sew-fee-za-mahN]

enter *(v)* entrer dans [ahN-tray-dahN]; (a country) entrer [ahN-tray]; (a room) entrer [ahN-tray]
entertaining distrayant(e) [dees-tray-yahN(t)]
enthusiastic about enthousiasmé(e) (par) [ahN-too-zyas-may-par]
entitled to autorisé(e) (à) [o-to-ree-zay-a]
entrance l'accès *(m)* [lak-say]; l'entrée *(f)* [lahN-tray]; **No (admittance)!** Entrée interdite! [ahN-tray-aN-tehr-deet]; **admission ticket** le billet d'entrée [luh-bee-yay-dahN-tray]; **admission price** le prix d'entrée [luh-pree-dahN-tray]; **main entrance** l'entrée *(f)* principale [lahN-tray-praN-see-pal]
environment l'environnement *(m)* [lahN-vee-rohn-mahN]
equivalent équivalent(e) [lay-kee-va-lahN(t)]
especially surtout [sewr-too]
estimate *(v)* estimer [ehs-tee-may]
Europe l'Europe *(f)* [luuh-rohp]
European l'Européen *(m)*, l'Européenne *(f)* [luuh-ro-pay-aN]/[luuh-ro-pay-ehn]
even même [mehm]
evening le soir [luh-swar]; la soirée [la-swa-ray]; **in the evening** le soir [luh-swar]; **this evening** ce soir [suh-swar]
event l'événement *(m)* [lay-vehn-mahN] la manifestation [la-ma-nee-fehs-ta-syohN]; *(show)* le spectacle [luh-spehk-takl]
every chaque *(adj)* [shak]; chacun(e) *(prn)* [sha-kaN]/[sha-kewn]; **every time** chaque fois [shak-fwa]
everything tout [too]
everywhere partout [par-too]
evidence le témoignage [luh-tay-mwa-nyazh]; le certificat [luh-sehr-tee-fee-ka]
evil méchant(e) [may-sahN(t)]
exact(ly) exact(e) [ehg-zakt]
exaggerated exagéré(e) [ehg-za-zhay-ray]
examination l'examen *(m)* [ehg-za-maN]
examine *(v)* examiner [ehg-za-mee-nay]
example l'exemple *(m)* [lehg-zahNpl]; **for example** par exemple [par-ehg-zahNpl]
excellent excellent(e) [ehk-seh-lahN(t)]
except hors de [ohr-duh]
exception l'exception [lehk-sehp-syohN]
exchange l'échange *(m)* [lay-shaNzh]
exchange *(v)* échanger [ay-shahN-zhay]
exchange rate le taux de change [to-duh-shahNzh]
excursion le tour [luh-toor]
excuse l'excuse *(f)* [lehk-skewz]
excuse *(v)* excuser [ehk-skew-zay]; **excuse me please!** excusez-moi [ehk-skew-zay-mwa]; **excuse oneself** s'excuser [sehk-skew-zay]

exhausted épuisé(e) [ay-pwee-zay]
exhibition la foire [la-fwar]
exit la sortie [la-sohr-tee]; *(freeway)* la sortie (d'autoroute) [la-sohr-tee-do-to-root]
expect *(v)* attendre [a-tahNdr]; *(to count on)* s'attendre à [sa-tahN-druh-a]
expenses les dépenses *(f pl)* [lay-day-pahNs]; les frais *(m pl)* [lay-fray]
expensive cher, chère [shehr]; coûteux, -euse [koo-tuuh(z)]
experience l'expérience *(f)* [lehk-spay-ryahNs]
experiment l'essai *(m)* [lay-say]
expire *(v) (go to the end)* se terminer [suh-tehr-mee-nay]; *(contract)* expirer [ehk-spee-ray]
explain *(v)* déclarer [day-kla-ray]; *(to make clear)* expliquer [ehk-splee-kay]
explicitly expressément [ehk-spray-say-mahN]
expression l'expression *(f)* [lehk-spray-syohN]
extend *(v)* allonger [a-lohN-zhay]
external externe [ehk-strehm]
extinguish éteindre [ay-taNdr]
extraordinary extraordinaire [ehk-stra-ohr-dee-nehr]
eye l'œil *(m)* [luhy]; **eyes** les yeux *(m pl)* [lay-zyuuh]

F

fabric le tissu [luh-tee-sew]
fact le fait [luh-fay]
factory l'usine *(f)* [lew-zeen]
fair loyal(e) [lwa-yal]
faith la foi [la-fwa]
fall la chute [la-shewt]
fall *(v)* tomber [tohN-bay]
false faux, fausse [fo(s)]
family la famille [la-fa-meey]
famous célèbre [say-lehbr]
farm la ferme [la-fehrm]
farmer le paysan [luh-pay-ee-sahN]
fashion la mode [la-mohd]
fashionable à la mode [a-la-mohd]; moderne [mo-dehrn]
fasten *(v)* lier [lee-yay]
fat gras, grasse [gra(s)]
father le père [luh-pehr]
fault le défaut [luh-day-fo]
faulty défectueux, -euse [day-fehk-twuuh(z)]; endommagé(e) [ahN-do-ma-zhay]
favor l'obligeance *(f)* [lo-blee-zhahNs]
favor le service [luh-sehr-vees]; **in favor of** en faveur de [ahN-fa-vuhr-duh]
favorable *(price)* intéressant [aN-tay-reh-sahN]
fear la crainte [la-kraNt], la peur [la-puhr]
fear *(v)* craindre [kraNdr]; avoir peur de [a-vwar-puhr-duh]
feather la plume [la-plewm]
fee les honoraires *(m pl)* [lay-zo-no-rehr]
feel *(v)* sentir [sahN-teer]
feeling le sentiment [luh-sahN-tee-mahN]
fees les droits *(m pl)* [lay-drwa]
feminine féminin(e) [fay-mee-naN]/[fay-mee-neen]
fetch *(v)* aller chercher [a-lay-shehr-shay]
fiancé/fiancée le fiancé, la fiancée [luh-fee-yahN-say]/[la-fee-yahN-say]
field le champ [luh-shahN]
fill *(v)* remplir [rahN-pleer]
fill up *(v)* prendre de l'essence [prahN-druh-duh-lay-sahNs]
film la pellicule [la-pay-lee-kewl]; *(cinema)* le film [luh-feelm]
filter le filtre [luh-feeltr]
finally en dernier lieu [ahN-dehr-nyay-lyuuh]; enfin [ahN-faN]
find *(v)* trouver [troo-vay]
fine fin(e) [faN]/[feen]; distingué(e) [dees-taN-gay]; délicat(e) [day-lee-ka(t)]; l'amende *(f)* [la-mahNd]
fingertip le bout des doigts [luh-boo-day-dwa]
finish *(v)* terminer [tehr-mee-nay]
fire l'incendie *(f)* [laN-sahN-dee]; le feu [luh-fuuuh]; **fire extinguisher** l'extincteur *(m)* [lehk-staNk-tuhr]; **fire alarm** l'avertisseur *(m)* d'incendie [la-vehr-tee-suhr-daN-sahN-dee]; **fire works** le feu d'artifice [luh-fuuh-daN-sahN-dee]
first d'abord [da-bohr]; premier, -ière [pruh-myay]/[pruh-myehr]; premièrement; [pruh-myehr-mahN]
first aid les premiers secours [lay-pruh-myah-suh-koor]
first, at d'abord [da-bohr]
first of all d'abord [da-bohr]
first class de premier ordre [duh-pruh-myeh-rohrdr]
fish *(v)* pêcher [peh-shay]
fish le poisson [luh-pwa-sohN]; **fish monger** le poissonnier [luh-pwa-so-nyay]
fit en forme [ahN-fohrm]
fix *(v)* fixer [fee-ksay]
flame la flamme [la-flam]

flat plat(e) [pla(t)]
flat rate le forfait [luh-fohr-fay]
fleece la peau [la-po]
flirt le flirt [luh-fuhrt]
floor l'étage *(m)* [lay-tazh]
flow *(v)* couler [koo-lay]
flow into *(v)* se jeter [suh-zhuh-tay]
flower la fleur [la-fluhr]
fly la mouche [la moosh]
fly *(v)* voler [vo-lay]
follow *(v)* suivre [sweevr]
food la nourriture [la-noo-ree-tewr]; **foods** les aliments *(m pl)* [lay-za-lee-mahN]; les denrées *(f pl)* alimentaires [lay-dahN-ray-za-lee-mahN-tehr]
for car [kar]; pour [poor]
for, to be être pour [eh-truh-poor]
for this reason pour cette raison [poor-seht-reh-zohN]
forbid *(v)* interdire [aN-tehr-deer]
forbidden interdit(e) [aN-tehr-dee(t)]
foreign *(from abroad)* étranger, -ère [ay-trahN-zhay]/[ay-trahN-zhehr]; *(unknown)* inconnu(e) [aN-ko-new]
foreign country l'étranger [lay-trahN-zhay]
foreigner l'étranger *(m)*, [lay-trahN-zhay]; l'étrangère *(f)*; [lay-trahN-zhehr]; l'in-connu(e) [laN-ko-new]
forget *(v)* oublier [oo-blee-yay]
forgive *(v)* pardonner [par-do-nay]
form le formulaire [luh-fohr-mew-lehr]; la formule [la-fohr-mewl]
form *(v)* former [fohr-may]
format le format [luh-fohr-ma]
forward en avant [ahN-na-vahN]
found, to be *(v)* se trouver [suh-troo-vay]
fountain la fontaine [la-fohN-tehn]
fragile fragile [fra-zheel]
France la France [la-frahNs]
free gratuit(e) [gra-twee(t)]; libre [libr]
free of charge gratuitement [gra-tweet-mahN]
freight le fret [luh-freht]; la cargaison [la-kar-geh-zohN]
French français(e) [frahN-seh(z)]
French person le/la Français(e) [luh/la-frahN-seh(z)]
frequently *(adv)* fréquemment [fray-ka-mahN]
fresh frais [fray]; fraîche [frehsh]; *(new)* nouveau [noo-vo]; nouvel(le) [noo-vehl]; *(linen)* propre [prohpr]
friend l'ami, l'amie [la-mee]; **boy friend** le petit ami [luh-puh-tee-ta-mee]; **girl friend** la petite amie [la-puh-tee-ta-mee]

friends, to be friends with être amis [eh-tra-mee]
friendly aimable [eh-mabl]
friendship l'amitié *(f)* [la-mee-tyay]
frighten *(v)* effrayer [ay-fray-yay]
from à partir de [a-par-teer-duh]; de [duh]; *(material)* en [ahN]; **from Paris** de Paris [duh-pa-ree]
front, in devant [duh-vahN]
frying pan la poêle [la-pwal]
fuel oil le mazout [luh-ma-zoot]
full plein(e) [plaN]/[plehn]; complet, -ète [kohN-play]/[kohN-pleht]; entier, -ière [ahNn-tyay]/[ahN-tyehr]; qui n'a plus faim [kee-na-plew-faN]; rassasié(e) [ra-sa-zyay]
fur la fourrure [la-foo-rewr]
furious furieux, -euse [few-ryuuh(z)]
furnish *(v)* meubler [muuh-blay]
furnishings *(apartment)* l'ameublement *(m)* [la-muh-bluuh-mahN]; le mobilier [luh-mo-bee-lyay]
furniture le meuble [luh-muhbl]
fuse *(el)* les plombs *(m pl)* [lay-plohN]; les fusibles *(m pl)* [lay-few-zeebl]
future l'avenir *(m)* [lav-neer]; futur(e) *(adj)* [few-tewr]

G

gain *(v)* gagner [ga-nyay]
gain weight *(v)* grossir [gro-seer]; aug-menter [ohg-mahN-tay]
game *(hunting)* le gibier [luh-zhee-byay]
garage le garage [luh-ga-razh]
garbage les ordures *(f pl)* [lay-zohr-dewr]
garden le jardin [luh-zhar-daN]
gas l'essence *(f)* [lay-sahNs]
gate le portail [luh-pohr-ta-yuh]
gateway l'entrée *(f)* [lahN-tray]
gear *(car)* la vitesse [la-vee-tehs]
general général; **in general** en général [ahN-zhay-nay-ral]
gentle affectueux, -euse, [a-fehk-twuuh(z)]; tendre [tahNdr]
genuine authentique [o-tahN-teek]
get *(v)* procurer [pro-kew-ray]; recevoir [ruh-suh-vwar]; obtenir [ob-tuh-neer]
get back *(v)* récupérer [ray-kew-pay-ray]
get up *(v)* se lever [suh-luh-vay]
giddy pris, e de vertige [pree(z)-duh-vehr-teezh]
gift le cadeau [luh-ka-do]
girl la jeune fille [la- zhuhn-feey]
give *(v)* donner [do-nay]

give back *(v)* rendre [rahNdr]
glad (about) heureux, -euse (de) [uuh-ruuh(z)-duh]
glad content(e) [kohN-tahN(t)]; heureux, -euse [uuh-ruuh(z)]; gai(e) [gay]
gladly volontiers [vo-lohN-tyay]; **not gladly** à contre-cœur [a-kohN-truh-kuhr]
glass *(pane)* la vitre [la-veetr]; *(drinking)* le verre [luh-vehr]
glasses les lunettes *(f pl)* [lay-lew-neht]
go *(v)* aller [a-lay]; *(on foot)* marcher [mar-shay]; *(by train, car, etc.)* aller [a-lay]; **go straight ahead** aller tout droit [a-lay-too-drwa]; **go on** avancer [a-vahN-say]; **go back** retourner [ruh-toor-nay]
go away partir [par-teer]; s'en aller [sahN-na-lay]
go for a walk *(v)* se promener [suh-pro-muh-nay]
go out *(v)* sortir [sohr-teer]
go up *(v)* monter [mohN-tay]; **go in** entrer [ahN-tray]; **go down** descendre [day-sahNdr]
God Dieu [dyuuh]; **Thank God** (goodness)! Dieu soit loué! [dyuuh-swa-lway]
good bon, bonne *(adj)* [bohN]/[bohn]; bien *(adv)* [byaN]; **to make good** rectifier [rehk-tee-fyay]
good le bien [luh-byaN]
goods la marchandise [la-mar-shaN-deez]
government le gouvernement [luh-goo-vehr-nuh-mahN]
grab *(v)* attraper [a-tra-pay]
grandfather le grand-père [luh-grahN-pehr]
grandmother la grand-mère [la-grahN-mehr]
grandson/daughter le petit-fils [luh-puh-tee-fees]; la petite-fille [la-puh-teet-feey]
grant *(v)* accorder [a-kohr-day]
great formidable [fohr-mee-dabl]
greet *(v)* saluer [sa-lew-ay]
grief le chagrin [luh-sha-graN]
ground le sol [luh-sohl]; le plancher [luh-plahN-shay]; le terrain [luh-tay-raN]
ground floor le rez-de-chaussée [luh-ray-duh-sho-say]
group le groupe [luh-groop]
grow *(v)* *(plant)* pousser [poo-say]; *(people)* grandir [grahN-deer]
grumble *(v)* protester [pro-tehs-tay]
guarantee la garantie [la-ga-rahN-tee]
guard *(v)* garder [gar-day]; surveiller [sewr-veh-yay]
guess la supposition [la-sew-po-zee-syohN]
guest l'hôte *(m)* [lot]; l'invité(e) [laN-vee-tay]
guide *(for foreigner)* le guide [luh-geed]
guilt la faute [la-fot]
guitar la guitare [la-gee-tar]

H

habit l'habitude [la-bee-tewd]
haggle *(v)* marchander [mar-shaN-day]
half *(adj)* demi(e) [duh-mee]; *(adv)* à demi [a-duh-mee]; à moitié [a-mwa-tyay]; la moitié [la-mwa-tyay]
hall la halle [la-al]; la salle [la-sal]
hammer le marteau [luh-mar-to]
hand la main [la-maN]
hand *(v)* over remettre [ruh-mehtr]
hand in *(v)* rendre [rahNdr]; remettre [ruh-mehtr]
handle la poignée [la-pwa—nyay]
handmade fait à la main [feh-maN]
handwriting l'écriture *(f)* [lay-kree-tewr]
hang *(v)* suspendre [sews-pahNdr]
happen *(v)* arriver [a-ree-vay]; se passer [suh-pa-say]; se produire [suh-pro-dweer]
happy heureux, -euse [uuh-ruuh(z)]
hard dur(e) [dewr]
hardly à peine [a-pehn]
hardness la dureté [la-dewr-tay]
harm *(v)* nuire [nweer]
harmful nuisible [nwee-zeebl]
harvest la récolte [la-ray-kohlt]
have *(v)* avoir [a-vwar]
have to *(v)* devoir [duh-vwar]; être obligé(e) de [eh-tro-blee-zhay-duh]
he il [eel]
health la santé [la-sahN-tay]
healthy en bonne santé [ahN-bohn-sahN-tay]
hear *(v)* entendre [ahN-tahNdr]
heart le cœur [luh-kuhr]
heat *(v)* chauffer [sho-fay]
heel *(shoe)* le talon [luh-ta-lohN]
height l'altitude *(f)* [lal-tee-tewd]
Hello! Salut! [sa-lew]
help l'aide *(f)* [lehd]
help s.o. *(v)* aider qn [eh-day-kehl-kaN]
her sa *(poss prn)* *(f)* [sa]; son *(m)* [sohN]; leur *(pl)* [luhr]
here ici [ee-see]
herring le hareng [luh-a-rahN]
hesitate hésiter [ay-zee-tay]
hide *(v)* cacher [ka-shay]; dissimuler [dee-see-mew-lay]
high haut(e) [o(t)]

hike *(v)* faire de la randonné pédestre [fehr-duh-la-rahN-do-nay-pay-dehstr]
hill la colline [la-ko-leen]
his son *(poss prn)* [sohN]
hobby le hobby [luh-o-bee]; le passe-temps [luh-pas-tahN]
hole le trou [luh-troo]
holiday le jour férié [luh-zhoor-fay-ryay]
holy saint(e) [saN(t)]
home, at à la maison [a-la-meh-zohN]
honor l'honneur *(m)* [lo-nuhr]
hook le crochet [luh-kro-shay]; *(coat)* le porte-manteau [luh-pohrt-mahN-to]
hope *(v)* espérer [ehs-pay-ray]
hospitality l'hospitalité *(f)* [lohs-pee-ta-lee-tay]
host/ess l'hôte *(m)* [lot]; l'hôtesse *(f)* [lo-tehs]
hot chaud(e) [sho(d)]
hotel l'hôtel *(m)* [lo-tehl]
hour l'heure *(f)* [luhr]; **a half hour** une demi-heure [ewn-duh-mee-uhr]; **a quarter of an hour** un quart d'heure [aN-kar-duhr]
hours, every two toutes les deux heures [toot-lay-duuh-zuhr]
house la maison [la-meh-zohN]
how comment [ko-mahN]
however pourtant [poor-tahN]
hug *(v)* serrer dans les bras [say-ray-dahN-lay-bra]
human humain(e) [ew-maN]/[ew-mehn]
hundred cent [sahN]; **one hundred times** cent fois [sahN-fwa]
hunger la faim [la-faN]
hungry, to be avoir faim [a-vwar-faN]
hurry *(v)* se dépêcher [suh-day-pay-shay]
hurt *(v)* faire mal [fehr-mal]

I

I je [zhuh]; moi [mwa]
ice *(sheet)* le verglas [luh-vehr-gla]; *(cream)* la glace [la-glas]
idea l'idée *(f)* [lee-day]; **no idea** aucune idée [o-kewn-ee-day]
identity card la pièce d'identité [la-pyehs-dee-dahN-tee-tay]
ill malade [ma-lad]; **to be taken ill** tomber malade [tohN-bay-ma-lad]
illuminated éclairé(e) [ay-klay-ray]; *(festive)* illuminé(e) [ee-lew-mee-nay]
immediately direct(e) [dee-rehkt]; directement *(adv)* [dee-rehk-tuh-mahN]; tout de suite [too-duh-sweet]

impertinent éhonté(e) [ay-ohN-tay]
impolite impoli(e) [aN-po-lee]
important important(e) [aN-pohr-tahN(t)]
impossible hors de question [ohr-duh-kehs-tyohN]; exclu(e) [ehk-sklew]; impossible [aN-po-seebl]
impractical peu pratique [puuh-pra-teek]
impression l'impression *(f)* [laN-pray-syohN]
improve *(v)* améliorer [a-may-lyo-ray]; *(mistake)* corriger [ko-ree-zhay]
in dans [dahN], en [ahN]; **in the street** dans la rue [dahN-la-rew]; **in French** en français [ahN-frahN-say]; **in France** en France [ahN-frahNs]; **in Rome** à Rome [a-rohm]; **in weather like this** avec un temps pareil [a-vehk-aN-tahN-pa-rehy]
incident l'incident *(m)* [laN-see-dahN]
included compris(e) [kohN-pree(z)]
incomplete incomplet, -ète [aN-kohN-play]/[aN-kohN-pleht]
inconsiderate sans gêne [sahN-zhehn]
increase *(v)* augmenter [ohg-mahN-tay]
incredible incroyable [aN-krwa-yabl]
indefinite indéterminé(e) [aN-day-tehr-mee-nay]
indispensable indispensable [aN-dees-pahN-sabl]
industrious travailleur, -euse [tra-va-yuhr]/[tra-va-yuuhz]
inevitable inévitable [ee-nay-vee-tabl]
inexact imprécis(e) [aN-pray-see(z)]
inexperienced inexpérimenté(e) [ee-nehk-spay-ree-mahN-tay]
inflammable inflammable [aN-fla-mabl]
inflate *(v)* gonfler [gohN-flay]
inform *(v)* annoncer [a-nohN-say]; *(news)* rapporter [ra-pohr-tay]; avertir [a-vehr-teer]; faire part de [fehr-par-duh]; informer [aN-fohr-may]
inform s.o. *(v)* prévenir qn [pray-vuh-neer]
information le renseignement [luh-rahN-seh-nyuh-mahN]; **ask for information** prendre des renseignements [prahN-druh-day-rahN-seh-nyuh-mahN]
inhabitant l'habitant *(m)* [la-bee-tahN]
injured person le blessé [luh-blay-say]; la blessée [la-blay-say]
injustice l'injustice *(f)* [laN-zhews-tees]
innocent innocent(e) [ee-no-sahN(t)]
innovation la nouveauté [la-noo-vo-tay]
inquire *(v)* se renseigner [suh-rahN-seh-nyay]
insect l'insecte *(m)* [laN-sehkt]
inside à l'intérieur [a-laN-teh-ryuhr]; dedans [duh-dahN]

insist on *(v)* insister sur [aN-sees-tay-sewr]
installation l'installation *(f)* [laNs-ta-la-syohN]
instead (of) au lieu de [o-lyuuh-duh]
insufficient insuffisant(e) [aN-sew-fee-zahN(t)]
insult l'offense *(f)* [lo-fahNs]; la vexation [la-vehk-sa-syohN]
insurance l'assurance *(f)* [la-sew-rahNs]
intelligence l'intelligence *(f)* [laN-tay-lee-zhahNs]; la raison [la-reh-zohN]
intend to *(v)* avoir l'intention de [a-vwar-laN-tahN-syohN-duh]
intention l'intention *(f)* [laN-tahN-syohN]
interest l'intérêt *(m)* [laN-tay-ray]
interested, to be interested (in) *(v)* s'intéresser (à) [saN-tay-reh-say]
interesting intéressant(e) [aN-tay-reh-sahN(t)]
international international(e) [aN-tehr-na-syo-nal]
interrupt *(v)* interrompre [aN-tay-rohNpr]
intolerable incapable [aN-ka-pabl], insupportable [aN-sew-pohr-tabl]
introduce *(v)* faire connaître [fehr-ko-nehtr], présenter [pray-zahN-tay]
invalid (not valid) périmé(e) [pay-ree-may]
invent *(v)* inventer [aN-vahN-tay]
invitation l'invitation *(f)* [laN-vee-ta-syohN]
invite *(v)* inviter [aN-vee-tay]
iron le fer, le fer à repasser [luh-fehr-a-ruh-pa-say]
irregular irrégulier, -ière [ee-ray-gew-lyehr]
island l'île *(f)* [leel]
isolated isolé(e) [ee-zo-lay]
itch *(v)* démanger [day-do-ma-zhay]; gratter [gra-tay]

J

jellyfish la méduse [la-may-dewz]
joke la plaisanterie [la-pleh-zahN-tuh-ree]
journey le voyage [luh-vwa-yazh]; le trajet [luh-tra-zhay]
journey, to go on a *(v)* partir en voyage [par-teer-ahN-vwa-yazh]
joy la joie [la-zhwa]
judge le juge [luh-zhewzh]
judge *(v)* juger [zhew-zhay]
judgment le jugement [luh-zhewzh-mahN]
jump *(v)* sauter [so-tay]
just *(time)* juste [zhewst]
just *(fair)* juste [zhewst]

K

keep *(v)* garder [gar-day]; conserver [kohN-sehr-vay]; tenir [tuh-neer]
kind aimable [eh-mabl]; bienveillant(e) [byaN-veh-yahN(t)]; la manière [la-ma-nyehr]; la façon [la-fa-sohN]; la sorte [la-sohrt]; *(cigarettes)* la marque [la-mark]
kindness l'amabilité *(f)* [la-ma-bee-lee-tay]
kiss le baiser [luh-beh-zay]
kiss *(v)* embrasser [ahN-bra-say]
kitchen la cuisine [la-kwee-zeen]
knock *(v)* frapper (à la porte) [fra-pay-a-la-pohrt]
knot le nœud [luh-nuuh]
know *(v)* connaître [ko-nehtr], savoir [sa-vwar]
knowledge la connaissance [la-ko-neh-sahNs]; le savoir [luh-sa-vwar]
known (well) connu(e) [ko-new]

L

lack le manque [luh-mahNk]
ladder l'échelle *(f)* [lay-shehl]
lady la dame [la-dam]
lamp la lampe [la-lahNp]
land le pays [luh-pay-ee]; *(as opposed to water)* la terre [la-tehr]
land *(v)* atterir [a-tay-reer]
landing stage la passerelle [la-pas-rehl]
landlord le patron [luh-pa-trohN]
language la langue [la-lahNg]
last dernier, -ière [dehr-nyay]/[dehr-nyehr]
last *(v)* durer [dew-ray]
last but one avant-dernier, -ière [a-vahN-dehr-nyay]/[a-vahN-dher-nyehr]
late tard [tar]
late, to be *(v)* être en retard [eh-trahN-ruh-tar]
later plus tard [plew-tar]
laugh *(v)* rire [reer]
laundry la lessive [la-leh-seev]
lawn la pelouse [la-puh-looz]
lazy paresseux, -euse [pa-reh-suuh(z)]
lead *(v)* conduire [kohN-dweer]
leaf la feuille [la-fuhy]
lean maigre [mehgr]
learn *(v)* apprendre [a-prahNdr]
least, at au moins [o-mwaN]
leather le cuir [luh-kweer]

leave *(v)* (for) partir (pour) [par-teer-poor]; *(v)* déposer [day-po-zay]; quitter le pays [kee-tay-luh-pay-ee; passer la frontière [pa-say-la-frohN-tyehr]; *(v)* quitter [kee-tay]
leave behind *(v)* laisser [leh-say]
left gauche [gosh]; restant(e) [rehs-tahN(t)]; **on the left** à gauche [a-gosh]
lend *(v)* prêter [preh-tay]
length la longueur [la-lohN-guhr]
let *(v)* laisser [leh-say]
letter la lettre [la-lehtr]
license plate la plaque [luh-plak]
lie le mensonge [luh-mahN-sohNzh]
life la vie [la-vee]
lift soulever [sool-vay]
light *(v)* allumer [a-lew-may]; *(match)* frotter [fro-tay]
light la lumière [la-lew-myehr]; **to switch on/off the light** allumer [a-lew-may] éteindre [ay-taNdr]
lighter le briquet [luh-bree-kay]
lighthouse le phare [luh-far]
lightning l'éclair *(m)* [lay-klehr]; *(photo)* le flash [luh-flash]
like *(v)* aimer [eh-may]
line la ligne [la-leeny]; le trajet [luh-tra-zhay]; *(train)* **line service** la ligne *(f)* [leeny]
lining *(cloth)* la doublure [la-doo-blewr]
liquid liquide [lee-keed]
list la liste [la-leest]
listen *(v)* écouter (qn) [ay-koo-tay-kehl-kaN]
little petit(e) [puh-tee(t)]; *(age)* jeune [zhuhn]; peu [puuh]; **a little** un peu [aN-puuh]; **a little bit of** un peu de [aN-puuh-duh]
live *(v)* habiter [a-bee-tay], vivre [veevr]
lively vif, vive [veef]/[veev]
load *(v)* charger [shar-zhay]
lock la fermeture [la-fehr-muh-tewr]; la serrure [la-say-rewr]; *(camera)* l'obturateur *(m)* [lob-tew-ra-tuhr]
lock *(v)* fermer [fehr-may] fermer à clé [fehr-may-a-klay]
lock in *(v)* inclure [aN-klewr]
lock up *(v)* fermer [fehr-may]
logic(ly) logique *(adj)* [lo-zheek]; logiquement *(adv)* [lo-zheek-mahN]
lonely seul(e) [suhl]; solitaire [so-lee-tehr]
long long [lohN]; longue [lohNg]
look le regard [luh-ruh-gar]
look *(v)* avoir l'air [a-vwar-lehr]; regarder [ruh-gar-day]
look after *(v)* s'occuper de [so-kew-pay-duh]; se soucier de [suh-soo-syay-duh]
look at *(v)* [ruh-gar-day]
look for *(v)* chercher [shehr-shay]
look forward *(v)* se réjouir à l'avance de [suh-ray-zhweer-a-la-vahNs-duh]
look like ressembler [ruh-sahN-blay]
Lorraine la Lorraine [la-lo-rehn]
lose *(v)* perdre [pehrdr]
lose one's way *(v)* s'égarer [say-ga-ray]
lose weight *(v)* maigrir [meh-greer]
loss la perte [la-pehrt]
lost and found office le bureau des objets trouvés [luh-bew-ro-day-zohb-zhay-troo-vay]
lot, a lot of un tas de [aN-ta-duh]
loud bruyant(e) [brew-yahN(t)]; **to be loud** parler fort [par-lay-fohr]; **loud speaker** le haut-parleur [luh-o-par-luhr]
love *(v)* aimer [eh-may]
love l'amour *(m)* [la-moor]
low bas, basse [ba(s)]
loyal fidèle [fee-dehl]
luck la chance [la-shahNs]; **Good luck!** Bonne chance! [bohn-shahNs]
luxurious luxueux, -euse [lewk-syuuh(z)]
luxury le luxe [luh-lewks]

M

machine la machine [la-ma-sheen]
mail la poste [la-pohst]
mail *(v)* *(letter)* envoyer [envoyer]
main(ly) principal(e) *(adj)* [praN-see-pal]; principalement *(adv)* [praN-see-pal-mahN]
maintain *(v)* affirmer [a-feer-may]
make *(v)* faire [fehr]
make-up, to put on *(v)* se maquiller [suh-ma-kee-yay]
man l'homme [lohm]; le mari [luh-ma-ree]
manager le directeur [luh-dee-rehk-tuhr]; la directrice [la-dee-rehk-trees]
manner la manière [la-ma-nyehr]
marriage le mariage [luh-ma-ryazh]
married (to) marié(e) (à) [ma-ryay-a]; **married couple** le couple [luh-koopl]; **married woman** la femme [la-fam]; **married man** le mari [luh-ma-ree]
marry *(v)* se marier [suh-ma-ryay]
masculine masculin(e) [mas-kew-laN]/[mas-kew-leen]
mass *(rel)* la messe [la-mehs]
match l'allumette *(f)* [la-lew-meht]; **match box** la boîte d'allumettes [la-bwat- da-lew-meht]

A/Z

material l'étoffe *(f)* [lay-tohf]; le matériel [luh-ma-tay-ryehl]
matter l'affaire *(f)* [la-fehr]; **to settle a matter** régler une affaire [ray-glay-ewn-a-fehr]
maybe peut-être [puuh-tehtr]
me me [muh], moi [mwa]; **to me** à moi [a-mwa]
meadow le pré [luh-pray]
meal le repas [luh-ruh-pa]
mean *(v)* signifier [see-nee-fyay]; vouloir dire [voo-lwar-deer]
mean méchant(e) [may-shahN(t)]
meaning la signification [la-see-nee-fee-ka-syohN]; l'importance *(f)* [laN-pohr-tahNs]
means le moyen [luh-mwa-yaN]
meanwhile entre-temps [ahN-truh-tahN]
measure la mesure [la-muh-zewr]
measure *(v)* mesurer [muh-zew-ray]
meat la viande [la-vyahNd]
Mediterranean Sea la Méditerranée [la-may-dee-tay-ra-nay]
meet *(v)* rencontrer [rahN-kohN-tray]
meet, to arrange to *(v)* se donner rendez-vous [suh-do-nay-rahN-day-voo]
mend *(v)* repriser [ruh-pree-zay]
merry gai(e) [gay]
message la nouvelle [la-noo-vehl]
middle le milieu [luh-mee-lyuuh]
midnight minuit *(m)* [mee-nwee]; **at midnight** à minuit [a-mee-nwee]
mild doux, douce [doo(s)]
mind, to make up one's *(v)* se décider [suh-day-see-day]
minus moins [mwaN]
minute la minute [la-mee-newt]
miscalculate faire une erreur de calcul [fehr-ewn-eh-ruhr-duh-kal-kewl]
misfortune le malheur [luh-ma-luhr]
miss *(v)* manquer [mahN-kay], rater [ra-tay]
Miss mademoiselle [mad-mwa-zehl]
missing, to be manquer [mahN-kay]
mistake l'erreur *(f)* [leh-ruhr]
mistake, to mistake for *(v)* confondre [kohN-fohNdr]
mistake la faute [la-fot], le défaut [luh-day-fo]
mistake, by par inadvertance [par-ee-nad-vehr-tahNs]
mistaken, to be *(v)* se tromper [suh-trohN-pay]
misty brumeux, -euse [brew-muuh(z)]
misunderstand *(v)* mal comprendre [mal-kohN-prahNdr]
misunderstanding le malentendu [luh-mal-ahN-tahN-dew]
mix up *(v)* échanger [ay-shahN-zhay], confondre [kohN-fohNdr]
mixed mixte [meeks]; mélangé(e) [may-lahN-zhay]
model le modèle [luh-mo-dehl]; *(trial)* l'échantillon *(m)* [lay-shaN-tee-yohN]
moderate modéré(e) [mo-day-ray]
moist humide [ew-meed]
moment le moment, [luh-mo-mahN]; l'instant *(m)*
money l'argent *(m)* [lar-zhaN]
month le mois [luh-mwa]
monthly mensuel(le) *(adj)* [mahN-swehl]; par mois *(adv)* [par-mwa]
mood l'humeur *(f)* [lew-muhr]
moon la lune [la-lewn]
more plus; **more than** plus que [plews-kuh]; plus de [plews-duh]; **more or less** plus ou moins [plew-zoo-mwaN]
morning le matin [luh-ma-taN]
mosquito le moustique [luh-moos-teek]
most, at the au plus [o-plews]; au maximum [o-mak-see-mohm]
mother la mère [la-mehr]
motherland la patrie [la-pa-tree]
mountain la montagne [la-mohN-tany]
mouth *(river)* l'embouchure *(f)* [lahN-boo-shewr]
move *(v)* déménager [day-may-na-zhay]; remuer [ruh-mew-ay]
movement le mouvement [luh-moov-mahN]
Mr. monsieur [muh-syuuh]
much beaucoup de [bo-koo-duh]
much, too trop [tro]
mud la boue [la-boo]
music la musique [la-mew-zeek]
my mon [mohN], ma [ma]
myself moi-même [mwa-mehm]

N

nail le clou [luh-kloo]; *(fingernail)* l'ongle *m* [lohNgl]
naked nu(e) [new]
name le nom [luh-nohN]
name *(v)* appeler [ap-lay]
narrow étroit(e) [ay-trwa]
nation la nation [la-na-syohN]
native natif, -ive [na-teef]/[na-teev]; originaire [o-ree-zhee-nehr]; local(e) [lo-kal]; national(e) [na-syo-nal]

native country le pays natal [luh-pay-ee-na-tal]
natural(ly) naturel(le) *(adj)* [na-tew-rehl]; naturellement *(adv)* [na-tew-rehl-mahN]
nature la nature [la-na-tewr]
near près de [pray-duh]; proche [prohsh]; **nearby** près de [pray-duh]
nearly presque [prehsk]
necessary nécessaire [nay-say-sehr]
necessity la nécessité [la-nay-say-see-tay]
need *(v)* avoir besoin de [a-vwar-buh-zwaN-duh]
needle l'aiguille *(f)* [leh-gweey]
negative négatif, -ive [nay-ga-teef]/[nay-ga-teev]
neglect *(v)* négliger [nay-glee-zhay]
negotiations les négociations *(f pl)* [lay-nay-go-sya-syohN]; les pourparlers *(m pl)* [lay-poor-par-lay]
neighbor le voisin [luh-vwa-zaN]; la voisine [la-vwa-zeen]
neither...nor ni...ni [nee]...[nee]
nephew le neveu [luh-nuh-vuuh]
nervous nerveux, -euse [nehr-vuuh(z)]
net le filet [luh-fee-lay]
never (ne É) jamais [zha-may]
new nouveau [noo-vo]; nouvel(le) [noo-vo]; *(unused)* neuf [nuhf]; neuve [nuhv]
news *(piece of)* la nouvelle [la-noo-vehl]
newsstand le journal [luh-zhoor-nal]; le kiosque à journaux [luh-kyohsk-a-zhoor-no]
next le suivant [luh-swee-vahN], la suivante [la-swee-vahNt]
next (to) à côté de [a-ko-tay-duh]
nice cher, chère [shehr]; joli(e) [zho-lee]; *(friendly)* gentil(le) [zhaN-tee(y)]
niece la nièce [la-nyehs]
night la nuit [la-nwee]; **tonight** cette nuit [seht-nwee]
no aucun(e) [o-kaN]/[o-kewn]
nobody (ne ...) personne [pehr-sohn]
noise le bruit [luh-brwee]
noon midi *(m)* [mee-dee]; **noon meal** le déjeuner [luh-day-zhuuh-nay]
no one personne [pehr-sohn]
nor, neither (ne É) pas non plus [pa-nohN-plew]
normal normal(e) [nohr-mal]
normally normalement [nohr-mal-mahN]
north le Nord [luh-nohr]
North Sea la mer du Nord [la-mehr-dew-nohr]
northern au nord de [o-nohr-duh]

not (ne ...) pas [nuh...pa]; **not even** (ne ...) même pas [nuh-...mehm-pa]; **not at all** (ne ...) pas du tout [nuh...pa-dew-too]; **not yet** (ne ...) pas encore [nuh-pa-zahN-kohr]
note la note [la-noht]
note, bank le billet [luh-bee-yay]
note, to make note of *(v)* prendre note [prahNdr-noht]
notebook le cahier [luh-ka-yay]
nothing (ne ...) rien [nuh...ryaN]; **nothing else** c'est tout [say-too]
nothing but rien que [ryaN-kuh]
notice *(v)* remarquer [ruh-mar-kay]
nourishing nourrissant(e) [noo-ree-sahN(t)]
now maintenant [mant-nahN]; à présent [a-pray-zahN]
nowhere nulle part [newl-par]
number le nombre [luh-nohNbr]; le numéro [luh-new-may-ro]
number *(v)* numéroter [new-may-ro-tay]
numerous nombreux, -euse [nohN-bruuh(z)]
nun la religieuse [la-ruh-lee-zhyuuhz]
nurse l'infirmière *(f)* [laN-feer-myehr]; **male nurse** l'infirmier [laN-feer-myay]

O

object l'objet *(m)* [lohb-zhay]; *(of a conversation)* le sujet [luh-sew-zhay]
obligation l'obligation *(f)* [lo-blee-ga-syohN]
obligation, without sans engagement [sahN-zahN-gazh-mahN]
obliged, to be to *(v)* être tenu de [eh-truh-tuh-new-duh]
observe *(v)* observer [ohb-sehr-vay]
obtain *(v)* obtenir [ohb-tuh-neer]; procurer [pro-kew-ray]
occasion *(opportunity)* l'occasion *(f)* [lo-ka-zyohN]
occasionally à l'occasion [a-lo-ka-zyohN]
occupied *(seat)* occupé(e) [o-kew-pay]
occurence le cas [luh-ka]; l'incident *(m)* [laN-see-dahN]
ocean l'océan *(m)* [lo-say-ahN]
offend *(v)* offenser [o-fahN-say]; vexer [vehk-say]
offer *(v)* offrir [o-freer]; proposer [pro-po-zay]
office *(kitchen)* l'office *(m)* [lo-fees]; l'agence *f* [la-zhahNs]

office le bureau [luh-bew-ro]; le cabinet [luh-ka-bee-nay]
office, box la caisse [la-kehs]
official officiel(le) [o-fee-syehl]
often souvent [soo-vahN]
oil l'huile *(f)*[lweel]
old vieux [vyuuh]; vieil(le) [vyehy]; *(from older times)* ancien(ne) [ahN-syaN]/[ahN-syehn]
old-fashioned démodé(e) [day-mo-day]
on à [a]; **on the Seine** sur les bords de la Seine [sewr-lay-bohr-duh-la-sehn]; **on Sunday** dimanche [dee-mahNsh]; sur [sewr]; **on a journey/trip** en voyage [ahN-vwa-yazh]
on time à l'heure [a-luhr]
once une fois [ewn-fwa]; **all at once** tout d'un coup [too-daN-koo]
once, at tout de suite [tood-sweet]
one and a half un et demi [aN-ay-duh-mee]; une et demie [ewn-ay-duh-mee]
one on [ohN]; un [aN], une [ewn]
only seul(e) [suhl] unique [ew-neek]; seulement [suhl-mahN]
open ouvert(e) [oo-vehr(t)]
open *(v)* ouvrir [oo-vreer]
operate *(v)* opérer [o-pay-ray]
opinion l'opinion *(f)* [lo-pee-nyohN]; **in my opinion** selon moi [suh-lohN-mwa]
opportunity l'occasion *(f)* [lo-ka-zyohN]
opposite en face de [ahN-fas-duh]; opposé(e) [o-po-zay]
or ou [oo]
order l'ordre *(m)* [lohrdr]; *(rel)* les ordres *(m pl)* [lay-zohrdr]
orderly *(organized)* en ordre [ahN-nohrdr]; *(person)* comme il faut [kohm-eel-fo]
organize *(v)* organiser [ohr-ga-nee-zay]; préparer [pray-pa-ray]
other, the l'autre [lotr]
otherwise autrement [o-truh-mahN]; *(opposite)* sinon [see-nohN]
our notre [nohtr]; nos [no]
outside à l'extérieur [a-lehk-stay-ryuhr]; **from the outside** de l'extérieur [duh-lehk-stay-ryuhr]; **outside of** à l'extérieur (de) [a-lehk-stay-ryuhr]
outskirts la périphérie [la-pay-ree-fay-ree]
over *(finished)* au-dessus (de) [o-duh-sew-duh]
over there de l'autre côté [duh-lo-truh-ko-tay]
overcrowded bondé(e) [bohN-day]
overseas outre-mer *(m)* [oo-truh-mehr]
overtake *(v)* dépasser [day-pa-say]
owe *(v)* devoir [duh-vwar]
own *(v)* posséder [po-say-day]
own propre [prohpr]
owner le propriétaire [luh-pro-pree-yay-tehr]

P

pack *(v)* emballer [ahN-ba-lay]
pack *(v) (suitcase)* faire sa valise [fehr-sa-va-leez]
package le paquet [luh-pa-kay]
packaging l'emballage *(m)* [lahN-ba-lazh]
page la page [la-pazh]
painful douloureux, -euse [doo-loo-ruuh(z)]
paint *(v)* peindre [paNdr]
pair, a pair of une paire de [ewn-pehr-duh]; le couple [luh-koopl]
pale pâle [pal]
panorama le panorama [luh-pa-no-ra-ma]
parcel le paquet [luh-pa-kay]
pardon? comment? [ko-mahN]; pardon? [par-dohN]
parents les parents *(m pl)* [lay-pa-rahN]
park le parc [luh-park]
park *(v)* se garer [suh-ga-ray]
part *(v)* prendre congé [prahN-druh-kohN-zhay]
part la partie [la-par-tee]; **take part** prendre part (à) [prahN-druh-par-a]
particulars des précisions *(f pl)* [day-pray-vee-zyohN]; le signalement [luh-see-nyal-mahN]
party la soirée [la-swa-ray]; la boum [la-boom]; la fête [la-feht]
pass *(v)* dépasser [day-pa-say]; passer (à côté) [pa-say-a-ko-tay]; passer [pa-say] *(time) (v)* passer [pa-say]
passage le passage [luh-pa-sazh]; la galerie [la-gal-ree]
passenger le passager [luh-pa-sa-zhay]
passing through *(v)* en transit [ahN-trahN-zeet]
passport le passeport [luh-pas-pohr]
past le passé [luh-pa-say]
path le sentier [luh-sahN-tyay]
patience la patience [la-pa-syahNs]
patient patient(e) [pa-syahN(t)]
pay *(v)* payer [peh-yay]
pay attention (to) *(v)* faire attention (à) [fehr-a-tahN-syohN-a]; respecter [rehs-pehk-tay]
pay cash *(v)* payer au comptant [peh-yay-o-kohN-tahN]; payer en liquide [peh-yay-ahN-lee-keed]

payment le paiement [luh-pehy-mahN]
peace la paix [la-peh]
pear la poire [la-pwar]; *(el)* l'ampoule *(f)* [lahN-pool]
pedestrian le piéton [luh-pyay-tohN]
people le peuple [luh-puhpl]; les gens *(m pl)* [lay-zhaN]
per par [par]
percent pour cent [poor-sahN]
perfect parfait(e) [par-feh(t)]
performance la présentation [la-pray-zhan-ta-syohN]; *(theater)* la représentation [la-ruh-pray-zhan-ta-syohN]
permission la permission [la-pehr-mee-syohN]
permission, to grant *(v)* autoriser [o-to-ree-zay]
permit *(v)* autoriser [o-to-ree-zay], permettre [pehr-mehtr]
permitted permis(e) [pehr-mee(z)]
person la personne [la-pehr-sohn]
personal personnel(le) [pehr-so-nehl]
perspire *(v)* transpirer [trahNs-pee-ray]
persuade *(v)* persuader [pehr-sew-a-day]
phone *(v)* téléphoner [tay-lay-fo-nay]
photo la photo [la-fo-to]
pick *(v)* cueillir [kuh-yeer]
pick out *(v)* sélectionner [say-lehk-syo-nay]
pick up *(v)* aller chercher [a-lay-shehr-shay]
picture *(photo)* la photo [la-fo-to]; *(painting)* le tableau [luh-ta-blo]; *(book)* l'illustration *(f)* [lee-lews-tra-syohN]
piece le morceau [luh-mohr-so]; **a piece of bread** un morceau de pain [aN-mohr-so]
pier la jetée [la-zhuh-tay]
pillow l'oreiller *(m)* [lo-reh-yay]; le coussin [luh-koo-saN]
pin l'épingle *(f)* [lay-paNgl]; **safety pin** l'épingle *(f)* de sûreté [lay-paNgl-duh-sewr-tay]
pipe *(gas, water)* la conduite [la-kohN-dweet]; la pipe [la-peep]; le tuyau [luh-twee-yo]
pity la pitié [la-pee-tyay]
pity, it is a c'est dommage [say-do-mazh]; **What a pity!** Quel dommage! [kehl-do-mazh]
place la place [la-plas]; place le lieu [luh-lyuuh]
plain la plaine [la-plehn]
plant la plante [la-plahNt]
plaster le plâtre [luh-platr]
plastic le plastique [luh-plas-teek]
plate l'assiette *(f)* [la-syeht]
play *(v)* jouer [zhoo-ay]
pleasant sympathique [saN-pa-teel]
please s'il te plaît [seel-tuh-play]; s'il vous plaît [seel-voo-play]
please *(v)* plaire [plehr]
pleased, to be *(v)* être content(e) de [eh-truh-kohN-tahN(t)-duh]
pleasure le plaisir [luh-pleh-zeer]
plugged bouché(e) [boo-shay]
plus plus [plews]
pocket la poche [la-pohsh]
point la pointe [la-pwaNt]; le point [luh-pwaN]; *(mountain)* le sommet [luh-so-may]
poison le poison [luh-pwa-zohN]
poisonous toxique [tohk-seek]
polite poli(e) [po-lee]
politeness la politesse [la-po-lee-tehs]
politics la politique [la-po-lee-teek]
poor pauvre [povr]
position la position [la-po-zee-syohN]; le poste [luh-pohst]
positive positif, -ive [po-zee-teef]/[po-zee-teev]
possession la possession [la-po-say-syohN]; *(property)* la propriété [la-pro-pree-yay-tay]
possibility la possibilité [la-po-see-bee-lee-tay]
possibly éventuellement *(adv)* [ay-vahN- tew-ehl-mahN]
possible possible [po-seebl]
possible, to make *(v)* rendre possible [rahN-druh-po-seebl]
poster l'affiche *(f)* [la-feesh]
postpone *(v)* remettre à plus tard [ruh-meh-tra-plew-tar]; repousser [ruh-poo-say]
pot la casserole [la-kas-rohl]
pottery la céramique [la-say-ra-meel]
powder la poudre [la-poodr]
power of attorney la procuration [la-pro-kew-ra-syohN]
practical pratique [pra-teek]
practice l'exercice *(m)* [lehg-zehr-sees]; la pratique [la-pra-teek]; *(doctor)* le cabinet [luh-ka-bee-nay]
practice *(v)* s'entraîner [sahN-tray-nay]; *(profession)* exercer [ehg-zehr-say]
praise *(v)* louer [loo-ay]; faire des compliments [fehr-day-kohN-plee-mahN]
pray *(v)* prier [pree-yay]
prayer la prière [la-pree-yehr]
prefer *(v)* préférer [pray-feh-ray]
preference la préférence [la-pray-feh-rahNs]; l'avantage *(m)* [la-vahN-tazh]

pregnant enceinte [ahN-saNt]

prepare *(v)* préparer [pray-pa-ray]

present présent(e) [pray-zahN(t)]

present, to give a present *(v)*, offrir [o-freer]

present, to be être là [eh-truh-la]; être présent(e) [eh-truh-pray-zhan(t)]

press *(v) (button)* pousser [poo-say]

pretext le prétexte [luh-pray-tehks]

pretty joli(e) [zho-lee]

prevent *(v)* empêcher [ahN-pay-shay]

price le prix [luh-pree]

priest le prêtre [luh-prehtr]

private privé(e) [pree-vay]

probability la probabilité [la-pro-ba-bee-lee-tay]

probably probable [pro-babl]; probablement *(adv)* [pro-ba-bluh-mahN]

procession la procession [la-pro-say-syohN]

produce *(v)* produire [pro-dweer]

product le produit [luh-pro-dwee]

profession la profession [la-pro-feh-syohN]

profit le gain [luh-gaN]; le bénéfice [luh-bay-nay-fees]

program le programme [luh-pro-gram]; *(radio, television)* l'émission *(f)* [lay-mee-syohN]

progress le progrès [luh-pro-gray]

promise la promesse [la-pro-mehs]

promise *(v)* promettre [pro-mehtr]

pronounce *(v)* prononcer [pro-nohN-say]

pronunciation la prononciation [la-pro-nohN-sya-syohN]

proof la preuve [la-pruhv]

prospectus le prospectus [luh-prohs-pehk-tews]

protect *(v)* protéger [pro-tay-zhay]

protection la protection [la-pro-tehk-syohN]

protest *(v)* protester [pro-tehs-tay]

prove *(v)* prouver [proo-vay]

provide with *(v)* fournir en [foor-neer-ahN]

provisions les provisions *(f pl)* [lay-pro-vee-zyohN]

proximity la proximité [la-prohk-see-mee-tay]

pub le café [luh-ka-fay]; *(with music)* la boîte [la-bwat]

public public, -ique [pew-bleek]

pull *(v)* tirer [tee-ray]

punishment la peine [la-pehn]; *(money)* l'amende *(f)* [la-mahNd]

purchase *(v)* acheter [ash-tay]

purchase l'achat *(m)* [la-sha]

purpose le but [luh-bewt]

purpose, on exprès [ehk-spray]

purse le sac à main [luh-sak-a-maN]

push *(v)* pousser [poo-say]

put *(v)* mettre [mehtr]

put down *(v)* poser [po-zay]

put on *(v)* mettre [mehtr]

put out *(v) (fire)* éteindre [ay-taNdr]

Q

quality la qualité [la-ka-lee-tay]

quantity la quantité [la-kahN-tee-tay]; *(people)* la foule [la-fool]

quarrel la dispute [la-dees-pewt]

quarrel *(v)* se quereller [suh-kuh-ray-lay]; se disputer [suh-dees-pew-tay]

quarter, a un quart [aN-kar]

question la question [la-kehs-tyohN]

quick rapide *(adj)* [ra-peed]; rapidement [ra-peed-mahN]; vite *(adv)* [veet]

quiet calme [kalm]

quietly doucement [doos-mahN]; **to speak quietly** parler à voix basse [par-lay-a-vwa-bas]

R

radiant brillant(e) [bree-yahN(t)]

radio la radio [la-ra-dyo]; le poste de radio [luh-pohst-duh-ra-dyo]

rage la colère [la-ko-lehr]

railings la grille [la-greey]

rain *(v)* pleuvoir [pluuh-vwar]

raise *(v) (price)* augmenter [og-mahN-tay]

rape *(v)* violer [vyo-lay]

rather assez [a-say]; plutôt [plew-to]

rather, to *(v)* préférer [pray-fay-ray]

reach *(v)* atteindre [a-taNdr]

read *(v)* lire [leer]

ready prêt(e) [preh(t)]; fini(e) [fee-nee]

real(ly) réel(le) [ray-ehl]; *(genuine)* vrai(e) [vray]; vraiment *(adv)* [vray-mahN]

reality la réalité [la-ray-a-lee-tay]

realize *(v)* réaliser [ray-a-lee-zay]

reason la raison [la-reh-zohN]

reasonable raisonnable [reh-zo-nabl]

receipt le reçu [luh-ruh-sew]; **to give a receipt** faire un reçu [fehr-aN-ruh-sew]

receive *(v)* recevoir [ruh-suh-vwar]; accueillir [a-kuh-yeer]; obtenir [ohb-tuh-neer]

reception *(broadcast)* la réception [la-ray-sehp-syohN]
recognize *(v)* reconnaître [ruh-ko-nehtr]
recommend *(v)* recommander [ruh-ko-mahN-day]
recommendation la recommandation [la-ruh-ko-mahN-da-syohN]
record le disque [luh-deesk]; **record player** le tourne-disque [luh-toor-nuh-deesk]
recover *(v)* se rétablir [suh-ray-ta-bleer]
recovery le rétablissement [luh-ray-ta-blees-mahN]
reduce *(v) (price)* baisser [beh-say]; diminuer [dee-mee-nway]
reduction la réduction [la-ray-dewk-syohN]
reeds le roseau [luh-ro-zo]
refer, refer to *(v)*, se référer à [suh-ray-fay-ray-a]
refreshment le rafraîchissement [ra-freh-shees-mahN]
refund *(v)* rembourser [rahN-boor-say]
refuse *(v)* refuser de [ruh-few-zay-duh]
regret le regret [luh-ruh-gray]
regret *(v)* regretter [ruh-gray-tay]
regular régulier, -ière *(adj)* [ray-gew-lyay]/ [ray-gew-lyehr]; régulièrement *(adv)* [ray- gew-lyehr-mahN]
reject *(v)* refuser [ruh-few-zay]
related parent(e) [pa-rahN(t)]
reliable sûr(e) [sewr]; fiable [fyabl]
reluctantly sans plaisir [sahN-pleh-zeer]
remain *(v)* rester [rehs-tay]
remainder le reste [luh-rehst]
remember *(v)* se souvenir [suh-soov-neer]
remind, remind s.o. of something *(v)*, rappeler qc à qn [rap-lay-kehl-kuh-shoz-a-kehl-kaN]
remote isolé(e) [ee-zo-lay]
renew *(v)* rénover [ray-no-vay]
rent le loyer [luh-lwa-yay]
rent *(v)* louer [loo-ay]
repair la réparation [la-ray-pa-ra-syohN]
repair *(v)* réparer [ray-pa-ray]
repeat *(v)* répéter [ray-pay-tay]
replace *(v)* remplacer [rahN-pla-say]; *(damages)* réparer [ray-pa-ray]
reply *(v)* répliquer [ray-plee-kay]; répondre à [ray-pohN-dra]
report le compte-rendu [luh-kohNt-rahN-dew]
request la demande [la-duh-mahNd]
reserve *(v)* réserver [ray-zehr-vay]
reserve a seat *(v)* réserver une place [ray-zehr-vay-ewn-plas]
residence le domicile [luh-do-mee-seel]
responsible compétent(e) [kohN-pay-tahN(t)]; responsable [rehs-pohN-sabl]
rest le repos [luh-ruh-po]
rest *(v)* se reposer [suh-ruh-po-zay]
restaurant le restaurant [luh-rehs-to-rahN]; la brasserie [la-bras-ree]
restless inquiet, -iète [aN-kyay]/[aN-kyeht]
result le résultat [luh-ray-zewl-ta]
retirement la retraite [la-ruh-treht]
return *(v)* rendre [rahNdr]; revenir [ruhv-neer]; retourner [ruh-toor-nay]
return journey le retour [luh-ruh-toor]
reverse en arrière [ahN-na-ryehr]; **in reverse** dans la direction opposée [dahN-la-dee-rehk-syohN-o-po-zay]
reward la récompense [la-ray-kohN-pahNs]
reward *(v)* récompenser [ray-kohN-pahN-say]
ribbon le ruban [luh-rew-bahN]
rich riche [reesh]
ridiculous ridicule [ree-dee-kewl]
right le droit [luh-drwa]; **to be right** avoir raison [a-vwar-reh-zohN]; juste [zhewst]; approprié(e) *(adj)* [a-pro-pree-yay]; *(direction)* **right**; **to the right** à droite [a-drwat]
right of way la priorité [la-pree-o-ree-tay]
ring la bague [la-bag]; **wedding ring** l'alliance *(f)* [la-lyahNs]
ring *(v)* sonner [so-nay]
ripe mûr(e) [mewr]
risk le risque [luh-reesk]
river la rivière [la-ree-vyehr]; le fleuve [luh-fluhv]
roast le rôti [luh-ro-tee]
roast *(v)* rôtir [ro-teer]
room l'espace *(f)* [lehs-pas]; la pièce [la-pyehs]; la salle [la-sal]
rooster le coq [luh-kohk]
rope la corde [la-kohrd]
rough *(sea)* agitée [a-zhee-tay]
round rond(e) [rohN(d)]
route l'itinéraire *(m)* [lee-tee-nay-rehr]
rude impoli(e) [aN-po-lee]
rule la prescription [la-prehs-kreep-syohN]; l'instruction *(f)* [laNs-trewk-syohN]
run *(v)* courir [koo-reer]; *(bus, train, etc.)* circuler [seer-kew-lay]
run into *(v)* déboucher [day-boo-shay]

S

sad triste [treest]
safe sûr(e) *(adj)* [sewr]; sûrement *(adv)* [sewr-mahN]
sale (clearance) les soldes *(m pl)* [lay-sohld]; la vente [la-vahNt]
same pareil(le) [pa-rehy]
same, the le/la même [luh/la-mehm]; la même chose [la-mehm-shoz]
satisfied content(e) [kohN-tahN(t)]; satisfait(e) [sa-tees-feh(t)]
save *(v)* sauver [so-vay]
save économiser [ay-ko-no-mee-zay]
say *(v)* dire [deer]
say goodbye *(v)* prendre congé [prahN-druh-kohN-zhay]
scales la balance [la-ba-lahNs]
school l'école *(f)* [lay-kohl]
scissors les ciseaux *(m pl)* [lay-see-zo]
scorpion le scorpion [luh-skohr-pyohN]
scream *(v)* crier [kree-yay]
sea la mer [la-mehr]
sea urchin l'oursin *(m)* [loor-saN]
seagull la mouette [la-mweht]; *(large seagull)* le goêland [luh-go-ay-lahN]
seaside resort la station balnéaire [la-sta-syohN-bal-nay-ehr]
season la saison [la-seh-zohN]; **off season** hors saison [ohr-seh-zohN]
seat le siège [luh-syehzh]
second deuxième [duuh-zyehm]; second(e) [suh-gohN(d)]; **secondly** deuxièmement [duuh-zyehm-mahN]
second, the la seconde [la-suh-gohNd]
secret secret *(adj)* [suh-kray]; secrète [suh-kreht]; en secret *(adv)* [ahN-suh-kray]
security la sécurité [la-say-kew-ree-tay]; *(guarantee)* la garantie [la-ga-rahN-tee]
see *(v)* voir [vwar]
see again *(v)* revoir [ruh-vwar]
seem *(v)* sembler [sahN-blay]; paraître [pa-rehtr]
seize *(v)* saisir [seh-zeer]
seldom rare *(adj)* [rar]; rarement *(adv)* [rar-mahN]
self-service le self-service [luh-sehlf-sehr-vees]
sell *(v)* vendre [vahNdr]
send *(v)* envoyer [ahN-vwa-yay]
send for *(v)* faire prendre [fehr-prahNdr]
send off *(v)* renvoyer [rahN-vwa-yay]
sense le sens [luh-sahNs]
sentence la phrase [la-fraz]
separate séparé(e) [say-pa-ray]
separate *(v)* séparer [say-pa-ray]
serious *(sickness)* grave [grav]; difficile [dee-fee-seel]; sérieux, -euse [say-ryuuh(z)]
sermon le sermon [luh-sehr-mohN]
serve *(v)* servir [sehr-veer]
service le service [luh-sehr-vees]
set *(radio)* le poste [luh-pohst]
settle *(v)* régler [ray-glay]
sex le sexe [luh-sehks]
shadow l'ombre *(f)* [lohNbr]
shape la forme [la-fohrm]
sharp fort(e) [fohrt]; pointu(e) [pwaN-tew]
shave *(v)* raser [ra-zay]
she elle [ehl]
sheep le mouton [luh-moo-tohN]
shine *(v)* briller [bree-yay]
shining lumineux, -euse [lew-mee-nuuh(z)]
shoe la chaussure [la-sho-sewr]
shoelace le lacet [luh-la-say]
shoot *(v)* tirer [tee-ray]
shop le magasin [luh-ma-ga-zaN]; la boutique [la-boo-teek]
shopping, to go *(v)* faire ses courses [fehr-say-koors]
short court(e) [koor(t)]; bref, brève [brehf]/[brehv]
shortcut le raccourci [luh-ra-koor-see]
shot le coup (de feu) [luh-koo-duh-fuuh]
shove le coup [luh-koo]
shove *(v)* pousser [poo-say]
show le spectacle [spehk-ta-kuhl]
show *(v)* montrer [mohN-tray]; indiquer [aN-dee-kay]; présenter [pray-zahN-tay]
shut *(v)* fermer [fehr-may]
shy timide [tee-meed]
side le côté [luh-ko-tay]
sight la vue [la-vew]
sign l'écriteau *(m)* [lay-kree-tewr]; le panneau [luh-pa-no]; le signe [luh-seeny]; l'indice *(m)* [laN-dees]; la preuve [la-pruhv]
sign *(v)* signer [see-nyay]
signal le signal [luh-see-nyal]
signal *(car)* clignoter [klee-nyo-tay]
signature la signature [la-see-nya-tewr]
silence le silence [luh-see-lahNs]
silent, to be *(v)* se taire [suh-tehr]
silly stupide [stew-peed]
similar semblable [sahN-blabl]
simple simple [saNpl]
simultaneous(ly) en même temps [ahN-mehm-tahN]
since depuis [duh-pwee]; depuis que [duh-pwee-kuh]; **since when?** depuis quand? [du-pwee-kahN]

sincere cordial(e) [kohr-dyal]
sing *(v)* chanter [shahN-tay]
singing le chant [luh-shahN]
single célibataire [say-lee-ba-tehr]
sip la gorgée [la-gor-zhay]
sister la sœur [la-suhr]
sit *(v)* être assis(e) [eh-tra-see(z)]; **sit down** *(v)* s'asseoir [sa-swar]
situation la situation [la-see-tew-a-syohN]
size l'étendue *(f)* [lay-tahN-dew]; la grandeur [la-grahN-duhr]; *(clothing)* la taille [la-ta-yuh]; *(shoe)* la pointure [la-pwaN-tewr]
skillful adroit(e) [a-drwa(t)]
sky le ciel [luh-syehl]
skyscraper le gratte-ciel [luh-grat-syehl]
sleep le sommeil [luh-so-mehy]
sleep *(v)* dormir [dohr-meer]
slender mince [maNs]
slide la diapo [la-dya-po]
slope la pente [la-pahNt]
slow(ly) lent(e) *(adj)* [lahN(t)]; lentement *(adv)* [lahNt-mahN]
small petit(e) [puh-tee(t)]; minime [mee-neem]; **smaller** moindre [mwaNdr]
smell *(v)* puer [pew-ay]; sentir [sahN-teer]
smell l'odeur *(f)* [lo-duhr]
smoke la fumée [la-few-may]
smoke *(v)* fumer [few-may]
smoker le fumeur [luh-few-muhr]
smuggle *(v)* faire de la contrebande [fehr-duh-la-kohN-truh-bahNd]
snack le casse-croûte [luh-cas-kroot]
snack bar le fast-food [luh-fast-food]; le snack [luh-snak]
snake le serpent [luh-sehr-pahN]
sneeze *(v)* éternuer [ay-tehr-new-ay]
snore *(v)* ronfler [rohN-flay]
snow *(v)* neiger [neh-zhay]
so comme ça [kohm-sa]; donc [dohNk]
soaked trempé(e) [trahN-pay]
sober à jeun [a-zhaN]
society la société [la-so-syay-tay]; la compagnie [la-kohN-pa-nee]
soft mou, molle [moo]/[mohl]; *(tone, color)* doux, douce [doo(s)]
solemn solennel(le) [so-la-nehl]
solid dur(e) [dewr]; solide [so-leed]
solve *(v)* résoudre [ray-zoodr]
some quelques [kehlk]
somebody quelqu'un [kehl-kaN]
somehow d'une façon ou d'une autre [dewn-fa-sohN-oo-dewn-otr]
something quelque chose [kehl-kuh-shoz]; *(a little)* un peu de [aN-puuh-duh]
somewhere quelque part [kehl-kuh-par]
son le fils [luh-fees]
song la chanson [la-shahN-sohN]
soon bientôt [byaN-to]; prochainement [pro-shehn-mahN]; **as soon as possible** dès que possible [day-kuh-po-seebl]
sound le son [luh-sohN]
sour acide [a-seed]; aigre [ehgr]
source la source [la-soors]
south le sud [luh-sewd]
southern au sud de [o-sewd-duh]
souvenir le souvenir [luh-soov-neer]
Spain l'Espagne *(f)* [lehs-pany]
Spaniard l'Espagnol(e) [lehs-pa-nyohl]
Spanish espagnol(e) [ehs-pa-nyohl]
spark l'étincelle *(f)* [lay-taN-sehl]
speak *(v)* parler [par-lay]
special spécial(e) [spay-syal]; à part [a-par]
spectator le spectateur [luh-spehk-ta-tuhr]
speed la vitesse [la-vee-tehs]
spell *(v)* épeler [ay-puh-lay]
spend *(v)* dépenser [day-pahN-say]; *(time)* passer [pa-say]
spend the night *(v)* coucher [koo-shay]; passer la nuit [pa-say-la-nwee]
spite, in spite of malgré [mal-gray]
splendid magnifique [ma-nee-feek]
spoil *(v)* abîmer [a-bee-may]
spoiled abîmé(e) [a-bee-may]; pourri(e) [poo-ree]; corrompu(e) [ko-rohN-pew]
sport le sport [luh-spohr]; **sport field** le terrain de sport [luh-tay-rahN-duh-spohr]; le stade [luh-stad]
spot l'endroit *(m)* [lahN-drwa]
square carré(e) [ka-ray]
staff le personnel [luh-pehr-so-nehl]
stain la tache [la-tash]
stairs l'escalier *(m)* [lehs-ka-lyay]
stamp le tampon [luh-tahN-pohN]; *(letter)* le timbre [luh-taNbr]; *(trade)* la marque [la-mark]
stand *(v)* être debout [eh-truh-duh-boo]
stand in line *(v)* faire la queue [fehr-la-kuuh]
star l'étoile *(f)* [lay-twal]
start (from) *(v)* partir (de) [par-teer-duh]
start *(v)* (car) démarrer [day-ma-ray]
state l'etat *(m)* [lay-ta]
statement la déclaration [la-day-kla-ra-syohN]; **to make a statement** faire une déclaration [fehr-ewn-day-kla-ra-syohN]
stay le séjour [luh-say-zhoor]
stay *(v)* rester [rehs-tay]; séjourner [say-zhoor-nay]
steal *(v)* voler [vo-lay]

steep raide [rehd]
stength la force [la-fohrs]
step le pas [luh-pa]
stick le bâton [luh-ba-tohN]
still encore [ahN-kohr]
sting *(v)* piquer [pee-kay]
stone la pierre [la-pyehr]
stony pierreux, -euse [pyay-ruuh(z)]; cailloteux, -euse [ka-yoo-tuuh(z)]
stop *(v)* interrompre [aN-teh-rohNpr]; arrêter [a-ray-tay]; s'arrêter [sa-ray-tay]
stop *(train)* l'arrêt *(m)* [la-ray]
Stop! Stop! [stohp]
stop doing sth *(v)* arrêter [a-ray-tay]
store le magasin [luh-ma-ga-zaN]; **store, department** le grand magasin [luh-grahN-ma-ga-zaN]
storm la tempête [la-tahN-peht]
story l'histoire *(f)* [lees-twar]
stout gros [gro], grosse [gros]; *(swollen)* enflé(e) [ahN-flay]
stove le poêle [luh-pwal]
straight droit(e) [drwa(t)]; **straight ahead** tout droit [too-drwa]
strap la courroie [la-koo-rwa]
street la rue [la-rew]
strength la force [la-fohrs]
strenuous fatigant(e) [fa-tee-gahN]
strict sévère [say-vehr]
strike *(v)* frapper [fra-pay]; *(hour)* sonner [so-nay]
string la ficelle [la-fee-sehl]
stroll la balade [la-ba-lad]; la virée [la-vee-ray]
strong fort(e) [fohr(t)]; corpulent(e) [kohr-pew-lahN(t)]; gros [gro]; grosse [gros], vigoureux, -euse [vee-goo-ruuh(z)]
study *(v)* faire des études [fehr-day-zay-tewd]
stupid bête [beht]
suburb la banlieue [la-bahN-lyuuh]
success le succès [luh-sewk-say]
such tel(le) [tehl]
suddenly soudain [soo-daN]; tout à coup [too-ta-koo]
sufficient, to be *(v)* suffire [sew-feer]
suggest *(v)* proposer [pro-po-zay]
suggestion la proposition [la-pro-po-zee-syohN]
suit *(v)* aller [a-lay]; convenir [kohN-vuh-neer]
suitable opportun(e) [o-pohr-taN]/[o-pohr-tewn]; *(useful)* utile [ew-teel]
suitcase la valise [la-va-leez]
summit le sommet [luh-so-may]
sun le soleil [luh-so-lehy]; **sun glasses** les lunettes *(f pl)* de soleil [lay-lew-neht-duh-so-lehy]; **at sun rise** au lever du soleil [o-luh-vay-dew-so-lehy]; **at sun set** au coucher du soleil [o-koo-shay-dew-so-lehy]
sunny ensoleillé(e) [ahN-so-leh-yay]
superfluous superflu(e) [sew-pehr-flew]
support le soutien [luh-soo-tyaN]
supporter le partisan [luh-par-tee-zahN]; l'adepte *(m/f)* [la-dehpt]
suppose *(v)* supposer [sew-po-zay]
surprised surpris(e) [sewr-preez]
surprised, to be about *(v)* s'étonner (de) [say-to-nay-duh]
suspicion le soupçon [luh-soop-sohN]
swamp le marais [luh-ma-ray]; le marécage [luh-ma-ray-kazh]
swap *(v)* échanger [ay-shahN-zhay]
sweet sucré(e) [sew-kray]
swim *(v)* nager [na-zhay]
swimming pool la piscine [la-pee-seen]
swindle l'escroquerie *(f)* [lehs-krohk-ree]; la fraude [la-frod]
swindler l'escroc *(m)* [lehs-kro]
Swiss person le Suisse [luh-swees]; la Suissesse [la-swees-sehs]
sister-in-law la belle-sœur [la-behl-suhr]
switch *(electricity)* l'interrupteur *(m)* [laN-tay-rewp-tuhr]
switch on *(v)* *(light)* allumer [a-lew-may]; brancher [brahN-shay]
Switzerland la Suisse [la-swees]

T

table la table [la-tabl]
take *(v)* prendre [prahNdr]; *(things)* emporter [ahN-pohr-tay]; *(people)* emmener [ahN-muh-nay]
take a picture *(v)* photographier [fo-to-gra-fyay]; **take a snapshot** prendre une photo [prahN-drewn-fo-to]
take away *(v)* emporter [ahN-pohr-tay]; enlever [ahN-luh-vay]
take off *(v)* quitter [kee-tay]; diminuer [dee-mee-nway]; *(plane)* décoller [day-ko-lay]
take over *(v)* se charger de [suh-shar-zhay-duh]
talk *(v)* parler [par-lay]
taste le goût [luh-goo]
taste *(v)* goûter [goo-tay]
taste good *(v)* être bon [eh-truh-bohN]

taxi le taxi [luh-tak-see]
teach *(v)* enseigner [ahN-seh-nyay]
team *(sport)* l'équipe *(f)* [lay-keep]; *(boat)* l'équipage *(m)* [lay-kee-pazh]
tear *(v)* déchirer [day-shee-ray]; se casser [suh-ka-say]; se déchirer [suh-day-shee-ray]
tell *(v)* raconter [ra-kohN-tay]
tell fibs *(v)* mentir [mahN-teer]; *(bluff)* bluffer [bluuh-fay]
temporary provisoire *(adj)* [pro-vee-zwar]; à titre provisoire *(adv)* [a-teetr-pro-vee-zwar]
temporarily provisoirement *(adv)* [pro-vee-zwar-mahN]
tender tendre [tahNdr]; délicat(e) [day-lee-la(t)]
term, short à court terme [a-koor-tehrm]
terrible affreux, -euse [a-fruuh(z)]
than *(comparison)* que [kuh]; **better than** mieux que [myuuh-kuh]
thank s.o. *(v)* remercier (qn) [ruh-mehr-syay-kehl-kaN]
thankful reconnaissant(e) [ruh-ko-neh-sahN(t)]
that que [kuh]
that/those celui-là [suh-lwee-la]; celle-là [sehl-la]; ceux-là [suuh-la]; celles-là [sehl-la]
then à l'époque [a-lay-pohk]; en ce temps-là [ahN-suh-tahN-la]; ensuite [ahN-sweet]
there là [la]; là-bas [la-ba]; **up/down there** là-haut [a-o]/là-bas [la-ba]
therefore c'est pourquoi [say-poor-kwa]
there is il y a [eel-ya]
thin mince [maNs]
thing la chose [la-shoz]
think *(v)* penser [pahN-say]; **think of** *(v)* penser à [pahN-say-a]
third le/la troisième [luh/la-trwa-zyehm]
third, one un tiers [aN-tyehr]
thirst la soif [la-swaf]
thirsty, to be *(v)* avoir soif [a-vwar-swaf]
this (these) ce, cet, cette, ces [suh/seht/seht/say]
thought l'idée *(f)* [lee-day]
thread le fil [luh-feel]
through à travers [a-tra-vehr]
throw *(v)* jeter [zhuh-tay]
thunderstorm l'orage *(f)* [lo-razh]
time la fois [la-fwa]; le temps [luh-tahN]; **one time** une fois [ewn-fwa]; **every time** chaque fois [shak-fwa]; **two times** deux fois [duuh-fwa]; **from time to time** de temps en temps [duh-tahN-zahN-tahN]
time, in à temps [a-tahN], à l'heure *(adj)* [a-luhr]
time, to have a good *(v)* s' amuser [sa-mew-zay]
tip le tuyau [luh-twee-yo], le conseil [luh-kohN-sehy]
tired fatigué(e) [fa-tee-gay]
to à [a]
tobacco le tabac [luh-ta-ba]
today aujourd'hui [o-zhoor-dwee]
together ensemble [ahN-sahNbl]
toilet les W.-C. [lay-vay-say] *(m pl)*; **toilet paper** le papier hygiénique [luh-pa-pyay-ee-zhyay-neek]
tolerate *(v)* supporter [sew-pohr-tay]
tone le ton [luh-tohN]; *(sound)* l'intonation *(f)* [laN-to-na-syohN]; *(color)* la teinte [la-taNt]
tongs la pince [la-paNs]
tonight cette nuit [seht-nwee]
touch *(v)* toucher [too-shay]
touched ému(e) [ay-mew]
tourist le/la touriste [luh/la-too-reest]
tourist office l'office *(m)* de tourisme [lo-fees-duh-too-reesm]; le syndicat d'initiative [luh-saN-kee-ka-dee-nee-sya-teev]
toy le jouet [luh-zhway]
trace la trace [la-tras]
traffic la circulation [la-seer-kew-la-syohN]
training la formation [la-fohr-ma-syohN]]
transfer *(v)* *(money)* virer [vee-ray]
transferable transmissible [trahNs-mee-seebl]
transit visa le visa de transit [luh-vee-za-duh-trahN-zeet]
translate *(v)* traduire [tra-dweer]
transport *(v)* transporter [trahNs-pohr-tay]
trash can la poubelle [la-poo-behl]
travel le voyage [luh-vwa-yazh]; **travel agency** l'agence *(f)* de voyages [la-zhahNs-duh-vwa-yazh]; **travel guide** le guide [luh-geed]; **group travel** le voyage organisé [luh-vwa-yazh-ohr-ga-nee-zay]; **travel** *(v)* voyager [vwa-ya-zhay]; **travel to** partir pour [par-teer-poor]
traveler le voyageur [luh-vwa-ya-zhuhr]; la voyageuse [la-vwa-ya-zhuuhz]
treat *(v)* soigner [swa-nyay]
treatment le traitement [luh-treht-mahN]
tree l'arbre [larbr]; **trimmings** l'accompagnement [la-kohN-pa-nyuuh-mahN]
trouble la peine [la-pehn]
true vrai(e) [vray]

trust *(v)* avoir confiance en [a-vwar-kohN-fyahNs-ahN]
truth la vérité [la-vay-ree-tay]
try *(v)* essayer [ay-say-yay]; *(dishes)* goûter [goo-tay]
try hard *(v)* s'efforcer de [say-fohr-say-duh]
try on *(v)* essayer [ay-say-yay]
tube le tube [luh-tewb]; le tuyau [luh-twee-yo]
tunnel le tunnel [luh-tew-nehl]
turn *(v)* tourner [toor-nay]; **turn to s.o.** s'adresser à [sa-dray-say-a]; **turn back** *(v)* faire demi-tour [fehr-duh-mee-toor]
turn on *(v)* *(light)* allumer [a-lew-may]; **turn off** *(v)* *(light, radio)* éteindre [ay-taNdr]
turn to the right/left *(v)* tourner à droite/à gauche [toor-nay-a-drwat/gosh]
typical (of) typique (de) [tee-peek-duh]; caractéristique (de) [ka-rak-tay-rees-teek-duh]

U

ugly laid(e) [leh(d)]
umbrella parapluie [pa-ra-plwee]
unload *(v)* décharger [day-shar-zhay]
uncertain incertain(e) [aN-sehr-taN]/[aN-sehr-tehn]
uncle l'oncle [lohNkl]
uncomfortable inconfortable [aN-kohN-fohr-tabl]; mal à l'aise [mal-a-lehz]
unconscious évanoui(e) [ay-va-noo-ee]; sans connaissance [sahN-ko-neh-sahNs]
undecided indécis(e) [aN-day-see]
under sous [soo]
underneath au-dessous (de) [o-duh-soo-duh]
underpass le passage souterrain [luh-pa-sazh-soo-teh-raN]
understand *(v)* comprendre [kohN-prahNdr]
undress *(v)* se déshabiller [suh-day-za-bee-yay]
unemployed au chômage [o-sho-mazh]
unexpected inattendu(e) [ee-na-tahN-dew]
unfair injuste [aN-zhewst]
unfavorable défavorable [day-fa-vo-rabl]
unfortunately malheureusement [ma-luuh-ruuhz-mahN]; par malheur [par-ma-luhr]
ungrateful ingrat(e) [aN-gra(t)]
unhappy malheureux, -euse [ma-luuh-ruuh(z)]
unhealthy malsain(e) [mal-saN]/[mal/sehn]
unimportant insignifiant(e) [aN-see-nee-fyahN(t)]; sans importance [sahN-zaN-pohr-tahNs]
unkind peu aimable [puuh-eh-mabl]
unknown inconnu(e) [aN-ko-new]
unlikely invraisemblable [aN-vreh-sahN-blabl]
unnecessary superflu(e) [sew-pehr-flew]
unpack *(v)* défaire ses valises [day-fehr-say-va-leez]
unpleasant désagréable [day-za-gray-abl]; fâcheux, -euse [fa-shuuh(z)]
unsafe pas sûr(e) [pa-sewr]; incertain [aN-sehr-taN]
unsuited impropre [aN-prohpr]
until jusqu'à [zhews-ka]; **until now** jusqu'à maintenant [zhews-ka-maNt-nahN]
unusual inhabituel(le) [ee-na-bee-tew-ehl]
unwelcome indésirable [aN-day-zee-rabl]
up en haut [ahN-o]; vers le haut [luh-o]; *(upstream)* en amont [ahN-na-mohN]; **up there** là-haut [la-o]; **upstairs** en haut [ahN-o]
uphill en montant [ahN-mohN-tahN]
urgent pressé(e) [pray-say]; **to be urgent** *(v)* être pressé(e) [eh-truh-pray-say]; urgent [ewr-zhaN]
us nous [noo]; to us à nous [a-noo]
use *(v)* employer [ahN-plwa-yay]; utiliser [ew-tee-lee-zay]; *(medication)* prendre [prahNdr]
use l'emploi *(m)* [lahN-plwa]; l'application *(f)* [la-plee-ka-syohN]; l'usage *(m)* [lew-zazh]
used, to be used to *(v)* être habitué(e) [eh-tra-bee-tway]
used, to get used to s'habituer à [sa-bee-tway-a]
useful utile [ew-teel]
useless inutile [ee-new-teel]
usual(ly) habituel(le) [a-bee-twehl]; *(ordinary)* commun(e) [ko-maN]/[ko-mewn]; habituellement [a-bee-twehl-mahN]

V

vacation le congé [luh-kohN-zhay]; **summer vacation** les vacances *(f pl)* [lay-va-kahNs]; les vacances *(f pl)* [lay-va-kahNs]; **on vacation** en vacances [ahN-va-kahNs]
vain, in inutilement [ee-new-teel-mahN]

valid valable [va-labl]
valid, to be *(v)* être valable [eh-truh-va-labl]
validity la validité [la-va-lee-dee-tay]
valuables les objets *(m pl)* de valeur [lay-zohb-zhay-duh-a-luhr]
variable *(people)* instable [aN-stabl]; inconsistant(e) [aN-kohN-sees-tahN(t)]; *(weather)* variable [va-ryabl]
vending machine *(goods)* le distributeur automatique [luh-dees-tree-bew-tuhr]
very très [tray]
view la vue [la-vew]; *(opinion)* l'avis *(m)* [la-vee]
villa la villa [la-vee-la]
village le village [luh-vee-lazh]
vineyard la vigne [la-veeny]
visible visible [vee-zeebl]
visit la visite [la-vee-zeet]
visit *(v)* visiter [vee-zee-tay]; **visit s.o.** *(v)* rendre visite à qn [rahN-druh-vee-zeet-a-kehl-kaN]
voice la voix [la-vwa]
voltage le volt [luh-vohlt]
volume le tome [luh-tohm]
voucher le bon [luh-bohN]

W

wages la paie [la-pay]; le salaire [luh-sa-lehr]
wait *(v)*, **wait for** *(v)* attendre [a-tahNdr]
wake *(v)* réveiller [ray-veh-yay]
wake up *(v)* se réveiller [suh-ray-veh-yay]; **wake s.o. up** réveiller [ray-veh-yay]
walk la promenade [la-pro-muh-nad]; **to take a walk** faire une promenade [fehr-ewn-pro-muh-nad]
wall le mur [luh-mewr]
wallet le portefeuille [luh-pohr-tuh-fuhy]
want *(v)* vouloir [voo-lwar]; *(wish)* désirer [day-zee-ray]
war la guerre [la-gehr]
warm chaud(e) [sho(d)]
warmth la chaleur [la-sha-luhr]; la cordialité [la-koh-dya-lee-tay]
warn about *(v)* mettre en garde (contre) [meh-trahN-gard]
wash *(v)* laver [la-vay]
wasp la guêpe [la-gehp]
watch la montre(-bracelet) [la-mohNtr-bras-lay]
watch *(v)* regarder [ruh-gar-day]
water l'eau *(f)* [lo]
watt le watt [luh-wat]

wave *(v)* faire signe [fehr-seeny]
way le chemin [luh-shuh-maN]; le sentier [luh-sahN-tyay]
way, by the au fait [o-feht]
way, on the en cours de route [ahN-koor-duh-root]
we nous [noo]
weak faible [fehbl]
weakness la faiblesse [la-feh-blehs]
wealth la richesse [la-ree-shehs]
wealthy aisé(e) [eh-zay]
weather le temps [luh-tahN]
wedding *(feast)* le mariage [luh-ma-ryazh]; la noce [la-nohs]
week la semaine [la-suh-mehn]; **in a week** dans une semaine [dahN-zewn-suh-mehn]
weekdays les jours ouvrables [lay-zhoor-oo-vrabl]; **on weekdays** pendant la semaine [pahN-dahN-la-suh-mehn]
weekly hebdomadaire *(adj)* [ehb-do-ma-dehr]; par semaine *(adv)* [par-suh-mehn]
weigh *(v)* peser [puh-zay]
weight le poids [luh-pwa]
welcome bienvenu(e) [byaN-vuh-new]
well sans doute *(adv)* [sahN-doot]
well-being le bien-être [luh-byaN-nehtr]; la bonne santé [la-bohn-sahN-tay]
West l'Ouest *(m)* [lwehst]
western à l'ouest de [a-lwehst-duh]
wet mouillé(e) [moo-yay]
what que [kuh]; qu'est-ce que [kehs-kuh]; **what kind of ... ?** quel(le) [kehl]
when quand [kahN]
whether si [see]
while, for a pendant un certain temps [pahN-dahN-aN-sehr-taN-tahN]
whistle le sifflet [luh-see-flay]
whole tout [too]; toute [toot]; tous *(pl)* [too]; toutes *(adv)* [toot]; complètement [kohN-pleht-mahN]; entier, -ère [ahN-tyay]/ [ahN-tyehr] complet, -ète [kohN-play]/[kohN-pleht]; le tout *(n))* [luh-too]
wide large [larzh]
wild sauvage [so-vazh]; féroce [fay-rohs]
window, store la vitrine [la-vee-treen]; **windowpane** la vitre [la-veetr]
wire *(el, tele)* la ligne [la-leeny]
wire le fil de fer [luh-feel-duh-fehr]
wish le désir [luh-day-zeer]
wish *(v)* désirer [day-zee-ray]
with avec [a-vehk]
withdraw *(v)* se retirer [suh-ruh-tee-ray]
within *(time)* en [ahN]

without sans [sahN]
witness le témoin [luh-tay-mwaN]
woman la femme [la-fam]
wonderful merveilleux, -euse [mehr-veh-yuuh(z)]
wood le bois [luh-bwa]
word le mot [luh-mo]
work le travail [luh-tra-vay]; *(occupation)* l'emploi *(m)* [lahN-plwa]
work *(v)* travailler [tra-va-yay]; *(appliance)* fonctionner [fohNk-syo-nay]
world le monde [luh-mohNd]
worm le ver [luh-vehr]
worry le souci [luh-soo-see]
worry *(v)* s'inquiéter [saN-kyay-tay]
worth la valeur [la-va-luhr]; **to be worth a lot** avoir beaucoup de valeur [a-vwar-bo-koo-duh-va-luhr]; **worthless** sans valeur [sahN-va-luhr]
wrap up *(v)* envelopper [ahN-vlo-pay]
wrapping l'emballage *(m)* [lahN-ba-lazh]
write *(v)* écrire [ay-kreer]
write (down) *(v)* noter [no-tay]
writing, in par écrit [par-ay-kree]
wrong faux, fausse [fo(s)]; **person who is wrong** trompeur, -euse [trohN-puuh(z)]
wrong, to be *(v)* avoir tort [a-vwar-tohr]

Y

yawn *(v)* bâiller [ba-yay]
year l'année *(f)* [la-nay]; l'an *(m)* [lahN]
you toi [twa]; te [tuh]; tu [tew]; vous [voo]; à vous [a-voo]
you, to te [tuh]; à toi [a-twa]
young jeune [zhuhn]
your ton [tohN]; ta [ta]; votre [vohtr]
youth la jeunesse [la-zhuh-nehs]

A/Z

French-English Dictionary

A

à *(time)* [a] at; *(direction)*to; **à la poste** [a-la-pohst] to the post office; **à table** [a-tabl] to the table
abeille *(f)* [a-behy] bee
abîmé(e) [a-bee-may] damaged, spoiled
abîmer [a-bee-may] to damage, to ruin
abondamment [a-bohN-da-mahN] copiously
d'abord [da-bohr] first
abréviation *(f)* [a-bray-vya-syohN] abbreviation
absent(e) [ab-sahN] absent
absolument [ab-so-lew-mahN] absolutely; **absolument pas** [ab-so-lew-mahN] absolutely not
abus *(m)* [a-bew] abuse, excess
abuser de [a-bew-zay-duh] to overuse, to abuse
accélérer [ak-say-lay-ray] to accelerate
acceptation *(f)* [ak-sehp-ta-syohN] acceptance, agreement
accepter [ak-sehp-tay] to accept, to agree
accès *(m)* [ak-say] access
accident *(m)* [ak-see-dahN] accident; **avoir un accident** [a-vwar-aN-ak-see-dahN] to have an accident
s'acclimater [sa-klee-ma-tay] to adapt, to get used to
accompagnement *(m)* [a-kohN-pa-nyuh-mahN] accompaniment
accompagner [a-kohN-pa-nyay] to accompany, to go with
accomplir [a-kohN-pleer] *(work)* to accomplish, to carry out
d'accord [da-kohr] agreed!, O.K.; **être d'accord** [eh-truh-da-kohr] to agree; **se mettre d'accord** [suh-meh-truh-da-kohr] to reach an agreement
accorder [a-kohr-day] to grant
accrocher [a-kro-shay] to hang
accueillir [a-kuuh-yeer] to welcome
accus [a-kew] *(car)* battery
achat *(m)* [a-sha] buy, purchase
acheter [ash-tay] to purchase, to buy
acheteur *(m)* [ash-tuhr] buyer
achever [ash-tay] to complete
acide [a-seed] acid
acte *(m)* [akt] act
action *(f)* [ak-syohN] action
activité *(f)* [ak-tee-vee-tay] activity
actuellement [ak-tew-ehl-mahN] at the moment
addition *(f)* [a-dee-syohN] *(in a restaurant, café)* bill, check
adepte *(m f)* [a-dehpt] follower
administration *(f)* [ad-(m)ee-nees-tra-syohN] administration
admirer [ad-mee-ray] to admire
adresse *(f)* [a-drehs] address
adresser [a-dray-say] to address; **s'adresser** [sa-dray-say] **à** to address
adroit(e) [a-drwa(t)] deft
adulte *(m f)* [a-dewlt] adult
aérer [a-ay-ray] to air
affaire *(f)* [a-fehr] matter, thing; *(econ)* business
affectueux, -euse [a-fehk-tew-uuh(z)] affectionate
affiche *(f)* [a-feesh] poster
affirmer [a-feer-may] to affirm, to assert
affreux, -euse [a-fruuh(z)] awful, terrible
âge *(m)* [azh] age
agence *(f)* [a-zhahNs] agency; *(service)* office; **agence de voyages** *(f)* [a-zhahNs- duh-vwa-yazh] travel agency
agitée [a-zhee-tay] *(sea)* rough, stormy
agréable [a-gray-abl] pleasant
agresser [a-gray-say] to attack
aide *(f)* [ehd] help
aider qn [eh-day-kehl-kaN] to help someone
aigre [ehgr] sour
aiguille *(f)* [eh-gweey] needle
ailleurs [a-yuhr] elsewhere
aimable [eh-mabl] nice, friendly
peu aimable [puuh-eh-mabl] unfriendly
aimer [eh-may] to like, to enjoy; **aimer** qn [eh-may-kehl-kaN] to love s.o.
air *(m)* [ehr] air; **en plein air** [ahN-pleh-nehr] in the fresh air; **avoir l'air** [a-vwar-lehr] to look
aisé(e) [eh-zay] well off
ajournement *(m)* [a-zhoor-nuh-mahN] postponement
ajouter [a-zhoo-tay] to add
alcool *(m)* [al-kohl] alcohol; **alcool à brûler** *(m)* [al-kohl-a-brew-lay] methylated spirits

algues *(f pl)* [alg] seaweed
aliments *(m pl)* [a-lee-(m)ahN] food
aller [a-lay] to go, to fit; **aller chercher** [a-lay-shehr-shay] to fetch; **aller se coucher** [a-lay-suh-koo-shay] to go to bed, **aller tout droit** [a-lay-too-drwa] to go straight; **s'en aller** [sahN-na-lay] to go, to die
alliance *(f)* [a-lyahNs] alliance, wedding band
allonger [a-lohN-zhay] to lengthen
allumer [a-lew-may] to light; *(light)* to turn on
allumette *(f)* [a-lew-meht] match
alors [a-lohr] *(time)* then
altitude *(f)* [al-tee-tewd] altitude
amabilité *(f)* [a- (m)a-bee-lee-tay] kindness, friendliness
ambassade *(f)* [ahN-ba-sad] embassy
ambulance *(f)* [ahN-bew-lahNs] ambulance
améliorer [a-may-lyo-ray] to improve
amende *(f)* [a-mahNd] fine
amer, -ère [a-mehr] bitter
ameublement *(m)* [a-muh-bluh-mahN] furniture
ami(e) [a-mee] friend; **petit ami** *(m)* [puh-tee-ta-mee] boyfriend, **petite amie** *(f)* [puh-tee-ta-mee] girlfriend; **être amis** [eh-tra-mee] to be friends
amitié *(f)* [a-mee-tyay] friendship
amont, en [ahn-na-mohN] upstream
amour *(m)* [a-moor] love
ampoule *(f)* [ahN-pool] blister; *(el)* bulb
amusement *(m)* [a-mewz-mahN] amusement, entertainment, diversion
s'amuser [sa-mew-zay] to amuse oneself, to play, to have fun
an *(m)* [ahN] year; **par an** *(adv)* [par-ahN] a year
ancien(ne) [ahN-syaN]/[ahN-syehn] *(from ancient time)* old
âne *(m)* [an] donkey
anglais(e) [ahN-gleh(z)] English
angle *(m)* [ahNgl] angle
animal *(m)* [a-nee-mal] animal
année *(f)* [a-nay] year
anniversaire *(m)* [a-nee-vehr-sehr] birthday
annonce *(f)* [a-nohNs] notification, advertisement
annoncer [a-nohN-say] to announce, to inform
annuel(le) [a-nwehl] *(adj)* yearly
annuler [a-new-lay] *(a trip, a flight)* to cancel
apparaître [a-pa-rehtr] to appear
appareil *(m)* [a-pa-rehy] device; **appareil-photo** *(m)* [a-pa-rehy] camera
apparemment [a-pa-ra-mahN] apparently *(adv)*
apparence *(f)* [a-pa-rahNs] appearance
appartement *(m)* [a-par-tuh-mahN] apartment
appartenir [a-par-tuh-neer] to belong
appeler [a-play] to call, to shout; **s'appeler** [sa-play] to be called
appétit *(m)* [a-pay-tee] appetite
applaudissements *(m pl)* [a-plo-dees-mahN] applause
application *(f)* [a-plee-ka-syohN] application, enforcement
appliquer [a-plee-kay] to apply
appoint *(m)* [a-pwaN] change
apporter [a-pohr-tay] to bring
apprendre [a-prahNdr] to learn, to hear
s'approcher [sa-pro-shay] to get closer, to approach
après [a-pray] *(time)* after
après-midi *(m)* [a-pray-mee-dee] afternoon
arbre *(m)* [arbr] tree
argent *(m)* [ar-zhahN] money, silver
arrêt *(m)* [a-reh] *(train)* stop, station
arrêter [a-ray-tay] to stop; **s'arrêter** [sa-ray-tay] to stop
arrière, en [ahN-na-ryehr] behind
arriver [a-ree-vay] to arrive, to come in
article *(m)* [ar-teekl] article
ascenseur *(m)* [a-sahN-suhr] elevator
s'asseoir [sa-swar] to sit down
assez [a-say] enough
assiette *(f)* [a-syeht] plate
assis(e) [a-zee(z)] to be seated
association *(f)* [a-so-sya-syohN] association; *(commercial)* partnership
assurance *(f)* [a-sew-rahNs] insurance
assurer [a-sew-ray] to insure
Atlantique *(m)* [at-lahN-teek] Atlantic
atteindre [a-taNdr] to reach
attendre [a-tahNdr] to wait, to expect; **s'attendre à** [sa-tahN-dra] to count on, to expect
attentif, -ive [a-tahN-teef]/[a-tahN-teev] attentive
attention! [a-tahN-syohN] Watch out!; **faire attention** (à) [fehr-a-tahN-syohN-a] to pay attention
attérir [a-tay-reer] to land
attester [a-tehs-tay] to attest, to certify
attraper [a-tra-pay] to catch
aucun(e) [o-kaN]/[o-kewn] no one, none

au-delà de [o-duh-la-duh] beyond
au-dessous (de) [o-duh-soo-duh] underneath
au-dessus (de) [o-duh-sew-duh] over
augmenter [ohg-mahN-tay] to increase, to grow; *(price)* to raise
aujourd'hui [o-zhoor-dwee] today
aussi [o-see] too; **aussi ... que [o-see] ...[kuh]** as ... as
authentique [o-tahN-teek] genuine
automatique [o-to-ma-teek] automatic
autorisé(e) (à) [o-to-ree-zay-a] authorized (to)
autoriser [o-to-ree-zay] to authorize; *(permission)* to allow
autour de [o-toor-duh] around
autre [otr] other; **une autre fois** [ew-no-truh-fwa] another time; **l'autre jour** [lo-truh-zhoor] the other day; **d'autre part** [do-truh-par] besides, on the other hand
autrefois [o-truh-fwa] once upon a time, previously
autrement [o-truh-mahN] otherwise, differently
avance *(f)* [a-vahNs] lead; **par avance** [par-a-vahNs] in advance
avancer [a-vahN-say] to go forward; *(hour)* to run fast
avant [a-vahN] *(time)* before; **avant que** [a-vahN-kuh] before; **avant tout** [a-vahN-too] first, before everything else; **en avant** [ahN-na-vahN] in front
avantage *(m)* [a-vahN-tazh] advantage
avantageux, -euse [a-vahN-ta-zhuuh(z)] profitable
avant-dernier, -ière [a-vahN-dehr-nyay]/[a-vahN-dehr-nyehr] the one before last
avec [a-vehk] with
avenir *(m)* [av-neer] future
avertir [a-vehr-teer] to warn
avertisseur d'incendie *(m)* [a-vehr-tee-suhr-daN-sahN-dee] fire alarm
aveugle [a-vuhgl] blind
avis *(m)* [a-vee] opinion, viewpoint
avoir [a-vwar] to have

B

bague *(f)* [bag] ring
se baigner [suh-beh-nyay] to swim, to bathe
bâiller [ba-yay] to yawn
bain *(m)* [baN] bath; **prendre un bain** [prahN-draN-baN] to take a bath *(big pool)*
baiser *(m)* [beh-zay] kiss
baisser [beh-say] *(price)* to lower
bal *(m)* [bal] *(party)* ball
balade *(f)* [ba-lad] stroll, walk
balance *(f)* [ba-lahNs] scale
balle *(f)* [bal] ball
ballon *(m)* [ba-lohN] ball
banc *(m)* [bahN] bench
banlieue *(f)* [bahN-lyuuh] suburb
banque *(f)* [bahNk] bank
barque *(f)* [bark] small boat
bas, basse [ba(s)] low, humble; cheap; **en bas** [ahN-ba] below; downstairs; **vers le bas** [vehr-luh-ba] down
bateau *(m)* [ba-to] boat
bâtiment *(m)* [ba-te-mahN] building
bâton *(m)* [ba-tohN] stick
batterie *(f)* [ba-tree] *(car)* battery
battre [batr] to beat
beau, bel, belle [bo]/[bel] beautiful
beaucoup de [bo-koo-duh] a lot of
beau-frère *(m)* [bo-frehr] brother-in-law
beauté *(f)* [bo-tay] beauty
bébé *(m)* [bay-bay] baby
Belge *(m f)* [behlzh] Belgian; **belge** [behlzh] Belgian
Belgique *(f)* [behl-zheek] Belgium
belle-sœur [behl-suhr] sister-in-law
bénéfice *(m)* [bay-nay-fees] profit
besoin *(m)* [buh-zwaN] need; **avoir besoin de** [a-vwar-buh-zwaN] to need
bête [beht] stupid
bien *(m)* [byaN] good; **bien** *(adv)* [byaN] well; **bien que** [byaN-kuh] although
bien-être *(m)* [byaN-nehtr] well-being
bientôt [byaN-to] soon
bienveillant(e) [byaN-veh-yahN(t)] kindliness
bienvenu(e) [byaN-vuh-new] welcome
billet *(m)* [bee-yay] *(money)* note, **billet d'entrée** *(m)* [bee-yay-dahN-tray] entrance ticket
blessé(e) [blay-say] *(m f)* wounded
bluffer [bluh-fay] to bluff
boire [bwar] to drink
bois *(m)* [bwa] wood
boîte *(f)* [bwat] box, can, nightclub; **boîte d'allumettes** *(f)* [bwat-da-lew-meht] box of matches; **boîte de conserve** *(f)* [bwat-duh-kohN-sehrv] tin, can
bon *(m)* [bohN] form, slip

bon, bonne *(adj)* [bohN]/[bohn] good, fine, correct; **bon marché** [bohN-mar-shay] cheap; **être bon** [eh-truh-bohN] to be good, tasty
bondé(e) [bohN-day] packed
bord *(m)* [bohr] (sea) side; embankment; **sur les bords de la Seine** [sewr-lay-bohr-duh-la-sehn] on the banks of the Seine
bouché(e) [boo-shay] blocked
boue *(f)* [boo] mud, sludge
bougie *(f)* [behzh] candle
bouillir [boo-yeer] to boil
boum *(f)* [boom] party
bouquet *(m)* [boo-kay] bunch of flowers, bouquet
boussole *(f)* [boo-sohl] compass
bout *(m)* [boo] end, tip; **bout des doigts** *(m)* tip of the fingers
bouteille *(f)* [boo-tehy] bottle
boutique *(f)* [boo-teek] store
bouton *(m)* [boo-tohN] button
brancher [brahN-shay] *(appliance)* to plug
brasserie *(f)* [bras-ree] restaurant
bref, brève [brehf]/[brehv] short, brief
brillant(e) [bree-yahN(t)] brilliant
briller [bree-yay] to shine, to glimmer
briquet *(m)* [bree-kay] lighter
bronzé(e) [brohN-zay] sunburned, tanned
brosse *(f)* [brohs] brush
brosser [bro-say] to brush
bruit *(m)* [brwee] noise, sound
brûler [brew-lay] to burn
brumeux, -euse [brew-muuh(z)] foggy
brun [braN] *(hair)* brown
bruyant(e) [brwee-yahN(t)] noisy
buisson *(m)* [bwee-sohN] bush
bureau *(m)* [bew-ro] office; **bureau des objets trouvés** *(m)* [bew-ro-day-zob-zhay-troo-vay] lost and found; **bureau des renseignements** *(m)* [bew-ro-day-rahN-seh-nyuh-mahN] information desk
but *(m)* [bewt] goal, objective

C

cabane *(f)* [ka-ban] hut
cabine *(f)* [ka-been] cabin
cabinet *(m)* [ka-bee-nay] *(doctors)* practice or office
cacher [ka-shay] to hide, to conceal
cadeau *(m)* [ka-do] present
café *(m)* [ka-fay] coffee; coffee shop
cahier *(m)* [ka-yay] notebook
caillouteux, -euse [ka-yoo-tuuh(z)] stony
caisse *(f)* [kehs] cashbox, cashier, box, chest
calculer [kal-kew-lay] to calculate
calme [kalm] calm, quiet; **se calmer** [suh-kal-may] to calm down
canal *(m)* [ka-nal] canal
capable [ka-pabl] capable, able; **être capable de** [eh-truh-ka-pa-bluh-duh] to be able to
capitale *(f)* [ka-pee-tal] capital
car [kar] for
caractéristique (de) [ka-rak-tay-rees-teek-duh] typical (of)
cargaison *(f)* [kar-gay-zohN] load, cargo
carré(e) [ka-ray] square
carrefour *(m)* [kar-foor] *(street)* intersection
carte *(f)* [kart] map, menu; **carte géographique** *(f)* [kart-zhay-o-gra-feek] topographical map **carte postale** *(f)* [kart-po-stal] postcard
cas *(m)* [ka] case, instance; **en cas d'urgence** [ahN-ka-dewr-zhahNs] in case of emergency; **au cas où** [o-ka-oo] in case
cassé(e) [ka-say] broken
casse-croûte *(m)* [kas-kroot] snack
casser [ka-say] to break; **se casser** [suh-ka-say] to break, to crack
casserole *(f)* [kas-rohl] saucepan
cause *(f)* [koz] cause, reason; **à cause de** [a-koz-duh] because
causer [ko-zay] to cause
caution *(f)* [ko-syohN] deposit
ce, cet, cette, ces [suh]/[seht]/[seht]/[say] this, these
célèbre [say-lehbr] famous
célibataire [say-lee-ba-tehr] bachelor
celle-là *(f)* [sehl-la] that one
celles-là *(f pl)* [sehl-la] those (ones)
celui-là *(m)* [suh-lwee-la] that one
cent [sahN] hundred; **cent fois** [sahN-fwa] hundred times
central(e) [sahN-tral] central
centre *(m)* [sahNtr] center
cependant [suh-pahN-dahN] however
céramique *(f)* [say-ra-meek] ceramics
certain(e) *(adj)* [sehr-taN] sure, some; **certainement** *(adv)* [sehr-tehn-mahN] certainly
certificat *(m)* [sehr-tee-fee-ka] certificate
ces pl [say] these
ceux-là *(m pl)* [suuh-la] those

chacun(e) [sha-kaN]/[sha-kewn] each one
chagrin *(m)* [sha-graN] sorrow
chaîne *(f)* [shehn] chain
chaise *(f)* [shehz] chair
chalet *(m)* [sha-lay] chalet *(in the Alps)*
chaleur *(f)* [sha-luhr] heat, warm
champ *(m)* [shahN] field
chance *(f)* [shahNs] luck; **Bonne chance!** [bohn-shahNs] Good Luck!
change *(m)* [shahNzh] change, exchange
changement *(m)* [shahNzh-mahN] change
changer [shahN-zhay] to change, to alter; *(money)* to exchange; **se changer** [suh-shahN-zhay] to change clothes
chanson *(f)* [shahN-sohN] song
chant *(m)* [shahN] song
chanter [shahN-tay] to sing
chapelle *(f)* [sha-pehl] chapel
chaque *(adj)* [shak] each
charbon *(m)* [shar-bohN] coal
charger [shar-zhay] to load; **se charger de** [suh-shar-zhay] to take care of
chat *(m)* [sha] cat
château *(m)* [zha-to] castle
chaud(e) [sho(d)] hot, warm
chauffer [sho-fay] to heat, to warm
chauffeur *(m)* [sho-fuhr] driver, chauffeur
chaussure *(f)* [sho-sewr] shoe
chemin *(m)* [shu-maN] way
cher, chère [shehr] dear, expensive
chercher [shehr-shay] to search; **aller chercher** [a-lay-shehr-shay] to go and look for
chéri(e) *(m f)* [shay-ree] darling
chewing-gum *(m)* [shweeng-gohm] chewing gum
chien *(m)* [shyaN] dog
chiffon *(m)* [shee-fohN] cloth, rag
choc *(m)* [shohk] collision
chœur *(m)* [kuhr] choir
choisir [shwa-zeer] to choose
choix *(m)* [shwa] choice, selection
chômage *(m)* [sho-mazh] unemployment; **au chômage** [o-sho-mazh] unemployed
chose *(f)* [shoz] thing, object
chute *(f)* [shewt] fall
ciel *(m)* [syehl] sky
cigare *(m)* [see-gar] cigar
cigarette *(f)* [see-ga-reht] cigarette
cigarillo *(m)* [see-ga-ree-yo] cigarillo
circonstances *(f pl)* [seer-cohN-stahNs] circumstances
circulation *(f)* [seer-kew-la-syohN] traffic
circuler [seer-kew-lay] *(traffic)* to move, to circulate
ciseaux *(m pl)* [see-zo] scissors
civilisation *(f)* [see-vee-lee-za-syohN] civilization
clair(e) [klehr] clear, light, obvious
classe *(f)* [klas] class
client(e) *(m f)* [klee-yahN(t)] customer, client
clignoter [klee-nyo-tay] to flicker, to signal
climat *(m)* [klee-ma] climate
clou *(m)* [kloo] nail
cœur *(m)* [kuhr] heart
coin *(m)* [kwaN] corner
col *(m)* [kohl] mountain pass
colère *(f)* [ko-lehr] anger; **en colère** [ahN-ko-lehr] angry; **se mettre en colère** [suh-meh-trahN-ko-lehr] to lose one's temper
collection *(f)* [ko-lehk-syohN] collection, sampling
collectionner [ko-lehk-syo-nay] to collect
collègue *(m)* [ko-lehg] colleague
collier *(m)* [ko-lyay] necklace
colline *(f)* [ko-leen] hill
collision *(f)* [ko-lee-zyohN] collision
coloré(e) [do-lo-ray] colored
comestible [ko-mehs-teebl] edible
comme [kohm] *(manner)* as; *(comparison)* like; **comme ça** [kohm-sa] like that; **comme il faut** [kohm-eel-fo] *(people)* respectable, proper; **comme si** [kohm-see] as if
commencement *(m)* [ko-mahNs-mahN] beginning
commencer [ko-mahN-say] to begin
comment [ko-mahN] how; **comment?** [ko-mahN] what?, pardon?
commun(e) *(adj)* [ko-maN]/[ko-mewn] common, shared, ordinary, coarse
communication *(f)* [ko-mew-nee-ka-syohN] *(tele)* communication
compagnie *(f)* [kohN-pa-nee] company
comparaison *(f)* [kohN-pa-reh-zohN] comparison
comparer [kohN-pa-ray] to compare
compatriote *(m)* [kohN-pa-tree-yoht] compatriot, fellow countryman
compensation *(f)* [kohn-pahN-sa-syohN] *(damages)* compensation
compétent(e) [kohN-pay-tahN(t)] competent
complet, -ète [kohN-play]/[kohN-pleht] full, complete

compliments, faire des [fehr-day-kohN-plee-mahN] to congratulate
composer [kohN-po-zay] (un numéro) *(tele)* to dial; **se composer de** [suh-kohN-po-zay-duh] to be made of
comprendre [kohN-prahndr] to understand; **mal comprendre** [mal-kohN-prahNdr] to misunderstand; **se faire comprendre** [suh-fehr-kohN-prahNdr] to make oneself understood
compris(e) [kohN-pree(z)] understood, included
comptant, payer [peh-yay-kohN-tahN] to pay cash
compter [kohN-tay] to count
compte-rendu *(m)* [kohNt-rahN-dew] report
concernant [kohN-sehr-nahN] regarding
concours *(m)* [kohN-koor] competition
condition *(f)* [kohN-dee-syohN] condition
condoléances *(f pl)* [kohN-do-lay-ahNs] condolences
conduire [kohN-dweer] to lead; *(transport)* to drive, to drive a car
conduite *(f)* [kohN-dweer] behavior; *(gas, water)* pipe
confiance *(f)* [kohN-fyahNs] confidence; **avoir confiance en** [a-vwar-kohN-fyahNs-ahN] to trust
confiant(e) [kohN-fyahN(t)] confident
confirmer [kohN-feer-may] to confirm
confondre [kohN-fohNdr] to mistake, to confuse
confort *(m)* [kohN-fohr] comfort
confortable [kohN-fohr-tabl] comfortable
confrère *(m)* [kohN-frehr] colleague
congé *(m)* [kohN-zhay] holiday; **prendre congé** [prahN-druh-kohN-zhay] to leave, to depart
connaissance *(f)* [ko-neh-sahNs] knowledge, acquaintance, consciousness; **faire la connaissance (de)** [fehr-ko-neh-sahNs-duh] to make acquaintance; **sans connaissance** [sahN-ko-neh-sahNs] unconscious
connaître [ko-nehtr] to know; **faire connaître** [fehr-ko-nehtr] to inform
connu(e) [ko-new] known; **être connu(e)** [eh-truh-ko-new] to be known
consciencieux, -euse [kohN-syahN-syuuh(z)] conscientious
conscient(e) [kohN-syahN(t)] conscious
conseil *(m)* [kohN-sehy] advice; council
conseiller [kohN-seh-yay] to advise
consentement *(m)* [kohN-sahNt-mahN] consent
consentir [kohN-sahN-teer] to grant; **consentir à** [kohN-sahN-teer-a] to agree to
conserver [kohN-sehr-vay] to keep
considérable [kohN-see-day-rabl] considerable
consigne *(f)* [kohN-seeny] *(bottle)* deposit
consommation *(f)* [kohN-so-ma-syohN] consumption
consommer [kohN-so-may] to consume, to use
constitution *(f)* [kohNs-tee-tew-syohN] constitution
construire [kohNs-trweer] to build
consulat *(m)* [kohN-sew-la] consulate
consulter [kohN-sewl-tay] to consult
contact *(m)* [kohN-takt] contact; touch
contenir [kohN-tuh-neer] to contain
content(e) [kohN-tahN(t)] pleased, content; **être content de** [eh-truh-kohN-tahN-duh] to be satisfied with
contenu *(m)* [kohN-tuh-new] content(s)
continuer [kohN-tee-nway] to carry on
contraceptif *(m)* [kohN-tra-sehp-teev] contraceptive
contrainte *(f)* [kohN-traNt] obligation
contraire *(m)* [kohN-trehr] contrary; **au contraire** [o-kohN-trehr] to the contrary
contrat *(m)* [kohN-tra] contract
contre [kohNtr] against; **être contre** [eh-truh-kohNtr] to be against; **à contre-cœur** [a-kohN-truh-kuhr] reluctantly
contrôler [kohN-tro-lay] to control
convaincre [kohN-vaNkr] to convince
convenir [kohN-vuh-neer] to agree, to suit; **convenir de** [kohN-vuh-neer-duh] to agree that, to admit
conversation *(f)* [kohN-vehr-sa-syohN] conversation, discussion
conversion *(f)* [kohN-vehr-syohN] conversion
copie *(f)* [ko-pee] copy
copieux, -euse *(adj)* [ko-pyuuh(z)] copious
coq *(m)* [kohk] rooster
corde *(f)* [kohrd] rope
cordial(e) [kohr-dyal] friendly
cordialité *(f)* [kohr-dya-lee-tay] warmth, friendliness
corps *(m)* [kohr] body
corpulent(e) [kohr-pew-lahN(t)] stout
correct(e) [ko-rehkt] correct

correspondance *(f)* [ko-rehs-pohN-dahNs] correspondance; *(train)* connection
corriger [ko-ree-zhay] to correct, to improve
corrompu(e) [ko-rohN-pew] corrupted
costume *(m)* [kos-tew (m)] suit; **costume régional/folklorique** *(m)* [kos-tewm-ray-zhyo-nal/fohl-klo-reek] regional costume
côte *(f)* [kot] slope; *(m)* [ko-tay] side; **à côté de** [a-ko-tay-duh] next; **de l'autre côté** (de) [duh-lo-truh-ko-tay-(duh)] on the other side (of)
coucher [koo-shay] to put to bed; **aller se coucher** [a-lay-suh-koo-shay] to go to bed; **au coucher du soleil** [o-koo-shay-dew-so-lehy] at sunset
couler [koo-lay] to run, to flow
couleur *(f)* [koo-luhr] color
couloir *(m)* [koo-lwar] corridor
coup *(m)* [koo] blow, knock; **coup (de feu)** *(m)* [koo-duh-fuuh] gunshot
couper [koo-pay] to cut
couple *(m)* [koopl] couple
cour *(f)* [koor] yard
courant *(m)* [koo-rahN] current; **courant d'air** *(m)* [koo-rahN-dehr] draft
courir [koo-reer] to run
courroie *(f)* [koo-rwa] strap
cours *(m)* [koor] course; rate; **en cours de route** [ahN-koor-duh-root] on the way
courses, faire ses [fehr-say-koors] to run errands
court(e) [koor(t)] *(space)* short; **à court terme** [a-koor-tehrm] in the short run
cousin(e) *(m f)* [koo-zaN]/[koo-zeen] cousin
coussin *(m)* [koo-saN] pillow
coût *(m)* [koo] cost
coûter [koo-tay] to cost
coûteux, -euse [koo-tuuh(z)] costly
couvert(e) [koo-vehr(t)] *(weather)* overcast, clouded over
couverture *(f)* [koo-vehr-tewr] blanket
couvrir [koo-vreer] to cover, to include
craindre [kraNdr] to fear, to be afraid of
crainte *(f)* [krahNt] fear
créatif, -ive [kray-a-teef]/[kray-a-teev] creative
crédit *(m)* [kray-dee] credit
crever [kruh-vay] *(tire)* to burst
crier [kree-yay] to scream
crique *(f)* [kreek] creek
critiquer [kree-tee-kay] to criticize
crochet *(m)* [kro-shay] hook
croire [krwar] to believe
cueillir [kuuh-yeer] to pick
cuir *(m)* [kweer] leather
cuisine *(f)* [kwee-zeen] kitchen; **faire la cuisine** [fehr-la-kwee-zeen] to cook
culture *(f)* [kewl-tewr] culture
curieux, -euse [kew-ryuuh(z)] curious, inquisitive, strange

D

d'abord [da-bohr] first
dame *(f)* [dam] lady
danger *(m)* [dahN-zhay] danger
dangereux, -euse [dahN-zhuh-ruuh(z)] dangerous
dans [dahN] in; **dans la rue** [dahN-la-rew] in the street; **dans une semaine** [dahN-zewn-suh-mehn] in a week
danse *(f)* [dahNs] dance
date *(f)* [dat] date; **date limite** *(f)* [dad-lee-meet] deadline
de [duh] from, of
déboucher [day-boo-shay] *(street)* to lead to
debout, être [eh-truh-duh-boo] to stand
début *(m)* [day-bew] beginning
débuter [day-bew-tay] to begin, to start
décharger [day-shar-zhay] to unload
déchirer [day-shee-ray] to tear; **se déchirer** [suh-day-shee-ray] to tear, to rip
décidé(e), être [eh-truh-day-see-day] to be decided
décider [day-see-day] to decide; **décider (de)** [day-see-day-duh] to decide to; **se décider** [suh-day-see-day] to make up one's mind
décision *(f)* [day-see-syohN] decision
déclarer [day-kla-ray] to declare
décoller [day-ko-lay] *(flight)* to take off
décommander [day-ko-mahN-day] *(room)* to cancel
découvrir [day-koo-vreer] to discover
décrire [day-kreer] to describe
déçu(e) [day-sew] disappointed
dedans [duh-dahN] inside
dédommagement *(m)* [day-do-mazh-mahN] compensation
dédouaner [day-dwa-nay] to clear customs
défaire ses valises [day-fehr-say-va-leez] to unpack
défaut *(m)* [day-fo] blemish, fault

défavorable [day-fa-vo-rabl] unfavorable
défectueux, -euse [day-fehk-twuuh(z)] defective
défendre [day-fahNdr] to defend
définitif, -ive *(adj)* [day-fee-nee-teef]/[day-fee-nee-teev] final; **définitivement** *(adv)* [day-fee-nee-teev-mahN] for good
dégât *(m)* [day-ga] damage
degré *(m)* [duh-gray] degree
dehors [duh-ohr] outside
déjà [day-zha] already
déjeuner *(m)* [day-zhuuh-nay] lunch; **petit déjeuner** *(m)* [puh-tee-day-zhuuh-nay] breakfast; **prendre son petit déjeuner** [prahN-druh-sohN-puh-tee-day-zhuuh-nay] to have breakfast
délai *(m)* [day-lay] extension; **délais** [day-lay] *(m pl)* time limit
délicat(e) [day-lee-ka(t)] delicate, fine
demande *(f)* [duh-mahNd] request
demander [duh-mahN-day] to request; **demander qch à qn** [duh-mahN-day-kehl-kuh-shoz-a-kehl-kaN] to ask smth from someone; **demander conseil à qn** [duh-mahN-day-kohN-sehy-a-kehl-kaN] to ask for advice from someone
démanger [day-mahN-zhay] to itch
démarrer [day-ma-ray] to start
déménager [day-may-na-zhay] to move
demi(e) *(adj)* [duh-mee] half; **à demi** *(adv)* [a-duh-mee] half; **une demi-heure** [ewn-duh-mee-uhr] a half hour; **faire demi-tour** [fehr-duh-mee-toor] to turn back
démodé(e) [day-mo-day] old-fashioned
denrées alimentaires *(f pl)* [dahN-ray-a-lee-mahN-tehr] foodstuffs
dentelle *(f)* [dahN-tehl] lace
départ *(m)* [day-par] departure
dépasser [day-pa-say] to pass, to overtake
se dépêcher [suh-day-pay-shay] to hurry
dépenser [day-pahN-say] to spend
dépenses *(f pl)* [day-pahNs] expenses
déposer [day-po-zay] to lay, to drop, to deposit
depuis [duh-pwee] since; **depuis quand?** [duh-pwee-kahN] since when?; **depuis que** [duh-pwee-kuh] since
dérangement *(m)* [day-rahNzh-mahN] inconvenience
déranger [day-rahN-zhay] to inconvenience
dernier, -ière [dehr-nyay]/[dehr-nyehr] last; **en dernier lieu** [ahN-dehr-nyay-lyuuh] finally
derrière [deh-ryehr] behind
dès que possible [day-kuh-po-seebl] as soon as possible
désagréable [day-za-gray-abl] unpleasant
descendre [day-sahNdr] to go down; **en descendant** [ahN-day-sahN-dahN] downward
désespéré(e) [day-zehs-pay-ray] desperate
se déshabiller [suh-day-za-bee-yay] to get undressed
désignation *(f)* [day-zee-nya-syohN] appointment
désir *(m)* [day-zeer] wish
désirer [day-zee-ray] to wish, to want
désordre *(m)* [day-zohrdr] mess
dessiner [day-see-nay] to draw
destination *(f)* [dehs-tee-na-syohN] destination
détail *(m)* [de-ta-yuh] detail; **en détail** [ahN-day-ta-yuh] in detail
détaillé(e) [day-ta-yay] detailed
détour *(m)* [day-toor] detour, bend
détruire [day-trweer] to destroy
dette *(f)* [deht] *(money)* debt
deux [duuh] two; **deux fois** [duuh-fwa] twice; **tous/toutes les deux** [too/toot-lay-duuh] both
deuxième [duuh-zyehm] second; **deuxièmement** [duuh-zyehm-mahN] secondly
devant [duh-vahN] in front, past
développement *(m)* [day-vlohp-m)ahN] development
développer [day-vlo-pay] to develop
devenir [duhv-neer] to become
deviner [duh-vee-nay] to guess
devoir [duh-vwar] must, to have to, to owe, *(m)* exercise
diagnostic *(m)* [dyag-nohs-teek] diagnosis
diapo *(f)* [dya-po] slide
Dieu [dyuuh] God; **Dieu soit loué!** [dyuuh-swa-lway] Thank God!
différence *(f)* [dee-fay-rahNs] difference
différent(e) *(adj)* [dee-fay-rahN(t)] different
différer [dee-fay-ray] to differ, to postpone
difficile [dee-fee-seel] difficult
difficulté *(f)* [dee-fee-kewl-tay] difficulty
diminuer [dee-mee-nway] to reduce *(price)*, to fall
dire [deer] to say
direct(e) [dee-rehkt] direct, straightforward; **directement** *(adv)* directly

directeur *(m)* [dee-rehk-tuhr] manager, director
direction *(f)* [dee-rehk-syohN] management, direction; **dans la direction opposée** [dahN-la-dee-rehk-syohN- o-po-zay] in the opposite direction
directrice *(f)* [dee-rehk-trees] manager, principal
disparaître [dees-pa-rehtr] to disappear
dispute *(f)* [dees-pewt] argument
se disputer [suh-dees-pew-tay] to argue, to fight
disque *(m)* [deesk] record
dissimuler [dee-see-mew-lay] to hide from sight
distance *(f)* [dees-tahNs] distance
distingué(e) [dees-taN-gay] distinguished, elegant
distinguer [dees-taN-gay] to distinguish; **se distinguer de** [suh-dees-taN-gay] to become famous, to distinguish o.s.
distraction *(f)* [dees-trak-syohN] amusement, entertainment
se distraire [suh-dees-trehr] to have fun, to enjoy o.s.
distrayant(e) [dees-tray-yahN(t)] amusing, entertaining
distributeur automatique *(m)* [dees-tree-bew-tuhr-o-to-ma-teek] vending machine, ATM
divertissant(e) [dee-vehr-tee-sahN(t)] *(entertainment)* amusing, entertaining
diviser [dee-vee-zay] to divide
docteur *(m)* [dohk-tuhr] doctor
document *(m)* [do-kew-mahN] document
domaine *(m)* [do-mehn] estate
domicile *(m)* [do-mee-seel] residence, domicile
dommage *(m)* [do-(m)azh] damage; **c'est dommage** [say-do-mazh] it is too bad, it's a pity; **Quel dommage!** [kehl-do-mazh] What a pity!
donc [dohNk] so
donner [do-nay] to give; **se donner du mal** [suh-do-nay-dew-mal] to take trouble; **se donner rendez-vous** [suh-do-nay-rahN-day-voo] to make an appointment
dormir [dohr-meer] to sleep
douane *(f)* [dwan] customs
double [doobl] double
doublure *(f)* [doo-blewr] lining
doucement [doos-mahN] gently, slowly
douloureux, -euse [doo-loo-ruuh(z)] painful
doute *(m)* [doot] doubt; **sans doute** *(adv)* [sahN-doot] probably; **sans aucun doute** [sahN-zo-kaN-doot] without any doubt
douter de [doo-tay-duh] to doubt
douteux, -euse [doo-tuuh(z)] doubtful
doux, douce [doo(s)] *(color)* soft, mild
drap *(m)* [dra] cloth; **draps** *(m pl)* [dra] bed linen
droit *(m)* [drwa] right; **droits** *(m pl)* [drwa] rights
droit(e) [drwa(t)] right; straight; **à droite** [a-drwat] to the right
dur(e) [dewr] hard, firm
durée *(f)* [dew-ray] duration
durer [dew-ray] to last, to go on
dureté *(f)* [dewr-tay] hardness

E

eau *(f)* [o] water
échange *(f)* [ay-shahNzh] exchange, swap
échanger [ay-shahN-zhay] to exchange, to swap
échantillon *(m)* [ay-shahN-tee-yohN] sample
échelle *(f)* [ay-shehl] ladder
éclair *(m)* [ay-klehr] lightning
éclairé(e) [ay-kleh-ray] lighted
éclater [ay-kla-tay] to burst
école *(f)* [ay-kohl] school
économiser [ay-ko-no-mee-zay] to save
écouter (qn) [ay-koo-tay-kehl-kaN] to listen to s.o.
écrire [ay-kreer] to write; **par écrit** [par-ay-kree] in writing
écriteau *(m)* [ay-kree-to] board, notice
écriture *(f)* [ay-kree-tewr] handwriting
éducation *(f)* [ay-dew-ka-syohN] education
effet *(m)* [ay-fay] effect; **en effet** [ahN-ay-fay] in fact, actually, indeed
efficace [ay-fee-kas] efficient
effort *(m)* [ay-fohr] effort
effrayer [ay-fray-yay] to scare
égards *(m pl)* [ay-gar] consideration
s'égarer [say-ga-ray] to get lost
éhonté(e) [ay-ohN-tay] shameless
élection *(f)* [ay-lehk-syohN] election
électricité *(f)* [ay-lehk-tree-see-tay] electricity; **à l'électricité** *(adv)* [a-lay-lehk-tree-see-tay] electric

électrique *(adj)* [ay-lehk-treek] electric
s'élever à [say-luh-vay-a] to rise
elle *(f sing)* [ehl] she; **elles** *(f pl)* [ehl] they
éloigné(e) [ay-lwa-nyay] distant, faraway
éloignement *(m)* [ay-lwa-nyuh-mahN] distance
émancipé(e) [ay-mahN-see-pay] emancipated
emballage *(m)* [ahN-ba-lazh] packaging, wrapping
emballer [ahN-ba-lay] to pack, to wrap
embouchure *(f)* [ahN-boo-shewr] *(river)* mouth
embrasser [ahN-bra-say] to kiss; to embrace
éméché(e) [ay-may-shay] tipsy
émission *(f)* [ay-mee-syohN] *(radio, TV)* broadcast
emmener [ahN-muh-nay] *(people)* to take along
empêcher [ahN-pay-shay] to prevent, to stop
emploi *(m)* [ahN-plwa] employment, job; work
employer [ahN-plwa-yay] to use, to employ
emporter [ahN-pohr-tay] *(things)* to take with, to remove, to carry
emprunter (à qn) [ahN-praN-tay] to borrow
ému(e) [ay-mew] *(feeling)* moved
en [ahN] by; *(material)* out of; *(time)* within; **en français** [ahN-frahN-say] in French; **en France** [ahN-frahNs] in France; **en outre** [ahN-nootr] furthermore; **en voyage** [ahN-vwa-yazh] on a trip
enceinte [ahN-saNt] pregnant
encore [ahN-kohr] more; **(ne ...) pas encore** [nuh-pa-ahN-kohr] not yet; **encore une fois** [ahN-kohr-ewn-fwa] one more time
endommagé(e) [ahN-do-ma-zhay] damaged
endommager [ahN-do-ma-zhay] to damage
s'endormir [sahN-dohr-meer] to fall asleep
endroit *(m)* [ahN-drwa] *(place)* spot
enfant *(m f)* [ahN-fahN] child
enfin [ahN-faN] finally
enflé(e) [ahN-flay] swollen
engagement *(m)* [ahN-gazh-mahN] commitment; **sans engagement** [sahN-zahN-gazh-mahN] without commitment
enlever [ahNl-vay] to remove
ennuyeux, -euse [ahN-nwee-yuuh(z)] boring
enregistrer, faire [fehr-ahN-ruh-zhees-tray] *(luggage)* to register, to check in
enseigner [ahN-seh-nyay] to teach
ensemble *(adv)* [ahN-sahNbl] together
ensoleillé(e) [ahN-so-leh-yay] sunny
ensuite [ahN-sweet] afterwards
entendre [ahN-tahNdr] to hear
enthousiasmé(e) (par) [ahN-too-zyas-may] filled with enthusiasm
entier, -ière [ahN-tyay] /[ahN-tyehr] full, whole
s'entraîner [sahN-treh-nay] to train, to practice
entre [ahNtr] between, among; **entre autres** [ahN-trotr] among others
entrée *(f)* [ahN-tray] entrance, admission; **entrée principale** *(f)* [ahN-tray-praN-see-pal] main entrance; **Entrée interdite!** [ahN-tray-aN-tehr-deet] No entrance!
entreprise [ahN-truh-preez] *(f)* firm, company
entrer [ahN-tray] to enter, to come in; to penetrate; to go in; **Entrez.** [ahN-tray] Come in!, **entrer dans** [ahN-tray-dahN] to go into
entre-temps [ahN-truh-tahN] in the meantime
envelopper [ahN-vlo-pay] to wrap
envie *(f)* [ahN-vee] desire, wish
environ [ahN-vee-rohN] about
environnement *(m)* [ahN-vee-rohn-mahN] environment
envoyer [ahN-vwa-yay] to send; *(post office)* to remit
épais(se) [ay-peh(s)] *(fog)* thick
épeler [ay-play] to spell
épingle *(f)* [ay-paNgl] pin; **épingle de sûreté** *(f)* [ay-paN-gluh-duh-sewr-tay] safety pin
époque *(f)* [ay-pohk] era; **à l'époque** [a-lay-pohk] at the time
épuisé(e) [ay-pwee-zay] exhausted
équipage *(m)* [ay-kee-pazh] *(ship)* crew
équipe *(f)* [ay-keep] *(sport)* team
équivalent *(m)* [ay-kee-va-lahN] equivalent; **équivalent(e)** [ay-kee-va-lahN(t)] equivalent
erreur *(f)* [eh-ruhr] mistake; **faire une erreur de calcul** [fehr-ewn-eh-ruhr-duh-kal-kewl] to make a miscalculation
escalier *(m)* [ehs-ka-lyay] staircase
escroc *(m)* [ehs-kro] swindler

escroquerie *(f)* [ehs-krohk-ree] swindle
espace *(m)* [ehs-pas] room
Espagne *(f)* [ehs-pany] Spain
Espagnol(e) [ehs-pa-nyohl] Spanish; **espagnol(e)** [ehs-pa-nyohl] Spanish
espérer [ehs-pay-ray] to hope
esquisse *(f)* [ehs-kees] sketch, draft
essai *(m)* [ay-say] trial, test, try
essayer [ay-say-yay] to try, to test
essence *(f)* [ay-sahNs] gas; **prendre de l'essence** [prahN-druh-duh-lay-sahNs] to fill the tank
Est *(m)* [ehst] east
estimer [ay-stee-may] to estimate
et [ay] and
étage *(m)* [ay-tazh] floor
état *(m)* [ay-ta] State; **état** *(m)* [ay-ta] condition, state
éteindre [ay-taNdr] *(light, radio)* to switch off, to turn off
s'étendre [say-tahNdr] to stretch; to lie down, to expand
étendue *(f)* [ay-tahN-dew] area, stretch
éternuer [ay-tehr-nway] to sneeze
étincelle *(f)* [ay-taN-sehl] spark
étoffe *(f)* [ay-tohf] fabric
étoile *(f)* [ay-twal] star
s'étonner (de) [say-to-nay-duh] to wonder
étranger *(m)* [ay-trahN-zhay] foreigner, stranger, **étranger, -ère** [ay-trahN-zhay]/[ay-trahN-zhehr] foreign; strange, unfamiliar; **à l'étranger** [a-lay-trahN-zhay] abroad
être [ehtr] *(v)* to be; **être contre** [eh-truh-kohN-truh] to be against; **être là** [eh-truh-la] to be here; **être pour** [eh-truh-poor] to be in favor of
étroit(e) [ay-trwa(t)] narrow
études *(f pl)* [ay-tewd] studies; **faire des études** [fehr-day-zay-tewd] to study
Europe *(f)* [uuh-rohp] Europe; **Européen(ne)** [uuh-ro-pay-aN]/[uuh-ro-ay-ehn] *(m f)* European; **Européen(ne)** [uuh-ro-pay-aN]/[uuh-ro-pay-ehn] European
évanoui(e) [ay-va-nwee] fainted
événement *(m)* [ay-vehn-(m)ahN] event
éventuellement *(adv)* [ay-vahN-twehl-mahN] possibly
éviter [ay-vee-tay] to avoid
exact(e) [ehg-zakt] exact; **être exact** [ehtr-ehg-zakt] to be exact, to add up
exactitude *(f)* [ehg-zak-tee-tewd] exactness
exagéré(e) [ehg-za-zhay-ray] excessive
examen *(m)* [ehg-za-maN] test, exam
examiner [ehg-za-mee-nay] to examine, to consider
excellent(e) [ehk-seh-lahN] outstanding
exception *(f)* [ehk-sehp-syohN] exception
exclu(e) [ehk-sklew] excluded
excuse [ehk-skewz] excuse
excuser [ehk-skew-zay] to excuse; **s'excuser** [sehk-skew-zay] to apologize; **excusez-moi** [ehk-skew-zay-mwa] excuse me please!; **Je m'excuse!** [zhuh-mehk-skewz] I'm sorry, excuse me!
exemple *(m)* [ehg-zahNpl] example; **par exemple** [par-ehg-zahNpl] for example
exercer [ehg-zehr-say] *(profession)* to practice; **s'exercer** [sehg-zehr-say] to practice
exercice *(m)* [ehg-zehr-sees] exercise, practice
exiger [ehg-zee-zhay] to demand
expédier [ehk-spay-dyay] to send, to dispatch
expérience *(f)* [ehk-spay-ryahNs] experience
expérimenté(e) [ehk-spay-ree-mahN-tay] *(adj)* experienced
expirer [ehk-spee-ray] *(contract)* to expire
expliquer [ehk-splee-kay] *(to make clearer)* to explain
exprès [ehk-sprehs] express
expressément [ehk-spray-say-mahN] expressly
expression *(f)* [ehk-spray-syohN] expression
extérieur *(m)* [ehk-stay-ryuhr] outside, outward appearance; **à l'extérieur** [a-lehk-stay-ryuhr] outside; **à l'extérieur (de)** [a-lehk-stay-ryuhr] outside, outdoors; **de l'extérieur** [duh-lehk-stay-ryuhr] from the outside
externe [ehk-stehrn] external
extincteur *(m)* [ehk-staNk-tuhr] extinguisher
extraordinaire [ehk-stra-ohr-dee-nehr] outstanding

F

face, en de [ahN-fas-duh] in front of
fâcheux, -euse [fa-shuu(z)] regretable; unfortunate

facile [fa-seel] easy
façon *(f)* [fa-sohN] manner; **d'une façon ou d'une autre** [dewn-fa-sohN-oo-dewn-otr] in one way or another
facture *(f)* [fak-tewr] invoice
faible [fehbl] weak
faiblesse *(f)* [feh-blehs] weakness, frailty
faim *(f)* [faN] hunger; **avoir faim** [a-vwar-faN] to be hungry; **qui n'a plus faim** [kee-na-plew-faN] satisfied
faire [fehr] to do, to make; **faire de la contrebande** [fehr-duh-la-kohN-truh-bahNd] to smuggle; **faire enregistrer** [fehr-ahN-ruh-zhees-tray] *(luggage)* to register; **faire faire** [fehr-fehr] to have something done; **faire mal** [fehr-mal] to hurt; **faire part de** [fehr-par-duh] to inform; **faire prendre** [fehr-prahNdr] to catch; **faire la queue** [fehr-la-kuuh] to stand in line; **faire le total de** [fehr-luh-to-tal-duh] to add up; **faire sa valise** [fehr-sa-va-leez] *(suitcase)* to pack; **fait à la main** [feh-maN] hand-made
fait *(m)* [feh] fact; **au fait** [o-feht] by the way; **en fait** *(adv)* [ahN-feht] in fact
famille *(f)* [fa-meey] family
fast-food *(m)* [fast-food] fast food restaurant
fatigant(e) [fa-tee-gahN(t)] tiring
fatigué(e) [fa-tee-gay] tired
faute *(f)* [fot] mistake, fault, responsibility
faux, fausse [fo(s)] false, wrong
faveur *(f)* [fa-vuhr] favor; **en faveur de** [ahN-fa-vuhr-duh] in favor of
félicitations *(f pl)* [fay-lee-see-ta-syohN] congratulations
féliciter [fay-lee-see-tay] to congratulate
féminin(e) [fay-mee-naN]/[fay-mee-neen] feminine
femme [fam] woman, wife
fer *(m)* [fehr] iron; **fer à repasser** *(m)* [fehr-a-ruh-pa-say] iron
ferme *(f)* [fehr(m)] farm
fermé(e) [fehr-may] closed
fermer [fehr-may] to close, to lock, to shut, to fasten; **fermer à clé** [fehr-may-a-klay] to lock
fermeture *(f)* [fehr-(m)uh-tewr] closing
feroce [fay-rohs] wild
fête *(f)* [feht] holiday, party, fair
feu *(m)* [fuuh] fire; **feu d'artifice** *(m)* [fuuh-dar-tee-fees] fireworks
feuille *(f)* [fuhy] leaf
fiable [fee-yabl] reliable
fiancé(e) *(m f)* [fee-yahN-say] engaged
se fiancer avec [suh-fee-yahN-say-a-vehk] to get engaged to
ficelle *(f)* [fee-sehl] string
fidèle [fee-dehl] faithful
fil *(m)* [feel] thread; **fil de fer** *(m)* [feel-duh-fehr] wire
filet *(m)* [fee-lay] net
fille *(f)* [feey] daughter; **jeune fille** *(f)* [zhuhn-feey] young lady
film *(m)* [feel (m)] film
fils *(m)* [fees] son
filtre *(m)* [feeltr] filter
fin *(f)* [faN] end
fin(e) [faN]/[feen] fine, slender
finalement [fee-nal-mahN] finally
fini(e) [fee-nee] finished, accomplished
fixer [fee-ksay] to stare, to pin
flamme *(f)* [fla(m)] flame
flash *(m)* [flash] *(photo)* flash
fleur *(f)* [fluhr] flower
fleurir [fluuh-reer] to be in bloom
fleuve *(m)* [fluhv] river
flirt *(m)* [fluhrt] flirt
foi *(f)* [fwa] faith
foire *(f)* [fwar] *(exhibition)* fair
fois *(f)* [fwa] time; **chaque fois** [shak-fwa] each time; **une fois** [ewn-fwa] once; **encore une fois** [ahN-kohr-ewn-fwa] one more time, once again
fonctionner [fohNk-syo-nay] to work
fontaine *(f)* [fohN-tehn] fountain
force *(f)* [fohrs] strength
forcer [fohr-say] to force, to compel
forfait *(m)* [fohr-say] flat rate
format *(m)* [fohr-ma] format
formation *(f)* [fohr-ma-syohN] training, formation
forme *(f)* [fohrm] form, shape, figure; **en forme** [ahN-fohrm] fit, in shape
former [fohr-may] to form, to put into shape
formidable [fohr-mee-dabl] incredible, tremendous
formulaire *(m)* [fohr-mew-lehr] form
formule *(f)* [fohr-mewl] formula, expression
fort(e) [fohr(t)] strong, big, powerful
fou, folle [foo]/[fohl] mad, insane
foulard *(m)* [foo-lar] scarf
foule *(f)* [fool] crowd
fournir en [foor-neer-ahN] to supply with
fourrure *(f)* [foo-reer] fur
fragile [fra-zheel] fragile, frail

A/Z

frais *(m pl)* [fray] cost, expenses, expenditure
frais, fraîche [fray]/[frehsh] fresh, cool
Français(e) [frahN-seh(z)] *(m f)* French; **français(e)** [frahN-seh(z)] French
France *(f)* [frahNs] France
frapper (à la porte) [fra-pay-a-la-pohrt] to knock on the door
fraude *(f)* [frod] fraud
fréquemment *(adv)* [fray-ka-mahN] frequently
frère *(m)* [frehr] brother
fret *(m)* [freht] freight
frire [freer] to fry
froid(e) [frwa(d)] cold; **avoir froid** [a-vwar-frwa] to be cold
frontière *(f)* [frohN-tyehr] border; **passer la frontière** [pa-say-la-frohN-tyehr] to pass the border
frotter [fro-tay] to scrub, *(wood)* to rub
fumée *(f)* [few-may] smoke
fumer [few-may] to smoke
fumeur *(m)* [few-may] smoker
furieux, -euse [few-ryuu(z)] furious
fusibles *(m pl)* [few-zeebl] *(el)* fuse
futur(e) [few-tewr] future

G

gage *(m)* [gazh] security
gagner [ga-nyay] to win, to earn
gai(e) [gay] cheerful, jolly, bright
gain *(m)* [gaN] earnings, winning
galerie *(f)* [gal-ree] passage
garage *(m)* [ga-razh] garage
garantie *(f)* [ga-rahN-tee] guarantee, warranty
garçon *(m)* [gar-sohN] boy
garde, mettre en (contre) [suh-mehtr-ahN-gard-kohNtr] to warn (against)
garder [gar-day] to keep, to look after, to guard
gardien *(m)* [gar-dyaN] guard
se garer [suh-ga-ray] to park
gauche [gosh] left; **à gauche** [a-gosh] to the left
gêne, sans [sahN-zhehn] inconsiderate
général [zhay-nay-ral] in general
gens *(m pl)* [zhahN] people
gentil(le) [zhaN-tee(y)] kind, friendly
gibier *(m)* [zhee-byay] *(hunting)* game
glace *(f)* [glas] ice
gobelet *(m)* [go-blay] tumbler
goêland *(m)* [go-ay-lahN] seagull
gonfler [gohN-flay] to inflate
gorgée *(f)* [gohr-zhay] gulp
goût *(m)* [goo] taste
goûter [goo-tay] to taste
goutte *(f)* [goot] drop; **tomber goutte à goutte** [tohN-bay-goot-a-goot] to drip
gouvernement *(m)* [goo-vehr-nuh-mahN] government
grâce à [gras-a] thanks to
grand(e) [grahN(d)] big
grandeur *(f)* [grahN-duhr] size
grandir [grahN-deer] *(people)* to grow
grand-mère *(f)* [grahN-mehr] grandmother
grand-père *(m)* [grahN-pehr] grandfather
gras, grasse [gra(s)] fat
gratte-ciel *(m)* [grat-syehl] skyscraper
gratter [gra-tay] to scratch
gratuit(e) [gra-twee(t)] free, gratuitous
gratuitement [gra-tweet-mahN] free, for no reason
grave [grav] solemn; *(sickness)* serious
grille *(f)* [greey] gate
gros, grosse [gro(s)] big, thick
grossir [gro-seer] to put on weight
groupe *(m)* [groop] group
guêpe *(f)* [gehp] wasp
guerre *(f)* [gehr] war
guichet *(m)* [gee-shay] *(Post etc.)* counter, window
guide *(m)* [geed] guide, leader, *(for foreigners)* travel guide
guitare *(f)* [gee-tar] guitar

H

s'habiller [sa-bee-yay] to get dressed
habitant *(m)* [a-bee-tahN] inhabitant, resident
habiter [a-bee-tay] to live in
habitude *(f)* [a-bee-tewd] habit
habituel(le) [a-bee-tew-ehl] *(adj)* usual, regular; **habituellement** *(adv)* usually [a-bee-tew-ehl-mahN]
s'habituer à [sa-bee-tew-ay-a] to get used to; **être habitué(e)** à [eh-tra-bee-tew-ay-a] to be used to
halle *(f)* [al] market *(covered)*
hareng *(m)* [a-rahN] herring
hasard *(m)* [a-zar] chance; **par hasard** [par-a-zar] by chance
haut(e) [o/ot] high; **en haut** [ahN-o] upstairs; at the top; **vers le haut** [vehr-luh-o] around the top
haut-parleur *(m)* [o-par-luhr] loudspeaker

hebdomadaire *(adj)* [ehb-do-ma-dehr] weekly
hébergement *(m)* [ay-behr-zhuh-mahN] lodging, accommodations
hésiter [e-zee-tay] to hesitate
heure *(f)* [uhr] hour; **à l'heure** [a-luhr] *(adv)* on time
heureux, -euse [uuh-ruuh]/[uuh-ruuhz] happy, glad; **heureux, -euse (de)** [duh] happy with
histoire *(f)* [ees-twar] story
hobby *(m)* [o-bee] hobby
homme *(m)* [ohm] man, humankind
honneur *(m)* [o-nuhr] honor
honoraires *(m pl)* [o-no-rehr] fees
horaires d'ouverture *(m pl)* [o-rehr-doo-vehr-tewr] business hours
hors de [ohr-duh] outside; **hors de question** [ohr-duh-kehs-tyohN] out of the question; **hors saison** [ohr-seh-zohN] off-season
hospitalité *(f)* [ohs-pee-ta-lee-tay] hospitality
hôte *(m)* [ot] host, guest
hôtel *(m)* [o-tehl] hotel, guesthouse
hôtesse *(f)* [o-tehs] hostess
huile *(f)* [weel] oil
humain(e) [ew-maN]/[ew-mehn] human
humeur *(f)* [ew-muhr] mood
humide [ew-meed] humid

I

ici [ee-see] here, at this point
idée *(f)* [ee-day] idea, thought, views; **aucune idée!** [o-kewn-ee-day] no idea!
il [eel] he
il y a [eel-ya] there is
île *(f)* [eel] island
illuminé(e) [ee-lew-mee-nay] illuminated
illustration *(f)* [ee-lews-tra-syohN] illustration
immédiatement *(adv)* [ee-may-dyat-mahN] immediately; at once
impoli(e) [aN-po-lee] rude, impolite
importance *(f)* [aN-pohr-tahNs] importance, significance; **sans importance** [sahN-zaN-pohr-tahNs] unimportant
important(e) [aN-pohr-tahN(t)] important, considerable, large
n'importe qui [naN-pohr-tuh-kee] anyone
importuner [aN-pohr-tew-nay] to bother, to disturb
impossible [aN-po-seebl] impossible
imprécis(e) [aN-pray-see(z)] imprecise, inaccurate
impression *(f)* [aN-pray-syohN] impression
impropre [aN-prohpr] unsuitable, inappropriate
imprudent(e) [aN-prew-dahN] careless
inadvertance *(f)* [ee-nad-vehr-tahNs] oversight; **par inadvertance** [par-ee-nad-vehr-tahNs] inadvertently
inattendu(e) [i-na-tahN-dew] unexpected
incapable [aN-ka-pabl] incapable, incompetent
incendie *(m)* [aN-sahN-dee] fire
incertain(e) [aN-sehr-taN/tehn] uncertain, unsure, doubtful
incident *(m)* [aN-see-dahN] incident, event
inclure [aN-klewr] to include
incomplet, -ète [aN-kohN-play]/[aN-kohN-pleht] unfinished
inconfortable [aN-kohN-fohr-tabl] uncomfortable, awkward
inconnu(e) [aN-ko-new] unknown; *(m f)* the unknown
inconsistant(e) [aN-kohN-sees-tahN(t)] *(person)* superficial
inconvénient *(m)* [aN-kohN-vay-nyahN] drawback
incroyable [aN-krwa-yabl] unbelievable
indécent(e) [aN-day-sahN(t)] indecent
indécis(e) [aN-day-see(z)] unsettled, undecided
indésirable [aN-day-zee-rabl] undesirable, unwanted
indéterminé(e) [aN-day-tehr-mee-nay] unspecified
indication *(f)* [aN-dee-ka-syohN] instruction **donner des indications** [do-nay-day-zaN-dee-ka-syohN] to give instructions
indice *(m)* [aN-dees] sign
indiquer [aN-dee-kay] to point out, to show
indispensable [aN-dees-pahN-sabl] indispensable
inévitable [ee-nay-vee-tabl] unavoidable
inexpérimenté(e) [ee-nehks-pay-ree-mahN-tay] inexperienced
infirmerie *(f)* [aN-feer-muh-ree] infirmary
infirmière *(f)* [aN-feer-myehr]; **infirmier** *(m)* nurse
inflammable [aN-fla-mabl] flammable
information *(f)* [aN-fohr-ma-syohN] information

A/Z

informer [aN-fohr-may] to inform, to advise
ingrat(e) [aN-gra(t)] thankless, ungrateful
inhabituel(le) [ee-na-bee-tew-ehl] unusual
injuste [aN-zhewst] unjust, unfair
injustice *(f)* [aN-zhews-tees] injustice, wrong
innocent(e) [ee-no-sahn] innocent
inquiet, -iète [aN-kyay]/[aN-kyeht] worried
insecte *(m)* [aN-sehkt] insect
insignifiant(e) [aN-see-nee-fyahN(t)] trivial, insignificant
insister sur [aN-sees-tay-sewr] to stress, to emphasize
instable [aN-stabl] *(person)* unsteady
installation *(f)* [aN-sta-la-syohN] installation
instant *(m)* [An-stahN] instant, moment
instruction *(f)* [aN-strewk-syohN] instruction; *(school)* education
insuffisant(e) [aN-sew-fee-zahn] insufficient
insupportable [aN-sew-pohr-tabl] unbearable
intelligence *(f)* [aN-teh-lee-zhahNs] intelligence
intelligent(e) [aN-tay-lee-zhahN(t)] clever
intention *(f)* [aN-tahN-syohN] intention; **avoir l'intention de** [a-vwar-laN-tahN-syohN-duh] to intend to
interdiction *(f)* [aN-tehr-deek-syohN] ban
interdire [aN-tehr-deer] to forbid
interdit(e) [aN-tehr-dee(t)] forbidden
intéressant(e) [aN-tay-ray-sahN(t)] interesting; (price) attractive
s'intéresser à [saN-tay-ray-say-a] to be interested in
intérêt *(m)* [aN-tay-ray] interest
intérieur *(m)* [aN-tay-ryuhr] inside; **à l'intérieur** [a-laN-tay-ryuhr] inside, in, within
intermédiaire *(m)* [aN-tehr-may-dyehr] go-between
international(e) [aN-tehr-na-syo-nal] international
interroger [aN-tay-ro-zhay] to ask
interrompre [aN-tay-rohNpr] to interrupt; to break
interrupteur *(m)* [aN-tay-rewp-tuhr] *(el)* switch
interruption *(f)* [aN-tay-rewp-syohN] interruption, breaking off
intervalle *(m)* [aN-tehr-val] interval
intonation *(f)* [aN-to-na-syohN] tone, intonation
inutile [ee-new-teel] useless, pointless, vain; **inutilement** needlessly, unnecessarily
inventer [aN-vahN-tay] to invent
inversement [aN-vehr-suh-mahN] conversely
invitation *(f)* [aN-vee-ta-syohN] invitation
invité(e) *(m f)* [aN-vee-tay] guest
inviter [aN-vee-tay] to invite, to call upon
invraisemblable [aN-vray-sahN-bla-bluh] unlikely
irrégulier, -ière [ee-ray-gew-lyay]/[ee-ray-gew-lyehr] irregular
s'irriter de [see-ree-tay-duh] to get annoyed
isolé(e) [ee-zo-lay] isolated
itinéraire *(m)* [ee-tee-nay-rehr] travel route, itinerary
ivre [eevr] drunk

J

jamais [zha-may] never; **ne (verb) jamais** [nuh] ... [zha-may] never
jardin *(m)* [zhar-daN] garden
je [zhuh]
jet d'eau *(m)* [zhay-do] water fountain
jetée *(f)* [zhuh-tay] pier, jetty
jeter [zhuh-tay] to throw; **se jeter** [suh-zhuh-tay] *(river)* to flow, to run into
jeu *(m)* [zhuuh] game; **jeu de cartes** *(m)* [zhuuh-duh-kart] card game
jeun, à [a-zhaN] on an empty stomach
jeune [zhuhn] young; early; **jeune fille** *(f)* [zhuhn-feey] young lady
jeunesse *(f)* [zhuuh-nehs] youth
joie *(f)* [zhwa] joy, delight
joli(e) [zho-lee] pretty, nice
jouer [zhoo-ay] to play
jouet [zhway] *(m)* toy
jouir de [zhweer-duh] to enjoy
jour *(m)* [zhoor] day; **jour férié** *(m)* [zhoor-fay-ryay] holiday; **de jour** [duh-zhoor] daytime; **les jours ouvrables** [lay-zhoor-zoo-vrabl] weekdays
journal *(m)* [zhoor-nal] newspaper
juge *(m)* [zhewzh] judge
jugement *(m)* [zhewzh-mahN] ruling
juger [zhew-zhay] to try, to judge
jumelles *(f pl)* [zhew-mehl] binoculars
jusqu'à [zhews-ka] up to; **jusqu'à maintenant** [zhews-ka-maNt-nahN] until now
juste [zhewst] right, appropriate, accurate

A/Z

K

kiosque (à journaux) *(m)* [kyohs-ka-zhoor-no] newsstand

L

là [la] here; **là-bas** [la-ba] down there; **là-haut** [la-o] up there; **là en bas** [la-ahN-ba] under there; **être là** [eh-truh-la] to be there
lac *(m)* [lak] lake
lacet *(m)* [la-say] shoelace
laid(e) [leh(d)] ugly
laisser [lay-say] to leave
lampe *(f)* [lahNp] lamp
langue *(f)* [lahNg] tongue, language
large [larzh] (cloth) wide, baggy
laver [la-vay] to wash
léger, -ère [lay-zhay]/[lay-zhehr] *(weight)* light
lent(e) *(adj)* [lahN(t)] slow; **lentement** *(adv)* [lahNt-mahN] slowly
lessive *(f)* [lay-seev] laundry
lettre *(f)* [lehtr] letter, character
leur [luhr] their
lever [luh-vay] to raise; **se lever** [suh-luh-vay] to get up; **au lever du soleil** [o-luh-vay-dew-so-lehy] at sunrise
libre [leebr] free
lier [lee-yay] to bind
lieu *(m)* [lyuuh] place; **au lieu de** [o-lyuuh-duh] instead of; **avoir lieu** [a-vwar-lyuuh] to take place
ligne *(f)* [leeny] line; (train) service; *(el, tele)* line
liquide [lee-keed] liquid
lire [leer] to read
liste *(f)* [leest] list, roll
lit *(m)* [lee] bed
livre *(m)* [leevr] book
livrer [lee-vray] to deliver
local(e) [lo-kal] local
localité *(f)* [lo-ka-lee-tay] village
logique(ment) [lo-zheek-(mahN)] logical(ly)
loin [lwaN] *(way)* far
long, longue [lohN]/[lohNg] long; **le long de** [luh-lohN-duh] along
longueur *(f)* [lohN-guhr] length
louer [loo-ay] to rent, to book, to hire
lourd(e) [loor(d)] heavy
loyal(e) [lwa-yal] faithful
loyer [lwa-yay] *(m)* rent
lui [lwee] his; him
lumière *(f)* [lew-myehr] light
lumineux, -euse [lew-mee-nuuh(z)] luminous
lune *(f)* [lewn] moon
lunettes *(f)* pl [lew-neht] glasses; **lunettes de soleil** *(f pl)* [lew-neht-duh-so-lehy] sunglasses
luxe *(m)* [lewks] luxury
luxueux, -euse [lewk-syuuh]/[lewk-syuuhz] luxurious

M

ma [ma] my
machine *(f)* [ma-sheen] machine
madame (before the name) [ma-dam] Mrs.
mademoiselle [mad-mwa-zehl] Miss
magasin *(m)* [ma-ga-zaN] store, shop; **grand magasin** *(m)* [grahN-ma-ga-zaN] department store
magnifique [ma-nee-feek] splendid
maigre [mehgr] thin
maigrir [meh-greer] to become thin, to lose weight
main *(f)* [maN] hand; **fait à la main** [feh-maN] handmade
maintenant [maNt-nahN] now
mais [meh] but
maison *(f)* [meh-zohN] house; **maison de campagne** *(f)* [meh-zohN-duh-kahN-pany] country home; **à la maison** [a-la-meh-zohN] at home
mal *(adv)* [mal] badly; **mal à l'aise** [ma-la-lehz] uneasy; **mal comprendre** [mal-kohN-prahNdr] to misunderstand; **faire mal** [fehr-mal] to hurt; **j'ai mal au cœur** [zhay-mal-o-kuhr] I feel sick
malade [ma-lad] sick; **tomber malade** [tohN-bay-ma-lad] to be taken ill
malentendu *(m)* [ma-lahN-tahN-dew] misunderstanding
malgré [mal-gray] in spite of; **malgré cela** [mal-gray-suh-la] despite this
malheur *(m)* [mal-uhr] misfortune; **par malheur** [par-mal-uhr] unfortunately
malheureusement [ma-luuh-ruuhz-mahN] unfortunately
malheureux, -euse [ma-luuh-ruuh]/[ma-luuh-ruuhz] unhappy
malsain(e) [mal-saN]/[mal-sehn] unhealthy
Manche *(f)* [mahNsh] English Channel

A/Z

manger [mahN-zhay] to eat; **en mangeant** [ahN-mahN-zhahN] by eating
manière *(f)* [ma-nyehr] way, manner
manifestation *(f)* [ma-nee-fehs-ta-syohN] demonstration
manque *(m)* [mahNk-duh] lack of, not enough
manquer [mahN-kay] to miss, to be absent, to lack
se maquiller [suh-ma-kee-yay] to make oneself up, to put on makeup
marais *(m)* [ma-ray] swamp
marchander [mar-shahN-day] to haggle over
marchandise *(f)* [mar-shahN-deez] merchandise, goods
marcher [mar-shay] to go *(on foot)*
marécage *(m)* [ma-ray-kazh] swamp
mari *(m)* [ma-ree] husband
mariage *(m)* [ma-ryazh] marriage, union, mixture
marié(e) à [ma-ryay-a] married to
se marier [suh-ma-ryay] to get married
marque *(f)* [mark] mark, label
marron [ma-rohN] brown
marteau *(m)* [mar-to] hammer
masculin(e) [mas-kew-laN]/[mas-kew-leen] masculin
matériel *(m)* [ma-tay-ryehl] material
matin *(m)* [ma-taN] morning
matinée *(f)* [ma-tee-nay] morning
mauvais(e) [mo-veh(z)] bad, faulty
maximum, au [o-mak-see-mohm] at the most
mazout *(m)* [ma-zoot] fuel oil
me [muh] me
méchant(e) [may-shahN(t)] nasty, wicked
mécontent(e) [may-kohN-tahN(t)] dissatisfied
Méditerranée *(f)* [may-dee-tay-ra-nay] Mediterranean Sea
méduse *(f)* [may-dewz] jellyfish
se méfier de [suh-may-fyay-duh] to mistrust
meilleur(e) [meh-yuhr] better
mélangé(e) [may-lahN-zhay] mixed
même [mehm] same; even; **le/la même** *(m f)* [luh/la-mehm] the same; **la même chose** *(f)* [la-mehm-shoz] the same thing; **même pas** [mehm-pa] not even
ménage, faire le [fehr-luh-may-nazh] to clean
mensonge *(m)* [mahN-sohNzh] lie
mensuel(le) *(adj)* [mahN-sew-ehl] monthly
mentir [mahN-teer] to lie
mer *(f)* [mehr] sea; **mer du Nord** *(f)* [mehr-dew-nohr] the North Sea
mère *(f)* [mehr] mother
mérite *(m)* [may-reet] merit, worth
mériter [may-ree-tay] to be worth, to deserve
merveilleux, -euse [mehr-veh-yuuh(z)] wonderful
messe *(f)* [mehs] *(religious)* Mass
mesure *(f)* [muh-zewr] measure
mesurer [muh-zew-ray] to measure
mettre [mehtr] to set, to put, to lay, to switch on; *(time)* to set; **mettre à la boîte** [mehtr-ahN-bwat] *(letter)* to mail; **mettre en garde contre** [meh-trahN-gard-kohNtr] to warn against; **se mettre d'accord** [suh-mehtr-da-kohr] to agree; **se mettre en colère** [suh-meh-trahN-ko-lehr] to get angry
meuble *(m)* [muhbl] furniture
meubler [muuh-blay] to furnish
midi *(m)* [mee-dee] noon
mieux [myuuh] *(adv)* better; **mieux que** [myuuh-kuh] better than
milieu *(m)* [mee-lyuuh] middle
mince [maNs] thin, slender
minime [mee-neem] minimal
minimum *(m)* [mee-nee-mohm] minimum
minuit [mee-nwee] midnight; **à minuit** [a-mee-nwee] at midnight
minute *(f)* [mee-newt] minute
mixte [meekst] mixed
mobilier *(m)* [mo-bee-lyay] *(apartment)* furniture
mode *(f)* [mohd] fashion; **à la mode** [a-la-mohd] fashionable
modèle *(m)* [mo-dehl] model
modéré(e) [mo-day-ray] moderate
moderne [mo-dehrn] modern
modifier [mo-dee-fyay] to modify, to alter
moi [mwa] me; **à moi** [a-mwa] mine
moindre [mwaNdr] lesser
moins [mwaN] less; minus; **au moins** [o-mwaN] at least
mois *(m)* [mwa] month; **par mois** *(adv)* [par-mwa] monthly
moitié *(f)* [mwa-tyay] half; **à moitié** *(adv)* [a-mwa-tyay] half
moment *(m)* [mo-mahN] moment
mon [mohN] my
monde *(m)* [mohNd] world
monnaie *(f)* [mo-nay] money; **pièce de monnaie** *(f)* [pyehs-duh-mo-nay] coin
monsieur [muh-syuuh] sir
montant *(m)* [mohN-tahN] amount, sum

monter [mohN-tay] to go up, to climb; **en montant** [ahN-mohN-tahN] going up; **monter à bord** [mohN-tay-a-bohr] to get on board
montre(-bracelet) *(f)* [bra-slay-mohNtr] watch(band)
montrer [mohN-tray] to show
morceau *(m)* [mohr-so] piece
mordre [mohr-druh] to bite
mort *(f)* [mohr] death
mort(e) [mohr(t)] dead
mot *(m)* [mo] word
motif *(m)* [mo-teef] reason, ground, design
mou *(m)*, **molle** *(f)* [moo]/[mohl] weak
mouche *(f)* [moosh] fly
mouette *(f)* [mweht] seagull
mouillé(e) [moo-yay] wet
mourir [moo-reer] to die
moustique *(m)* [moos-teek] mosquito
mouton *(m)* [moo-tohN] sheep
mouvement *(m)* [moov-mahN] movement
moyen *(m)* [mwa-yaN] mean, way
moyen, ne [mwa-yaN]/[mwa-yehn] *(adj)* middle
moyenne *(f)* [mwa-yehn] average; **en moyenne** *(adv)* [ahN-mwa-yehn] on average
multicolore [mewl-tee-ko-lohr] colorful, many-colored
mur *(m)* [mewr] wall
mûr(e) [mewr] ripe
musique *(f)* [mew-zeek] music

N

nager [na-zhay] to swim
naissance *(f)* [nay-sahNs] birth
natif, -ive [na-teef]/[na-teev] native
nation *(f)* [na-syohN] nation
national(e) [na-syo-nal] national
nature *(f)* [na-tewr] nature
naturel(le) *(adj)* [na-tew-rehl] natural; **naturellement** *(adv)* [na-tew-rehl-mahn] naturally
ne...que [nuh]...[kuh] no earlier than, only
né(e) [nay] born
nécessaire [nay-say-sehr] necessary
nécessité *(f)* [nay-say-see-tay] necessity, need
négatif, -ive [nay-ga-teef]/[nay-ga-teev] negative
négligent(e) [nay-gli-zhahN(t)] careless
négliger [nay-glee-zhay] to neglect, to disregard
négociations *(f pl)* [nay-go-sya-syohN] negociations
neiger [nay-zhay] to snow
nerveux, -euse [nehr-vuuh]/[nehr-vuuhz] nervous
n'est-ce pas? [nehs-pa] is it not?
nettoyer [nay-twa-yay] to clean
neuf, neuve [nuhf]/[nuhv] new, not used
neveu *(m)* [nuh-vuuh] nephew
ni ... ni [nee]...[nee] neither ... nor
nièce *(f)* [nyehs] niece
nier [nee-ay] to deny
noce *(f)* [nohs] wedding party
nœud *(m)* [noht] knot
nom *(m)* [nohN] name
nombre *(m)* [nohN-bruh] number
nombreux, -euse [nohN-bruuh]/[nohN-bruuhz] many, numerous
Nord *(m)* [nohr] North; **au nord de** [o-nohr-duh] to the north of
normal(e) [nohr-mal] normal; **normalement** [nohr-mal-mahN] normally
nos [no] our
note *(f)* [noht] grade; *(hotel)* bill
noter [no-tay] to take note
notre [nohtr] our
nourrissant(e) [noo-ree-sahN(t)] nourishing
nourriture *(f)* [noo-ree-tewr] food
nous [noo] we, us; **à nous** [a-noo] ours
nouveau [noo-vo] **nouvel(le)** [noo-vehl] new, latest; **de nouveau** [duh-noo-vo] again
nouveauté *(f)* [noo-vo-tay] novelty
nouvelle *(f)* [noo-vehl] news
nu(e) [new] naked
nuire [nweer] to harm
nuisible [nwee-zeebl] harmful
nuit *(f)* [nwee] night; **cette nuit** [seht-nwee] tonight
nulle part [newl-par] nowhere
numéro *(m)* [new-may-ro] number

O

objet *(m)* [ohb-zhay] object; **objets de valeur** *(m pl)* [ohb-zhay-duh-va-luhr] valuables
obligation *(f)* [o-blee-ga-syohN] obligation
obligé(e) être de [eh-tro-blee-zhay-duh] to have to
obligeance *(f)* [o-blee-zhahNs] kindness
obscur(e) [ohb-skewr] dark
observer [ohb-sehr-vay] to observe

obtenir [ohb-tuh-neer] to obtain, to get, to receive
obturateur *(m)* [ohb-tew-ra-tuhr] *(photo)* shutter
occasion *(f)* [o-ka-syohN] occasion, opportunity
occupé(e) [o-kew-pay] busy; *(seat)* occupied
s'occuper de [so-kew-pay-duh] to take care of, to deal with
océan *(m)* [o-say-ahN] ocean
odeur *(f)* [o-duhr] smell
œil *(m)* [uhy] eye
œuf *(m)* [uhf] egg; **œufs** *(m pl)* [uuh] eggs
offense *(f)* [o-fahNs] insult
offenser [o-fahN-say] to insult, to offend
office *(m)* [o-fees] *(kitchen)* pantry; **office de tourisme** *(m)* [o-fees-duh-too-reesm] tourist office
officiel(le) [o-fee-syehl] official, formal
offrir [o-freer] to offer, to give, to present
oiseau *(m)* [wa-zo] bird
ombre *(f)* [ohNbr] shadow
on [ohN] one
oncle *(m)* [ohNkl] uncle
ongle *(m)* [ohNgl] fingernail
opérer [o-pay-ray] to operate on, to carry out
opinion *(f)* [o-pee-nyohN] opinion
opportun(e) [o-pohr-taN]/[o-pohr-tewn] opportune
opposé(e) [o-po-zay] opposite; **dans la direction opposée** [dahN-la-dee-rehk-syohN-o-po-zay] in the opposite direction
orage *(m)* [o-razh] storm
orchestre *(m)* [ohr-kehstr] orchestra
ordre *(m)* [ohrdr] order; **ordres** *(m pl)* [ohrdr] *(religious)* orders; **en ordre** [ahN-nohrdr] orderly; **de premier ordre** [duh-pruh-myehr-ohrdr] first-class
ordures *(f pl)* [ohr-dewr] garbage, rubbish
oreiller *(m)* [o-reh-yay] pillow
organiser [ohr-ga-nee-zay] to organize
originaire [o-ree-zhee-nehr] native of; **être originaire de** [ehtr-o-ree-zhee-nehr-duh] to come from, to be born in
oser [o-zay] to dare
ou [oo] or; **ou...ou** [oo]...[oo] either...or; **ou bie ...ou bien** [oo-byaN]...[oo-byaN] or...or
oublier [oo-blee-yay] to forget, to leave out
Ouest *(m)* [wehst] West
oursin *(m)* [oor-saN] sea urchin
outre, en [ahN-nootr] furthermore
outre-mer *(m)* [oo-truh-mehr] overseas
ouvert(e) [oo-vehr(t)] open
ouvrir [oo-vreer] to open

P

page *(f)* [pazh] *(book)* page
paie *(f)* [pehy] pay, wages
paiement *(m)* [peh-mahN] payment
paire *(f)* [pehr] pair
paix *(f)* [peh] peace
pâle [pal] pale
panier *(m)* [pa-nyay] basket
panne *(f)* [pan] breakdown; **en panne** [ahN-pan] broken down
panneau *(m)* [pa-no] notice, sign *(road)*
panorama *(m)* [pa-no-ra-ma] panorama
pansement *(m)* [pahNs-mahN] *(med)* dressing, bandage
papier *(m)* [pa-pyay] paper; **papier hygiénique** *(m)* [pa-pyay-ee-zhyay-neek] toilet paper
paquet *(m)* [pa-kay] packages, parcel; **petit paquet** *(m)* [puh-tee-pa-kay] small package
par [par] per, by
paraître [pa-rehtr] to appear
parapluie *(m)* [pa-ra-plwee] umbrella
parc *(m)* [park] park
parce que [par-suh-kuh] because
pardon [par-dohN] *(m)* forgiveness; **pardon?** [par-dohN] sorry?
pardonner [par-do-nay] to forgive
pareil(le) [pa-rehy] same
parent(e) [pa-rahN(t)] related
parents *(m pl)* [pa-rahN] parents
paresseux, -euse [pa-ray-suuh]/[pa-ray-suuhz] lazy
parfait(e) [par-feh(t)] perfect
pari *(m)* [pa-ree] bet
parier [pa-ryay] to bet
parler [par-lay] to speak, to talk; **parler fort** [par-lay-fohr] to speak loudly; **parler à voix basse** [par-lay-a-vwa-bas] to speak in a low voice
parmi [par-mee] among *(several)*
part *(f)* [par] part; **à part** [a-par] aside; **à part ça** [a-par-sa] aside from this
partager [par-ta-zhay] to share
parti(e) [par-tee] gone
partie *(f)* [par-tee] part
partir [par-teer] to leave, to set off;

partir de [par-teer-duh] to start from; **partir pour** [par-teer-poor] to set off (for)
partisan *(m)* [par-tee-zahN] partisan
partout [par-too] everywhere
pas *(m)* [pa] step
(ne ...) pas [pa] not; **(ne ...) pas du tout** [pa-dew-too] not at all, not in the least; **(ne ...) pas encore** [pa-zahN-kohr] not yet; **(ne ...) pas non plus** [pa-nohN-plew] not either; **(ne ...) même pas** [mehm-pa] not even
passage *(m)* [pa-sazh] crossing, traffic, way, passage; **passage souterrain** *(m)* [pa-sazh-soo-tay-raN] underground passage
passager *(m)* [pa-sa-zhay] passenger
passé *(m)* [pa-say] past
passé(e) [pa-say] past
passeport *(m)* [pas-pohr] passport
passer [pa-say] to go past; *(time)* to spend, to pass; **passer quelqu'un** [pa-say-kehl-kaN] *(tele)* to put s.o. on the line; **passer (à côté)** [pa-say-a-ko-tay] to go by; **passer la frontière** [pa-say-la-frohN-tyehr] to cross the border; **passer la nuit** [pa-say-la-nwee] to spend the night; **se passer** [suh-pa-say] to happen, occur
passerelle *(f)* [pas-rehl] gangway
passe-temps *(m)* [pas-tahN] hobby
patience *(f)* [pa-syahNs] patience
patient(e) [pa-syahN(t)] patient
patrie *(f)* [ap-tree] motherland
patron *(m)* [pa-trohN] boss, manager
pauvre [povr] poor
payer [pay-yay] to pay; **payer comptant/en liquide** [pay-yay [kohN-tahN]/ahN-lee-keed] to pay cash
pays *(m)* [peh-ee] country; **pays natal** *(m)* [peh-ee-na-tal] native land
paysan *(m)* [peh-ee-zahN] peasant
pêcher [pay-shay] to fish, to track down
peindre [paNdr] to paint
peine *(f)* [pehn] penalty, trouble; **à peine** [a-pehn] barely
pellicule *(f)* [pay-lee-kewl] film
pelouse *(f)* [puh-looz] lawn
pendant prep [pahN-dahN] while; **pendant un certain temps** [pahN-dahN-aN-sehr-taN-tahN] for a while; **pendant la semaine** [pahN-dahN-la-smehn] during the week; **pendant que** *(conj)* [pahN-dahN-kuh] while
pendule *(f)* [pahN-dewl] clock
penser [pahN-say] to think; to consider; **penser à** [pahN-say-a] to think about
pension de famille *(f)* [pahN-syohN] guesthouse
pente *(f)* [pahNt] slope
perdre [pehrdr] to lose
père *(m)* [pehr] father
périmé(e) [pay-ree-may] out-of-date
périphérie *(f)* [pay-ree-fay-ree] periphery
permettre [pehr-mehtr] to allow
permis(e) [pehr-mee(z)] permitted
permission *(f)* [pehr-mee-syohN] permission
personne *(f)* [pehr-sohn] person; **ne personne** *(v)* [nuh]...[pehr-sohn] no one
personnel *(m)* [pehr-so-nehl] workforce
personnel(le) [pehr-so-nehl] personal
persuader [pehr-sew-a-day] to convince
perte *(f)* [pehrt] loss
peser [puh-zay] to weigh
petit(e) [puh-tee(t)] small
petite-fille *(f)* [puh-teet-feey] granddaughter
petit-fils *(m)* [puh-tee-fees] grandson
peu [puuh] little; **à peu près** [a-puuh-pray] almost; **un peu** [aN-puuh] a little
peuple *(m)* [puhpl] people
peur *(f)* [puhr] fear; **avoir peur de** [a-vwar-puhr-duh] to be afraid of
peut-être [puuh-tehtr] maybe
phare *(m)* [far] lighthouse
photo *(f)* [fo-to] photo, picture; **prendre une photo** [prahNdr-ewn-fo-to] to take a picture
photographier [fo-to-gra-fyay] to photograph; to take pictures
phrase *(f)* [fraz] sentence
pièce *(f)* [pyehs] piece; room; **pièce d'identité** *(f)* [pyehs-dee-dahN-tee-tay] ID, proof of identity; **pièce de monnaie** *(f)* [pyehs-duh-mo-nay] coin; **pièce(s) jointe(s)** *(f pl)* [pyehs-zhwaNt] *(letter)* enclosures
pierre *(f)* [pyehr] stone
pierreux, -euse [pyay-ruuh(z)] stony
piéton *(m)* [pyay-tohN] pedestrian
pile *(f)* [peel] *(flashlight)* battery
pince *(f)* [paNs] pliers
pipe *(f)* [peep] pipe
piquer [pee-kay] to prick
piquet *(m)* [pee-kay] stake
pire [peer] worse; **le pire** [luh-peer] the worst
piscine *(f)* [pee-seen] swimming pool
pitié *(f)* [pee-tyay] pity
place *(f)* [plas] place
plafond *(m)* [pla-fohN] ceiling

plage *(f)* [plazh] beach
se plaindre (de) [suh-plaN-druh-duh] to complain *(about)*
plaine *(f)* [plehn] plain
plainte *(f)* [plaNt] complaint
plaire [plehr] to please
plaisanterie *(f)* [pleh-zahN-tuh-ree] joke
plaisir *(m)* [play-zeer] pleasure, fun; **sans plaisir** [sahN-play-zeer] without pleasure
plan *(m)* [plahN] plan; **plan de la ville** *(m)* [plahN-duh-la-veel] city map
plancher *(m)* [plahN-shay] floor
plante *(f)* [plahNt] plant
plaque *(f)* [plak] license plate
plastique *(m)* [plas-teek] plastic
plat *(m)* [pla] dish, course, platter
plat(e) [pla(t)] flat
plâtre *(m)* [platr] plaster
plein(e) [plaN]/[plehn] full, loaded; **en plein air** [ahN-pleh-nehr] in the open
pleurer [pluuh-ray] to cry
pleuvoir [pluuh-vwar] to rain
plombs [plohN] *(m pl) (el)* fuse
plume *(f)* [plewm] feather
plus [plew] more, plus; **plus de** [plew-duh] more than; **plus que** [plew-kuh] more than; **plus ou moins** [plew-zoo-mwaN] more or less; **au plus** [o-plews] at the most; **en plus** [ahN-plews] moreover
plutôt [plew-to] rather, instead
poche *(f)* [pohsh] pocket
poêle *(m)* [pwal] frying pan, stove
poids *(m)* [pwa] weight
poignée *(f)* [pwa-nyay] handshake, handful
point *(m)* [pwaN] point; **à point** [a-pwaN] *(cooking)* well-done
pointe *(f)* [pwaNt] peak, point
pointu(e) [pwaN-tew] sharp
pointure *(f)* [pwaN-tewr] *(shoe)* size
poire *(f)* [pwar] pear
poison *(m)* [pwa-zohN] poison
poisson *(m)* [pwa-sohN] fish
poissonnier *(m)* [pwa-sohn-ree] fish-monger
poli(e) [po-lee] polite
politesse *(f)* [po-lee-tehs] politeness
politique *(f)* [po-lee-teek] politics
pompiers *(m pl)* [pohN-pyay] firemen
portail [pohr-tay] *(m)* gate
porte *(f)* [pohrt] door; **porte d'entrée** *(f)* [pohrt-dahN-tray] entrance gate; **porte de la maison/de l'immeuble** *(f)* [pohrt-duh-[la-meh-zohN]/[lee-muhbl]] front door
porte-documents *(m)* [pohrt-do-kew-mahN] document case
portefeuille *(m)* [pohr-tuh-fuhy] wallet
porte-manteau *(m)* [pohrt-mahN-to] coat hanger
porte-monnaie *(m)* [pohrt-mo-nay] coin purse
porter [pohr-tay] to carry
poser [po-zay] to lay
positif, -ive [po-zee-teef]/[po-zee-teev] positive
position *(f)* [po-zee-syohN] position
posséder [po-say-day] to own
possession *(f)* [po-say-syohN] ownership
possibilité *(f)* [po-see-bee-lee-tay] possibility
possible [po-seebl] possible; **rendre possible** [rahN-druh-po-seebl] to make possible
poste *(f)* [pohst] post; **poste (de radio)** *(m)* [pohs-tuh-duh-ra-dyo] receiving set
potable [po-tabl] potable
poterie *(f)* [poh-tree] pottery
poubelle *(f)* [poo-behl] garbage can, trash can
poudre *(f)* [poodr] powder
poupée *(f)* [poo-pay] doll
pour [poor] for; (reason) for; **être pour** [eh-truh-poor] to be in favor of; **pour cette raison** [poor-seht-reh-zohN] for this reason; **pour ma part** [poor-ma-par] as for me; **pour cent** [poor-sahN] per cent
pourcentage *(m)* [poor-sahN-tazh] percentage
pourparlers *(m pl)* [poor-par-lay] negotiations
pourquoi [poor-kwa] why; **c'est pourquoi** [say-poor-kwa] therefore, it is why
pourri(e) [poo-ree] rotten, spoiled
pourrir [poo-reer] to become rotten, to decay, to rot
pourtant [poor-tahN] yet, even so
pousser [poo-say] to push, to shove, to utter; *(plant)* to grow
poussière *(f)* [poo-syehr] dust
pouvoir [poo-vwar] to be able to
pratique *(f)* [pra-teek] practice; *(adj)* practical; **peu pratique** [puuh-pra-teek] impractical
pré *(m)* [pray] meadow
précaution *(f)* [pray-ko-syohN] precaution

précision *(f)* [pray-see-zyohN] preciseness; **précisions** *(f pl)* [pray-see-zyohN] information, details

préférence *(f)* [pray-fay-rahNs] preference

préférer to [pray-fay-ray] prefer

premier, -ière [pruh-myay]/[pruh-myehr] first; **de premier ordre** [duh-pruh-myay-rohrdr] first class; **le premier venu** [luh-pruh-myay-vuh-new] first one to come; **premiers secours** [pruh-myay-suh-koor] *(m pl)* first aid; **premièrement** [pruh-myehr-mahN] firstly

prendre [prahNdr] to take; to pick up; *(means of transport)* to take; **prendre congé** [prahN-druh-kohN-zhay] to take leave; **prendre note** [prahN-druh-noht] to take note; **prendre part (à)** [prahN-druh-par-a] to take part (in); **faire prendre** [fehr-prahNdr] to have s.o. take

préparer [pray-pa-ray] to prepare, to be working on; *(food)* to prepare, to make

près de [pray-duh] nearby; **à peu près** [a-puuh-pray] about, around

prescription *(f)* [prehs-kreep-syohN] prescription

présent(e) [pray-zahN(t)] present; **être présent** [eh-truh-pray-zahN] to be present; **à présent** [a-pray-zahN] now

présentation *(f)* [pray-zahN-ta-syohN] presentation

présenter [pray-zahN-tay] to introduce, to present

préservatif *(m)* [pray-zehr-va-teef] condom

presque [prehsk] almost, nearly

pressé(e) [pray-say] in a hurry; **être pressé(e)** [eh-truh-pray-say] to be in a hurry

prêt(e) [preh(t)] ready; willing

prêter [pray-tay] to lend to s.o.

prétexte *(m)* [pray-tehks] pretext

prêtre *(m)* [prehtr] priest

preuve *(f)* [pruhv] proof

prévenir quelqu'un [pray-vuh-neer-kehl-kaN] to inform s.o., to warn s.o.

prier [pree-yay] to request

prière *(f)* [pree-yehr] request

principal(e) [praN-see-pal] *(adj)* main; **principalement** *(adv)* [praN-see-pal-mahN] mainly

priorité *(f)* [pree-yo-ree-tay] priority, right of way

privé(e) [pree-vay] private

prix *(m)* [pree] price; **prix d'entrée** *(m)* [pree-dahN-tray] entrance fee

probabilité *(f)* [pro-ba-bee-lee-tay] probability

probable(ment) [pro-ba-bluh-(mahN)] probable(ly)

procession *(f)* [pro-say-syohN] procession

prochainement [pro-shay-nuh-mahN] shortly, soon

proche [prohsh] nearby

procuration *(f)* [pro-kew-ra-syohN] power

procurer [pro-kew-ray] to provide, to bring

produire [pro-dweer] to produce; **se produire** [suh-pro-dweer] to happen

produit *(m)* [pro-dwee] product, article

profession *(f)* [pro-fay-syohN] occupation

profond(e) [pro-fohN(d)] deep

programme *(m)* [pro-gram] program

progrès *(m)* [pro-gray] progress

projet *(m)* [pro-zhay] plan

promenade *(f)* [pro-muh-nad] walk, stroll; **faire une promenade** [fehr-ewn-pro-muh-nad] to take a walk

se promener [suh-pro-muh-nay] to go for a walk

promesse *(f)* [pro-mehs] promise

promettre [pro-mehtr] to promise

prononcer [pro-nohN-say] to pronounce

prononciation *(f)* [pro-nohN-sya-syohN] pronunciation

proposer [pro-po-say] to offer, to propose, to suggest

proposition *(f)* [pro-po-zee-syohN] suggestion

propre [prohpr] clean, tidy; own

propriétaire *(m)* [pro-pree-yay-tehr] owner

propriété *(f)* [pro-pree-yay-tay] ownership, property, estate

prospectus *(m)* [prohs-pehk-tews] leaflet

protection *(f)* [pro-tehk-syohN] protection

protéger [pro-tay-zhay] to protect

protester [pro-tehs-tay] to protest

prouver [proo-vay] to prove, to show

proviseur *(m)* [pro-vee-zuhr] (high school) principal, headmaster

provisions *(f pl)* [pro-vee-zyohN] shopping, groceries

provisoire *(adj)* [pro-vee-zwar] temporary, provisional; **à titre provisoire** [a-teetr-pro-vee-zwar] *(adv)* temporarily; **provisoirement** *(adv)* [pro-vee-zwar-mahN] temporarily

A/Z

proximité *(f)* [pro-ksee-mee-tay] closeness, proximity
prudent(e) [prew-dahN(t)] cautious
public *(m)* [pew-bleek] public
public, -ique [pew-bleek] public, well-known
publicité *(f)* [pew-blee-see-tay] advertising
puer [pew-ay] to stink
puissant(e) [pwee-sahN(t)] powerful

Q

qualité *(f)* [ka-lee-tay] quality
quand [kahN] *(time)* when, as; *(question)* when?
quantité *(f)* [kahN-tee-tay] quantity
quart *(m)* [kar] quarter; **un quart d'heure** [aN-kar-duhr] a quarter of an hour
quartier *(m)* [kar-tyay] district, area
que [kuh] *(interr prn)* what; *(comparison)* as, than; *(conj)* that; **ne...que** [nuh]...[kuh] *(not later than)* only
quel(le) [kehl] which one...?
quelque chose [kehl-kuh-shoz] something
quelque part [kehl-kuh-par] somewhere
quelques [kehlk] a few
quelqu'un [kehl-kaN] someone
se quereller [suh-kuh-ray-lay] to quarrel
qu'est-ce que [kehs-kuh] what; **Qu'est-ce qui est arrivé?** [kehs-kee-ay-ta-ree-vay] What happened?
question *(f)* [kehs-tyohN] question
quitter [kee-tay] to leave, to take off; **quitter le pays** [kee-tay-luh-peh-ee] to leave the country

R

raccourci *(m)* [ra-koor-see] shortcut
raconter [ra-kohN-tay] to tell
radio *(f)* [ra-dyo] radio
rafraîchissement *(m)* [ra-fray-shees-mahN] refreshments
raide [rehd] stiff
raison *(f)* [reh-zohN] ground, reason, mind; **avoir raison** [a-vwar-reh-zohN] to be right
raisonnable [reh-zo-nabl] sensible
randonné, [rahN-do-nay] **faire de la pédestre** [fehr-duh-la-pay-dehstr] to hike
rapide *(adj)* [ra-peed] fast, quick; **rapidement** *(adv)* [ra-peed-mahN] quickly
rappeler qch à qqn [rap-lay-kehl-kuh-shoz-a-kehl-kaN] to remind s.o. of something
rapporter [ra-pohr-tay] to bring back, to take back, to return
rare *(adj)* [rar] rare; **rarement** *(adv)* [rar-mahN] rarely
raser [ra-zay] to shave
rater [ra-tay] to miss
ravi(e) [ra-vee] delighted
ravissant(e) [ra-vee-sahN(t)] beautiful, delightful
rayon *(m)* [ray-yohN] beam
réaliser [ray-a-lee-zay] to carry out
réalité *(f)* [ray-alee-tay] reality
réception *(f)* [ray-sehp-syohN] receipt, reception
recevoir [ruh-suh-vwar] to receive, to get, to greet
récipient *(m)* [ray-see-pyahN] container, receptacle
réclamation *(f)* [ray-kla-ma-syohN] complaint; **faire une réclamation** [fehr-ewn-ray-kla-ma-syohN] to lodge a complaint
réclamer [ray-kla-may] to demand, to call for, to complain
récolte *(f)* [ray-kohlt] harvest, crop
recommandation *(f)* [ruh-ko-mahN-da-syohN] advice, recommendation
recommander [ruh-ko-mahN-day] to recommend
récompense *(f)* [ray-kohN-pahNs] reward
récompenser [ray-kohN-pahN-say] to reward
reconnaissant(e) [ruh-ko-nay-sahN(t)] thankful
reconnaître [ruh-ko-nehtr] to recognize
rectifier [rehk-tee-fyay] to correct, to adjust
reçu *(m)* [ruh-sew] receipt; **faire un reçu** [fehr-aN-ruh-sew] to write a receipt
recueillir [ruh-kuuh-yeer] to gather
récupérer [ray-kew-pay-ray] to recover
réduction *(f)* [ray-dewk-syohN] discount
réel(le) [ray-ehl] genuine, real
se référer à [suh-ray-fay-ray-a] to refer to
refuser [ruh-few-say] to refuse, to reject; **refuser de** [ruh-few-zay-duh] to refuse to
regard *(m)* [ruh-gar] look
regarder [ruh-gar-day] to look, to watch, to concern, to view
région *(f)* [ray-zhyohN] area, region
régler [ray-glay] to settle, to pay; **régler une affaire** [ray-glay-ewn-a-fehr] to settle a matter

regret *(m)* [ruh-gray] regret
regretter [ruh-gray-tay] to regret
régulier, -**ière** *(adj)* [ray-gew-lyay]/[ray-gew-lyehr] regular; **régulièrement** *(adv)* [ray-gew-lyehr-mahN] regularly
se réjouir [suh-ray-zhweer] to rejoice; **se réjouir à l'avance de** [suh-ray-zhweer-a-la-vahNs-duh] to be delighted in advance
relation *(f)* [ruh-la-syohN] relation
relier [ruh-lyay] to link up
religieuse *(f)* [ruh-lee-zhyuuhz] nun
remarquer [ruh-mar-kay] to notice, to remark; **faire remarquer** [fehr-ruh-mar-kay] to remark (to say)
rembourser [rahN-boor-say] to pay back
remède *(m)* [ruh-mehd] remedy
remercier (qn) [ruh-mehr-syay] to thank (s.o.)
remettre [ruh-mehtr] to put back, to get something going again, to deliver; **remettre à plus tard** [ruh-meh-tra-plew-tar] to postpone, to put off
remise *(f)* [ruh-meez] rebate
remplacer [rahN-pla-say] to replace, to substitute
remplir [rahN-pleer] to fill
remuer [ruh-mew-ay] to move, to shift
rencontre *(f)* [rahN-kohNtr] encounter
rencontrer [rahN-kohN-tray] to meet, to come across
rendez-vous *(m)* [rahN-day-voo] appointment; **prendre rendez-vous avec qq** [prahN-druh-rahN-day-voo-a-vehk-kehl-kaN] to make an appointment with someone
rendre [rahNdr] to return, to give back, to capture; *(money)* to give back change, **rendre possible** [rahN-druh-po-seebl] to make possible; **rendre visite à qn** [rahN-druh-vee-zeet-a-kehl-kaN] to pay a visit to s.o.
rénover [ray-no-vay] to renovate
renseignement *(m)* [rahN-seh-nyuh-mahN] information; **prendre des renseignements** [prahN-druh-day-rahN-seh-nyuh-mahN] to make inquiries about
se renseigner [suh-rahN-seh-nyay] to inquire
renvoyer [rahN-vwa-yay] to return
réparation *(f)* [ray-pa-ra-syohN] repair
réparer [ray-pa-ray] to repair; to make up for
répartir [ray-par-teer] to divide up
répartition *(f)* [ray-par-tee-syohN] distribution
repas *(m)* [ruh-pa] meal, feed
répéter [ray-pay-tay] to repeat
répliquer [ray-plee-kay] to reply
répondre [ray-pohNdr] to answer; **répondre à** [ray-pohNdr] to fulfill, to live up to
réponse *(f)* [ray-pohNs] answer
repos *(m)* [ruh-po] rest
se reposer [suh-ruh-po-zay] to rest
repousser [ruh-poo-say] *(time)* to defer, to postpone
représentation *(f)* [ruh-pray-zahN-ta-syohN] *(theater)* performance
repriser [ruh-pree-zay] to mend
réserver [ray-zehr-vay] to reserve, to save; (seat) to book; **réserver une place** [ray-zehr-vay-ewn-plas] to reserve a seat
résistant(e) [ray-zees-tahN(t)] strong
résoudre [ray-zoodr] to solve
respecter [rehs-pehk-tay] to respect
responsable [rehs-pohN-sabl] responsible, liable
ressembler [ruh-sahN-blay] to look like
ressort *(m)* [ruh-sohr] *(elastic)* spring
restant(e) [rehs-tahN(t)] remaining
restaurant *(m)* [rehs-to-rahN] restaurant
reste *(m)* [rehst] rest
rester [rehs-tay] to remain, to be left
résultat *(m)* [ray-zewl-ta] result
se rétablir [suh-ray-ta-bleer] to restore
rétablissement *(m)* [ray-ta-blees-mahN] recovery
retard *(m)* [ruh-tar] delay; **être en retard** [ehtr-ahN-ruh-tar] to be late
retenir [ruh-tuh-neer] to hold; *(seat)* to book; **retenir qch** [ruh-tuh-neer-kehl-kuh-shoz] to retain
se retirer [suh-ruh-tee-ray] to withdraw
retour *(m)* [ruh-toor] return, reappearance, journey back; **de retour** [duh-ruh-toor] back
retourner [ruh-toor-nay] to turn around; to send back
retraite *(f)* [ruh-treht] retirement
rêve *(m)* [rehv] dream
réveil *(m)* [ray-vehy] waking
réveillé(e) [ray-veh-yay] awake
réveiller [ray-veh-yay] to wake up; **se réveiller** [suh-ray-veh-yay] to awaken
revendication *(f)* [ruh-vahN-dee-ka-syohN] demand
revenir [ruh-vuh-neer] to come back, to return

rêver [reh-vay] to dream
revoir [ruh-vwar] to see again
rez-de-chaussée *(m)* [ray-duh-sho-say] ground floor
riche [reesh] rich
richesse *(f)* [ree-shehs] wealth
rideau *(m)* [ree-do] curtain
ridicule [ree-dee-kewl] ridiculous
rien, [ryaN]**; (ne...) rien** [nuh]...[ryaN] nothing; **rien que** [ryaN-kuh] only
rire [reer] to laugh
risque *(m)* [reesk] hazard
rivage *(m)* [ree-vazh] *(sea)* shore
rive *(f)* [reev] *(river)* bank
rivière *(f)* [ree-vyehr] river
robinet *(m)* [ro-bee-nay] tap
rocher *(m)* [ro-shay] rock
rond(e) [rohN(d)] round
ronfler [rohN-flay] to snore
roseau *(m)* [ro-zo] reed
rôti *(m)* [ro-tee] roast
rôtir [ro-teer] to roast
route *(f)* [root] *(street)* way; country road; **en cours de route** [ahN-koor-duh-root] on the way
ruban *(m)* [rew-bahN] ribbon
rue *(f)* [rew] street; **dans la rue** [dahN-la-rew] in the street
rusé(e) [rew-zay] crafty

S

sa *(poss prn)* [sa] her
sac *(m)* [sak] bag; **sac à dos** *(m)* [sa-ka-do] back pack; **sac à main** *(m)* [sa-ka-maN] handbag; **sac de montagne** *(m)* [sak-duh-mohN-tany] back-pack
sachet *(m)* [sa-shay] small bag
saint(e) [saN(t)] saint
saisir [say-zeer] to grab
saison *(f)* [seh-zohN] season; **hors saison** [ohr-seh-zohN] off-season
salaire *(m)* [sa-lehr] salary
sale [sal] dirty
saleté *(f)* [sal-tay] dirt
salle *(f)* [sal] room, hall
salon de thé *(m)* [sa-lohN-duh-tay] tearoom
saluer [sa-lew-ay] to greet, to take one's leave of s.o.
Salut! [sa-lew] hello!
sans [sahN] without **sans aucun doute** [sahN-zo-kaN-doot] without any doubt; **sans importance** [sahN-zaN-pohr-tahNs] unimportant
santé *(f)* [sahN-tay] health; **bonne santé** *(f)* [sohn-sahN-tay] good health; **en bonne santé** [ahN-bohn-sahN-tay] healthy
satisfait(e) [sa-tees-feh(t)] happy
sauter [so-tay] to jump
sauvage [so-vazh] wild
sauver [so-vay] to save
savoir [sa-vwar] knowledge; to know *(learn)* to be able to
savourer [sa-voo-ray] to enjoy
scorpion *(m)* [skohr-pyohN] scorpio
sculpture *(f)* [skewl-tewr] sculpture
sec, sèche [sehk]/[sehsh] dry; *(wine)* dry
sécher [say-shay] to dry
second(e) *(adj)* [suh-gohN(d)] second
seconde *(f) (n)* [suh-gohNd] second
secret, secrète *(adj)* [suh-kray]/[suh-kreht] secret, reserved; **en secret** *(adv)* [ahN-suh-kray] secretly; **tenir secret** [tuh-neer-suh-kray] to keep secret
sécurité *(f)* [say-kew-ree-tay] security
séjour *(m)* [say-zhoor] stay
séjourner [say-zhoor-nay] to stay
sélectionner [say-lehk-syo-nay] to select
self-service *(m)* [sehlf-sehr-vees] self-service
selon moi [suh-lohN-mwa] in my mind
semaine *(f)* [suh-mehn] week; **dans une semaine** [dahN-zewn-suh-mehn] in a week; **pendant la semaine** [pahN-dahN-la-smehn] during the week; **par semaine** *(adv)* [par-suh-mehn] weekly
semblable [sahN-blabl] similar
sembler [sahN-blay] to seem
sens *(m)* [sahNs] sense
sentier *(m)* [sahN-tyay] path, footpath
sentiment *(m)* [sahN-tee-mahN] feeling
sentir [sahN-teer] to feel, to smell
séparé(e) [say-pa-ray] separate
séparer [say-pa-ray] to separate
sérieux, -euse [seh-ryuuh(z)] solemn
sermon *(m)* [sehr-mohN] sermon
serpent *(m)* [sehr-pahN] snake
serrure *(f)* [seh-rewr] lock *(door)*
service *(m)* [sehr-veer] duty, service, department
servir [sehr-veer] to serve, to be in service with, to be of service to, **se servir** [suh-sehr-veer] to help s.o.
seul(e) [suhl] alone, lonely, lonesome
seulement [suhl-mahN] only; *(no earlier than)* first
sévère [say-vehr] strict
sexe *(m)* [sehks] sex

si [see] whether, if **si!** [see] indeed
siège *(m)* [syehzh] seat
sifflet *(m)* [see-flay] whistle
signal [see-nyal] *(m)* signal
signalement *(m)* [see-nyal-mahN] description, particulars
signature *(f)* [see-nya-tewr] signature
signe *(m)* [seeny] sign, mark; **faire signe** [fehr-siny] to make a sign
signer [see-nyay] to sign
signification *(f)* [see-nee-fee-ka-syohN] meaning
signifier [see-nee-fyay] to mean, to imply
silence *(m)* [see-lahNs] silence
silencieux, -euse [see-lahN-syuuh(z)] quiet, silent
s'il te plaît [seel-tuh-play] please (informal)
s'il vous plaît [seel-voo-lay] please (formal)
simple [saNpl] simple
sinon [see-nohN] otherwise
situation *(f)* [see-tew-a-syohN] situation
snack *(m)* [snak] snack
société *(f)* [so-syay-tay] company, firm
sœur *(f)* [suhr] sister
soif *(f)* [swaf] thirst; **avoir soif** [a-vwar-swaf] to be thirsty
soigner [swa-nyay] to nurse, to look after
soigneusement [swa-nyuuhz-mahN] carefully
soin *(m)* [swaN] care
soir *(m)* [swar] evening; **ce soir** [suh-swar] tonight; **le soir** [luh-swar] in the evening
soirée *(f)* [swa-ray] evening, party
soit [swa] that is to say
sol *(m)* [sohl] soil
soldes *(m pl)* [sohld] sale
soleil *(m)* [so-lehy] sun
solennel(le) [so-la-nehl] solemn, formal
solide [so-leed] solid
solitaire [so-lee-tehr] lonely
sombre [sohNbr] dark
somme *(f)* [sohm] amount
sommeil *(m)* [so-mehy] sleep
sommet *(m)* [so-may] summit, top, highest point
son *(m)* [sohN] sound
son *(poss prn)* [sohN] his
sonner [so-nay] to ring, to chime; *(hour)* to strike
sonnette *(f)* [so-neht] doorbell
sorte *(f)* [sohrt] sort, kind
sortie *(f)* [sohr-tee] exit; **sortie (d'autoroute)** *(f)* [sohr-tee-do-to-root] highway exit
sortir [sohr-teer] to go out, to come out
souche *(f)* [soosh] stock, stump
souci *(m)* [soo-see] worry; **se faire du souci pour** [suh-fehr-dew-soo-see-poor] to worry for
se soucier de [suh-soo-syay-duh] to worry about
soucieux, -euse [soo-syuuh]/[soo-syuuhz] worried
soudain [soo-daN] suddenly
souffle *(m)* [soofl] blow
soûl(e) drunk
soulever [sool-vay] to lift
soupçon *(m)* [sews-pee-syohN] suspicion
source *(f)* [soors] source
sous [soo] under
sous-vêtements *(m pl)* [soo-veht-mahN] underware
soutien *(m)* [sew-pohr] support
souvenir *(m)* [soo-vuh-neer] memory
se souvenir [suh-soo-vuh-neer] to remember
souvent [soo-vahN] often
spécial(e) [spay-syal] special, distinctive
spectacle *(m)* [spehk-takl] show, sight
spectateur *(m)* [spehk-ta-tuhr] spectator
sport *(m)* [spohr] sport
stade *(m)* [stad] stadium
station balnéaire *(f)* [sta-syohN-bal-nay-ehr] spa, resort
Stop! [stohp] Stop!
stupide [stew-peed] stupid
succès *(m)* [sewk-say] success
succursale *(f)* [sew-kewr-sal] branch
sucré(e) [sew-kray] sweet
Sud *(m)* [sewd] South; **au sud de** [o-sewd-duh] to the south of
suffire [sew-feer] to be enough
suffisamment [sew-fee-za-mahN] enough
Suisse *(f)* [swees] Switzerland; *(m)* Swiss; **Suissesse** *(f)* [swee-sehs] Swiss
suivant(e) [swee-vahN(t)] following
suivre [sweevr] to follow, to undergo
sujet *(m)* [sew-zhay] topic, theme
superflu(e) [sew-pehr-flew] superfluous, unnecessary
supplémentaire [sew-play-mahN-tehr] additional
supporter [sew-pohr-tay] to support, to assume
supposer [sew-po-zee-syohN] to suppose, to assume
supposition *(f)* [sew-po-zee-syohN] assumption, supposition

A/Z

supprimer [sew-pree-may] to stop
sur [sewr] on
sûr(e) [sewr] sure, certain; **pas sûr(e)** [pa-sewr] unsure
sûrement [sewr-mahN] surely, certainly
surpris(e) [sewr-pree(z)] surprised
surtout [sewr-too] above all
surveiller [sewr-veh-yay] to watch, to supervise
suspendre [sews-pahNdr] to hang
sympathique [saN-pa-teek] likeable
syndicat d'initiative *(m)* [saN-dee-ka-dee-nee-sya-teev] tourist office

T

ta [ta] your
tabac *(m)* [ta-ba] tobacco
table *(f)* [tabl] table
tableau *(m)* [ta-blo] painting, picture
tache *(f)* [tash] stain
taille *(f)* [tay] *(clothing)* size
taire [tehr] to keep secret; **se taire** [suh-tehr] to keep quiet
talon *(m)* [ta-lohN] heel; *(shoe)* heel
tampon *(m)* [tahN-pohN] ink pad, tampon
tante [tahNt] *(f)* aunt
tard [tar] late; **plus tard** [plew-tar] later
tas, un de [aN-ta-duh] heap, pile
taux de change *(m)* [to-duh-shahNzh] exchange rate
taxi *(m)* [tak-see] taxi
te [tuh] you
teinte *(f)* [taNt] *(color)* shade
teinturerie *(f)* [taN-tewr-ree] *(business)* dry cleaner
tel(le) [tehl] such
téléphoner [tay-lay-fo-nay] to phone, to call
témoignage *(m)* [tay-mwa-nyazh] testimony, evidence
témoin *(m)* [tay-mwaN] witness
tempête *(f)* [tahN-peht] storm
temps *(m)* [tahN] time; weather; **à temps** [a-tahN] *(adv)* in time; **avec un temps pareil** [a-vehk-aN-tahN-pa-rehy] with such a weather; **de temps en temps** [duh-tahN-zahN-tahN] from time to time; **en ce temps-là** [ahN-suh-tahN-la] at that time; **en même temps** [ahN-mehm-tahN] at the same time; **pendant un certain temps** [pahN-dahN-aN-sehr-taN-tahN] for a time
tendre [tahNdr] to give, to offer
tendre [tahNdr] tender
tenir [tuh-neer] to hold; **être tenu de** [eh-truh-tuh-new-duh] to have to
terminer [tehr-mee-nay] to finish; **se terminer** [suh-tehr-mee-nay] to draw to a close, to end
terrain *(m)* [tay-raN] ground; **terrain de sport** [tay-raN-duh-spohr] *(m)* sportground
terre *(f)* [tehr] earth, land
tiers *(m)* [tyehr] third
timbre *(m)* [taNbr] stamp
timide [tee-meed] shy
tirer [tee-ray] to pull, to drag
tissu *(m)* [tee-sew] fabric
toi [twa] you; **à toi** [a-twa] yours
tomber [tohN-bay] to fall, to collapse; **tomber malade** [tohN-bay-ma-lad] to fall ill; **tomber goutte à goutte** [tohN-bay-goot-a-goot] to drip
tome *(m)* [tohm] volume
ton *(m)* [tohN] tone
ton [tohN] your
tort, avoir ____ [a-vwar-tohr] to be wrong
tôt [to] early; **plus tôt** [plew-to] earlier
total, faire le...de [fehr-luh-to-tal-duh] to up the total
toucher [too-shay] to touch
toujours [too-zhoor] always
tour *(m)* [toor] tour
touriste *(m f)* [too-reest] tourist
tourne-disque *(m)* [toor-nuh-deesk] record player
tourner [toor-nay] to revolve; **tourner à droite/à gauche** [toor-nay-[a-drwat]/[a-gosh] to turn right/left
tousser [too-say] to cough
tout, toute [too]/[toot] all; **tous, toutes** [toos]/[toot] all; **tous les jours** [too-lay-zhoor] every day; **toutes les deux heures** [toot-lay-duuh-zuhr] every two hours
tout *(adv)* [too] all; **tout à coup** [too-ta-koo] suddenly; **tout d'un coup** [too-daN-koo] all of a sudden; **tout droit** [too-drwa] straight ahead; **tout près** [too-pray] quite close by; **tout de suite** [toot-sweet] immediately
toxique [tohk-seek] toxic
trace *(f)* [tras] trail
traduire [tra-dweer] to translate
traitement [treht-mahN] *(m)* treatment
trajet *(m)* [tra-zhay] journey, distance
tranche *(f)* [trahNsh] *(slice of bread)*
tranquillité *(f)* [trahN-kee-lee-tay] *(of a place)* quietness

transit, en [ahN-trahN-zeet] in transit
transmissible [trahNs-mee-seebl] transmittable
transpirer [trahNs-pee-ray] to sweat
transporter [trahNs-pohr-tay] to carry, to convey
travail *(m)* [tra-vay] work
travailler [tra-va-yay] to work
travailleur, -euse [tra-va-yuhr]/[tra-va-yuuhz] hard-working
travers, à [a-tra-vehr] through
traversée *(f)* [tra-vehr-say] crossing, through route
traverser [tra-vehr-say] to cross
trempé(e) [trahN-pay] drenched
très [tray] very
tribunal *(m)* [tree-bew-nal] court
triste [treest] sad
troisième [trwa-zyehn] third; **troisièmement** [trwa-zyehm-mahN] thirdly
tromper [trohN-pay] to deceive; **se tromper** [suh-trohN-pay] to make a mistake
trompeur, -euse [trohN-puhr]/[trohN-puuhz] deceitful
trop [tro] too much; with *(adj)* **trop** [tro] too
trou *(m)* [troo] hole
trouble [troobl] confusion
trouver [troo-vay] to find; **se trouver** [suh-troo-vay] to happen, to be located
tu [tew] you
tube *(m)* [tewb] tube
tunnel *(m)* [tew-nehl] tunnel
tuyau [twee-yo] *(m)* pipe
typique (de) [tee-peek][duh] typical

U

un, une [aN]/[ewn] one; **un/une et demi** [aN]/[ewn]-[ay-duh-mee] one and a half
unique [ew-neek] unique
urgent(e) [ewr-zhahN(t)] urgent
usage *(m)* [ew-zazh] usage
usine *(f)* [ew-zeen] factory
usuel(le) [ew-zwehl] usual
utile [ew-teel] useful, necessary
utiliser [ew-tee-lee-zay] to use, to utilize

V

vacances *(f pl)* [va-kahNs] vacation; **en vacances** [ahN-va-kahNs] on vacation
vache *(f)* [vash] cow
valable [va-labl] valid; **être valable** [eh-truh-va-labl] to be valid
valeur *(f)* [va-luhr] value; **avoir beaucoup de valeur** [a-vwar-bo-koo-duh-va-luhr] to be very valuable **sans valeur** [sahN-va-luhr] worthless
validité *(f)* [va-lee-dee-tay] validity
valise *(f)* [va-leez] suitcase; **faire sa valise** [fehr-sa-va-leez] to pack
variable [va-ryabl] *(weather)* unsettled
varié(e) [va-ryay] varied
vendre [vahNdr] to sell
venir [vuh-neer] to come
vente *(f)* [vahNt] sale; **ventes** *(f pl)* [vahNt] sales promotion; **en vente** [ahN-vahNt] on sale
ver *(m)* [vehr] worm
verglas *(m)* [vehr-gla] sheet of ice
vérifier [vay-ree-fyay] to check
véritable *(adj)* [vay-ree-tabl] genuine
vérité *(f)* [vay-ree-tay] truth
verre *(m)* [vehr] glass
verrou *(m)* [vay-roo] bolt
vers [vehr] toward, around, about; *(time)* around; **vers le bas** [vehr-luh-ba] downward; **vers le haut** [vehr-luh-o] upward
vertige *(m)* [vehr-teezh] vertigo; **pris de vertige** [pree-duh-vehr-teezh] suffering from vertigo
vêtements *(m pl)* [veht-mahN] clothing
vexation *(f)* [veh-ksa-syohN] snub
vexer [vehks] to hurt s.o.'s feelings
viande *(f)* [vyahNd] meat
vide [veed] empty
vie *(f)* [vee] life
vieux, vieil, vieille [vyuuh]/[vyehy]/[vyehy] old
vif, vive [veef]/[veev] lively
vigne *(f)* [veeny] vineyard
vigoureux, -euse [vee-goo-ruuh(z)] vigorous
villa *(f)* [vee-la] villa
village *(m)* [vee-lazh] village
ville *(f)* [veel] town
virage *(m)* [vee-razh] curve
virée *(f)* [vee-ray] *(promenade)* ride
virer [vee-ray] *(money)* to transfer
visible [vee-zeebl] visible
visite *(f)* [vee-zeet] visit; **rendre visite à qn** [rahN-druh-vee-zeet-a-kehl-kaN] to pay a visit to s.o.
visiter [vee-zee-tay] to visit
vite *(adv)* [veet] quickly, fast
vitesse *(f)* [vee-tehs] speed

vitre *(f)* [veetr] window pane
vitrine *(f)* [vee-treen] display window
vivant(e) [vee-vahN(t)] alive
vivre [veevr] to live
voir [vwar] to see, to picture
voisin(e) *(m f)* [vwa-zaN]/[vwa-zeen] neighbor
voiture *(f)* [vwa-tewr] car
voix *(f)* [vwa] voice
voler [vo-lay] to fly, to steal
volonté *(f)* [a-vo-lohN-tay] will; **à volonté** [a-vo-lohN-tay] as much as you want
volontiers [vo-lohN-tyay] gladly
volt *(m)* [vohlt] voltage
voter [vo-tay] to vote
votre [vohtr] your
vouloir [voo-lwar] to want, to expect; **vouloir dire** to mean
vous [voo] you
voyage *(m)* [vwa-yazh] travel, trip; **voyage organisé** *(m)* [vwa-yazh-ohr-ga-nee-zay] organized trip; **en voyage** [ahN-vwa-yazh] on a trip
voyager [vwa-ya-zhay] to travel
voyageur, -euse *(m f)* [vwa-ya-zhuhr]/[vwa-ya-zhuuhz] traveler
vrai(e) [vray] right, true; genuine; **être vrai(e)** [eh-truh-vray] to be true; **à vrai dire** [a-vray-deer] *(adv)* in actual fact
vraiment *(adv)* [vray-mahN] really
vue [vew] *(f)* sight, eyesight, view, opinion
vulgaire [vewl-gehr] ordinary, common

W

W.-C. *(m pl)* [vay-say] toilets
watt *(m)* [wat] Watt

Y

y [ee] there
yeux *(m pl)* [yuuh] eyes

Notes

Notes

Notes

Notes

Notes

Notes

Notes

Notes